Studies in Development Economics and Policy

General Editor: **Anthony Shorrocks**

UNU WORLD INSTITUTE FOR DEVELOPMENT ECONOMICS RESEARCH (UNU-WIDER) was established by the United Nations University as its first research and training centre and started work in Helsinki, Finland, in 1985. The purpose of the Institute is to undertake applied research and policy analysis on structural changes affecting the developing and transitional economies, to provide a forum for the advocacy of policies leading to robust, equitable and environmentally sustainable growth, and to promote capacity strengthening and training in the field of economic and social policy-making. Its work is carried out by staff researchers and visiting scholars in Helsinki and through networks of collaborating scholars and institutions around the world.

UNU World Institute for Development Economics Research (UNU-WIDER)
Katajanokanlaituri 6B, FIN-00160 Helsinki, Finland

Titles include:

Tony Addison and Alan Roe (*editors*)
FISCAL POLICY FOR DEVELOPMENT
Poverty, Reconstruction and Growth

Tony Addison, Henrik Hansen and Finn Tarp (*editors*)
DEBT RELIEF FOR POOR COUNTRIES

George G. Borjas and Jeff Crisp (*editors*)
POVERTY, INTERNATIONAL MIGRATION AND ASYLUM

Ricardo Ffrench-Davis and Stephany Griffith-Jones (*editors*)
FROM CAPITAL SURGES TO DROUGHT
Seeking Stability for Emerging Economies

David Fielding (*editor*)
MACROECONOMIC POLICY IN THE FRANC ZONE

Basudeb Guha-Khasnobis (*editor*)
THE WTO, DEVELOPING COUNTRIES AND THE DOHA DEVELOPMENT AGENDA
Prospects and Challenges for Trade-led Growth

Aiguo Lu and Manuel F. Montes (*editors*)
POVERTY, INCOME DISTRIBUTION AND WELL-BEING IN ASIA DURING THE TRANSITION

Robert J. McIntyre and Bruno Dallago (*editors*)
SMALL AND MEDIUM ENTERPRISES IN TRANSITIONAL ECONOMIES

Vladimir Mikhalev (*editor*)
INEQUALITY AND SOCIAL STRUCTURE DURING THE TRANSITION

E. Wayne Nafziger and Raimo Väyrynen (*editors*)
THE PREVENTION OF HUMANITARIAN EMERGENCIES

Matthew Odedokun (*editor*)
EXTERNAL FINANCE FOR PRIVATE SECTOR DEVELOPMENT
Appraisals and Issues

Laixiang Sun (*editor*)
OWNERSHIP AND GOVERNANCE OF ENTERPRISES
Recent Innovative Developments

UNU-WIDER
WIDER PERSPECTIVES ON GLOBAL DEVELOPMENT

Studies in Development Economics and Policy
Series Standing Order ISBN 0–333–96424–1
(*outside North America only*)

You can receive future titles in this series as they are published by placing a standing order. Please contact your bookseller or, in case of difficulty, write to us at the address below with your name and address, the title of the series and the ISBN quoted above.

Customer Services Department, Macmillan Distribution Ltd, Houndmills, Basingstoke, Hampshire RG21 6XS, England

Wider Perspectives on Global Development

UNU-WIDER

Anthony B. Atkinson
Kaushik Basu
Jagdish N. Bhagwati
Douglass C. North
Dani Rodrik
Frances Stewart
Joseph E. Stiglitz
Jeffrey G. Williamson

in association with the United Nations
University – World Institute for Development
Economics Research

First published in 2005 by
PALGRAVE MACMILLAN
Houndmills, Basingstoke, Hampshire RG21 6XS and
175 Fifth Avenue, New York, N.Y. 10010
Companies and representatives throughout the world.

PALGRAVE MACMILLAN is the global academic imprint of the Palgrave
Macmillan division of St. Martin's Press, LLC and of Palgrave Macmillan Ltd.
Macmillan® is a registered trademark in the United States, United Kingdom
and other countries. Palgrave is a registered trademark in the European
Union and other countries.

ISBN-13: 978–1–4039–9626–8 hardback
ISBN-10: 1–4039–9626–1 hardback
ISBN-13: 978–1–4039–9631–2 paperback
ISBN-10: 1–4039–9631–8 paperback

This book is printed on paper suitable for recycling and made from fully
managed and sustained forest sources.

A catalogue record for this book is available from the British Library.

Library of Congress Cataloging-in-Publication Data
    Wider perspectives on global development / edited by UNU-WIDER.
        p. cm.—(Studies in development economics and policy)
    "This volume reproduces the first eight [WIDER] Annual Lectures
[inaugurated in 1997]"–P. xviii.
    Includes bibliographical references and index.
        ISBN 1–4039–9626–1 (cloth)—ISBN 1–4039–9631–8 (paper)
    1. Economic development. 2. Development economics. 3. Developing
countries – Economic policy. I. World Institute for Development Economics
Research. II. WIDER annual lectures. III. Series.
HD72.W54 2005
338.9—dc22   2005048741

10 9 8 7 6 5 4 3 2 1
14 13 12 11 10 09 08 07 06 05

Printed and bound in Great Britain by
Antony Rowe Ltd, Chippenham and Eastbourne

Contents

List of Tables and Box   vi

List of Figures   vii

Acknowledgements   x

List of Abbreviations   xi

Notes on the Contributors   xiii

   Introduction: Wider Perspectives on Global Development   xvi
   Giovanni Andrea Cornia, Matti Pohjola and Anthony Shorrocks

1 The Contribution of the New Institutional Economics to an
   Understanding of the Transition Problem   1
   Douglass C. North

2 More Instruments and Broader Goals: Moving toward the
   Post-Washington Consensus   16
   Joseph E. Stiglitz

3 Is Rising Income Inequality Inevitable? A Critique of the
   Transatlantic Consensus   49
   Anthony B. Atkinson

4 Globalization and Appropriate Governance   74
   Jagdish N. Bhagwati

5 Horizontal Inequalities: A Neglected Dimension of Development   101
   Frances Stewart

6 Winners and Losers over Two Centuries of Globalization   136
   Jeffrey G. Williamson

7 Global Labour Standards and Local Freedoms   175
   Kaushik Basu

8 Rethinking Growth Strategies   201
   Dani Rodrik

Index   225

List of Tables and Box

Tables

2.1	Fiscal costs of banking crises, selected countries	26
5.1	Sources of differentiation among groups	110
5.2	Inequalities between Indian-origin Fijians (I) and local-origin Fijians (F)	115
5.3	Some indicators of horizontal inequality in Uganda, 1959–91	117
5.4	Ratio of black/white performance in Brazil	126
6.1	Trade policy orientation and growth rates in the Third World, 1963–92	144
6.2	Wealth bias during the two global centuries	158
6.3	Tariff impact of GDP *per capita* growth, by region	161
8.1	World Bank's 'star globalizers'	205
8.2	East Asian anomalies	206
8.3	The indeterminacy of institutional forms: a Chinese counterfactual	208
8.4	The Washington Consensus and 'Augmented' Washington Consensus: what to avoid	212
8.5	Episodes of rapid growth, by region, decade and magnitude of acceleration, 1957–92	215
8.6	Predictability of growth accelerations	217

Box

8.1	Chinese shortcuts	210

List of Figures

2.1 Public sector deficits: Latin America versus East Asia 19
2.2 Inflation: Latin America versus East Asia, 1980–95 20
2.3 Inflation rates in developing countries, 1985 and 1995 22
2.4 Volatility of GDP growth, 1970–95 25
2.5 GDP growth before and after banking crises, 1975–94 26
2.6 Government spending in selected countries 35
2.7 Tertiary-level students in technical fields 38
3.1 Changes in income inequality, 1977–99 52
3.2 Changes in earnings inequality, 1977–99 54
3.3 Earnings distribution in France and the United States, 1977–97 56
3.4 Tilt in UK earnings distribution, 1977 and 1998 59
3.5 Redistributive impact of budget, 1977–97 65
5.1 Chiapas compared with all Mexico 114
5.2 Malaysia and the NEP 119
5.3 Changing horizontal inequalities in Sri Lanka 120
5.4 Black/white inequalities in South Africa 121
5.5 Horizontal inequalities in Northern Ireland 123
5.6 Horizontal inequalities in the United States 125
6.1 Global inequality of individual incomes, 1820–1992 137
6.2 Explaining the European trade boom, 1500–1800 139
6.3 Average world tariffs, 1865–1945 141
6.4 Initial real wage versus subsequent inequality
trends, 1870–1913 151
6.5 Unweighted average of regional tariffs, 1865–1939 151
6.6 Real wage dispersion in the Atlantic economy, 1854–1913 155
8.1 Structural reform index for Latin American countries, 1985–99 202
8.2 Response to reforms has been weak at best 203
8.3 Economic performances, 1960–2002 204
8.4 The Indian economic take-off, 1960–2000 206
8.5 Growth accelerations: what does the theory say?
Effect of improvement in growth fundamentals at time t 213
8.6 Problem: low levels of private investment and
entrepreneurship 219

UNU World Institute for Development Economics Research

UNU-WIDER was established by the United Nations University as its first research and training centre and started work in Helsinki, Finland in 1985. The purpose of the institute is to undertake applied research and policy analysis on structural changes affecting developing and transitional economies, to provide a forum for the advocacy of policies leading to robust, equitable, and environmentally sustainable growth, and to promote capacity strengthening and training in the field of economic and social policy making. Its work is carried out by staff researchers and visiting scholars in Helsinki and via networks of collaborating scholars and institutions around the world.

World Institute for Development Economics Research of the United Nations University (UNU-WIDER)

Katajanokanlaituri 6B, FIN-00160 Helsinki, Finland
www.wider.unu.edu

Acknowledgements

UNU-WIDER relies on the hospitality, support and financial contributions of various donors. Since 1997 WIDER has received important contributions to the research programme from the governments of Denmark, Finland, Italy, Norway, Sweden and the United Kingdom. In addition, special acknowledgement for sponsorship of the WIDER Annual Lectures is due to the following: WIDER Annual Lectures 1997 and 1998 in Helsinki with thanks to Oracle; WIDER Annual Lecture 1999 in Oslo with thanks to Norway's Royal Ministry of Foreign Affairs and the University of Oslo; WIDER Annual Lectures 2000, 2001 and 2003 in Helsinki with thanks to Finland's Ministry for Foreign Affairs; WIDER Annual Lecture 2002 in Copenhagen with thanks to Denmark's Royal Ministry of Foreign Affairs and Copenhagen University; and WIDER Annual Lecture 2004 in Stockholm with thanks to the Swedish International Development Cooperation Agency (Sida) and the Stockholm School of Economics.

List of Abbreviations

AFL–CIO	American Federation of Labor–Congress of Industrial Organizations
CAP	Common Agricultural Policy
CEA	Council of Economic Advisers
CEPR	Center for Economic Policy Research
CPI	Consumer Price Index
CRISE	Centre for Research on Inequality, Human Security and Ethnicity
CUTS	Consumer Unity and Trust Society
DFI	direct foreign investment
DFID	Department for International Development
EC	European Community
EMU	European Monetary Union
EPA	Environmental Protection Agency
EPZ	export processing zone
EU	European Union
EZ	Euro zone
EZLN	*Ejército Zapatisto de Liberación Nacional* (Zapatista Army of National Liberation)
FDI	foreign direct investment
Fed	Federal Reserve Bank (US)
FES	Family Expenditure Survey
FSU	former Soviet Union
GATT	General Agreement on Tariffs and Trade
GDP	gross domestic product
GERC	general-equilibrium reversal claim
GNP	gross national product
HDI	Human Development Index
HI	horizontal inequality
ICC	International Criminal Court
ICFTU	International Confederation of Free Trade Unions
IFI	international financial institution
ILO	International Labour Organization
IMF	International Monetary Fund
INTRAC	International NGO Training and Research Centre
IP	intellectual property
IT	information technology
LO	trade union federation (Norway)

LSE	London School of Economics and Political Science
MDG	Millennium Development Goal
MNC	multinational corporation
NAFTA	North American Free Trade Agreement
NBER	National Bureau of Economic Research
NEP	New Economic Policy (Malaysia)
NGO	non-governmental organization
NHO	employers' organization (Norway)
NIC	newly industrializing country
NIEO	New International Economic Order
NRM/NRA	National Resistance Movement/National Resistance Army (Uganda)
NTB	non-tariff barriers
OECD	Organisation for Economic Cooperation and Development
PPF	production possibility frontier
PPP	purchasing power parity
PRSPs	poverty reduction and growth strategies
QR	quantitative restriction
R&D	research and development
RUC	Royal Ulster Constabulary
SEZ	special economic zone (China)
SOE	state-owned enterprise
SSA	sub-Saharan Africa
TFP	total factor productivity
TVEs	township and village enterprises
UNIFEM	United Nations Development Fund for Women
UNRISD	United Nations Research Institute for Social Development
UNU	United Nations University
USSR	Union of Soviet Socialist Republics
WIDER	World Institute for Development Economics Research, UNU
WTO	World Trade Organization

Notes on the Contributors

Sir Anthony B. Atkinson is Warden of Nuffield College, Oxford. He was previously Professor of Political Economy at the University of Cambridge, Tooke Professor of Economic Science and Statistics, LSE, Professor of Political Economy and Head of Department, University College, London, Visiting Professor of Economics at MIT and Professor of Economics, University of Essex. He is a Fellow of the British Academy and an Honorary Member of the American Economic Association. He is past President of the Royal Economic Society, the Econometric Society, the European Economic Association and the International Economic Association, and has served on the Royal Commission on the Distribution of Income and Wealth, the Pension Law Review Committee and the Commission on Social Justice.

Kaushik Basu is the C. Marks Professor of International Studies in the Economics Department of Cornell University. Previously he taught at Princeton, MIT and the LSE, and founded the Centre for Development Economics in Delhi. A Fellow of the Econometric Society and a recipient of the Mahalanobis Memorial Award, he is editor of *Social Choice and Welfare*, and has served on the editorial boards of the *Journal of Development Economics* and the *World Bank Economic Review*.

Jagdish N. Bhagwati is University Professor, Columbia University and Senior Fellow in International Economics at the Council on Foreign Relations, New York. He is an External Adviser to the WTO and a member of UN Secretary General Kofi Annan's High-Level Advisory Group on the NEPAD process in Africa. He is also a Director of the National Bureau of Economic Research, on the Academic Advisory Board of Human Rights Watch (Asia) and was a member of the Advisory Board of the Council on Economic Priorities Accreditation Agency. Professor Bhagwati has been Arthur Lehman Professor of Economics and Professor of Political Science at Columbia, Ford International Professor of Economics at MIT and Professor of International Trade at the Delhi School of Economics.

Douglass C. North is Spencer T. Olin Professor in Arts and Sciences, Washington University in St Louis, having been the Henry R. Luce Professor of Law and Liberty in the Department of Economics in Arts and Sciences and serving as director of the Center in Political Economy. In 1992 he became the first economic historian to win one of the economics profession's most prestigious honours, the John R. Commons Award. A fellow of the British Academy he was also elected to the American Academy of Arts and Sciences.

He has been editor of the *Journal of Economic History*, is past President of the Economic History Association and a twenty-five-year member of the Board of Directors of the National Bureau of Economic Research. The Nobel Memorial Prize in Economics in 1993 was awarded jointly to Professor North and Professor Robert W. Fogel of the University of Chicago, 'for having renewed research in economic history by applying economic theory and quantitative methods in order to explain economic and institutional change'.

Dani Rodrik is Professor of International Political Economy at the John F. Kennedy School of Government, Harvard University. He is affiliated with the National Bureau of Economic Research, the Centre for Economic Policy Research (London), the Center for Global Development, the Institute for International Economics and the Council on Foreign Relations. Among other honours, in 2002 he was presented the Leontief Award for Advancing the Frontiers of Economic Thought. He has published widely in the areas of international economics, economic development and political economy, and is an editor of the *Review of Economics and Statistics* and an associate editor of the *Journal of Economic Literature*.

Frances Stewart is Professor of Development Economics and Director of the Centre for Research on Inequality, Human Security and Ethnicity (CRISE), Queen Elizabeth House, University of Oxford. She is a Fellow of Somerville College. A former Council member of the United Nations University, she is currently a Board Member of the International Food Policy Research Institute and an Overseer of the Thomas Watson Institute for International Studies, Brown University. Formerly Director of the International Development Centre, Queen Elizabeth House, she has also been special adviser to UNICEF on Adjustment (1985–86) and has been one of the chief consultants for the Human Development Report since its inception.

Joseph E. Stiglitz is University Professor at Columbia University. He has taught at Princeton, Stanford, Yale and MIT and was the Drummond Professor at All Souls College, Oxford. In 1979 he was awarded the John Bates Clark Award, given biennially by the American Economic Association to the economist under forty who has made the most significant contribution to the field. In 2001 he was awarded the Nobel Prize in Economics. He was a member of the Council of Economic Advisors from 1993 to 1995, during the Clinton Administration, and served as CEA chairman from 1995 to 1997. He then became Chief Economist and Senior Vice-President of the World Bank from 1997 to 2000.

Jeffrey G. Williamson is the Laird Bell Professor of Economics, Center for International Development at Harvard University where he was Chair of the Economics Department. He is also Research Associate at the National Bureau of Economic Research. He taught at the University of Wisconsin for twenty years before joining the Harvard faculty in 1983. Professor Williamson has served as President of the Economic History Association and is the author of more than twenty scholarly books and almost 200 articles on economic history, international economics and economic development.

Introduction: Wider Perspectives on Global Development

Giovanni Andrea Cornia, Matti Pohjola and Anthony Shorrocks

UNU-WIDER is one of the world's leading research institutes on development economics. It strives to provide original analysis of important global issues and to offer policy advice aimed at the sustainable economic and social development of the poorest nations. Established in 1984 in Helsinki, Finland, as the first research and training centre of the United Nations University, UNU-WIDER is part of an international academic community which promotes the United Nations' aims of peace and progress. One aspect of this role is to provide a forum for bringing together leading scholars from around the world to address urgent global problems.

The WIDER Annual Lecture was inaugurated in 1997 to allow a distinguished scholar to offer his or her analysis and views on a topic relevant to the work of UNU-WIDER. This volume reproduces the first eight Annual Lectures. The authors are universally recognized as among the most prominent contributors in their fields, and the range of themes captures the vitality, breadth, detail and quality associated with the research of UNU-WIDER on international development. Most of the core issues in the field of development are included among the topics: governance and institutions, trade and globalization, inequality and conflict, growth and employment. The individual contributions offer great insights into the role of economic, political and social factors in global development, and into the way that effective structures and institutions can be designed in order to improve the well-being of the poor.

Institutions are the formal and informal rules that structure human interaction. The way that they evolve shapes economic development via the costs of transactions and production. In Chapter 1, Douglass North develops a theory of institutions which is then used to examine organizational problems in the modern world and to look at the challenges that these problems pose for low-income countries. He goes on to show how the theory of institutions can be used to improve economic performance in transitional economies. By focusing on deep-rooted institutional obstacles and their evolution, rather than on macroeconomic issues, North provides a more realistic and original assessment of the momentous changes faced by nations in transition and of the sources of the difficulties encountered. This chapter is also a key contribution to the analysis of the appropriate way to proceed with policy reforms and policy implementation in transitional and developing economies.

Chapter 2, by Joseph Stiglitz, provides a thorough critique of the 'Washington Consensus'. His analysis shows that while certain elements of the Washington Consensus – for example, low inflation and low budget deficits – might have been relevant for addressing the economic crises of Latin America in the 1980s, they are not sufficient for achieving long-term growth, or even macroeconomic stability, under different circumstances. Stiglitz emphasizes the lack of attention of the Washington Consensus to developing sound financial markets (as opposed to mere financial liberalization), a neglect evident in the problems in the financial sector across much of East Asia in the late 1990s.

It is now widely accepted that governments complement markets. A market economy cannot thrive, and the majority of people cannot benefit, without wise government and effective state institutions. Stiglitz stresses that developing and transition economies need to do more that just liberalize in order to build markets: they need to build regulatory capacity and to establish truly competitive markets in order to overcome asymmetric information and market imperfections, especially in sectors which have undertaken large-scale privatization of state enterprises. Otherwise, the new market economies will be inefficient, and will not yield the broad-based growth which is so essential to raising living standards. In addition to these tasks, state action is required to support public investment in human capital – which raises living standards and growth – and to assist countries in adopting new technologies.

Income inequality has been a core interest of UNU-WIDER over the years. In Chapter 3, Anthony Atkinson examines the rise in income inequality in a large number of industrialized countries since the late 1970s. This phenomenon, which first became apparent in the United States and the United Kingdom, has subsequently become evident across much of the developing and developed world. However, the experience is not uniform across countries. This suggests that rising inequality is not inevitable, a conclusion that contrasts with the widely held belief that it is an unavoidable consequence of the present revolution in information technology, and/or the globalization of trade and finance.

Atkinson's analysis suggests that the world is working in more complex ways than those described in simple technological and trade explanations of the level and trend of inequality. The latter theories see wage differentials as nothing more than the outcome of supply and demand, thereby ignoring the role of conventions and social norms. More recent economic theories show that supply and demand only places limits on possible wage differentials, while social forces determine where wages actually lie between those limits. These newer models also indicate that shifts in pay norms can result in widening wage differentials, and thus higher income inequality. Moreover, Chapter 3 reminds us that progressive income taxation and social transfers can substantially reduce the income inequalities that may arise in the market place. Thus national governments do have room for manoeuvre, especially in influencing the social norms which are as important – perhaps even more important – in determining the distribution of income as the much-cited trends in trade and technology.

Jagdish Bhagwati, in Chapter 4, presents us with a quite different perspective on globalization than we typically get in the polarized debates in the media between its proponents and opponents. He first points out that the different dimensions of globalization may have different impacts; therefore, to analyse the debate, globalization needs to be disaggregated instead of being treated as a gigantic whole. Concentrating on international trade and direct foreign investment (DFI), Bhagwati shows that these two dimensions of globalization are economically benign. He then argues that they can also be socially benign – that is, they can produce beneficial consequences for a variety of social objectives. However, this holds only as a general tendency, so undesirable outcomes can occur. Consequently, appropriate governance is needed at both national and international levels to manage globalization.

In Chapter 5, Frances Stewart expands on some of the central themes of her studies for UNU-WIDER: the causes of humanitarian emergencies, and institutions and group behaviour. Stewart documents the ways in which political power, social demarcations and economic differences combine to produce horizontal inequalities between population subgroups within countries, and the impact of these horizontal inequalities on social cohesion. The case studies leave no doubt that inequitable treatment of groups – either real or perceived – can be a major source of social instability and hence a major obstacle to improvements in well-being. Yet, as emphasized in the title of the chapter, these phenomena are routinely neglected in the design of development policies, which tend to focus on outcomes for individuals rather than groups.

The evidence indicates that historical patterns of privilege can be redressed, particularly if the privileged groups are a minority. In other circumstances, however, the interplay of political and economic forces may exacerbate the underlying problems. In strongly divided countries, Stewart suggests that donor countries and international organizations must ensure that their policies take account of horizontal inequity, recognizing that this stance may conflict with narrowly defined efficiency objectives.

Jeffrey Williamson's research covers a wide range of historical and contemporary topics, including growth, trade, migration, living standards and inequality. All these themes are evident in Chapter 6, which offers a broad perspective on the global impact of trade and factor flows over many centuries. Noting that while world inequality has been trending upwards for most of the past 500 years, 'globalization' – defined in terms of commodity price convergence across regions of the world – began only around 1820. During the 'first global century' up to 1913, lower transport costs and tariffs stimulated trade which, together with relatively free factor mobility, created powerful egalitarian forces on a world scale. However, as Williamson stresses, not everyone stood to benefit from a continuation of these policies, and the period from 1913 to 1950 was characterized by an anti-globalization back-lash under which restrictions on migration and rising tariffs resulted in price divergence across countries.

The period from 1950 until the present day constitutes the second global-ization era. It differs, however, from the first global century in one important respect – the mass labour migrations that were the main globalization force in the nineteenth century have been replaced by immigration controls, leaving trade (aided by tariff reductions) as the principal source of interna-tional price convergence. Weaving together the economic, political and demographic factors, which help to explain the pattern of living standards across countries and over time, Williamson offers a vision of the way in which the world is likely to develop over the next half-century.

Kaushik Basu is known for the creative way in which he brings the tools of economic and philosophical analysis to bear on current development issues. In recent years his interests have included questions concerned with international labour standards and worker rights, particularly those related to the use of child labour in developing countries. Chapter 7 begins by not-ing that one of the consequences of globalization is an erosion of democracy, with the lives of individuals in developing nations becoming increasingly dependent on decisions taken in other countries over which they have no influence. The imposition of global labour standards – however well-meaning the motivation of the proponents – risks adding to this disenfran-chisement as well as hurting the intended beneficiaries. Hence the need for a thorough assessment of the rationale for international intervention.

Respect for personal liberty leads Basu to argue that individuals should be allowed to enter into a labour contract that would be outlawed in the developed world, provided that the contract does not involve coercion and provided that the parties concerned fully comprehend the implications of their agreement. Those who favour imposing external constraints on such free market activities must offer convincing counterarguments. Individual ignorance or irrationality is one possible route, along with explicit or implicit coercion. Another possible justification rests on the existence of multiple equilibria, when an external 'benign intervention' might result in a switch to a stable and mutually preferred equilibrium. A third, more subtle, line of reasoning is that while individual free market transactions may be justifiable, certain *classes* of contracts can have such severe repercussions that these undermine the case for respecting individual freedom. Basu expands on these ideas and examines their implications for global labour standards in the context of such issues as child labour, hazardous working conditions and workplace harassment. The attention to the detail of the argument is a welcome contrast to what Basu refers to as the 'muscular desire' of international bureaucrats to get on with the business of crafting legislation.

In Chapter 8, Dani Rodrik addresses one of the core issues in development: how can low-income countries achieve faster rates of economic growth? Reviewing the lessons to be drawn from recent history, particularly with regard to Latin America and Asia, Rodrik concludes that successful policies are invariably built on sensible general principles such as a desire to interact more closely with the global economy, to maintain fiscal discipline and to establish a strong and supportive institutional environment. However, attempts to translate these general principles into a collection of orthodox liberal policies have a patchy record of success, at best. This conclusion is reinforced by the fact that the vast majority of significant growth accelerations over the past fifty years fail to reveal any clear link with economic liberalization.

The alternative framework proposed by Rodrik involves a move away from a blanket prescription and towards a more nuanced strategy, which focuses on the particular constraints that prevent a given country from growing faster. The consequent policy recommendations may be quite different for countries that appear superficially to share similar problems, or for the same country at different points of time. Rodrik makes a persuasive case for an alternative strategy which has profound implications for the construction of economic policy in developing countries.

Overall, the contributions in this volume address many of the core issues in the field of global development. It is hoped that the lessons drawn, and the policy advice offered, will contribute significantly to the efforts of UNU-WIDER to promote the sustainable economic and social development of the poorest nations and to assist in the eradication of the blight of poverty from the world.

Giovanni Andrea Cornia
University of Florence
(Director of UNU-WIDER, 1996–99)

Matti Pohjola
Helsinki School of Economics
(Director i. a. of UNU-WIDER, 2000)

Anthony Shorrocks
Director of UNU-WIDER

1
The Contribution of the New Institutional Economics to an Understanding of the Transition Problem

Douglass C. North

Introduction

Institutions and the way they evolve shape economic performance. Institutions affect economic performance by determining (together with the technology employed) the cost of transacting and producing. They are composed of formal rules, of informal constraints and of their enforcement characteristics; while formal rules can be changed overnight by the polity, informal constraints change very slowly. Both are ultimately shaped by the subjective perceptions people possess to explain the world around them which in turn determine explicit choices of formal rules and evolving informal constraints. Institutions differ from organizations. The former are the rules of the game; the latter are groups of individuals bound together by a common objective function (economic organizations are firms, trade unions, cooperatives; political organizations are political parties, legislative bodies, etc.).

This chapter develops this analytical framework which is then applied to explore the underlying organizational problems of economies in the modern world. We then analyse the problems these changes pose for Third World and transition economies, and go on to apply the analysis in order to improve our understanding of transition economies.

Institutions and efficient markets

Institutions are the rules of the game in a society; more formally, they are the humanly devised constraints that shape human interaction. In consequence they structure incentives in exchange, whether political, social or economic.

That institutions affect economic performance is hardly controversial. That the differential performance of economies over time is fundamentally influenced by the way institutions evolve is also not controversial. But because Western neoclassical economic theory is devoid of institutions, it is of little help in analysing the underlying sources of economic performance. It would be little exaggeration to say that, while neoclassical theory is focused on the operation of efficient markets, few Western economists understand the institutional requirements essential to the creation of such markets, since they simply take them for granted. A set of political and economic institutions that provides low-cost transacting and credible commitment makes possible the efficient factor and product markets underlying economic growth.

Four major variables determine the costliness of transacting in exchange. The first is the *cost of measuring the valuable attributes* of the goods and services or the performance of agents in exchange. Property rights consist of a bundle of rights and, to the degree that we cannot measure precisely the valuable attributes of the separable rights being exchanged, then the costs of transacting and the uncertainties associated with transacting rise dramatically. Measurement consists of defining the physical dimensions of the rights exchanged (colour, size, weight, number, etc.), but also the property rights dimensions of the exchange (rights defining uses, income to be derived and alienation). When such costs are high or unforeseeable, the rights are imperfectly and incompletely specified. In consequence, the other variables in the cost of transacting become important.

The second variable in the costliness of the exchange process is the *size of the market*, which determines whether personal or impersonal exchange occurs. In personal exchange, kinship ties, friendship, personal loyalty and repeat dealings all play a part in constraining the behaviour of participants and reduce the need for costly specification and enforcement. In contrast, in impersonal exchange there is nothing to constrain the parties from taking advantage of each other. Accordingly the cost of contracting rises with the need for more elaborate specification of the rights exchanged. Effective competition acts as an essential constraint in efficient impersonal markets.

The third variable is *enforcement*. In a world of perfect enforcement, there would be, ideally, a third party impartially (and costlessly) evaluating disputes and awarding compensation to the injured party when contracts are violated. In such a world opportunism, shirking and cheating would never pay. But such a world does not exist. Indeed, the problems of creating a relatively impartial judicial system that enforces agreements have been a critical stumbling block in the path of economic development. In the Western world the evolution of courts, legal systems and a relatively impartial body of judicial enforcement has played a major role in permitting the development of a complex system of contracting that can extend over time and space, an essential requirement for a world of specialization.

If we retain the neoclassical behavioural assumption of wealth maximization, then these three variables alone determine the cost of exchange; that is, individuals would maximize at every margin (if cheating pays, one cheats; if loafing on the job is possible, one loafs; if one could with impunity burn down a competitor, one would do so). But it is hard to imagine that complex exchange and organization would be possible if this assumption accurately described human behaviour; the costliness of measuring performance, of contract fulfilment and of enforcing agreements would foreclose a world of specialization (and division of labour). *Ideological attitudes and perceptions*, the fourth variable, matter.

Ideology – consisting of the subjective 'models' individuals possess to explain and evaluate the world around them – not only plays an essential role in political choices, but also is a key to the individual choices that affect economic performance. Individual perceptions about the fairness and justice of the rules of the game obviously affect performance; otherwise we would be at a loss to explain a good deal of schooling, as well as the immense investment made by politicians, employers, labour leaders and others in trying to convince participants of the fairness or unfairness of contractual arrangements. The importance of ideology is a direct function of the degree to which the measurement and enforcement of contracts are costly. If the measurement and enforcement of contract performance can be done at low cost, then it makes very little difference whether people believe that the rules of the game are fair or unfair. But because measurement and enforcement are costly, ideology matters.

Efficient markets are a consequence of institutions that provide the low-cost measurement and enforcement of contracts at a moment of time, but we are interested in markets with such characteristics over time. Essential to efficiency over time are institutions that provide economic and political flexibility to adapt to new opportunities. Such adaptively efficient institutions must provide incentives for the acquisition of knowledge and learning, induce innovation and encourage risk taking and creative activity. In a world of uncertainty, no one knows the correct solution to the problems we confront, as Hayek has persuasively argued. Institutions should therefore encourage trials and eliminate errors. A logical corollary is decentralized decision making that will allow a society to explore many alternative ways to solve problems. It is equally important to learn from and eliminate failures. The institutions therefore must not only provide low-cost measurement of property rights and bankruptcy laws, but also provide incentives to encourage decentralized decision making and effective competitive markets.

The composition of institutions

Formal rules include political (and judicial) rules, economic rules and contracts. *Political rules* broadly define the hierarchy of the polity, its basic decision structure and the explicit characteristics of agenda control. *Economic rules* define property rights. *Contracts* contain the provisions specific to a particular agreement in exchange. Given the initial bargaining strength of the decision making parties, the function of rules is to facilitate exchange, political or economic.

Informal constraints cannot be as precisely defined as formal rules. They are extensions, elaborations and qualifications of rules that 'solve' innumerable exchange problems not completely covered by formal rules and that in consequence have tenacious survival ability. They allow people to go about the everyday process of making exchanges without the necessity of thinking out exactly at each point and in each instance the terms of exchange. 'Routines', 'customs', 'traditions' and 'culture' are words we use to denote the persistence of informal constraints. They include conventions that evolve as solutions to coordination problems and that all parties are interested in having maintained (such as, for example, the rules of the road), norms of behaviour that are recognized standards of conduct (such as codes of conduct that define interpersonal relationships in the family, business, school, etc.) and self-imposed codes of conduct (such as standards of honesty or integrity). Conventions are self-enforcing. Norms of behaviour are enforced by the second party (retaliation) or by a third party (societal sanctions or coercive authority), and their effectiveness will depend on the effectiveness of enforcement.

Self-imposed codes of conduct, unlike conventions and norms of behaviour, do not obviously entail wealth maximizing behaviour, but rather entail the sacrifice of wealth or income for other values. Their importance in constraining choices is the subject of substantial controversy, for example, in modelling voting behaviour in the US Congress (see Kalt and Zupan, 1984). Most of the controversy has missed the crucial reason why such behaviour can be and is important. That is that formal institutions (rules) frequently deliberately, sometimes accidentally, lower the costs to individuals of such behaviour and can make their normative standards embodied in self-imposed codes of conduct matter a great deal. Individual votes do not (usually) matter, but in the aggregate they shape the political world of democratic polities and they cost the voter very little; legislators commonly find ways by strategic voting to vote for their personal preferences rather than those of the electorate (Denzau, Riker and Shepsle, 1985), and judges with lifetime tenure are deliberately shielded from interest group pressures so that they can make decisions on the basis of their interpretation (subjective models) of the law. In each case, the choices that are made may be different from what they would be if the individual bore the full cost that resulted from these actions. It is the institutions that deliberately or accidentally create the externalities that alter choices. The lower the cost we incur for our convictions (ideas, dogmas, prejudices), the more they contribute to outcomes (see Nelson and Silberberg, 1987, for empirical evidence).

Agreements may be enforced by a third party (societal sanctions or the coercive force of the state), by the other party to the agreement (retaliation), or by self-imposed standards of conduct. How effectively agreements are enforced is the single most important determinant of economic performance. The ability to enforce agreements across time and space is the central under-pinning of efficient markets. On the surface it would appear to be an easy requirement to fulfil. All one needs is an effective, impartial system of laws and courts for the enforcement of formal rules, the 'correct' societal sanctions to enforce norms of behaviour and strong normative personal standards of honesty and integrity to underpin self-imposed standards of behaviour.

The creation and enforcement of efficient property rights depend on the polity, but it is difficult, if not impossible, to derive a model of a polity that produces such results with a strictly wealth maximizing behavioural assumption employing the time horizons that characterize political decisions. It is equally difficult to create normative standards of behaviour that will reinforce formal rules and make them effective. Yet when economists talk about 'efficient markets', they have implicitly assumed that all of the above conditions exist.

The historical evidence upon which to build generalizations about the evolution of efficient markets is slim indeed. We cannot explain the ascendancy of the Western world in the past six centuries purely in terms of the simple restructuring of property rights and the evolution of more efficient political markets. We must invoke the cultural and specifically ideological constraints that altered attitudes and made such property rights effective. While the Weberian heritage of the role of the Protestant ethic in the rise of capitalism has been discredited in its crude form, cultural beliefs were an important (and at least partially independent) source of the successful development of the Western world. Nor has the issue been resolved with respect to Japan and the newly industrializing economies in Asia. We know all too little about the role of cultural beliefs in shaping economic performance.

Institutional change

Understanding institutional change entails an understanding of:

(1) the stability characteristics of institutions
(2) the sources of change
(3) the agent of change, and
(4) the direction of change and path dependence.

A basic function of institutions is to provide stability and continuity by dampening the effects of relative price changes. It is institutional stability that makes possible complex exchange across space and time. A necessary condition for efficient markets is channels of exchange, both political and economic, which make possible credible agreements. This condition is accomplished by the complexity of the set of constraints that constitute institutions – by rules nested in a hierarchy, each level more costly to change than the previous one. In the United States, the hierarchy moves from constitutional rules to statute law and common law to individual contracts. Political rules are nested in a hierarchy even at the level of specific bills before Congress. The structure of committees and agenda control assures that the status quo is favoured over change.

Informal constraints are even more important anchors of stability. However, it is important to stress that these stability features in no way guarantee that the institutions are *efficient* (in the sense of producing economic growth). Stability is a necessary condition for complex human interaction, but it is not a sufficient condition for efficiency.

The sources of institutional change are changing perceptions, sometimes reflecting changes in relative prices and/or changes in preferences. Historically, fundamental changes in relative prices – such as changes in land/labour ratios as a consequence of population growth or decline – have been a key source of change. Thus, the decline of manorialism is linked to the population decline in the era that followed the fourteenth-century plague. But the associated decline of feudalism was also linked to another fundamental relative price change – alterations in military technology (the pike, cross-bow, long-bow and, of course, gunpowder) which altered the viable size and fiscal needs of polities. Changes in the relative stock of capital (both physical and human) are key sources of the institutional change of the past 200 years and will be discussed in more detail below.

But preferences change as well. For example, there may be no way to explain the demise of slavery that does not take into account the growing abhorrence on the part of civilized human beings of ownership of one person by another. Slavery was both profitable and viable in many parts of the New World in the nineteenth century. Moreover, slavery had persisted for millennia without incurring the opprobrium that began to crystallize in the Western world in the late eighteenth and early nineteenth centuries and led to the demise of slavery in the British West Indies, the US abolitionist movement and finally the end of New World slavery in Brazil in the 1880s. Ideas matter, and as they evolve they do alter preferences and hence choices.

The agent of change is the entrepreneur – political or economic. So far, we have left organizations and their entrepreneurs out of the analysis, and the definition of institutions has focused on the rules of the game rather than the players. Left out was the purposive activity of human beings to achieve objectives which in turn result in altering constraints. Organizations consist of firms, trade unions, political parties, regulatory bodies, churches and so forth. Organizations and learning alter outcomes, but how?

The institutional constraints, together with the traditional constraints of economic theory, define the potential wealth maximizing opportunities of entrepreneurs (political and economic). If the constraints result in the highest payoffs in the economy being criminal activity, or the payoff to the firm being highest from sabotaging or burning down a competitor, or to a union from engaging in slowdown and make-work, then we can expect that the organization will be shaped to maximize at those margins. On the other hand, if the payoffs come from productivity enhancing activities, then economic growth will result. In either case, the entrepreneur and his/her organization will invest in acquiring knowledge, coordination and 'learning by doing' skills in order to enhance the profitable potential. As the organization evolves to capture the potential returns, it will gradually alter the institutional constraints. It will do so either indirectly, via interaction between maximizing behaviour and its effect on gradually eroding or modifying informal constraints; or directly via investing in altering the formal rules. The relative rate of return on investing within the formal constraints or devoting resources to altering constraints will depend on the structure of the polity, the payoffs to altering the rules and the costs of political investment.

But it is not just the efforts of organizations to alter the rules that shape long-run economic performance. It is also the kind of skills and knowledge that they will induce the society to invest in. Investment in formal education, new technologies and pure science have been a derived demand from the perceived payoffs to such investment.

Institutional change, then, is an incremental process in which the short-run profitable opportunities cumulatively create the long-run path of change. The long-run consequences are often unintended for two reasons. First, the entrepreneurs are seldom interested in the larger (external to them) consequences, but the direction of their investment influences the extent to which there is investment in adding to or disseminating the stock of knowledge, encouraging or discouraging factor mobility, etc. Second, there is frequently a significant difference between intended outcomes and actual outcomes. Outcomes frequently diverge from intentions because of the limited capabilities of the individuals and the complexity of the problems to be solved.

The second economic revolution

Let us now turn to applying the foregoing analytical framework to the problems of modern economies. A little history is a prerequisite.

The tension between population and resources first popularized by Malthus has fundamentally shaped the long-run pattern of economic change. The potential economic well-being of human beings has been limited by the productivity of the technology human beings have developed. That has imposed an upper bound on their possible well-being. The lower bound has been imposed by the degree of success of human beings in exploiting that technology.

There have been two basic breakthroughs in economic history which have altered the ratio of population to resources. The first economic revolution was the creation of agriculture, which permitted an expansion of population for 10 millennia (albeit with widely varying success at solving problems and exploiting the technology). We live in the midst of the second economic revolution.

The term 'economic revolution' is intended to describe three distinct changes in an economic system:

(1) a change in the productive potential of a society which is a consequence of
(2) a basic change in the stock of knowledge and which entails
(3) an equally basic change in organization to realize that productive potential.

The second economic revolution came about in the last half of the nineteenth century as a consequence of the changes in the stock of knowledge arising from the development and implementation of modern scientific disciplines. It resulted in the systematic wedding of science and technology. The technology that characterized this revolution was one in which there were significant indivisibilities in the production process and large fixed capital investment. The overall implications for economies that could take advantage of this technology were the increasing returns and consequent high rates of economic growth that have characterized the last 150 years of the Western world. But taking advantage of this technology entailed fundamental reorganization of economies to realize this potential. In those Western economies that have, at least partially, realized this potential the result has been stresses and strains that have threatened and do threaten their continued adaptive efficiency. For the rest of the world the inability to reorganize has prevented them from realizing this productive potential and produced 'underdevelopment' and political instability. It is an extraordinary irony that Karl Marx, who first pointed out the necessity of restructuring societies in order to realize the potential of a new technology, should have been responsible for the creation of economies that have foundered on this precise issue. We shall examine the micro-level characteristics of the organizational requirements before turning to the macro-level implications.

Realizing the gains from a world of specialization requires occupational and territorial specialization on an unprecedented scale, and in consequence the number of exchanges grows exponentially. In fact, in order to realize the gains from the productive potential associated with a technology of increasing returns, one has to invest enormous resources in transacting. In the United States, for example, the labour force grew from 29 million to 80 million between 1900 and 1970. During that period the number of production workers rose from 10 million to 29 million and of white-collar workers (the majority of whom are engaged in transacting) from 5 million to 38 million; the transaction sector (that part of transaction costs that goes through the market) in 1970 made up 45 per cent of gross national product (GNP) (Wallis and North, 1986).

Let us briefly elaborate some of the measurement and enforcement problems that determine the size of the transaction sector. Necessary requirements to be able to realize the gains of a world of specialization are control over quality in the lengthening production chain and a solution to the problems of increasingly costly principal/agent relationships. Much technology, indeed, is designed to reduce transaction costs by substituting capital for labour or by reducing the degrees of freedom of the worker in the production process and by automatically measuring the quality of intermediate goods. An underlying problem is that of measuring inputs and outputs so that one can ascertain the contribution of individual factors at successive stages of production. For inputs, there is no agreed measure of the contribution of an individual input. Equally, there is room for conflict over the consequent payment to factors of production. For output, not only is there residual unpriced output – that is, waste and pollutants – but there are also complicated costs of specifying the desired properties of the goods and services produced at each stage in the production process.

Another characteristic of this new technology is that it requires large fixed capital investments with a long life and (frequently) low alternative scrap value. As a result, the exchange process embodied in contracts has to be extended over long periods of time, which entails uncertainty about prices and costs and the possibilities for opportunistic behaviour on the part of one party or the other in exchange. A number of organizational dilemmas result from these problems.

First, there are the *increased resources* necessary to measure the quality of output. Sorting, grading, labelling, trade marks, warranties and licensing are all, albeit costly and imperfect, devices to measure the characteristics of goods and services. Despite their existence, the dissipation of income is evident all around us in the difficulties of measuring automobile repairs, in evaluating the safety characteristics of products or the quality of medical services, or in measuring educational output.

Second, while team production permits economies of scale, it does so at the cost of *worker alienation and shirking*. The 'discipline' of the factory is nothing more than a response to the control problem of shirking in team production. From the perspective of the employer, discipline consists of rules, regulations, incentives and punishment essential to effective performance. Innovations such as time and motion studies are methods of measuring individual performance. From the viewpoint of the worker, they are inhuman devices to foster speed-ups and exploitation. Since there is no agreed-upon measure of output that constitutes contract performance, both are right.

Third, the potential gains from opportunistic behaviour increase and lead to *strategic behaviour* both within the firm (in labour–employer relations, for example) and in contractual behaviour among firms. Everywhere in factor and product markets the gains from withholding services or altering the terms of agreement at strategic points are potentially large.

Fourth, the development of large-scale hierarchies produces the familiar problems of *bureaucracy*. The multiplication of rules and regulations inside large organizations to control shirking and principal/agent problems results in rigidities, income dissipation and the loss of the flexibility essential to adaptive efficiency.

Fifth, and finally, there are the *external effects*: the unpriced costs reflected in the modern environmental crisis. The interdependence of a world of specialization (and division of labour) raises exponentially the imposition of costs on third parties.

The institutional and organizational restructuring necessary to take advantage of this technology is, however, much more fundamental than simply restructuring economic organization – although that task, the creation of efficient markets, is complicated enough. The entire structure of societies must be transformed. This technology and accompanying scale economies entail specialization, minute division of labour, impersonal exchange and urban societies. Uprooted are all of the old informal constraints built around the family, personal relationships and repetitive individual exchanges. Indeed, the basic traditional functions of the family, education, employment (the family enterprise) and insurance are either eliminated, or severely circumscribed. New formal rules and organizations and a greater role of government replace them.

Adaptive efficiency and modern technology

The contention of Marxists was that these problems were a consequence of capitalism and that the inherent contradictions between the new technology and the consequent organization of capitalism would lead to its demise. The Marxists were wrong that the problems were a consequence of capitalism; they are ubiquitous for any society that attempts to adopt the technology of the second economic revolution. However, as the foregoing paragraphs have attempted to make clear, Marxists were right in viewing the tensions arising between the new technology and organization as a fundamental dilemma. These tensions have only very partially been solved in the market economies of the Western world. The growth of government, the disintegration of the family and the incentive incompatibilities of many modern political and economic hierarchical organizations are all symptoms of the consequent problems besetting Western economies.

However, it has been the relative flexibility of the institutions of the Western world – both economic and political – that has been the mitigating factor in dealing with these problems. Adaptive efficiency, while far from perfect in the Western world, accounts for the degree of success that such institutions have experienced. The basic institutional framework has encouraged the development of political and economic organizations that have replaced (however imperfectly) the traditional functions of the family, mitigated the insecurity that is associated with a world of specialization, evolved flexible economic organization that has induced the low-cost transacting that has resolved some of the incentive incompatibilities of hierarchies and that has encouraged creative entrepreneurial talent and tackled (again very imperfectly) the external effects that are not only environmental, but also social in an urban world.

It is easy in the abstract to state the conditions that underlie adaptive efficiency. There must be formal rules (both political and economic) that result in well-specified property rights, effective competition, decentralized decision making and the elimination of failures. But such formal rules are by themselves no guarantee of adaptive efficiency, as illustrated by Latin American economies that adopted the US Constitution (or variants thereof) when they became independent. In fact, the simple-minded notion that 'privatization' is all that is needed to set faltering and failed economies on the path to growth is a travesty of institutional reasoning that reflects the primitive understanding of most economists about the nature of institutions. Creating efficient factor and product markets is a complicated process about which we know all too little. It does necessitate coming to grips with the transaction costs that arise from the deployment of this technology and creating the institutions that induce the development of organizations to mitigate and reduce these costs of transacting. Formal rules must be complemented by informal constraints and effective enforcement to produce such markets. Shaping the choices made about formal rules that a society adopts, the complementarity of informal constraints and the effectiveness of enforcement are the subjective frameworks that individuals employ to explain the world around them.

Ideology, choices and adaptive efficiency

While the subjective models individuals employ may be, and usually are, a hodgepodge of beliefs, dogmas, 'sound theories' and myths, there are usually elements of an organized structure to them that make them an economizing device for receiving and interpreting information.

Ideology plays no role in neoclassical economic theory. 'Rational choice' models assume that the actors possess correct models by which to interpret the world around them or receive information feedback that will lead them to revise and correct their initially incorrect models. Actors and their organizations that fail to so act will perish in the competitive markets that characterize societies. At issue is the information feedback that individuals receive and that will lead them to update their subjective models. If, in fact, the instrumental rationality postulate of economic theory were correct, we would anticipate that 'false' theories would be discarded and, to the extent that wealth maximizing was a basic behavioural trait of human beings, that economic growth would be a universal feature of economies. With a sufficiently long time horizon, that may be true; but in 10,000 years of human economic history we are still a long way from universal economic growth. The plain fact is that we do not possess the information to update our subjective theories to arrive at one true theory; in consequence, no one equilibrium is the outcome, but rather multiple equilibria exist that can take us in many directions, including stagnation and the decline of economies. Ideology matters. But where do individuals' subjective models come from and how do they get altered?

The subjective models individuals use to decipher the environment are in part a consequence of the growth and transmission of 'scientific' knowledge and in part a consequence of the socially transmitted knowledge that is the cultural heritage of every society. To the extent that the former type of knowledge determines choices, an instrumental rationality approach is the correct one in analysing economic performance. But from the beginning of human socialization, humans have created myths, taboos, religions and dogmas to account for much of their environment that defied 'scientific' explanation. They still do. Culture is more than a blending of different kinds of knowledge; it is value-laden with standards of behaviour that have evolved to solve 'local' exchange problems (be they social, political, or economic). In all societies there evolves an informal framework to structure human interaction. This framework is the basic 'capital stock' that defines the culture of a society. Culture, then, provides a language-based conceptual framework for encoding and interpreting the information that the senses are presenting to the brain. As a consequence, culture not only plays a role in shaping the formal rules, but also underlies the informal constraints that are a part of the makeup of institutions.

The ideological constructs individuals possess to explain their environment do change. They are clearly influenced by fundamental changes in relative prices which result in persistent inconsistency between the outcomes 'predicted' by the subjective models individuals possess and perceived outcomes. But that is not all. Ideas matter, and it is the combination of changes in relative prices filtered through the culturally conditioned ideas that are generated that accounts for the evolving subjective models that shape choices in a society.

The second economic revolution induced a change not only in institutions, but also in individual perceptions. It brought into question many traditional values and beliefs that had been associated with the traditional role of the family, polity and economic organization. Indeed, the intellectual ferment of the past 150 years, including the diverse perceptions of economists from Marx to Keynes to Hayek, has been an integral part of this change in perceptions that has, in turn, shaped the ideological constructs – and, therefore, the choices – of the players. But neither the constructs of economists, nor the subjective perceptions of those making choices over political and economic institutions have been independent of the evolving external political and economic environment. Or, to restate the proposition made above, it is the interplay among the evolution of culturally conditioned ideas, the constraints imposed by the existing institutional framework and the consistency or inconsistency between the perceived and predicted outcomes that shapes the evolving subjective models humans employ to make choices.

The institutional framework of market economies has both adjusted partially to resolve the costs associated with the second economic revolution and permitted the realization of the productive potential of the new technology to create the high-income economies that characterize the Western world. For the Third World and transition economies the institutional framework has imposed such high transaction costs that, while these economies have incurred the costs of the second economic revolution, they have realized only very partially the productive potential of the new technology.

Path dependence

'Path dependence', a term originally employed to describe the way a particular technological development shaped subsequent downstream technological choices, is used here to account for the parallel characteristic of an institutional framework that has shaped downstream institutional choices and in consequence makes it difficult to alter the direction of an economy once it is on a particular institutional path. The reason is that the organizations of an economy and the interest groups they produce are a consequence of the opportunity set provided by the existing institutional framework. The resulting complementarities, economies of scope and network externalities reflect the symbiotic interdependence among the existing rules, the complementary informal constraints and the interests of members of organizations created as a consequence of the institutional framework. In effect, an institutional matrix creates organizations and interest groups whose welfare depends on that institutional framework.

The dramatic fall in information costs resulting from modern technology has not only sharpened the perceived inconsistencies between predicted outcomes (of policies) and observed results, but also has made people acutely aware of alternative models that exist and that appear to offer improved solutions to economic problems. But it is one thing to become disenchanted with the old subjective models that one has employed; it is much more difficult to arrive at a new 'equilibrium' in the context of rapidly changing external events. Not only must the formal rules be changed in the face of the opposition of existing interest groups, but the ideological perceptions of the participants must change also. Moreover, the information feedback typically produces confused signals which will be interpreted differently by different individuals and groups. The result is political and social fragmentation and political instability. For example, a change in the formal rules – and, specifically, property rights – must be complemented by consistent informal constraints and effective enforcement to produce the desired results. But norms of behaviour, conventions and self-imposed codes of conduct change very slowly; moreover, enforcement will have to be undertaken, at least partially, by organizations and interest groups whose interests rest with the old institutional matrix.

Understanding transition economies

Let us state clearly and unambiguously the fundamental policy issue. If the institutional matrices of economies did not result in path dependence (that is, were not characterized by complementarities, economies of scope and network externalities) and if instrumental rationality characterized the way choices were made, then institutions would not matter, and overnight the policy maker could impose efficient rules upon an economy and alter its direction to a productive economy. Such, in essence, are the implicit assumptions that underlie neoclassical reasoning and led to the policy conclusions associated with 'privatization' as the answer to the problems of transition economies.

The Eastern European demise of communism in 1989 reflected a collapse of the perceived legitimacy of the existing belief system and consequent weakening of the supporting organizations. The result was the destruction of most of the formal institutional framework, but the survival of many of the informal constraints. Policy makers were confronted not only with restructuring an entire society, but also with the blunt instrument that is inherent in policy changes that can only alter the formal rules but cannot alter the accompanying norms and have had only limited success in even inducing enforcement of policies. The relative success of policy measures (such as the auctioning of state assets and the re-establishment of a legal system) in the Czech Republic compared to Russia resulted from the heritage of informal norms from the precommunist (and Nazi) era that made for the relatively harmonious establishment of the new rules in the former country. Russia (and the other republics of the former Soviet Union), without the heritage of a market economy and democracy, had no such norms to provide a hospitable foundation for the establishment of formal rules for such an economy and polity.

A major complicating issue was our lack of understanding about political economy. We simply do not know how to create efficient political markets. They entail not simply a set of formal rules, but complementary norms that will underpin such rules and also enforcement mechanisms (such as the rule of law). None of these existed in Russia and the other republics, and the consequences have been high costs of transacting without secure property rights and with enforcement undertaken by Mafia-like groups. We simply have no good models of polities in Third World, transition, or other economies. The interface between economics and politics is still in a primitive state in our theories, but its development is essential if we are to implement policies consistent with our intentions.

Let us conclude by talking about time. If you accept the crude schematic outline of the process of change laid out above, it is clear that change is an ongoing affair and that typically our institutional prescriptions reflect the learning from experience. But there is no guarantee that the past experiences are going to equip us to solve new problems. Indeed, an historic dilemma of fundamental importance has been the difficulties of economies shifting from a political economy based on personal exchange to one based on impersonal exchange. An equally disruptive change can be the movement from a 'command' economy to a market economy. In both cases, the necessary institutional restructuring – both economic and political – has been a major obstacle to development and still is the major obstacle for transition economies. The difficulty comes from the belief system that has evolved as a result of the cumulative past experiences of that society not equipping its members to confront and solve the new problems. Path dependence, again, is a major factor in constraining our ability to alter performance for the better in the short run.

References

Denzau, A., W. Riker and K. Shepsle (1985) 'Farquharson and Fenno: Sophisticated Voting and Home Style', *American Political Science Review* 79: 1117–34.

Kalt, M. and M. Zupan (1984) 'Capture and Ideology in the Economic Theory of Politics', *American Economic Review* 75: 279–300.

Nelson, D. and E. Silberberg (1987) 'Ideology and Legislator Shirking', *Economic Inquiry* 25: 15–25.

Wallis, J. and D. North (1986) 'Measuring the Transaction Sector in the American Economy', in S. Engerman and R. Gallman (eds), *Long-Term Factors in American Economic Growth*, Chicago: University of Chicago Press: 95–148.

2
More Instruments and Broader Goals: Moving toward the Post-Washington Consensus

Joseph E. Stiglitz

Introduction

I would like to discuss improvements in our understanding of economic development, in particular the emergence of what is sometimes called the 'post-Washington Consensus'. My remarks elaborate on two themes. The first is that we have come to a better understanding of what makes markets work well. The Washington Consensus held that good economic performance required liberalized trade, macroeconomic stability and getting prices right (see Williamson, 1990). Once the government dealt with these issues – essentially, once the government 'got out of the way' – private markets would allocate resources efficiently and generate robust growth. To be sure, all of these are important for markets to work well: it is very difficult for investors to make good decisions when inflation is running at 100 per cent a year and highly variable. But the policies advanced by the Washington Consensus are not complete, and they are sometimes misguided. Making markets work requires more than just low inflation; it requires sound financial regulation, competition policy and policies to facilitate the transfer of technology and to encourage transparency, to cite some fundamental issues neglected by the Washington Consensus.

Our understanding of the instruments to promote well-functioning markets has also improved, and we have broadened the objectives of development to include other goals, such as sustainable development, egalitarian development and democratic development. An important part of development today is seeking complementary strategies that advance these goals simultaneously. In our search for these policies, however, we should not ignore the inevitable trade-offs. This is the second theme I shall address.

Some lessons of the East Asian financial crisis

Before discussing these themes, I would like to address the implications of the East Asian crisis for our thinking about development. Observation of the successful – some even say miraculous – East Asian development was one of the motivations for moving beyond the Washington Consensus. After all, here was a regional cluster of countries that had not closely followed the Washington Consensus prescriptions but had somehow managed the most successful development in history. To be sure, many of their policies – such as low inflation and fiscal prudence – were perfectly in line with the Washington Consensus. Several aspects of their strategy, such as an emphasis on egalitarian policies, while not at odds with the Washington Consensus, were not emphasized by it. Their industrial policy, designed to close the technological gap between them and the more advanced countries, was actually contrary to the spirit of the Washington Consensus. These observations were the basis for the World Bank's *East Asian Miracle* study (World Bank, 1993), and it stimulated the recent rethinking of the role of the state in economic development.

Since the financial crisis, the East Asian economies have been widely condemned for their misguided economic policies, which are seen as responsible for the mess in which those economies find themselves today. Some ideologues have taken advantage of the current problems in East Asia to suggest that the system of active state intervention is the root of the problem. They point to the government-directed loans and the cosy relations between the government and the large *chaebol* in the Republic of Korea. In doing so, they overlook the successes of the past three decades, to which the government, despite occasional mistakes, has certainly contributed. These achievements, which include not only large increases in *per capita* GDP but also increases in life expectancy, the extension of education and a dramatic reduction in poverty, are real and will prove more lasting than the current financial turmoil.

Even when the governments directly undertook actions themselves, they made notable advances. The fact that they created the most efficient steel plants in the world challenges the privatization ideologues who suggested that such successes are at best a fluke, and at worst impossible. Nevertheless, I agree that, in general, government should focus on what it alone can do and leave the production of commodities such as steel to the private sector. But the heart of the current problem in most cases is not that government has done too much in every area but that it has done too little in some areas. In Thailand, the problem was not that the government directed investments into real estate; it was that government regulators failed to halt it. Similarly, the Republic of Korea suffered from problems including overlending to companies with excessively high leverage and weak corporate governance. The fault is not that the government misdirected credit – the fact that the current turmoil was precipitated by loans by so many US, European and Japanese banks suggests that *market* entities also may have seriously misdirected credit. Instead the problem was the government's lack of action, the fact that the government underestimated the importance of financial regulation and corporate governance.[1]

The East Asian crisis is not a refutation of the East Asian miracle. The basic facts remain: no other region in the world has ever seen incomes rise so dramatically and seen so many people move out of poverty in such a short time. The more dogmatic versions of the Washington Consensus fail to provide the right framework for understanding either the success of the East Asian economies or their current troubles. Responses to East Asia's crisis grounded in these views of the world are likely to be, at best, badly flawed and, at worst, counterproductive.

Making markets work better

The Washington Consensus was catalysed by the experience of Latin American countries in the 1980s. At the time, markets in the region were not functioning well, partly the result of dysfunctional public policies. GNP declined for three consecutive years. Budget deficits were very high – some were in the range of 5–10 per cent of GDP[2] – and the spending underlying them was being used not so much for productive investments as for subsidies to the huge and inefficient state sector. With strong curbs on imports and relatively little emphasis on exports, firms had insufficient incentives to increase efficiency or maintain international quality standards. At first deficits were financed by borrowing – including very heavy borrowing from abroad. Bankers trying to recycle petrodollars were quick to lend and low real interest rates made borrowing very attractive, even for low-return investments. After 1980, though, real interest rate increases in the United States restricted continued borrowing and raised the burden of interest payments, forcing many countries to turn to seigniorage to finance the gap between the continued high level of public spending (augmented by soaring interest payments) and the shrinking tax base. The result was very high and extremely variable inflation. In this environment, money became a much costlier means of exchange, economic behaviour was diverted toward protecting value rather than making productive investments and the relative price variability induced by the high inflation undermined one of the primary functions of the price system: conveying information.

The so-called 'Washington Consensus' of US economic officials, the International Monetary Fund (IMF) and the World Bank, was formed in the midst of these serious problems. Now is a good time to re-examine this consensus. Many countries, such as Argentina and Brazil, have pursued successful stabilizations; the challenges they face are in designing the second generation of reforms. Still other countries have always had relatively good policies or face problems quite different from those of Latin America. East Asian governments, for instance, have been running budget surpluses; inflation is low and, before the devaluations, was falling in many countries (see Figures 2.1, 2.2). The origins of the current financial crises lie elsewhere, and their solutions will not be found in the Washington Consensus.

The focus on inflation – the central macroeconomic malady of the Latin American countries, which provided the backdrop for the Washington Consensus – has led to macroeconomic policies that may not be the most conducive for long-term economic growth, and it has detracted attention from other major sources of macro-instability – namely, weak financial sectors. In the case of financial markets the focus on freeing up markets may have had the perverse effect of contributing to macroeconomic instability by weakening the financial sector. More broadly, in focusing on trade liberalization, deregulation and privatization, policy makers ignored other important ingredients, most notably competition, that are required to make an effective market economy and which may be at least as important as the standard economic prescriptions in determining long-term economic success.[3]

Other essential ingredients were also left out or underemphasized by the Washington Consensus. One – education – has been widely recognized within the development community; others, such as the improvement of technology, may not have received the attention they deserve.

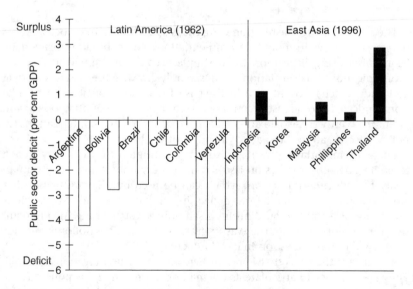

Figure 2.1   Public sector deficits: Latin America versus East Asia

Notes: Calculations based on data from IMF International Statistics Database. Figures for Thailand are from 1995.

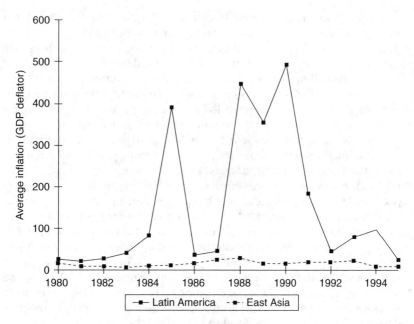

Figure 2.2   Inflation: Latin America versus East Asia, 1980–95
Note: Unweighted regional averages based on World Bank (1997d) data.

The success of the Washington Consensus as an intellectual doctrine rests on its simplicity: its policy recommendations could be administered by economists using little more than simple accounting frameworks. A few economic indicators – inflation, money supply growth, interest rates, budget and trade deficits – could serve as the basis for a set of policy recommendations. Indeed, in some cases economists would fly into a country, look at and attempt to verify these data and make macroeconomic recommendations for policy reforms, all in the space of a couple of weeks.[4]

There are important advantages to the Washington Consensus approach to policy advice. It focuses on issues of first-order importance, it sets up an easily reproducible framework which can be used by a large organization worried about recommendations depending on particular individuals' viewpoints and it is frank about limiting itself only to establishing the prerequisites for development. But the Washington Consensus does not offer answers to every important question in development.

In contrast, the ideas that I present here are, unfortunately, not so simple. They are not easy to articulate as dogma nor to implement as policy. There are no easy-to-read thermometers of the economy's health, and worse still, there may be trade-offs, in which economists, especially outside economists, should limit their role to describing consequences of alternative policies. The political process may actually have an important say in the choices of economic direction. Economic policy may not be just a matter for technical experts! These conflicts become all the more important when we come to broaden our objectives, in the final part of this chapter.

This section focuses on enhancing the efficiency of the economy. I will discuss macro-stability and liberalization – two sets of issues which the Washington Consensus was concerned about – as well as financial sector reform, the government's role as a complement to the private sector, and improving the state's effectiveness – issues that were not included in the Consensus. I shall argue that the Washington Consensus' messages in the two core areas are at best incomplete and at worse misguided. While macro-stability is important, for example, inflation is not always its most essential component. Trade liberalization and privatization are key parts of sound macroeconomic policies, but they are not ends in themselves. They are the means to the end of a less distorted, more competitive, more efficient market place and must be complemented by effective regulation and competition policies.

Achieving macroeconomic stability

Controlling inflation

Probably the most important policy prescription of the stabilization packages promoted by the Washington Consensus was controlling inflation. The argument for aggressive, pre-emptive strikes against inflation is based on three premises. The most fundamental is that inflation is costly and should therefore be averted or lowered. The second premise is that once inflation starts to rise, it has a tendency to accelerate out of control. This belief provides a strong motivation for pre-emptive strikes against inflation, with the risk of an increase in inflation being weighed far more heavily than the risk of adverse effects on output and unemployment. The third premise is that increases in inflation are very costly to reverse. This line of thought implies that even if maintaining low unemployment were valued more highly than maintaining low inflation, steps would still be taken to keep inflation from increasing today in order to avoid having to induce large recessions to bring the inflation rate down later on. All three of these premises can be tested empirically.

I have discussed this evidence in more detail elsewhere (Stiglitz, 1997a). Here I would like to summarize briefly. The evidence has shown only that high inflation is costly. Bruno and Easterly (1996) found that when countries cross the threshold of 40 per cent annual inflation, they fall into a high-inflation/low-growth trap. Below that level, however, *there is little evidence that inflation is costly.* Barro (1997) and Fischer (1993) also confirm that high inflation is, on average, deleterious for growth, but they, too, fail to find any evidence that low levels of inflation are costly. Fischer finds the same results for the variability of inflation.[5] Research by Akerlof, Dickens and Perry (1996) suggests that low levels of inflation may even improve economic performance relative to what it would have been with zero inflation.

The evidence on the accelerationist hypothesis (also known as 'letting the genie out of the bottle', the 'slippery slope' or the 'precipice theory') is unambiguous: there is no indication that the increase in the inflation rate is related to past increases in inflation. Evidence on reversing inflation suggests that the Phillips curve may be concave and that the costs of reducing infla-tion may thus be smaller than the benefits incurred when inflation is rising.[6]

In my view the conclusion to be drawn from this research is that controlling high- and medium-rate inflation should be a fundamental policy priority but that pushing low inflation even lower is not likely significantly to improve the functioning of markets.

In 1995, more than half the countries in the developing world had inflation rates of less than 15 per cent a year (Figure 2.3). For these seventy-one coun-tries, controlling inflation should not be an overarching priority. Controlling inflation is probably an important component of stabilization and reform in the twenty-five countries, almost all of them in Africa, Eastern Europe and the former Soviet Union (FSU), with inflation rates of more than 40 per cent a year. The single-minded focus on inflation may not only distort economic policies – preventing the economy from living up to its full growth and output potentials – but also lead to institutional arrangements that reduce economic flexibility without gaining important growth benefits.[7]

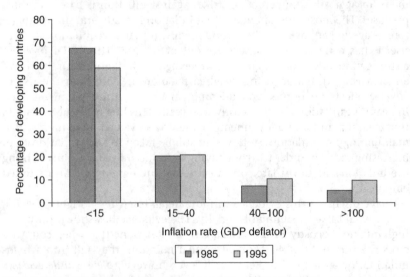

Figure 2.3   Inflation rates in developing countries, 1985 and 1995

Note: 121 of 158 low- and middle-income countries.
Source: World Bank (1997d).

Managing the budget deficit and the current account deficit

A second component of macroeconomic stability has been reducing the size of government, the budget deficit and the current account deficit. I shall return to the issue of the optimal size of government later; for now I would like to focus on the twin deficits. Much evidence shows that sustained, large budget deficits are deleterious to economic performance (Fischer, 1993; Easterly, Rodriguez and Schmidt-Hebbel, 1994).[8] The three methods of financing deficits all have drawbacks: internal finance raises domestic interest rates, external financing can be unsustainable and money creation causes inflation.[9]

There is no simple formula for determining the optimum level of the budget deficit. The optimum deficit – or the range of sustainable deficits[10] – depends on circumstances, including the cyclical state of the economy, prospects for growth, the uses of government spending, the depth of financial markets and the levels of national savings and national investment. The United States, for example, is currently trying to balance its budget. I have long argued that the low private saving rate and the ageing of the 'baby boom' generation suggest that the United States should probably be aiming for budget surpluses. In contrast, the case for maintaining budget surpluses in the East Asian countries in the face of an economic downturn, where the rate of private saving is high and the public debt–GDP ratios are relatively low, is far less compelling.

The experience of Ethiopia emphasizes another determinant of optimal deficits, the source of financing. For the last several years Ethiopia has a run a deficit of about 8 per cent of GDP. Some outside policy advisers would like Ethiopia to lower its deficit. Others have argued that the deficit is financed by a steady and predictable inflow of highly concessional foreign assistance, which is driven not by the necessity of filling a budget gap but by the availability of high returns to investment. Under these circumstances – and given the high returns to government investment in such crucial areas as primary education and physical infrastructure (especially roads and energy) – it may make sense for the government to treat foreign aid as a legitimate source of revenue, just like taxes, and balance the budget inclusive of foreign aid.

The optimal level of the current account deficit is difficult to determine. Current account deficits occur when a country invests more than it saves. They are neither inherently good nor inherently bad but depend on circumstances and especially on the uses to which the funds are put. In many countries, the rate of return on investment far exceeds the cost of international capital. In these circumstances, current account deficits are sustainable.[11]

The form of the financing also matters. The advantage of foreign direct investment (FDI) is not just the capital and knowledge that it supplies, but also the fact that it tends to be very stable. In contrast, Thailand's 8 per cent current account deficit in 1996 was not only large but came in the form of short-term, dollar-denominated debt that was used to finance local currency-denominated investment, often in excessive and unproductive uses such as real estate. More generally, short-term debt and portfolio flows can bring the costs of high volatility without the benefits of knowledge spillovers.[12]

Stabilizing output and promoting long-run growth

Ironically, macroeconomic stability – as conceived by the Washington Consensus – typically downplays stabilizing output or unemployment. Minimizing or avoiding major economic contractions should be one of the most important goals of policy. In the short run large-scale involuntary unemployment is clearly inefficient – in purely economic terms, it represents idle resources that could be used more productively. The social and economic costs of these downturns can be devastating: lives and families are disrupted, poverty increases, living standards decline and, in the worst cases, social and economic costs translate into political and social turmoil.

Moreover, business cycles themselves can have important consequences for long-run growth (see Stiglitz, 1994). The difficulty of borrowing to finance research and development (R&D) means that firms will need to reduce drastically their R&D expenditures when their cash flow decreases in downturns. The result is slower total factor productivity (TFP) growth in the future. This effect appears to have been important in the United States; whether or not it matters in countries in which R&D plays a less important role requires further study. Generally, however, variability of output almost certainly contributes to uncertainty and thus discourages investment.[13]

Variability of output is especially pronounced in developing countries (see Pritchett, 1997). The median high-income country has a standard deviation of annual growth of 2.8 per cent (Figure 2.4). For developing countries the standard deviation is 5 per cent or higher, implying huge deviations in the growth rate. Growth is especially volatile in Europe and Central Asia, the Middle East and North Africa, and sub-Saharan Africa (SSA).

How can macroeconomic stability, in the sense of stabilizing output or employment, be promoted? The traditional answer is good macroeconomic policy, including countercyclical monetary policy and a fiscal policy that allows automatic stabilizers to operate. These policies are certainly necessary, but a growing literature, both theoretical and empirical, has emphasized the important microeconomic underpinnings of macroeconomic stability. This literature emphasizes the importance of financial markets and explains economic downturns through such mechanisms as credit rationing and banking and firm failures.[14]

In the nineteenth century most of the major economic downturns in industrial countries resulted from financial panics that were sometimes preceded by and invariably led to precipitous declines in asset prices and widespread banking failures. In some countries, improvement in regulation and supervision, the introduction of deposit insurance and the shaping of

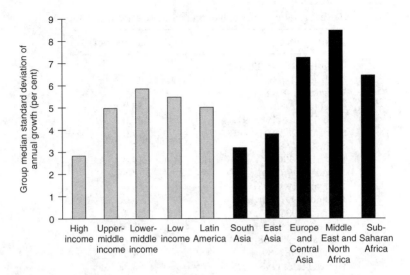

Figure 2.4 Volatility of GDP growth, 1970–95

Source: Calculations based on real annual growth rates from World Bank (1997d).

incentives for financial institutions reduced the incidence and severity of financial panics. But financial crises continue to occur, and there is some evidence that they have become more frequent and more severe in recent years (Caprio and Klingebiel, 1997). Even after adjusting for inflation, the losses from the notorious savings and loan débâcle in the United States were several times larger than the losses experienced in the Great Depression. Yet when measured relative to GDP, this débâcle would not make the list of the top twenty-five international banking crises since the early 1980s (Table 2.1).

Banking crises have severe macroeconomic consequences, affecting growth over the five following years (Figure 2.5). During the period 1975–94 growth edged up slightly in countries that did not experience banking crises; countries with banking crises saw growth slow by 1.3 percentage points in the five years following the crisis. Clearly, building robust financial systems is a crucial part of promoting macroeconomic stability.

The process of financial reform

The importance of building robust financial systems goes beyond simply averting economic crises. The financial system can be likened to the 'brain' of the economy. It plays an important role in collecting and aggregating savings from agents who have excess resources today. These resources are allocated to others – such as entrepreneurs and home builders – who can make productive use of them. Well-functioning financial systems do a very good job of selecting the most productive recipients for these resources. In

Table 2.1   Fiscal costs of banking crises, selected countries

Country (date)	Cost (percentage of GDP)
Argentina (1980–82)	55.3
Chile (1981–83)	41.2
Uruguay (1981–84)	31.2
Israel (1977–83)	30.0
Côte d'Ivoire (1988–91)	25.0
Senegal (1988–91)	17.0
Spain (1977–85)	16.8
Bulgaria (1990s)	14.0
Mexico (1995)	13.5
Hungary (1991–95)	10.0
Finland (1991–93)	8.0
Sweden (1991)	6.4
Sri Lanka (1989–93)	5.0
Malaysia (1985–88)	4.7
Norway (1987–89)	4.0
United States (1984–91)	3.2

Source: Caprio and Klingebiel (1996).

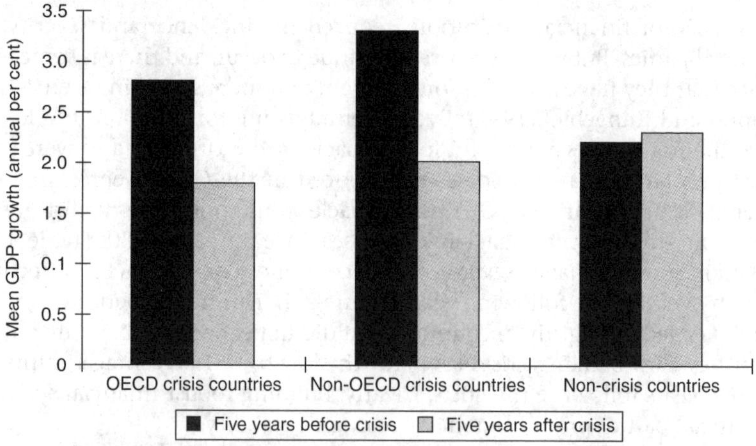

Figure 2.5   GDP growth before and after banking crises, 1975–94
Source: Caprio (1997).

contrast, poorly functioning financial systems often allocate capital to low-productivity investments. Selecting projects is only the first stage. The financial system must continue to monitor the use of funds, ensuring that they continue to be used productively. In the process financial markets serve a number of other functions, including reducing risk, increasing liquidity and conveying information. All of these functions are essential to both the growth of capital and the increase in TFP.

Left to themselves, financial systems will not do a very good job of performing these functions. Problems of incomplete information, incomplete markets and incomplete contracts are all particularly severe in the financial sector, resulting in an equilibrium that is not even constrained Pareto efficient (Greenwald and Stiglitz, 1986).[15]

The emphasis on 'transparency' in recent discussions of East Asia demonstrates our growing recognition of the importance of good information for the effective function of markets. Capital markets, in particular, require auditing standards accompanied by effective legal systems to discourage fraud, provide investors with adequate information about the firms' assets, liabilities and protect minority shareholders.[16] But transparency by itself is not sufficient, in part because information is inevitably imperfect. A sound legal framework combined with regulation and oversight is necessary to mitigate these informational problems and foster the conditions for efficient financial markets.

Regulation serves four purposes in successful financial markets: maintaining safety and soundness (prudential regulation), promoting competition, protecting consumers and ensuring that underserved groups have some access to capital. In many cases the pursuit of social objectives – such as ensuring that minorities and poor communities receive funds, as the US Community Reinvestment Act does, or ensuring funds for mortgages, the essential mission of the government-created Federal National Mortgage Association – can, if done well, reinforce economic objectives. Similarly, protecting consumers is not only good social policy; it also builds confidence that there is a 'level playing field' in economic markets. Without such confidence, those markets will remain thin and ineffective.

At times, however, policy makers face trade-offs among conflicting objectives. The financial restraints adopted by some of the East Asian economies, for example, increased the franchise values of banks, discouraging them from taking unwarranted risks that otherwise might have destabilized the banking sector. Although there were undoubtedly some economic costs associated with these restraints, the gains from greater stability almost surely outweighed those losses. As I comment below, the removal of many of these restraints in recent years may have contributed in no small measure to the current instability that these countries are experiencing.

The World Bank and others have tried to create better banking systems. But changing the system – through institutional development, transformations in credit culture and creation of regulatory structures which reduce the likelihood of excessive risk taking[17] – has proved more intractable than finding short-term solutions, such as recapitalizing the banking system. In the worst cases the temporary fixes may even have undermined pressures for further reform. Since the fundamental problems were not addressed, some countries have required assistance again and again.

The Washington Consensus developed in the context of highly regulated financial systems, in which many of the regulations were designed to limit competition rather than promote any of the four legitimate objectives of regulation. But all too often the dogma of liberalization became an end in itself, not a means of achieving a better financial system. I do not have space to delve into all of the many facets of liberalization, which include freeing up deposit and lending rates, opening up the market to foreign banks and removing restrictions on capital account transactions and bank lending. But I do want to make a few general points.

First, the key issue should not be liberalization or deregulation but construction of the *regulatory framework* that ensures an effective financial system. In many countries, this will require changing the regulatory framework by eliminating regulations that serve only to restrict competition but also accompanying these changes with increased regulations to ensure competition and prudential behaviour (and to ensure that banks have appropriate incentives).

Second, even once the design of the desired financial system is in place, care will have to be exercised in the *transition*. Attempts to initiate overnight deregulation – sometimes known as the 'big bang' – ignore the very sensitive issues of sequencing. Thailand, for instance, used to have restrictions on bank lending to real estate. In the process of liberalization it got rid of these restrictions without establishing a more sophisticated risk-based regulatory regime. The result, together with other factors, was the large-scale misallocation of capital to fuel a real estate bubble, an important factor in the financial crisis.

It is important to recognize how difficult it is to establish a *vibrant financial sector*. Even economies with sophisticated institutions, high levels of transparency, and good corporate governance such as the US and Sweden have faced serious problems with their financial sectors. The challenges facing developing countries are far greater, while the institutional base from which they start is far weaker.

Third, in all countries a primary objective of regulation should be to ensure that participants face the right *incentives*: government cannot and should not be involved in monitoring every transaction. In the banking system liberalization will not work unless regulations create incentives for bank owners, markets and supervisors to use their information efficiently and act prudentially.

Incentive issues in securities markets also need to be addressed. It must be more profitable for managers to create economic value than to deprive minority shareholders of their assets: rent-seeking can be every bit as much a problem in the private as in the public sector. Without the appropriate legal framework, securities markets can simply fail to perform their vital functions – to the detriment of the country's long-term economic growth. Laws are required to protect the interests of shareholders, especially minority shareholders.

The focus on the microeconomic – particularly the financial – underpinnings of the macroeconomy also has implications for responses to currency turmoil. In particular, where currency turmoil is the consequence of a failing financial sector, the conventional policy response to rising interest rates may be counterproductive.[18] The maturity and structure of bank and corporate assets and liabilities are frequently very different, in part because of the strong incentives for banks to use short-term debt to monitor and influence the firms they lend to and for depositors to use short-term deposits to monitor and influence banks (Rey and Stiglitz, 1993). As a result interest rate increases can lead to substantial reductions in bank net worth, further exacerbating the banking crisis.[19] Empirical studies by IMF and World Bank economists have confirmed that interest rate rises tend to increase the probability of banking crises and that currency devaluations have no significant effect (Demirgüç-Kunt and Detragiache, 1997).[20]

Advocates of high interest rate policies have asserted that such policies are necessary to restore confidence in the economy and thus stop the erosion of the currency's value. Halting the erosion of the currency, in turn, is important to both restore the economy's underlying strength and prevent a burst of inflation from the rise of the price of imported goods.[21] This prescription is based on assumptions about market reactions – i.e. what will restore confidence – and economic fundamentals.

Ultimately confidence and economic fundamentals are inextricably intertwined. Are measures that weaken the economy, especially the financial system, likely to restore confidence? To be sure, if an economy is initially facing high levels of inflation caused by high levels of excess aggregate demand, increases in the interest rate will be seen to strengthen the economic fundamentals by restoring macro-stability. For an economy where there is little initial evidence of macro-imbalances but a predicted large exogenous fall in aggregate demand, high interest rates will lead to an economic slump and the slump will combine with the interest rates themselves to undermine the financial system.

Fostering competition

So far, I have argued that macroeconomic policy needs to be expanded beyond a single-minded focus on inflation and budget deficits; the set of policies that underlay the Washington Consensus is not sufficient for macroeconomic stability or long-term development. Macroeconomic stability and long-term development require sound financial markets. But the agenda for creating sound financial markets should not confuse means with ends; redesigning the regulatory system, not financial liberalization, should be the issue.

I now want to argue that competition is central to the success of a market economy. Here, too, there has been some confusion between means and ends. Policies that should have been viewed as the means to achieve a more competitive market place were seen as ends in themselves. As a result, in some instances they failed to attain their objectives.

The fundamental theorems of welfare economics, the results that establish the efficiency of a market economy, assume that both private property and competitive markets exist in the economy. Many countries – especially developing and transition economies – lack both. Until recently, however, emphasis was placed almost exclusively on creating private property and liberalizing trade – trade liberalization being confused with establishing competitive markets. Trade liberalization is important, but we are unlikely to realize the full benefits of liberalizing trade without creating a competitive economy.

Promoting free trade

Trade liberalization, leading eventually to free trade, was a key part of the Washington Consensus. The emphasis on trade liberalization was natural: the Latin American countries had stagnated behind protectionist barriers.[22] Import substitution proved a highly ineffective strategy for development. In many countries industries were producing products with negative value added, and innovation was stifled. The usual argument – that protectionism itself stifled innovation – was somewhat confused. Governments could have created competition among domestic firms, which would have provided incentives to import new technology. It was the failure to create competition internally, more than protection from abroad, which was the cause of the stagnation. Of course, competition from abroad would have provided an important source of competition. But it is possible that in the one-sided race, domestic firms would have dropped out of the competition rather than enter the fray. Consumers might have benefited, but the effects on growth might have been more ambiguous.

Trade liberalization may create competition, but it does not do so automatically. If trade liberalization occurs in an economy with a monopoly importer, the rents may simply be transferred from the government to the monopolist, with little decrease in prices. Trade liberalization is thus neither necessary nor sufficient for creating a competitive and innovative economy.

At least as important as creating competition in the previously sheltered import-competing sector of the economy is promoting competition on the export side. The success of the East Asian economies is a powerful example of this point. By allowing each country to take advantage of its comparative advantage, trade increases wages and expands consumption opportunities. Since the 1980s, years trade has been doing just that – with world trade growing at 5 per cent a year, nearly twice the rate of world GDP growth.

Interestingly, the process by which trade liberalization leads to enhanced productivity is not fully understood. The standard Heckscher–Ohlin theory predicts that countries will shift intersectorally, moving along their production possibility frontier (PPF), producing more of what they are better at and trading for what they are worse at. In reality, the main gains from trade seem to come intertemporally, from an outward shift in the PPF as a result of increased efficiency, with little sectoral shift. Understanding the causes of this improvement in efficiency requires an understanding of the links between trade, competition and liberalization. This is an area that needs to be pursued further.[23]

Facilitating privatization

State monopolies in certain industries have stifled competition. But the emphasis on privatization over the 1990s stemmed less from concern over lack of competition than from a focus on profit incentives. In a sense, it was natural for the Washington Consensus to focus more on privatization than on competition. Not only were state enterprises inefficient, their losses contributed to the government's budget deficit, adding to macroeconomic instability. Privatization would kill two birds with one stone, simultaneously improving economic efficiency and reducing fiscal deficits.[24] The idea was that if property rights could be created, the profit maximizing behaviour of the owners would eliminate waste and inefficiency. At the same time the sale of the enterprises would raise much-needed revenue.

Although in retrospect the process of privatization in the transition economies was, in several instances at least, badly flawed, at the time it seemed reasonable to many. Although most people would have preferred a more orderly restructuring and the establishment of an effective legal structure (covering contracts, bankruptcy, corporate governance and competition) prior with or at least simultaneous with promulgations, no one knew how long the reform window would stay open. At the time, privatizing quickly and comprehensively – and then fixing the problems later on – seemed a reasonable gamble. From today's vantage point, the advocates of privatization may have overestimated the benefits of privatization and underestimated the costs, particularly the political costs of the process itself and the impediments it might pose to further reform. Taking that same gamble today, with the benefit of seven more years of experience, would be much less justified.

Even at the time many of us warned against hastily privatizing without creating the needed institutional infrastructure, including competitive markets and regulatory bodies. David Sappington and I showed in the fundamental theorem on privatization that the conditions under which privatization can achieve the public objectives of efficiency and equity are very limited and are very similar to the conditions under which competitive markets attain Pareto efficient outcomes (Sappington and Stiglitz, 1987). If, for instance, competition is lacking, creating a private, unregulated monopoly will likely result in even higher prices for consumers. And there is some evidence that, insulated from competition, private monopolies may suffer from several forms of inefficiency and may not be highly innovative.

Indeed, both large-scale public and private enterprises share many similarities and face many of the same organizational challenges (Stiglitz, 1989). Both involve substantial delegation of responsibility – neither legislatures nor shareholders in large companies directly control the daily activities of an enterprise. In both cases the hierarchy of authority terminates in managers who typically have a great deal of autonomy and discretion. Rent-seeking occurs in private enterprises, just as it does in public enterprises. Shleifer and Vishny (1989) and Edlin and Stiglitz (1995) have shown that there are strong incentives not only for private rent-seeking on the part of management but for taking actions that increase the scope for such rent-seeking. In the Czech Republic the bold experiment with voucher privatization seems to have foundered on these issues, as well as the broader issues of whether, without the appropriate legal and institutional structures, capital markets can provide the necessary discipline to managers as well as allocate scarce capital efficiently.

Public organizations typically do not provide effective incentives and often impose a variety of additional constraints. When these problems are effectively addressed, when state enterprises are embedded in a competitive performance-based environment, performance differences may narrow (Caves and Christenson, 1980).

The differences between public and private enterprises are hazy, and there is a continuum of arrangements in between. Corporatization, for instance, maintains government ownership but moves firms toward hard budget constraints and self-financing; performance-based government organizations use output-oriented performance measures as a basis for incentives. Some evidence suggests that much of the gains from privatization occur before privatization as a result of the process of putting in place effective individual and organizational incentives (Pannier, 1996).

The importance of competition rather than ownership has been most vividly demonstrated by the experience of China and the Russian Federation. China extended the scope of competition without privatizing state-owned enterprises (SOEs). To be sure, a number of problems remain in the state-owned sector, which may be addressed in the next stage of reform. In contrast, Russia has privatized a large fraction of its economy without doing much to promote competition. The contrast in performance could not be greater, with Russia's output below the level attained almost a decade ago, while China has managed to sustain double-digit growth for almost two decades. Though the differences in performance may be only partially explained by differences in the policies they have pursued, both the Chinese and Russian experiences pose quandaries for traditional economic theories.

In particular, the magnitude and duration of Russia's downturn is itself somewhat of a puzzle: the Soviet economy was widely considered rife with inefficiencies, and a substantial fraction of its output was devoted to military expenditures. The elimination of these inefficiencies should have raised GDP, and the reduction in military expenditures should have increased personal consumption still farther.[25] Yet neither seems to have occurred.

The magnitude and success of China's economy since the 1980s also represents a puzzle for standard theory. Chinese policy makers not only eschewed a strategy of outright privatization, they also failed to incorporate numerous other elements of the Washington Consensus. Yet China's recent experience is one of the greatest economic success stories in history. If China's thirty provinces were treated as separate economies – and many of them have populations exceeding those of most other low-income countries – the twenty fastest-growing economies between 1978 and 1995 would all have been Chinese provinces (World Bank, 1997a). Although China's GDP in 1978 represented only about one-quarter of the aggregate GDP of low-income countries and its population represented only 40 per cent of the total, almost two-thirds of aggregate growth in low-income countries between 1978 and 1995 was accounted for by the increase in China's GDP.

While measurement problems make it difficult to make comparisons between Russia and China with any precision, the broad picture remains persuasive: real incomes and consumption have fallen in the FSU, and real incomes and consumption have risen rapidly in China.

One of the important lessons of the contrast between China and Russia is for the political economy of privatization and competition. It has proved difficult to prevent corruption and other problems in privatizing monopolies. The huge rents created by privatization will encourage entrepreneurs to try to secure privatized enterprises rather than invest in creating their own firms. In contrast, competition policy often undermines rents and creates incentives for wealth creation. The sequencing of privatization and regulation is also very important. Privatizing a monopoly can create a powerful entrenched interest that undermines the possibility of regulation or competition in the future.

The Washington Consensus is right – privatization is important. The government needs to devote its scarce resources to areas the private sector does not and is not likely to enter. It makes no sense for the government to be running steel mills. But there are critical issues about both the sequencing and the scope of privatization. Even when privatization increases productive efficiency, it may be difficult to ensure that broader public objectives are attained, even with regulation. Should prisons, social services, or the making of atomic bombs (or the central ingredient of atomic bombs, highly enriched uranium) be privatized, as some in the United States have advocated? Where are the boundaries? More private sector activity can be introduced into public activities (through contracting, for example, and incentive-based mechanisms, such as auctions). How effective are such mechanisms as substitutes for outright privatization? These issues were not addressed by the Washington Consensus.

Establishing regulation

Competition is an essential ingredient in a successful market economy. But competition is not viable in some sectors – the so-called 'natural monopolies'. Even there, however, the extent and form of actual and potential competition are constantly changing. New technologies have expanded the scope for competition in many sectors that have historically been highly regulated, such as telecommunications and electric power.

Traditional regulatory perspectives, with their rigid categories of regulation versus deregulation and competition versus monopoly, have not been helpful guides to policy in these areas. These new technologies do not call for wholesale deregulation, because not all parts of these industries are adequately competitive. Instead, they call for appropriate changes in *regulatory structure* to meet the new challenges. Such changes must recognize the existence of hybrid areas of the economy, parts of which are well suited to competition, while other parts are more vulnerable to domination by a few producers. Allowing a firm with market power in one part of a regulated industry to gain a stranglehold over other parts of the industry will severely compromise economic efficiency.

Forging competition policy

Although the scope of viable competition has expanded, competition is often imperfect, especially in developing countries. Competition is suppressed in a variety of ways, including implicit collusion and predatory pricing. Control of the distribution system may effectively limit competition even when there are many producers. Vertical restraints can restrict competition. And new technologies have opened up new opportunities for anti-competitive behaviour, as recent cases in the US airline and computer industry have revealed.

The establishment of effective anti-trust laws for developing countries has not been examined adequately. The sophisticated and complicated legal structures and institutions in place in the United States may not be appropriate for many developing countries, which may have to rely more on *per se* rules.

Competition policy also has important implications for trade policy. Currently, most countries have separate rules governing domestic competition and international competition (Australia and New Zealand are exceptions). With little if any justification, rules governing competition in international trade (such as anti-dumping provisions and countervailing duties) are substantially different from domestic anti-trust laws (see Stiglitz, 1997b); much of what we consider as healthy price competition domestically would be classified as dumping.[26] These abuses of fair trade were pioneered in the industrial countries but are now spreading to the developing countries – which surpassed industrial countries in the initiation of anti-dumping actions reported to the General Agreement on Tariffs and Trade (GATT) and the World Trade Organization (WTO) for the first time in 1996

(World Bank, 1997b). The best way to curtail these abuses would be to integrate fair trade and fair competition laws based on the deep understanding of the nature of competition that anti-trust authorities and industrial organization economists have evolved over the course of a century.

Government acting as a complement to markets

For much of this century, people have looked to government to spend more and intervene more. Government spending as a share of GDP has grown with these demands (Figure 2.6). The Washington Consensus policies were based on a rejection of the state's activist role and the promotion of a minimalist, non-interventionist state. The unspoken premise is that governments are worse than markets. Therefore the smaller the state, the better the state.

It is true that states are often involved in too many things, in an unfocused manner. This lack of focus reduces efficiency; trying to get government better focused on the fundamentals – economic policies, basic education, health, roads, law and order, environmental protection – is a vital step. But focusing on the fundamentals is not a recipe for minimalist government. The state has an important role to play in appropriate regulation, social protection and welfare. The choice should not be whether the state should be involved, but how it gets involved. The central question should thus not be the size of the government, but the activities and methods of the government.

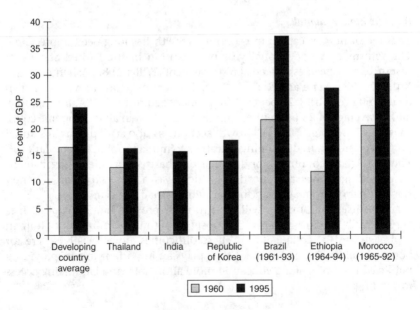

Figure 2.6 Government spending in selected countries (as a per cent of GDP)
Source: Data from IMF Government Financial Statistics.

Countries with successful economies have governments that are involved in a wide range of activities.

Over the past several decades there has been an evolving framework within which the issue of the role of the government can be addressed: the recognition that markets might not always yield efficient outcomes – let alone socially acceptable distributions – led to the 'market failures' approach.[27] There was a well-defined set of market failures, associated with externalities and public goods, which justified government intervention. This list of market failures was subsequently expanded to include imperfect information and incomplete markets, but the market failure approach continued to focus on dividing sectors and activities into those which should be in the government domain and those that fell within the province of the private sector. More recently, there has been a growing recognition that the government and private sector are much more intimately entwined. The government should serve as a *complement* to markets, undertaking actions that make markets work better and correcting market failures. In some cases the government has proved to be an effective catalyst – its actions have helped solve the problem of undersupply of (social) innovation, for example. But once it has performed its catalytic role, the state needs to withdraw.[28]

I cannot review all of the areas in which government can serve as an important complement to markets. I shall discuss briefly only two, building human capital and transferring technology.

Building human capital

The role of human capital in economic growth has long been appreciated. The returns to an additional year of education in the United States, for instance, have been estimated at 5–15 per cent (Willis, 1986; Ashenfelter and Krueger, 1994; Kane and Rouse, 1995). The rate of return is even higher in developing countries: 24 per cent for primary education in SSA, for example, and an average of 23 per cent for primary education in all low-income countries (Psacharopoulos, 1994). Growth accounting also attributes a substantial portion of growth in developing countries to human capital accumulation.[29] The East Asian economies, for instance, emphasized the role of government in providing universal education, which was a necessary part of their transformation from agrarian to rapidly industrializing economies.

Left to itself, the market will tend to underprovide human capital. It is very difficult to borrow against the prospects of future earnings since human capital cannot be collateralized. These difficulties are especially severe for poorer families. The government thus plays an important role in providing public education, making education more affordable, and enhancing access to funding.

Transferring technology

Studies of the returns to R&D in industrial countries have consistently found individual returns of 20–30 per cent and social returns of 50 per cent or higher – far exceeding the returns to education (Nadiri, 1993). Growth accounting usually attributes the majority of *per capita* income growth to improvements in TFP – Solow's pioneering analysis (1957) attributed 87.5 per cent of the increase in output per man-hour between 1909 and 1949 to technical change. Based on a standard Cobb–Douglas production function, *per capita* income in the Republic of Korea in 1990 would have been only $2,041 (in 1985 international dollars) if it had relied solely on capital accumulation, far lower than actual *per capita* income of $6,665. The difference comes from increasing the amount of output per unit of input, which is partly the result of improvements in technology.[30]

Left to itself, the market underprovides technology. Like investments in education, investments in technology cannot be used as collateral. Investments in R&D are also considerably riskier than other types of investment and there are much larger asymmetries of information that can impede the effective workings of the market.[31] Technology also has enormous positive externalities that the market does not reward. Indeed, in some respects, knowledge is like a classical public good. The benefits to society of increased investment in technology far outweigh the benefits to individual entrepreneurs. As Thomas Jefferson said, ideas are like a candle, you can use them to light other candles without diminishing the original flame. Without government action there will be too little investment in the production and adoption of new technology.

For most countries not at the technological frontier, the returns associated with facilitating the transfer of technology are much higher than the returns from undertaking original R&D. Policies to facilitate the transfer of technology are thus one of the keys to development. One aspect of these policies is investing in human capital, especially in tertiary education. Funding of universities is justified not because it increases the human capital of particular individuals but because of the major externalities that come from enabling the economy to import ideas. Of course, unemployment rates for university graduates are high in many developing countries, and many university graduates hold unproductive civil service jobs. These countries have probably overemphasized liberal arts educations.[32] In contrast, the Republic of Korea and Taiwan (China) have narrowed the productivity gap with the leading industrial countries by training scientists and engineers (Figure 2.7).

Another policy that can promote the transfer of technology is FDI. Singapore, for example, was able to assimilate rapidly the knowledge that came from its large FDI inflows.

Policies adopted by the technological leaders also matter. There can be a tension between the incentives to produce knowledge and the benefits from more dissemination. In recent years concern has been expressed that the balance industrial countries have struck – often under pressure from special interest groups – underemphasizes dissemination. The consequences may slow the overall pace of innovation and adversely affect living standards in both richer and poorer countries.[33]

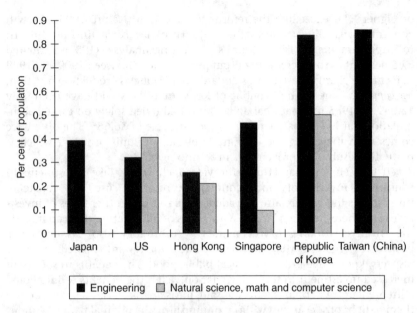

Figure 2.7 Tertiary-level students in technical fields (percentage of population)

Source: *UNESCO Statistical Yearbook 1995*; Government of Taiwan, *Taiwan Statistical Yearbook, 1994*; Ministry of Education (Singapore).

Making government more effective

How can policies be designed that increase the productivity of the economy? Again, the ends must not be confused with the means. The elements stressed by the Washington Consensus may have been reasonable means for addressing the particular set of problems confronting the Latin American economies in the 1980s, but they may not be the only, or even the central, elements of policies aimed at addressing problems in other circumstances.

Part of the strategy for a more productive economy is ascertaining the appropriate role for government – identifying, for instance, the ways in which government can be a more effective complement to markets. I now want to turn to another essential element of public policy – namely, how we can make government more effective in accomplishing whatever tasks it undertakes.

The *World Development Report 1997* shows that an effective state is vital for development (World Bank, 1997c). Using data from ninety-four countries over three decades, the study shows that it is not just economic policies and human capital but the quality of a country's *institutions* that determines economic outcomes. Those institutions in effect determine the environment within which markets operate. A weak institutional environment allows greater arbitrariness on the part of state agencies and public officials.

Given very different starting points – unique histories, cultures and societal factors – how can the state become effective? Part of the answer is that the state should match its role to its capability. What the government does, and how it does it, should reflect the capabilities of the government – and those of the private sector. Low-income countries often have weaker markets and weaker government institutions. It is especially important, therefore, that they focus on how they can most effectively complement markets.

But capability is not destiny. States can improve their capabilities by reinvigorating their institutions. This means not only building administrative or technical capacity but instituting rules and norms that provide officials with incentives to act in the collective interest while restraining arbitrary action and corruption. An independent judiciary, institutional checks and balances through the separation of powers and effective watchdogs can all restrain arbitrary state action and corruption. Competitive wages for civil servants can attract more talented people and increase professionalism and integrity.

Perhaps some of the most promising and least explored ways to improve the function of government is to use markets and market-like mechanisms. There are several ways the government can do this:

(1) It can use auctions both for procuring goods and services and for allocating public resources
(2) It can contract out large portions of government activity
(3) It can use performance contracting, even in those cases where contracting out does not seem feasible or desirable
(4) It can design arrangements to make use of market information – for instance, it can rely on market judgements of qualities for its procurement (off-the-shelf procurement policies); it can use information from interest rates paid to, say, subordinated bank debt to ascertain appropriate risk premiums for deposit insurance.

At the same time, governments are more effective when they respond to the needs and interests of their citizens, while at the same time giving them a sense of ownership and stake in the policies. Michael Bruno emphasized the importance of consensus building in ending inflations. The reason for this should be obvious: if workers believe that they are not being fairly treated, they may impose inflationary wage and other demands, making the resolution of the inflationary pressures all but impossible (see Bruno, 1993).

At the microeconomic level, governments, aid agencies and non-governmental organizations (NGOs) have been experimenting with ways of providing decentralized support and encouraging community participation in the selection, design and implementation of projects. Research provides preliminary support for this approach: a study by Isham, Narayan and Pritchett (1995) found the success rate for rural water projects that involved participation was substantially higher than the success rate for those that did not. It is not just that localized information is brought to bear in a more effective way; the commitment to the project leads to the long-term support (or 'ownership' in the popular vernacular) which is required for sustainability.

Broadening the goals of development

The Washington Consensus advocated use of a small set of instruments (including macroeconomic stability, liberalized trade and privatization) to achieve a relatively narrow goal (economic growth). The post-Washington Consensus recognizes both that a broader set of instruments is necessary and that our goals are also much broader. We seek increases in living standards – including improved health and education – not just increases in measured GDP. We seek sustainable development, which includes preserving natural resources and maintaining a healthy environment. We seek equitable development, which ensures that all groups in society, not just those at the top, enjoy the fruits of development. And we seek democratic development, in which citizens participate in a variety of ways in making the decisions that affect their lives.

Knowledge has not kept pace with this proliferation of goals. We are only beginning to understand the relationship between democratization, inequality, environmental protection and growth. What we do know holds out the promise of developing complementary strategies that can move us toward meeting all of these objectives. But we must recognize that not all policies will contribute to all objectives. Many policies entail trade-offs. It is important to recognize these trade-offs and make choices about priorities. Concentrating solely on 'win–win' policies can lead policy makers to ignore important decisions about 'win–lose' policies.

Achieving multiple goals by improving education

Promoting human capital is one example of a policy that can help promote economic development, equality, participation and democracy. In East Asia universal education created a more egalitarian society, facilitating the political stability that is a precondition for successful long-term economic development. Education – especially education that emphasizes critical, scientific thinking – can also help train citizens to participate more effectively and more intelligently in public decisions.

Achieving multiple goals through joint implementation of environmental policy

To minimize global climate change, the nations of the world need to reduce the production of greenhouse gases, especially carbon dioxide, which is produced primarily by combustion. The reduction of carbon emissions is truly a global problem. Unlike air pollution (associated with sulphur dioxide or nitrogen dioxide), which primarily affects the polluting country, all carbon emissions enter the atmosphere, producing global consequences that affect the planet as a whole.

Joint implementation gives industrial countries (or companies within them) credit for emissions reductions they would not otherwise have undertaken anywhere in the world. It may be a feasible first step toward designing an efficient system of emission reductions because it requires commitments only from industrial countries and therefore does not entail resolving the huge distributional issues involved either in systems of tradable permits or the undertaking of obligations by developing countries.

The premise of joint implementation is that the marginal cost of carbon reductions may differ markedly in different countries. Because developing countries are typically less energy efficient than industrial countries, the marginal cost of carbon reduction in developing countries may be substantially lower than in industrial countries. The World Bank has offered to set up a carbon investment fund that would allow countries and companies that need to reduce emissions to invest in carbon-reducing projects in developing countries. For developing countries this plan would offer increased investment flows and pro-environment technology transfers. These projects would also be likely to reduce the collateral environmental damage caused by dirty air. Joint implementation allows industrial countries to reduce carbon emissions at a lower cost. This strategy is designed to benefit the developing countries as it improves the global environment.

Recognizing the trade-offs involved in investing in technology

One important example of a potential trade-off is investment in technology. Earlier I discussed the way investments in tertiary technical education promote the transfer of technology and thus economic growth. The direct beneficiaries of these investments, however, are almost inevitably better off than the average. The result is thus likely to be increased inequality.

The transfer of technology may also increase inequality. Although some innovations benefit the worst off, much technological progress raises the marginal products of those who are already more productive. Even when it does not, the opportunity cost of public investment in technology may be forgone investment in anti-poverty programmes. By increasing output, however, these investments can benefit the entire society. The potential trickle down, however, is not necessarily rapid or comprehensive.

Recognizing the trade-off between protecting the environment and increasing participation

A second example of a trade-off is the choice between environmental goals and participation. Participation is essential. It is not, however, a substitute for expertise. Studies have shown, for instance, that popular views on the ranking of various environmental health risks are uncorrelated with the scientific evidence (US EPA, 1987; Slovic, Layman and Flynn, 1993). In pursuing environmental policies, do we seek to make people feel better about their environment, or do we seek to reduce real environmental health hazards? There is a delicate balance here, but at the very least, more dissemination of knowledge can result in more effective participation in formulating more effective policies.

Concluding remarks

The goal of the Washington Consensus was to provide a formula for creating a vibrant private sector and stimulating economic growth. In retrospect the policy recommendations were highly risk-averse – they were based on the desire to avoid the worst disasters. Although the Washington Consensus provided some of the foundations for well-functioning markets, it was incomplete and sometimes even misleading.

The World Bank's East Asian miracle project was a significant turning-point in the discussion. It showed that the stunning success of the East Asian economies depended on much more than just macroeconomic stability or privatization. Without a robust financial system – which the government plays a huge role in creating and maintaining – it is difficult to mobilize savings or allocate capital efficiently. Unless the economy is competitive, the benefits of free trade and privatization will be dissipated in rent-seeking, not directed toward wealth creation. And if public investment in human capital and technology transfers is insufficient, the market will not fill the gap.

Many of these ideas – and more still that I have not had time to discuss – are the basis of what I see as an emerging consensus, a post–Washington Consensus consensus. One principle that emerges from these ideas is that whatever the new consensus is, it cannot be based on Washington. If policies are to be sustainable, developing countries must claim ownership of them. It is relatively easier to monitor and set conditions for inflation rates and current account balances. Doing the same for financial sector regulation or competition policy is neither feasible nor desirable.

A second principle of the emerging consensus is that a greater degree of humility is called for, acknowledgment of the fact that we do not have all of the answers. Continued research and discussion, not just between the World Bank and the IMF but throughout the world, are essential if we are to better understand how to achieve our many goals.

Notes

1. There are, to be sure, many other dimensions to the turmoil. Misguided foreign exchange policies and the potential for political instability are a few other significant issues that I discuss at more length in Stiglitz (1998).
2. Argentina, for example, had a deficit of over 5 per cent of GDP in 1982 and 7 per cent in 1983, Colombia's budget deficit was over 4 per cent from 1982 to 1984 and Brazil's deficit had increased from 11 per cent in 1985 to 16 per cent by 1989 (World Bank, 1997d).

3. See Vickers and Yarrow (1988) for a fuller discussion of privatization, competition and incentives.
4. These issues came up in the management of the US economy. Although much research showed that the United States was able to operate at lower levels of unemployment without an acceleration of inflation, reports from some international institutions, using oversimplified models of the US economy, recommended tightening monetary policy. Had this advice been followed, the remarkable economic expansion, and the resulting low unemployment rate which has brought marginalized groups into the labour force, reduced poverty and contributed substantially to the reduction of welfare rolls, would all have been thwarted (see US CEA, 1997, Chapter 2, for some of this analysis).
5. Because the level and variability of inflation are correlated, Fischer reported great difficulty in disentangling their separate effects at any level/variance of inflation. This point holds true generally: any study of the consequences of inflation probably also picks up costs associated with the variability of inflation.

   The strength of non-linearity in the relationship between inflation and social welfare is clear from the outcome of research conducted by the US Fed. Despite the efforts of their first-rate economists – some of them working full time on the costs of inflation – the Fed has still failed to find definitive evidence of costs of inflation in the United States. Should they eventually succeed in finding such results, they will have proven only that data-mining works, not that inflation is costly.
6. Stiglitz (1997c) discusses the evidence in the United States. Tentative research at the World Bank (discussed in Stiglitz, 1997a) extends the results to a number of other countries, including Australia, Brazil, Canada, France, Germany, Italy and Japan. Mexico was the only country with adequate data to run the tests where the Phillips curve appeared convex.
7. Some have argued that central banks should have an exclusive mandate to maintain price stability. This perspective has even been introduced into IMF programmes in economies such as Korea *with no history of an inflation problem*. There is no evidence that such constraints (whether embodied in legislation or formal commitments such as inflation targets) improve *real* economic performance as measured by growth (see Alesina and Summers, 1993). Such results are consistent with the earlier empirical evidence concerning the real effects of inflation. More importantly, these issues involve fundamental political judgements, values and trade-offs in addition to technical expertise. For example, I – as well as most other members of the Clinton Administration's economics team – strongly opposed proposals to change the charter of the Fed to make price stability its primary or sole mandate. Such proposals might well have been the centre of a major political debate if they had been pushed. See Stiglitz (1997a) for a broader discussion of these issues.
8. The theoretical literature on Ricardian equivalence (Barro, 1974) criticizes the view that the deficit *by itself* has significant economic effects. The Washington Consensus was not based on models that explicitly addressed the issue of Ricardian equivalence.
9. Easterly and Fischer (1990) summarize the simple analytics of the macroeconomic effects of government budget deficits.
10. I use the terms 'optimum' and 'sustainable' loosely. In this context, 'sustainable' does not necessarily mean 'sustained' at a high level indefinitely. Rather, it refers to situations such as when large deficits are used to stimulate the economy out of

an economic downturn expected to be of short duration. 'Optimum' has to be defined relative to a clearly articulated objective such as maximizing in an intertemporal social welfare function. There are circumstances and reasonable social welfare functions that give markedly different values for today's optimal level of deficit – one cannot assert that desirable level of deficit without knowing both factors. The same observation applies to the following discussion of the optimal level of the current account deficit.

11. The current account deficit is an endogenous variable. Assessing whether it is too 'high' depends on the source of its size. If, for example, misguided foreign exchange policies account for the deficit, it is too high.

12. Traditional government macro-policies focus on aggregates such as capital flows and budget deficits and do not deal directly with these issues. If the maturity structure of foreign borrowing leads to significant risks, other capital restraints or interventions may be necessary.

13. There are also other channels through which economic downturns leave a longer-term adverse legacy: the attrition of human capital has, for instance, been emphasized in the literature on the hysteresis effect and may be a factor in the sustained high levels of unemployment in Europe (see Blanchard and Summers, 1987). As I discuss in the following section, economic downturns, when severe enough, can undermine the strength of the financial system.

14. In the Great Depression, falling prices combined with fixed interest payments reduced firms' net cash flows, eroding net worth and decreasing their investment and further weakening the economy. As a result, these models are sometimes called 'debt–deflation models'. See Greenwald and Stiglitz (1988, 1993a, 1993b).

15. The term 'constrained Pareto efficient' means that there are (in principle) government interventions which can make some people better off without making anyone else worse off *which respect the imperfections of information and the incompleteness of markets – and, more broadly, the costs of offsetting these imperfections.*

16. For a fuller discussion of the role of these protections as part of the basic architecture of modern capitalism, see Greenwald and Stiglitz (1992).

17. This is sometimes referred to as the problem of *moral hazard.*

18. Supporters of these policies, while recognizing these problems, argue that a *temporary* increase in interest rates is required to restore confidence and that as long as the interest rate measures are very short term, little damage will be done. Whether increases in interest rates will, or should, restore confidence has been much debated. The evidence from the recent experience is not fully supportive. Thailand and Indonesia have been pursuing high-interest rate policies since the summer of 1997.

19. Most analyses of the US saving and loan crisis place the ultimate blame on the unexpectedly large increases in interest rates that began in the late 1970s under Fed chairman Paul Volcker. This increase in interest rates caused the value of their assets to plunge, leaving many with low or negative net worth. Attempts to allow individual savings and loans to try to solve their own problems (part of regulatory forbearance) failed, worsening the eventual débâcle.

20. There is another reason that government should perhaps be more sensitive to interest rate changes than to exchange rate changes: while there is an economic logic to maturity mismatches, there is no corresponding justification for exchange rate mismatches. There is a real cost associated with forcing firms to reduce maturity mismatches. Exchange rate mismatches, in contrast, simply represent speculative behaviour. In practice, policy cannot rely on these general

nostrums but needs to look carefully at the situation within the country in crisis. It is possible that currency mismatches are far larger than maturity mismatches, and while future actions may be directed at correcting such speculation with its systemic effects, current policy must deal with the realities of today.

21. The persistence of the inflationary effects of a devaluation raises subtle questions. Earlier I argued against the 'precipice' theory of inflation. One might argue that an increase in the price level associated with a devaluation is even less likely to give rise to inflation inertia than other sources of increases in prices, particularly when there may be a perception that the exchange rate has overshot.

22. Advocates of import substitution point out that during certain periods countries that pursued protectionist policies – notably Brazil and Taiwan (China) in the 1950s – did achieve strong economic growth.

23. The adverse effects associated with protectionism may come more from its impact on competition and its inducement to rent-seeking behaviour. These forces are so strong that even when there may be seemingly strong arguments for trade interventions in particular cases, most economists view intervention in trade policy with considerable scepticism.

24. Short-term impacts on deficits were, however, often markedly different from the long-term impacts. In those cases where the state enterprises were reasonably well run, the latter could be negligible or even negative while the former could be substantial. In response, some governments disallowed the inclusion of capital transactions in the annual budget – an accounting practice consistent with views that such public sector financial reorganization may have little impact on macro-behaviour, or at least far different effects.

25. This can be thought of either as a movement toward the production possibilities curve or as an outward shift of the production possibilities curve (a 'technological improvement', where the curve has embedded in it the institutional constraints reflecting how production and distribution is organized).

26. Lester Thurow has noted that, 'if the [anti-dumping] law were applied to domestic firms, eighteen out of the top twenty firms in Fortune 500 would have been found guilty of dumping in 1982' (Thurow, 1985: 359).

27. See Stiglitz (1989) for an extended discussion of the economic role of the state from this perspective.

28. The US government, for example, established a national mortgage system, which lowered borrowing costs and made mortgages available to millions of Americans. Having done so, however, it may be time for this activity to be turned over to the private sector.

29. Mankiw, Romer and Weil (1992).

30. While more recent studies (Young, 1994, for example) have questioned the robustness of these results and some growth accounting exercises for the United States suggest little increase in TFP growth over the past quarter-century, the observation that changes in technology have played a major role in improvements in standards of living seems uncontroversial.

31. The innovator will be reluctant to describe his innovation to a provider of capital, lest he steal his idea; but the provider of capital will be reluctant to supply capital without an adequate disclosure. A clear regulatory structure for protecting intellectual property (IP) rights is necessary, but not sufficient, to overcome these sorts of problems.

32. There may also be an absence of complementary factors, such as the conditions required for new enterprises to develop to use these skills.

33. Knowledge is a key input into the production of knowledge; an increase in the 'price' of knowledge (as a result of stricter IP standards) may thereby reduce the production of knowledge. There is also a concern that an excessive amount of expenditures on research is directed at trying to convert 'common knowledge' into a form that can be appropriated. While in principle 'novelty' standards are intended to guard against this, in practice the line is never perfectly clear, and stricter IP regimes are more likely to commit 'errors' of privatizing public knowledge, thereby creating incentives for misdirecting intellectual energies in that direction.

References

Akerlof, G., W. Dickens and G. Perry (1996) 'The Macroeconomics of Low Inflation', *Brookings Papers on Economic Activity* 1: 1–76.
Alesina, A. and L. Summers (1993) 'Central Bank Independence and Macroeconomic Performance: Some Comparative Evidence', *Journal of Money Credit and Banking* 25(2).
Ashenfelter, O. and A. Krueger (1994) 'Estimates of Economic Returns to Schooling from a New Sample of Twins', *American Economic Review* December.
Barro, R. (1974) 'Are Government Bonds Net Wealth?', *Journal of Political Economy* 81(6): 1095–117.
——— (1997) *Determinants of Economic Growth*, Cambridge, MA: MIT Press.
Blanchard, O. and L. Summers (1987) 'Hysteresis and the European Unemployment Problem', in S. Fischer (ed.), *NBER Macroeconomics Annual*, 1, Cambridge, MA: MIT Press.
Bruno, M. (1993) *Crisis, Stabilization, and Economic Reform: Therapy by Consensus*, Oxford: Clarendon Press.
Bruno, M. and W. Easterly (1996) 'Inflation and Growth: In Search of a Stable Relationship', *Federal Reserve Bank of St Louis Review* 78(3): 139–46.
Caprio, G. (1997) 'Safe and Sound Banking in Developing Countries: We're Not in Kansas Anymore', *Research in Financial Services: Private and Public Policy* 9: 79–97.
Caprio, G. and D. Klingebiel (1996) 'Bank Insolvencies: Cross-Country Experience', World Bank Policy Research Working Paper 1620, Washington, DC: World Bank.
——— (1997) 'Bank Insolvency: Bad Luck, Bad Policy, or Bad Banking?', in M. Bruno and B. Pleskovic (eds), *Annual World Bank Conference on Development Economics 1996*, Washington, DC: World Bank.
Caves, D. and L. Christensen (1980) 'The Relative Efficiency of Public and Private Firms in a Competitive Environment: The Case of Canadian Railroads', *Journal of Political Economy* 88(5): 958–76.
Demirgüç-Kunt, A. and E. Detragiache (1997) 'The Determinants of Banking Crises: Evidence from Industrial and Developing Countries', World Bank Policy Research Working Paper 1828, Washington, DC: World Bank.
Easterly, W. and S. Fischer (1990) 'The Economics of the Government Budget Constraint', *World Bank Research Observer* 5(2): 127–42.
Easterly, W., C. Rodriguez and K. Schmidt-Hebbel (eds) (1994) *Public Sector Deficits and Macroeconomic Performance*, Washington, DC: World Bank.
Edlin, A. and J. E. Stiglitz (1995) 'Discouraging Rivals: Managerial Rent-Seeking and Economic Inefficiencies', *American Economic Review* 85(5): 1301–12.
Feldstein, M. (1996) 'The Costs and Benefits of Going from Low Inflation to Price Stability', *NBER Working Paper* 5469, Cambridge, MA: NBER.

Fischer, S. (1993) 'The Role of Macroeconomic Factors in Growth', *Journal of Monetary Economics* 32: 485–512.

Greenwald, B. and J. E. Stiglitz (1986) 'Externalities in Markets with Imperfect Information and Incomplete Markets', *Quarterly Journal of Economics* 101: 229–64.

———— (1988) 'Examining Alternative Macroeconomic Theories', *Brookings Papers on Economic Activity* 1: 207–70.

———— (1992) 'Information, Finance and Markets: The Architecture of Allocative Mechanisms', *Industrial and Comporate Change* 1(1): 37–63.

———— (1993a) 'Financial Market Imperfections and Business Cycles', *Quarterly Journal of Economics* 108(1): 77–114.

———— (1993b) 'New and Old Keynesians', *Journal of Economic Perspectives* 7(1): 23–44.

Isham, J., D. Narayan and L. Pritchett (1995) 'Does Participation Improve Performance? Establishing Causality with Subjective Data', *World Bank Economic Review* 9(2): 175–200.

Kane, T. and C. Rouse (1995) 'Labor Market Returns to Two- and Four-Year College: Is a Credit a Credit and Do Degrees Matter?', *American Economic Review* 85(3): 600–14.

Mankiw, N. G., D. Romer and D. N. Weil (1992) 'A Contribution to the Empirics of Economic Growth', *Quarterly Journal of Economics*, 107(2): 407–37.

Nadiri, I. (1993) 'Innovations and Technological Spillovers', NBER Working Paper 4423, Cambridge, MA: NBER.

Pannier, D. (ed.) (1996) *Corporate Governance of Public Enterprises in Transitional Economies*, World Bank Technical Paper 323. Washington, DC: World Bank.

Pritchett, L. (1997) *Patterns of Economic Growth: Hills, Plateaus, Mountains, Cliffs, and Plains*, Washington, DC: Policy Research Department, World Bank.

Psacharopoulos, G. (1994) 'Returns to Investment in Education: A Global Update', *World Development* 22(9): 1325–43.

Rey, P. and J. E. Stiglitz (1993) 'Short-term Contracts as a Monitoring Device', NBER Working Paper 4514, Cambridge, MA: NBER.

Sappington, D. and J. E. Stiglitz (1987) 'Privatization, Information and Incentives,' *Journal of Policy Analysis and Management* 6(4): 567–82.

Shleifer, A. and R. Vishny (1989) 'Management Entrenchment: The Case of Manager-Specific Investments', *Journal of Financial Economics* 25(1): 123–39.

Slovic, P., M. Layman and J. Flynn (1993) 'Perceived Risk, Trust, and Nuclear Waste: Lessons from Yucca Mountain', in R. Dunlap, M. Kraft and E. Rosa (eds), *Public Reactions to Nuclear Waste*, Durham, NC: Duke University Press.

Solow, R. (1957) 'Technical Change and the Aggregate Production Function', *Review of Economics and Statistics* August.

Stiglitz, J. E. (1989) 'The Economic Role of the State: Efficiency and Effectiveness,' in A. Heertje (ed.), *The Economic Role of the State*, London: Basil Blackwell and Bank Insinger de Beaufort NV.

———— (1994) 'Endogenous Growth and Cycles', in Y. Shionoya and M. Perlman (eds), *Innovation in Technology, Industries, and Institution*, Ann Arbor, MI: University of Michigan Press.

———— (1997a) 'Central Banking in a Democratic Society', The Tinbergen Lecture.

———— (1997b) 'Dumping on Free Trade: The US Import Trade Laws', *Southern Economic Journal* 64(2), 402–24.

———— (1997c) 'Reflections on the Natural Rate Hypothesis', *Journal of Economic Perspectives* 11(1): 3–10.

———— (1998) 'The Role of International Institutions in the Current Global Economy', speech to the Council on Foreign Relations in Chicago, 27 February.

Thurow, L. (1985) *The Zero-Sum Solution: Building a World-Class American Economy*, New York: Simon & Schuster.

US CEA (United States Council of Economic Advisers) (1997) *Economic Report of the President 1997*, Washington, DC: Government Printing Office.

US EPA (United States Environmental Protection Agency) (1987) *Unfinished Business: A Comparative Assessment of Environmental Problems*, Washington, DC: Government Printing Office.

Vickers, J. and G. Yarrow (1988) *Privatization: An Economic Analysis*, Cambridge, MA: MIT Press.

Williamson, J. (1990) 'What Washington Means by Policy Reform', in J. Williamson (ed.), *Latin American Adjustment: How Much Has Happened?* Washington, DC: Institute for International Economics.

Willis, R. (1986). 'Wage Determinants: A Survey and Reinterpretation of Human Capital Earnings Functions', in O. Ashenfelter and R. Layard (eds), *Handbook of Labor Economics I*, Amsterdam: Elsevier Science/North-Holland.

World Bank (1993) *The East Asian Miracle*, New York: Oxford University Press.

———— (1997a) *China 2020*, Washington, DC: World Bank.

———— (1997b) *Global Economic Prospects and the Developing Countries*, Washington, DC: World Bank.

———— (1997c) *World Development Report 1997: The State in a Changing World*, New York: Oxford University Press.

———— (1997d) *World Development Indicators 1997*, Washington, DC: World Bank.

Young, A. (1994) 'The Tyranny of Numbers: Confronting the Statistical Realities of the East Asian Growth Experience', *Quarterly Journal of Economics* 110: 641–80.

3
Is Rising Income Inequality Inevitable? A Critique of the Transatlantic Consensus

Anthony B. Atkinson

Introduction: is rising income inequality inevitable?

This chapter addresses one of the most important economic issues facing our societies and the world as a whole: rising income inequality. There is a widely held belief that rising inequality is inevitable. Increased inequality is the result of forces, such as technological change, over which we have no control, or the globalization of trade, which people believe, despite historical evidence to the contrary, to be irreversible. Kuznets (1955) suggested that income inequality might be expected to follow an inverse-U shape, first rising with industrialization and then declining. Today, the Kuznets curve is commonly believed to have doubled back on itself: the period of falling inequality has been succeeded by a reversal of the trend. Seen in this way, the third quarter of the twentieth century was a Golden Age not just for growth and employment, but also for its achievement in lowering economic inequality. On this basis, the marked rise in wage and income inequality observed in the United States and the United Kingdom in recent decades will unavoidably be followed by rises in other countries, and indeed worldwide. Policy can make little difference.

In this chapter, I take issue with the assertion that rising inequality is inevitable. It may in fact turn out that the twenty-first century sees rising inequality, but this is not inescapable. We do have some choice. In challenging the popular position, I focus on the experience of Organization for Economic Cooperation and Development (OECD) countries, since it is these that I know best, but what is happening in industrialized economies cannot be divorced from what is happening in developing countries. Indeed, one frequently expressed view is that increased wage dispersion in the OECD countries is due to increased competition from low-wage economies. This is a view which it seems particularly appropriate to examine in the WIDER Annual Lecture. (I have discussed the rival view that increased wage dispersion is due to technological change in Atkinson, 2000.)

The chapter comprises three sections. In the first, I present a critique of the 'Transatlantic Consensus', a term I use to describe what has rapidly become the generally accepted explanation of the rise in inequality in OECD countries. Economists are sometimes accused of being slow to react to changing events – that they are always seeking to explain the last generation's economic problems. In my view, economists are in fact quick to respond to changing issues; indeed they could rather be faulted for being too fashion conscious. In the field of income inequality, there has been a swift response. There has become established a Transatlantic Consensus that increased income inequality in the United States and high unemployment in Continental Europe are due to a shift of demand away from unskilled workers towards skilled workers. I refer to it as a 'Transatlantic Consensus' because it provides a unified explanation as to how a single cause has a differential impact on the United States and on mainland Europe. It also captures the fact that this view has been widely influential in the policy making of international institutions on both sides of the Atlantic, such as the IMF and the OECD. This consensus is, however, open to question. The first section of this chapter elaborates the underlying theory of distribution, treating in particular the international trade aspects, and argues that the Consensus view has so far fallen short of providing a complete explanation.

Is there an alternative? The second section of the chapter seeks to describe a different approach to explaining rising earnings inequality. One ingredient is a move from a simple skilled/unskilled dichotomy of the labour force to the more realistic assumption of a continuum of earnings capacity. This allows us to focus on the fact that it is not just the unskilled who have lost relative to the median but that the median worker has lost relative to high earners. There has in fact been a 'tilt' in the earnings/skill nexus. The second ingredient in the alternative approach proposed here is the explicit recognition of the role of social conventions or social codes in pay determination. Social conventions may allow the resolution of problems of incomplete contracting, where supply and demand considerations place limits only on the possible wage differentials. Changes in wage differentials may reflect shifts in such social conventions. Social codes, or pay norms, may play an intrinsic, and not just an instrumental, role, where people attach weight to the loss of reputation that follows from breach of the code. The cost of breaking the code depends on the degree of adherence, which is endogenous, and increased pay dispersion may have arisen on account of a shift from a high- to a low-adherence equilibrium.

The first two sections therefore concentrate on the determinants of what people receive as wages in the market place. (Capital incomes are also important, but are not discussed here.) But market incomes are significantly modified by government policy. Many people in OECD countries, like the retired or the unemployed, receive very little in the way of market incomes. They survive because of state transfers (retirement pensions, unemployment insurance, etc.) financed by social security and other taxes. In the third section I show how the government budget has played a major role in off-setting the rise in inequality in market incomes – a rise that pre-dates the present concerns. The degree of offset differs, however, across countries, and across time in any one country. This suggests that national policy may be influential, but also raises the question as to the degree to which national governments can preserve autonomy in their redistributive policy in an increasingly integrated world.

Rising inequality and the Transatlantic Consensus

The phenomenon of rising inequality of income in industrialized countries[1] was first noticed in the United States, where inequality as measured by the Gini coefficient began to rise in the 1970s – see Figure 3.1. (The Gini coefficient is a summary measure of inequality, varying between 0 when we all have identical incomes and 100 per cent when one person scoops the entire pool.) The rise in the United States has attracted most attention, but my own country, the United Kingdom, has seen an even larger increase. In the period 1977–90, the Gini coefficient for the distribution by individuals of equivalent household disposable income in the United Kingdom rose by some 10 percentage points, from around 23 per cent to around 33 per cent (see Figure 3.1). This increase is 2.5 times the increase in the United States over that period.[2]

The first point that I therefore want to make is that experience is not uniform across OECD countries. Even if it were true that all OECD countries have seen increased income inequality, the extent and timing of the increase have differed. Among Anglo-Saxon countries, there has been a sharp rise in income inequality in New Zealand, but little apparent increase in Canada. The last of these is striking, as Smeeding (1999) has emphasized. We have two North American countries, sharing a long frontier, with considerable cross-border economic flows, where the degree of integration has increased with the North American Free Trade Agreement (NAFTA), and yet the time paths of income inequality are noticeably different. In the Nordic countries there has also been a variety of experience. In their study of the distributional impact of rising unemployment, Aaberge *et al.* (1997) found that, in the period in question, inequality of disposable income did not respond at all in Finland and relatively little in Denmark, but rose, albeit modestly, in Sweden and Norway – the situation for Norway is shown in Figure 3.1. In other European countries, there is a similar diversity of experience. In Germany, taking the Western *Länder* for purposes of comparability over time, the Gini coefficient has increased by some 3 percentage points since the 1970s, as may be seen by piecing together the two series in Figure 3.1, and the increase in the Netherlands in the second half of the 1980s was similar in magnitude. In France, there was no increase in the 1980s.

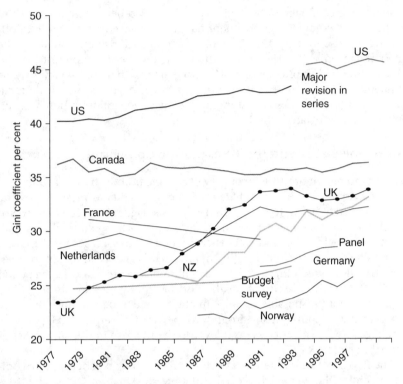

Figure 3.1   Changes in income inequality, 1977–99

Sources: Canada, Statistics Canada (1996: Text Table VI) and Statistics Canada (1999: Appendix Table III); France, (1975 = 100) Atkinson (1997b: Table FR2 Synthèses series); (West) Germany (1978 = 100), Becker (1996: Tabelle 1) and Hauser (1996: Tabelle 1) linked at 1993 using Becker (1998: Tabelle 4); Netherlands, supplied by Central Bureau of Statistics; New Zealand, Statistics New Zealand (1999); Norway, Epland (1998); United Kingdom, up to 1993 from Atkinson (1997b: Table UK3) series constructed by Goodman and Webb (1994), 1994/5–1997/8 from Clark and Taylor (1999: Figure 2 and text). Figures prior to 1993 from Family Expenditure Survey (FES); figures from 1994/5 from Family Resources Survey; United States, US Department of Commerce (1999: Table B-3, B-6).

The figures just cited refer to the inequality of *disposable household incomes*; there is similar diversity in the experience with regard to *gross individual earnings*. Figure 3.2 shows estimates (based largely on data assembled by the OECD) of the changes since 1977 in the ratio of earnings at the top decile to those at the bottom decile (the 'decile ratio').[3] The picture is again one of diversity. The United States, the United Kingdom and New Zealand are in this case more similar in the extent of the increase in dispersion. For other countries, the pattern is mixed, with a rise and then a fall in Canada and Norway, a fall in Germany, a rise in the Netherlands and variation about a level trend in France. Certainly for the first half of the 1990s there is no dominating pattern. As has been observed by the OECD, drawing on evidence for a larger number of countries, 'No clear tendency emerges of a generalized increase in earnings inequality over the first half of the 1990s. Of the 16 countries ... dispersion increased in half, and was either broadly unchanged or declined somewhat in the rest' (OECD, 1996: 63).

The second point to be made about the evidence for incomes and earnings is that, while economists tend to talk glibly about 'trends' in income inequality, this is not necessarily a good way of describing the observed changes over time. As I argued in my Presidential Address to the Royal Economic Society (Atkinson, 1997a), it may be more instructive to think in terms of 'episodes' when inequality rose or fell. This is well illustrated by the United Kingdom in Figure 3.1. There has not been a continuous upward trend in the United Kingdom. In the 1980s, inequality increased, and it then accelerated. But from 1990 to 1997, under the premiership of John Major, the Gini coefficient appears to have cycled rather than trended upward. Equally, the 1999 report of the US Department of Commerce (1999: xiii) commented that there had been no significant annual increase since 1993 (when there was a major revision in the methodology). While there may be cyclical influences in operation disguising the trend, the 1990s do not look like the 1980s in the United States and the United Kingdom. A third example is provided by the Netherlands. Inequality in disposable income clearly increased, but it appears to have been a step increase in the second half of the 1980s, not a continuing trend (the same appears to be true of earnings dispersion in Figure 3.2). To describe recent experience as an inexorable trend is not therefore correct empirically, and it may well put us on the wrong track when seeking to explain the evolution of inequality, which is my main concern here.

The Transatlantic Consensus

As already noted, economists seem to have moved rapidly to a consensus view, where increased income inequality is identified with increased inequality of potential earnings (and hence actual earnings or employment), and where increased wage inequality is attributed to a shift in relative demand away from unskilled to skilled workers. There is debate about the causes of the shift in relative demand – see, for example, Burtless (1995) and Dewatripont, Sapir and Sekkat (1999). It may be liberalization of international trade and increased trade flows; it may be heightened competition from newly industrializing countries (NICs) (Wood, 1994). Or, the shift may be the result of technical change biased towards skilled labour, with the introduction of automation and information technology (IT). Or it could be the outcome of technical change biased towards sectors using skilled labour. In this chapter, given its international focus, I concentrate on the international trade version of the story,[4] without in any way suggesting that technological change is unimportant.

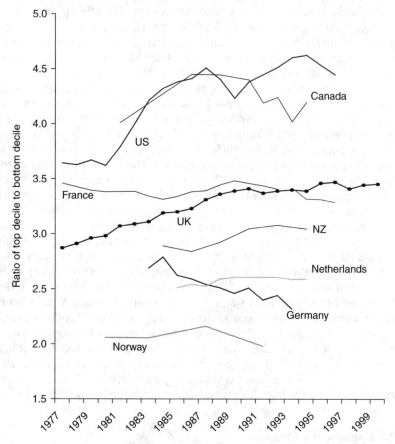

Figure 3.2   Changes in earnings inequality, 1977–99

Sources: Canada (1981 = 100), (West) Germany (1983 = 100), Netherlands (1985 = 100), New Zealand (1984 = 100) and Norway (1980 = 100), OECD (1996: Table 3.1); France, Bayet and Julhès (1996: 48); United Kingdom, Atkinson and Micklewright (1992: Table BE1) linked at 1990 to Department of Employment (1999: Table A30.2); United States, Karoly (1994: Table 2B.2), weekly (consistent) wage and salary income, linked at 1979 and 1987, linked in 1989 to OECD (1996: Table 3.1, which refers to male earnings).

The trade story is well summarized in a 1999 CEPR bulletin: 'developed countries have become increasingly open to trade with developing countries. The latter are rich in unskilled labour, it is argued: they can supply goods where production is "unskilled-intensive", such as T-shirts from China, at a fraction of developed country costs. Hence unskilled wages in developed countries must fall' (CEPR, 1999: 5).

This can be formally demonstrated in a standard trade theory model of the Heckscher–Ohlin type, where there are two blocs of countries (industrialized and newly industrializing, respectively), each with two sectors of production. The sectors produce tradable goods using two different types of labour (skilled and unskilled) in different mixes: one 'high-technology' sector uses skilled labour relatively intensively (at all relative wage rates), whereas the other sector is relatively unskilled-intensive (for simplicity, other factors of production such as capital or land are ignored, as are non-traded goods and services). A reduction in the barriers to trade leads to a new equilibrium where the industrialized countries expand their output of the high-technology sector and contract that of the other good, and the relative wage of skilled labour rises.

All models are abstractions, but that just sketched is an oversimplification in one important respect: the industrialized countries have very different structures. We need to allow for at least two distinct groupings within the OECD: Continental Europe and the United States (plus probably the United Kingdom and other Anglo-Saxon countries; Japan should perhaps be treated on its own). In what follows, I posit a three-bloc model, referred to as US, EZ (Euro zone) and NIC (newly industrializing). The relevant difference here between the two industrialized blocs (US and EZ) is the existence in the latter of effective minimum wage protection, or social security benefit levels, preventing wages from falling at the bottom. The demand shift story then predicts not increased wage dispersion but increased unemployment. According to Krugman, 'the upward trend in unemployment [in Europe] is the result of market forces that "want" to produce greater inequality of earnings. The collision between these market forces and the attempts of the welfare state to limit inequality then lead to higher unemployment' (Krugman, 1994: 60).

So we appear to have unified explanation for what is happening on both sides of the Atlantic: widening wage dispersion in the US and raised unemployment in the EZ. The position as far as earnings are concerned is shown for France and the United States in Figure 3.3. In the French case, the bottom decile of earnings for male workers was 59 per cent of the median in 1977 and had actually risen slightly to 62 per cent in 1987, whereas the US percentage fell from 50 per cent to 44 per cent over the same period. I will return later to what happened post-1987.

Moreover, even though the step is not usually taken, we could explain differences *within* the two industrialized blocs in the speed and timing of the rise in earnings inequality by reference to changes in the supply of skilled labour in response to the emerging increased skill premium. Differential performance across countries in the race between technological development and education, as it was described by Tinbergen (1975), does not, in the Heckscher–Ohlin model, cause the unskilled/skilled wage relationship to differ across countries, but the distribution of earnings *is* potentially affected by changes in the proportions of unskilled workers (and of the unemployed). The unskilled/skilled wage differential is not a complete summary statistic,

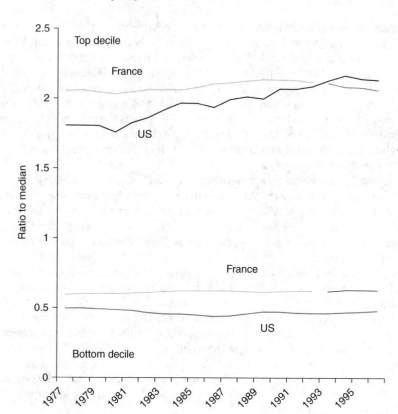

Figure 3.3   Earnings distribution in France and the United States, 1977–97
Sources: Bernstein and Mishel (1997: Table 4); Friez and Julhès (1998: 43).

as is obvious from considering the case of the decile ratio where one group is more than 90 per cent of the total.

Unresolved questions

The relation between wage dispersion and increased international competition has been seen as a classic example of the power of economic theorizing. A textbook model can be applied directly to explain real-world observations. At the end of his survey on growing world trade, Krugman (1995) observes that 'the time has come' for general equilibrium trade theory. By this, he meant that one of the most important contributions of trade theory is its general equilibrium perspective, of seeing the world economy as a whole. But in seeing the world as a whole, we need to go beyond the two-country model which has dominated trade theory since, as has been brought out by Davis (1998a, 1998b), the conclusions can be misleading. In drawing its conclusions, the 'Transatlantic Consensus' in effect carries out parallel analyses of the impact on the United States and the impact on Europe of the opening of trade with the NICs. As noted earlier, we require at least a three-bloc model. When we look at the world in this way, we see, extending the analysis of Davis, that the standard Heckscher–Ohlin trade theory falls short of yielding the predictions assumed in the Transatlantic Consensus.

Suppose first that the conditions for factor price equalization hold. These conditions are strong, requiring that countries differ in their productive capacities only in their factor endowments, having identical (constant returns to scale) production functions. The conditions require that there be equal numbers of goods and factors, and that countries produce all goods. From strong assumptions follow strong implications. In particular, where there are no factor-intensity reversals, free international trade leads to the equalization of factor prices – see, for example, Bhagwati (1964), Chipman (1966) and Dixit and Norman (1980). Put in terms of two factors (skilled and unskilled labour) and two goods, there is a one-to-one relation between the relative goods prices and the skilled/unskilled wage ratio (the assumption that there are no factor-intensity reversals, means that one of the two goods uses skilled labour relatively intensively at all relative wage rates). If we now suppose that one of the two industrialized blocs (the EZ) imposes a minimum relative wage for unskilled labour, then this determines the goods' relative prices and the wage of skilled labour. In the absence of specialization, the US will adjust to the EZ-determined relative price. The United States has a flexible wage, but the wages of the unskilled rise to the European level (and those of the skilled fall) as the US expands its exports to the EZ of the good which uses unskilled labour intensively. There will be unemployment of unskilled labour in the EZ, but not in the US.

Before questioning the underlying assumptions, we should note the implications of this analysis for the Transatlantic Consensus. If the combined US + EZ trading economy is opened to trade with the NIC, then, provided that the EZ continues to produce the good intensive in unskilled labour, the goods' price remains unchanged. The US is unaffected and the impact of the trade is entirely on unemployment in the EZ. In neither region is wage inequality affected. We have one part of the Transatlantic Consensus but not the other. As put by Davis: 'So long as Europe maintains a commitment to both free trade and a high-wage policy, America is fully insulated from the NIC shock' (1998a: 485). The factor price equalization result should not be taken too literally: '[it is] a very ambitious proposition ... One ought to be satisfied with the more plausible Marshallian way of putting things: free trade sets up a tendency to factor price equalization' (Hahn, 1998: 18). But, translated to the present context, this means that there is a *tendency* for the low paid in the United States to be sheltered by European unemployment.

On this basis, trade theory can explain the widening of wage inequality in the United States only to the extent that the conditions of the standard Heckscher–Ohlin model do *not* hold. In order for this to be satisfactorily treated, we need to model the reasons why the factor price equalization theorem does not apply. One reason is that the EZ, with its minimum wage, may cease to produce the good in which unskilled labour is used intensively; it becomes specialized in the high-technology good, importing the other good from the US, where the wages of the unskilled are no longer tied to those in Europe. In this case, opening of trade with NIC will drive the relative price of the high-technology good higher and, reading across from goods prices to factor prices, hence widen wage differentials in the US. The US side of the story is now in place. In the EZ, however, wage inequality will rise, and unemployment fall (as unskilled labour is substituted for skilled in the production of the high-technology good). The effect will be intensified if there are also non-traded goods and services which use unskilled labour. We lose therefore the EZ arm of the Consensus.

In brief, the theoretical basis for the Consensus does not appear to be a simple application of standard international trade theory of the Heckscher–Ohlin variety. The model needs to be richer. This enrichment could take the form of more realistic assumptions about the trading economies, such as introducing imperfect competition and product differentiation, or non-traded goods, or allowing for productivity differences, or for transport costs, or incorporating the effect of the Common Agricultural Policy (CAP) in the EZ. All of these could well lead to an enhanced trade theory which can explain the observed changes in the US and the EZ, but work remains to be done. Alternatively, we could look elsewhere.

An alternative approach to explaining earnings inequality

In this section, I want to suggest two ingredients of an alternative approach to explaining earnings dispersion. The first is to abandon the simple unskilled/skilled distinction. A century ago, it might have been relatively easy to apply such a dichotomy. In Aldous Shipyard in Brightlingsea, where my sailing boat was built in 1899, the shipwrights were skilled craftsmen and the men with brooms who kept the slipways free of mud were unskilled. Today's attempts to implement the distinction are less satisfactory. As noted by Cooper (1995: 366), the practice adopted in many studies of treating all production workers as unskilled and non-production as skilled seems too coarse. In some cases, skill is equated with formal education, and increased wage inequality is associated with the increased return to college-educated workers since the 1970s. But identifying 'skilled' with 'college-educated' shifts the basis for the definition, and makes no allowance for mismatch between the educational qualifications of workers and the requirements of the job they hold.

What I would like to consider instead is a *continuum of earnings*. One reason for so doing is empirical. From Figure 3.3, it may be seen that the most significant widening is not that at the bottom of the US earnings distribution. In fact, the bottom decile, where the unskilled may be expected to be found, was actually rising relative to the median in the United States through the 1990s, rather than falling. Between 1987 and 1996 the ratio increased from the 44 per cent mentioned earlier back to 48 per cent. It is true that earnings dispersion has been widening, but this is because of what is happening higher up the scale. From Figure 3.3, it may be seen that in the United States the top decile's pay rose over the two decades from around 1.8 times the median to around 2.15. In contrast, in France the top decile did not go up significantly relative to the median over the period as a whole. Of course, the ratio in France was initially higher,[5] so that one can represent the US widening as 'catching up', but in terms of changes over time the main phenomenon which needs to be explained is the rotation of the wage/rank relationship. This tilt is illustrated for the United Kingdom in Figure 3.4. It is not just a question of those at the bottom losing out (the downward arrow) – indeed, in the second ten-year period from 1989 to 1999 the ratio of the

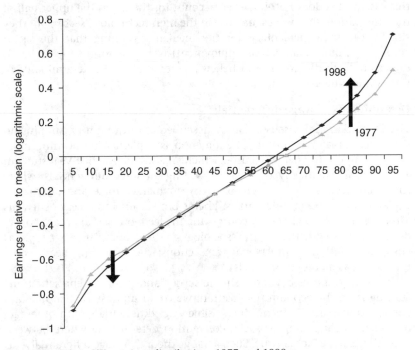

Figure 3.4 Tilt in UK earnings distribution, 1977 and 1998

Sources: 1977 earnings data for all workers whose pay was not affected by absence from Atkinson and Micklewright (1992: Table BE1), 1998 from Department of Employment, *New Earnings Survey* (1998: Table UK 9.1) for all workers whose pay was not affected by absence, paid at adult rates. The former covers Great Britain, the latter the United Kingdom.

bottom decile to the median in the United Kingdom rose slightly. Increased wage dispersion is due more to what has happened in the upper part of the distribution (upward arrow).

In order to understand this, we have to move to a continuum of earnings. This is not of course new. A continuum of earnings has been studied in labour economics and in public economics (as in the optimum income tax literature). But it has not been treated explicitly in the present context. Krugman drew just such a tilt in his popular exposition (1994), but did not carry it through to the more formal model (1995). In order to see the implications for international trade, let us suppose that there are two goods, in one of which (the 'high-technology' sector) output is proportional to individual productivity, but in the other (the 'low-technology' sector), all workers are equally productive. Average productivity in the high-technology sector depends on the proportion of the labour force employed. The expansion of international trade, so that the relative price of the low-technology good falls, means that wages fall relatively in that sector, although the proportion employed also falls (the number of less favoured workers is endogenous in this case).[6] This does not, however, account for the tilt in the upper half of the distribution. Real wages may rise in the high-technology sector, but they rise by the same percentage for the median (assuming that the sector accounts for more than half of employment) as they do for the top decile. To understand the tilt, we have, I believe, to investigate the determinants of wage differentials.

Determinants of wage differentials

The Transatlantic Consensus can be described as a triumph of 'supply and demand'. A major economic phenomenon is explained by nothing more than the supply and demand curves which are learned by a first-year student. This contrasts markedly with earlier writing on wage differentials, where there has been a creative tension between market force and alternative explanations of wage differentials. Phelps Brown, for instance, opened his *The Inequality of Pay* (1977) by contrasting the 'economist's' approach to pay determination with that of the 'sociologist': the economist sees people as engaged in rational, impersonal transactions; the sociologist sees people interacting as members of a society.

How can we move beyond a simple supply and demand representation? Starting from the economist's position, we could suppose that supply and demand only place limits on the possible wage differentials, with other factors such as bargaining or social convention determining where between these limits wages actually lie. Such a 'range theory' of wage differentials was advanced by Lester (1952) and the way in which a range of negotiation can arise has been illustrated by models of job matching: 'Having come together, the firm and worker have a joint surplus ... there is a wage that makes the worker indifferent between taking this job and waiting for his next job opportunity. There is a wage that makes the firm indifferent between hiring this worker and waiting for the next available worker. The bargaining problem is to agree on a wage between these two limits' (Diamond, 1982: 219).

The quasi-rents are typically assumed in the job search literature to be shared out as a result of a process of bilateral bargaining, the division reflecting relative bargaining power. On this basis, the tilt in the wage distribution could reflect changes in the relative bargaining power at different points on the wage scale (see, for example, Fortin and Lemieux, 1997). Decline in trade union membership and diminution of union power may have reduced the union wage premium in the lower part of the distribution, whereas individual negotiation higher up the scale may have allowed the better paid to capture more of the gains from productivity increases. Or, where wage dispersion is negatively correlated with the degree of centralization of wage bargaining (Rowthorn, 1992), increased dispersion may be due to a decline in centralized bargaining.

Where there is a degree of indeterminacy of the market equilibrium, pay norms may play a role. Introduction of a notion of 'fairness' or 'equity' provides a route to removing the indeterminacy where 'individual incentives are not by themselves generally sufficient to determine a unique equilibrium' (MacLeod and Malcomson, 1998: 400).

In this context, observance of social norms may be consistent with individual rationality and indeed instrumental in achieving efficient outcomes. Where contracts are not legally enforceable, then general acceptance of a convention may allow firms or workers to make investments which would not be profitable if there were a risk that the agreement would later be renegotiated in breach of the convention. This view of social norms attributes no weight to any intrinsic value attached to respecting the convention: 'A central assumption of the strategic interpretation of custom is that the rules selected as coordination devices are used *in a purely instrumental manner*. All phenomena of rule obedience, commitment, etc., are assumed to be of only secondary importance' (Schlicht, 1998: 132).

In this regard, economists can learn from sociology and anthropology, as stressed by Akerlof (1980), who describes a model where individual utility depends not only on income but also on *reputation*, which is based on conformity with the social code. The loss of reputation if one departs from the social code depends on the proportion who believe in the code, which is undermined if people cease to observe it. Akerlof shows that there may be a long-run equilibrium with the persistence of a 'fair', rather than market-clearing, wage and involuntary unemployment.

The reputational approach

This reputational approach can be applied to the relation between wages and productivity. Suppose that there is a social code, or pay norm, that limits the extent to which individual earnings increase with earnings potential. Where this code is followed, people are paid a fraction of their productivity plus a uniform amount. Such a policy involves a degree of redistribution and low productivity workers can be expected to subscribe to the pay norm. But other workers will also accept it even where they could be paid more if they broke the norm, since – if they believe in the norm – by breaking it they would suffer a loss of reputation.[7] The extent of the loss rises with the proportion of the population who at that time believe in the norm, a proportion which is assumed to adjust over time in a way described below. Employers are also concerned with their reputations. When they create a job, it is determined in advance whether or not it is paid according to the pay norm. The profitability of the job depends not only on the pay but also on the acceptance of the job by the worker with whom it is matched. Matching is assumed to follow a random process, but is successful only where employer and worker either both observe the code or both do not.[8] Employers determine their pay policy (i.e. whether or not to observe the social code) on the basis of comparing expected profitability, which depends on the proportion, and characteristics, of workers who accept different pay offers.[9] The expected profitability of breaking the social code has to exceed the consequential loss of reputation, which is assumed to vary across employers, so that some employers may observe the code while others depart from it. There will therefore be a proportion of jobs which accord with the pay norm. If the proportion of the population who believe in the pay norm is less (greater) than this, then the extent of belief grows (falls).

There is therefore a dynamic process of adjustment. As Akerlof has shown, the process is likely to be of the 'tipping' kind identified by Schelling (1978). Interior equilibria for the proportion believing in the social code may be unstable and, depending on the initial conditions, a society converges to a high level of conformity with the social code, or to the virtual absence of conformity. In this kind of situation, an exogenous shock may shift the key relationship and switch the society from an equilibrium with conformity to the pay norm, and hence relatively low wage differentials, to an equilibrium where everyone is paid on the basis of their productivity. Such an exogenous shock may have been a fall in the weight attached by employers to reputation. Or, reflecting changes in the capital market, it may be that greater weight is attached to short-run profits. As a result, there are, as it has been put by Summers, 'market forces that have tended to pay everyone more like salespersons – on the basis of what they produce' (Summers, 1999: 102).

We may therefore observe a discrete change in the wage distribution: an episode of increasing dispersion (not a continuing trend). Such periods of rapid change in differentials have been noted at earlier times. In his account of wage differentials moving in the opposite direction, Reder states that, 'the long-run decline in the skill margin in advanced countries has not occurred slowly and steadily. Instead, the skill margin appears to have remained constant for relatively long periods of time and then to have declined sharply within a very few years' (Reder, 1962: 408).

One route by which shifts in pay norms may be brought about is government incomes policy. In the United Kingdom, it is worth remembering that in 1973 the Conservative government's Stage Two Incomes Policy set a group pay limit of GB£1 plus 4 per cent, with an individual maximum increase of GB£250 a year. Although now distant history, Labour's *Attack on Inflation* in 1975 restricted increases to GB£6 a week, with no increase for those earning more than GB£8,500 a year. The wage norm may, alternatively, be enforced through the process of collective bargaining. In Norway, according to Kahn (1998), the agreement negotiated between the LO (trade union federation) and the employers' organization (NHO) allowed in 1989 for a uniform 3 kronor per hour increase (with a 1 kronor supplement in export industries), and the 1990 contract allowed for a larger absolute increase for the low paid. (Evidence about the role of fairness in collective bargaining at the micro-level in Norway is provided by Strøm, 1995.)

The pay norm model, in addition to helping explain episodes of rising or falling wage dispersion, can also be used to explain differences across countries. The support for pay norms depends, for instance, on the extent of differences in underlying productivity. Where people are relatively homogeneous then there is more likely to be adherence to an egalitarian pay norm, so that the two elements – one exogenous (productivity differences) and one endogenous (degree of adherence to the code) – combine to explain smaller wage dispersion. Moreover, the shifting pay norm explanation can be introduced into the model of trade with a continuum of abilities. A shift from a redistributive pay norm to a payment strictly on the basis of productivity can have the effect of reducing the supply of the high-technology good at any relative price. This arises because the condition for equilibrium in the labour market is based on the marginal worker, who ceases to gain from the redistributive pay norm. Paying wages purely on productivity benefits those higher up the scale. There is a shift in the offer curve. If there is a bloc of countries, say the EZ, where no such shift in the pay norm has happened, then they will see an increased demand for their exports. This clearly not the whole story, but – just as international trade theory has begun to incorporate considerations of efficiency wages[10] – a model with a richer treatment of the labour market seems well worth exploring.

The view of rising wage dispersion advanced here is certainly not the only way of explaining what has happened in the upper part of the earnings distribution in the United States and the United Kingdom. At the very top, particularly when one introduces the value of stock options, the 'superstar theory' of Rosen (1981) appears to have considerable relevance. But the reputational approach to pay norms seems well worth exploring further, and it has a number of implications for policy. In part, the widely advocated policies of skills acquisition remain valid, although the mechanism by which they operate is rather different. The support for a redistributive pay norm depends on the extent of dispersion of productive abilities. Ensuring relatively homogeneous skills in the population may ensure continued support for a redistributive pay norm. In part, the policy implications are different. The role of public sector pay policy is an example. The adoption of performance-related pay in the public sector can be expected to influence pay norms elsewhere. Such a shift in the public sector may cause a discrete change in the economy as a whole.

Can redistribution offset market inequality?

To this juncture, I have considered what people receive as wages in the market place. But market incomes are significantly modified by income taxation and by social transfers financed out of the government budget. In this section, I examine how far fiscal redistribution offsets any rise in inequality in market incomes.

Actual redistributive experience

In Figure 3.5 are assembled estimates of the overall degree of inequality (measured by the Gini coefficient) before and after redistribution for three OECD countries. The selection of countries is determined by the availability in each country of a long time series of official estimates of the redistributive impact of the government budget,[11] but they have in common a rise over the two decades in the inequality of market incomes, shown by the dashed lines in Figure 3.5. In Canada the Gini coefficient for market income increased by some 5 percentage points, in the United Kingdom by around 8 points and in Finland (from 1981) by more than 10 points.

There is again diversity of experience across both countries and across time. Here I focus on the difference between the market and disposable income series. In the case of the United Kingdom, inequality of market income increased over the period as a whole, but the Gini coefficient for disposable income showed scarcely any rise over the first part of the period. From 1977 to 1984, the redistributive impact of cash transfers and taxation increased by enough to offset the more unequal market incomes: the Gini coefficient for market income rose by 6 percentage points but that for disposable income by only 1 point. After 1984, however, the story in the United Kingdom is quite different, reflecting a major reduction in the progressivity of income taxation and cutbacks in benefit levels and coverage. Inequality in market income continued to rise, but between 1984 and 1990 the Gini coefficient for post-tax income increased much more sharply (marked by the upward arrow in Figure 3.5). Measured in terms of the difference between the two coefficients, the redistributive contribution of transfers and taxes fell from 19 percentage points (the difference between the two Gini coefficients in 1984) to 11 percentage points in 1990. The reduction in redistributive impact was attributable to a smaller impact of cash transfers (−5 percentage

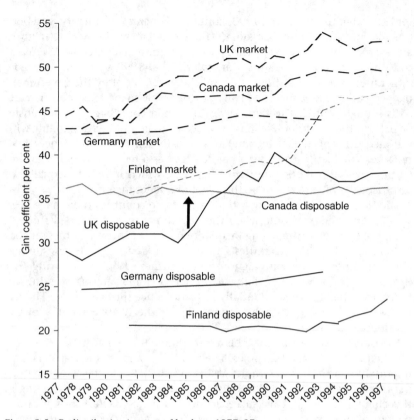

Figure 3.5 Redistributive impact of budget, 1977–97

Sources: UK distribution among households of equivalized original income and post-tax income. There are breaks in the series in 1990, 1992 and 1996/97 (although a figure is given for this year on the previous basis). Office for National Statistics (1998, April: 58, for 1977, 1979, 1981, 1983, 1985, 1987, 1989, 1991, 1993/94 to 1996/97), (1994, December: 65, for 1978, 1980, 1982, 1984, 1986, 1988, 1992) and (1993, January: 159, for 1990). It should be noted that the definition of the post-tax series differs from the disposable income series in Figure 3.1. Canada, Statistics Canada (1996: Text Table VI) and Statistics Canada (1999: Appendix Table III); Finland, Statistics Finland (1999: Asetelma 3).

points), less progressive direct taxes (−1 percentage point) and more regressive indirect taxes (−2 percentage points).

The UK experience may be contrasted with that of Canada. The coverage of the Canadian data is different, in that disposable income refers to income after direct taxes but before indirect taxes. This may affect the comparison not only of *levels* but also of *trends*. However, the difference in trends from the United Kingdom is so striking that this cannot be explained solely by definitions. Over the period 1980–94 as a whole, the Gini coefficient for market income rose by some 5 percentage points, whereas that for disposable income in 1994 was not significantly higher than seventeen years earlier. The picture for Finland in the 1980s and 1990s contains elements of similarity with both Canada and the United Kingdom. The 'Canadian' period was that up to 1994. From 1981 to 1994 the Gini coefficient for market income in Finland rose by 10 percentage points, particularly post-1990 with the economic difficulties faced at that time. This was, however, offset by the government budget to the extent that inequality in disposable income did not increase. As is brought out by Uusitalo (1998), the main contributors were transfer payments; the redistributive impact of taxation did not increase in line with the inequality of market income, and actually fell after 1989. Since 1994, however, the picture in Finland has changed as a result of policy measures cutting the redistributive impact of transfers, which have led inequality of disposable income to rise more than that of market income.

The first conclusion I draw is that in all three countries there have been substantial periods of time when the government has succeeded through fiscal policy in offsetting rising inequality of market incomes. The same has been observed in other countries. In the case of France, Piketty has summarized the findings of Bourguignon and Martinez (1997) as showing that (from 1979 to 1994) 'inequality of primary incomes among working-age households has grown substantially in France since the late 1970s. [The rise in social transfers] is entirely responsible for the relative stability of the distribution of disposable income' (Piketty, 1999: 842).

Of course, it is possible that the redistributive policy has itself caused rising inequality of market incomes. The incidence of taxes and transfers is an important issue (see, for example, Atkinson, 1999). But to the extent that rising market inequality is due to outside factors, as I have been discussing in this chapter, countries have succeeded in offsetting its effect for significant periods of time. We would indeed expect the government budget to attenuate the impact of rising wage inequality on household disposable incomes. Progressive income taxation should mean that the Gini coefficient of disposable income rises less than that of market incomes. Where a shift in demand away from unskilled workers leads to a rise in unemployment, as posited by the Transatlantic Consensus in the case of Europe, the impact on household disposable incomes is moderated by the existence of other income sources within the household and by the payment of unemployment benefit. An unskilled man who becomes unemployed may be supported by his skilled partner who keeps her job. Countries differ in the rate of replacement in unemployment insurance, but even the least generous systems in OECD countries offer some financial protection against unemployment.

Fiscal policy would therefore moderate rising market inequality. The same is true where the explanation of rising wage inequality is the alternative one advanced here, based on changes in pay norms. A tilt in the wage/skill nexus would lead to increased revenue from a progressive tax. The distribution of disposable income would again show less increase in inequality. This alternative approach does however raise the issue of *changes* in fiscal policy.

There is the possibility that the shift in norms may extend beyond the labour market to influence attitudes to redistribution. The shift from a relatively egalitarian pay norm to one where pay is related more closely to productivity may be accompanied by shifts in the attitudes of voters to redistributive policy, causing governments to become less willing to finance transfers and to levy progressive taxes. The fiscal changes may reinforce, rather than moderate, the tilt in the wage distribution.

As we have seen, there have been periods in two of the three countries when inequality of disposable income has increased as a result of policy choices. The United Kingdom and Finnish governments have, to varying degrees, scaled back redistributive transfers. This raises the question as to whether the explanation for these policy shifts is to be found in the national political economy of these countries or whether they, too, are the product of external forces. Do national governments in fact have room to manoeuvre? Are these fiscal choices, reducing tax progression and cutting the welfare state, in fact ones that all governments will in time be forced to follow?

How much freedom do national governments possess?

The constraints on national policy choices could take several different forms. They may be external economic forces, common to many countries, such as those that arise from increased competitiveness in international trade or increased factor mobility. Where social transfers are financed by payroll taxes on employers, these taxes enter wage costs and raise the prices of the country's goods and services. Firms find it harder, or less profitable, to sell their products abroad. However, in the standard trade model, the exchange rate would adjust, with a depreciation of the currency offsetting the price rise, shifting the burden onto the factors of production (assumed to be in fixed supply). Of course, this assumes that the exchange rate can adjust, and we have to distinguish here between trade between currency unions and trade within currency areas. Within the European Monetary Union (EMU) this instrument of correction is not available, and this may limit the autonomy of individual member states. On the other hand, the costs of the European welfare state as a whole can be offset by depreciation of the euro *vis-à-vis* other currencies, such as the dollar. Autonomy still remains, but at the European level. The constraints on governments could be those of factor mobility. An increased tax burden resulting from social transfers could lead to the outmigration of capital or labour. In the case of labour, there are reasons to doubt whether this will be of sufficient quantitative importance, at least in the foreseeable future. The position with regard to capital is more difficult, and it is possible that this may limit the choice of tax base, but this still leaves open possibilities for the progressive taxation of wage income.

There remains, however, a further dimension to the argument – and perhaps the more important. Rather than *real* tax competition, based on external economic changes, there may be *virtual* tax competition, based on national threats of the movement of labour or capital. Hirschman (1970) distinguished between 'exit' and 'voice' as reactions to economic change. Workers who perceive that taxes are lower in other member states may not migrate but may seek to exercise political power to achieve lower taxes at home. Comparisons of personal, or corporate, tax rates with those in other member countries may play a role in national election campaigns. I believe that these public choice aspects may be the most important restrictions on the freedom of national governments to carry out social protection. They cannot, however, be described as purely external, since they arise as a result of interaction with domestic politics. This brings one back to the different explanations of rising wage inequality. As already noted, if one adopts the alternative approach outlined here, based on shifting pay norms, then one has to recognize that the same norms are likely to influence public as well as private decisions. A society which shifts away from redistributive pay norms is likely to shift away from fiscal redistribution. But this is not inevitable, and can be influenced, just as the pay distribution can be influenced, by public policy. National governments are not, on this approach, faced with absolute external constraints. There is scope for political leadership.

Conclusions

In Carol Shields' novel, *Happenstance* (1991), one reads the book from one end and gets the wife's story, and then can turn it upside down and read from the other end the husband's story of the same five days. The husband's story is, in broad terms, one of a person whose five days were at the mercy of outside disturbing events. The wife's story, again loosely interpreted, is influenced and constrained by social custom (the original version of this half was called *A Fairly Conventional Woman*).

Equally, I have presented in this chapter two different perspectives. One, the husband's story, is the Transatlantic Consensus which sees rising inequality as the product of exogenous, inevitable events. Wage inequality in industrialized OECD countries, or unemployment, is increasing on account of technical change biased against unskilled workers or, the explanation on which I have focused here, on account of the liberalization of international trade and increased competition from newly industrializing countries. The other version, the wife's story, sees inequality as at least in part socially generated. There has been a tilt in the wage/productivity relationship, affecting the well paid as well as the low paid. There has been a shift away from a redistributive pay norm to one where market forces dominate. Social conventions in the labour market have changed within individual countries, and this may spill over into other spheres and to other countries.

What do these two stories imply for the inevitability of rising inequality? How do they affect the way in which we see the two key elements on which I have focused: increased inequality of earning power and redistribution through the government budget? On the first view – the Transatlantic Consensus – there is nothing to be done about rising market inequality. It is pure supply and demand. On the other hand, this does not imply rising inequality of disposable income: there are steps which governments can take to offset rising inequality of market incomes. The experience of a range of countries has shown that tax and transfer systems have been remarkably successful in counteracting the rise in inequality due to unemployment (Atkinson, 1998). The differing experience across OECD countries, as described earlier, with regard to inequality in disposable household income is in part a reflection of differences in national redistributive policies.

What about the alternative view which I have put forward because I have doubts about the Transatlantic Consensus on both theoretical and empirical grounds? The Consensus has been advertised as a triumph of trade theory, but in fact the conclusions do not follow directly from standard application of international trade theory of the Heckscher–Ohlin variety. The model needs to be richer. Empirically, the Consensus does not readily explain the tilt in the upper part of the distribution (to understand which, a simple unskilled/skilled distinction does not seem adequate). The alternative approach described here argues that the relation between skill and pay reflects social conventions, where adherence to the pay norm is endogenously determined. A view which gives prominence to norms about pay has of course to recognize that the same norms may govern redistribution. If, as I am suggesting, widening wage dispersion in part arises on account of shifting norms, then the same shift may have reduced the willingness of governments to redistribute. Both elements move in the same direction. But the fact that the driving force is social in origin, rather than trade or technology, means that there is more scope for political leadership. The evolution of social norms is influenceable by policy decisions.

In any two accounts of a marriage, there are undoubtedly elements of truth on both sides, even if one tends to sympathize more with one than the other. However, whether the reader adheres to the Transatlantic Consensus, or is persuaded of the need to look at the role of social norms, it remains the case that rising inequality is not inevitable.

Notes

Thanks to Andrea Cornia and Matti Pohjola for helpful comments.

1. I do not discuss income inequality in developing countries. For general surveys, see Adelman and Robinson (1989) and Kanbur (2000); for discussion of the determinants of income distribution in developing countries, see, among others, Bourguignon and Morrisson (1998), Cornia (1999) and Stewart and Berry (1999).
2. It should be noted that the series for different countries are based on different definitions. The US figures are for gross income and are unadjusted for household size, whereas the UK figures relate to disposable income adjusted for household size using an equivalence scale. Not only are the levels not comparable, but differences in definition may also affect the measurement of trends over time.

3. Cross-country earnings data are usually made available in the form of decile ratios, rather than Gini coefficients, and I have followed this convention. Again it should be stressed that the data are not comparable across countries: some, for instance, relate to male workers, others to all workers.
4. Increased competition from imports from NICs is only one aspect of the globalization of the economy. Among the important dimensions not discussed here is the globalization of capital markets, allowing the free movement of financial capital, which may well have had a significant effect on income inequality.
5. There are also issues of comparability of the data – in particular, the degree to which remuneration in kind and stock options are omitted.
6. As a result, the mean earnings may fall in the high-technology sector, as well. This aspect of the 'Roy model' of self-selection by workers, applied to international trade, is noted in the survey of assignment models by Sattinger (1993).
7. They may also accept wage compression as a form of insurance against wage risk, given that this cannot be secured through private insurance. Agell and Lommerud (1992) examine the arguments why unions may on this ground adopt strongly egalitarian wage policies (see also Agell, 1999).
8. It might be the case that a worker would prefer a job paying according to the norm but that the loss of reputation from breaking the code would be less than the loss from unemployment. However, it is assumed that employers do not engage workers who take a different view of the social code on the grounds that they will lack motivation.
9. In the model considered, differences in productivity lead to differences in wages (even if not proportionately). The case where firms have a company wage policy, paying a rate for the job, unrelated to productivity, is analysed by Manning (1994).
10. A different model of fair wages in an open economy is provided by Agell and Lundborg (1995).
11. Evidence from academic studies exists for other OECD countries: for example, for Germany, see Becker and Hauser (1997) and Hauser (1999).

References

Aaberge, R., A. Björklund, M. Jäntti, P. J. Pedersen, N. Smith and T. Wennemo (1997) 'Unemployment Shocks and Income Distribution', Statistics Norway Research Department Discussion Paper 201, Oslo: Statistics Norway.
Adelman, I. and S. Robinson (1989) 'Income Distribution and Development', in H. Chenery and T. N. Srinivasan (eds), *Handbook of Development Economics*, 2, Amsterdam: North-Holland.
Agell, J. (1999) 'On the Benefits from Rigid Labour Markets: Norms, Market Failures, and Social Insurance', *Economic Journal* 109: F143–F164.
Agell, J. and K. E. Lommerud (1992) 'Union Egalitarianism as Income Insurance', *Economica* 59: 295–310.
Agell, J. and P. Lundborg (1995) 'Fair Wages in an Open Economy', *Economica* 62: 335–51.
Akerlof, G. A. (1980) 'A Theory of Social Custom, of Which Unemployment may be one Consequence', *Quarterly Journal of Economics* 95: 749–75.
Atkinson, A. B. (1997a) 'Bringing Income Distribution in from the Cold', *Economic Journal* 107: 297–321.
——— (1997b) 'Measurement of Trends in Poverty and the Income Distribution', Microsimulation Unit Working Paper MU9701, Cambridge: Department of Applied Economics, University of Cambridge.

Atkinson, A. B. (1998) *Three Lectures on Poverty in Europe*, Oxford: Basil Blackwell.
———— (1999) 'Increased Income Inequality in OECD Countries and the Redistributive Impact of the Government Budget', Paper presented at UNU-WIDER conference on Income Inequality and Poverty Reduction, Helsinki, July, published in G. A. Cornia (ed.), *Inequality, Growth, and Poverty in an Era of Liberalization and Globalization*, Oxford: Oxford University Press, 2004.
———— (2000) 'The Changing Distribution of Income: Evidence and Explanations', *German Economic Review* 1(1): 3–18.
Atkinson, A. B. and J. Micklewright (1992) *Economic Transformation in Eastern Europe and the Distribution of Income*, Cambridge: Cambridge University Press.
Bayet, A. and M. Julhès (1996) *Séries longues sur les salaires, Emploi-Revenus* 105, Paris: INSEE.
Becker, I. (1996) 'Die Entwicklung der Einkommensverteilung und der Einkommensarmut in den alten Bundesländern von 1962 bis 1988', in I. Becker and R. Hauser, 'Einkommensverteilung und Armut in Deutschland von 1962 bis 1995', EVS-Projekt, Arbeitspapier 9, Frankfurt: Universität Frankfurt am Main.
———— (1998) 'Zur personellen Einkommensverteilung in Deutschland', EVS-Projekt, Arbeitspapier 13, Frankfurt: Universität Frankfurt am Main.
Becker, I. and R. Hauser (1997) 'Abgaben- und Transfersystem wirkt Polarisierungstendenzen entgegen', EVS-Projekt, Arbeitspapier 12, Frankfurt: Universität Frankfurt am Main.
Bernstein, J. and L. Mishel (1997) 'Has Wage Inequality Stopped Growing?', *Monthly Labor Review* December: 3–16.
Bhagwati, J. N. (1964) 'The Pure Theory of International Trade: A Survey', *Economic Journal* 74: 1–84.
Bourguignon, F. and M. Martinez (1997) 'Decomposition of the Changes in the Distribution of Primary Family Incomes: A Microsimulation Approach Applied to France, 1979–1994', Paris: DELTA.
Bourguignon, F. and C. Morrisson (1998) 'Inequality and Development: the Role of Dualism', *Journal of Development Economics* 57: 233–57.
Burtless, G. (1995) 'International Trade and the Rise in Earnings Inequality', *Journal of Economic Literature* 33: 800–16.
CEPR (Centre for Economic Policy Research) (1999) 'The Full Monty', *European Economic Perspectives* 22 (June): 5–6.
Chipman, J. S. (1966) 'A Survey of the Theory of International Trade: Part 3, The Modern Theory', *Econometrica* 34: 18–76.
Clark, T. and J. Taylor (1999) 'Income Inequality: a Tale of Two Cycles?', *Fiscal Studies* 20: 387–408.
Cooper, R. A. (1995) 'Discussion of Krugman', *Brookings Papers*, 1.
Cornia, G. A. (1999) 'Liberalization, Globalization and Income Distribution', WIDER Working Papers 157, Helsinki: UNU-WIDER, published in G. A. Cornia (ed.), *Inequality, Growth, and Poverty in an Era of Liberalization and Globalization*, Oxford: Oxford University Press, 2004.
Davis, D. R. (1998a) 'Does European Unemployment Prop Up American Wages? National Labor Markets and Global Trade', *American Economic Review* 88: 478–94.
———— (1998b) 'Technology, Unemployment and Relative Wages in a Global Economy', *European Economic Review* 42: 1613–33.
Department of Employment (1998) *New Earnings Survey*, London: HMSO.
———— (1999) *New Earnings Survey*, London: HMSO.

Dewatripont, M., A. Sapir and K. Sekkat (1999) *Trade and Jobs in Europe*, Oxford: Oxford University Press.
Diamond, P. A. (1982) 'Wage Determination and Efficiency in Search Equilibrium', *Review of Economic Studies* 49: 217–27.
Dixit, A. K. and V. Norman (1980) *Theory of International Trade*, Cambridge: Cambridge University Press.
Epland, J. (1998) 'Endringer i fordelingen av husholdningsinntekt 1986–1996', *Statistics Norway Reports* 98/17, Oslo: Statistics Norway.
Fortin, N. M. and T. Lemieux (1997) 'Institutional Changes and Rising Wage Inequality: Is There a Linkage?', *Journal of Economic Perspectives* 11(2): 75–96.
Friez, A. and M. Julhès (1998) 'Séries longues sur les salaires', *Emploi-Revenus* 136, Paris: INSEE.
Goodman, A. and S. Webb (1994) 'For Richer, For Poorer', *Institute for Fiscal Studies Commentary* 42 (June).
Hahn, F. H. (1998) 'Reconsidering Free Trade', in G. Cook (ed.), *The Economics and Politics of International Trade, Freedom and Trade*, II, London: Routledge.
Hauser, R. (1996) 'Vergleichende Analyse der Einkommensverteilung und der Einkommensarmut in den alten und neuen Bundesländern von 1990 bis 1995', in I. Becker and R. Hauser, 'Einkommensverteilung und Armut in Deutschland von 1962 bis 1995', EVS-Projekt, Arbeitspapier 9, Frankfurt: Universität Frankfurt am Main.
———— (1999) 'Personelle Primär- und Sekundärverteilung der Einkommen under dem Einfluss sich ärnderner wirtschaftlicher und sozialpolitischer Rahmenbedingungen – eine empirische Analyse auf der Basis der Einkommens- und Verbrauchstichproben 1973–1993', *Allgemeines Statistisches Archiv* 83: 88–110.
Hirschman, A. O. (1970) *Exit, Voice and Loyalty*, Cambridge, MA: Harvard University Press.
Kahn, L. M. (1998) 'Against the Wind: Bargaining Recentralization and Wage Inequality in Norway 1987–91', *Economic Journal* 108: 603–45.
Kanbur, R. (2000) 'Income Distribution and Development', in A. B. Atkinson and F. Bourguignon (eds), *Handbook of Income Distribution*, Amsterdam: Elsevier.
Karoly, L. A. (1994) 'The Trend in Inequality Among Families, Individuals, and Workers in the United States: A Twenty-Five Year Perspective', in S. Danziger and P. Gottschalk (eds), *Uneven Tides*, New York: Russell Sage Foundation.
Krugman, P. (1994) 'Past and Prospective Causes of High Unemployment', *Reducing Unemployment: Current Issues and Policy Options*, Kansas City: Federal Reserve Bank of Kansas City.
———— (1995) 'Growing World Trade: Causes and Consequences', *Brookings Papers* 1: 327–62.
Kuznets, S. (1955) 'Economic Growth and Income Inequality', *American Economic Review* 45: 1–28.
Lester, R. A. (1952) 'A Range Theory of Wage Differentials', *Industrial and Labor Relations Review* 5: 483–500.
MacLeod, W. B. and J. M. Malcomson (1998) 'Motivation and Markets', *American Economic Review* 88: 388–411.
Manning, A. (1994) 'Labour Markets with Company Wage Policies', Centre for Economic Performance Discussion Paper 214, London: LSE.
OECD (1996) *Employment Outlook*, Paris: OECD.
Office for National Statistics (various years) 'The Effects of Taxes and Benefits on Household Income', *Economic Trends*.
Phelps Brown, E. H. (1977) *The Inequality of Pay*, Oxford: Oxford University Press.

Piketty, T. (1999) 'Can Fiscal Redistribution Undo Skill-Biased Technical Change? Evidence from the French Experience', *European Economic Review* 43: 839–51.

Reder, M. W. (1962) 'WAGES: Structure', *International Encyclopaedia of the Social Sciences*, 16, New York: Macmillan: 403–14.

Rosen, S. (1981) 'The Economics of Superstars', *American Economic Review* 71: 845–58.

Rowthorn, R. E. (1992) 'Corporatism and Labour Market Performance', in J. Pekkarinen, M. Pohjola and R. E. Rowthorn (eds), *Social Corporatism: A Superior Economic System?*, Oxford: Clarendon Press for UNU-WIDER.

Sattinger, M. (1993) 'Assignment Models of the Distribution of Earnings', *Journal of Economic Literature* 31: 831–80.

Schelling, T. C. (1978) *Micromotives and Macrobehavior*, New York: Norton.

Schlicht, E. (1998) *On Custom in the Economy*, Oxford: Clarendon Press.

Shields, C. (1991) *Happenstance*, London: Fourth Estate.

Smeeding, T. (1999) *Income Inequality: Is Canada Different or Just Behind the Times?*, Invited plenary lecture presented to the Canadian Economic Association, Toronto, 30 May.

Statistics Canada (1996) *Income After Tax, Distributions by Size in Canada, 1994*, Ottawa: Statistics Canada.

——— (1999) *Income After Tax, Distributions by Size in Canada, 1997*, Ottawa: Statistics Canada.

Statistics Finland (1999) *Income Distribution Statistics, 1997*, Helsinki: Statistics Finland.

Statistics New Zealand (1999) *Incomes*, Wellington: Statistics New Zealand.

Stewart, F. and A. Berry (1999) 'Globalization, Liberalization, and Inequality: Expectations and Experience', in A. Hurrell and N. Woods (eds), *Inequality, Globalization, and World Politics*, Oxford: Oxford University Press.

Strøm, B. (1995) 'Envy, Fairness and Political Influence in Local Government Wage Determination: Evidence from Norway', *Economica* 62: 389–409.

Summers, L. (1999) 'Equity in a Global Economy', in V. Tanzi, K. Chu and S. Gupta (eds), *Economic Policy and Equity*, Washington, DC: IMF.

Tinbergen, J. (1975) *Income Distribution*, Amsterdam: North-Holland.

US Department of Commerce (1999) *Money Income in the United States: 1998*, Washington, DC: Government Printing Office.

Uusitalo, H. (1998) *Changes in Income Distribution during a Deep Recession and After*, Helsinki: STAKES.

Wood, A. (1994) *North–South Trade, Employment and Inequality*, Oxford: Clarendon Press.

4
Globalization and Appropriate Governance

Jagdish N. Bhagwati

Introduction

I am overwhelmed by the generosity of Professor Pohjola's welcoming remarks. It is customary to say, on such occasions, that my mother would have believed every compliment that he directed at me, that she might even have considered the praise wanting, but that I realize that I do not deserve it. But that is unlikely to work tonight. Too many of you know well my wife, Padma Desai, who directed a successful project for UNU-WIDER some years ago and is also a frequent visitor to Finland in other capacities. So you can believe me that, if she were present, she would have responded mischievously, since she moves between putting me on a pedestal and putting me in my place: 'Professor Pohjola, you have said nothing that my husband does not say better about himself.'

When I was invited to give the 2000 WIDER Annual Lecture, I must say that I was delighted. Partly, it was because the economists who had given two earlier Annual Lectures were eminent scholars whom I hold in the highest regard; Tony Atkinson and Joe Stiglitz (the latter winning subsequently the Nobel Prize for 2001). But it was also because, if I may be frank, WIDER had secured a reputation among trade economists worldwide for being sceptical of, if not hostile to, freer trade. This reputation, or shall I say notoriety, was all the more strange because Finland certainly has thrived thanks to trade. And, as for direct foreign investments, even its great firm Nokia is now owned, I am told, more than three-quarters, by foreign shareholders (among whom I am proud to include myself). I thought it would therefore be a great opportunity to be able to come to WIDER, and talk to a distinguished audience such as I have, on the upside of globalization, contesting in a nuanced way the fears and worries that have come to dominate the so-called 'anti-globalizers'. In fact, I hoped that my being invited to give the 2000 Annual Lecture was probably a sign of a change in the intellectual orientation of WIDER on the merits and demerits of global integration. How could I not rise to the occasion?

74

But let me assure you that I intend to present to you a rather different perspective on globalization than you routinely get in the polarized debates between its proponents and its opponents in the streets and in polemical magazines. To be precise:

- I intend to argue at the outset that (economic) globalization needs to be *disaggregated* instead of being treated as one gigantic whole, with the possible vices of one type of globalization (e.g. gung-ho liberalization of financial flows) being visited upon the virtues of another (e.g. freeing of trade). I will then concentrate, for reasons of brevity, on just trade and direct foreign investment (DFI or what the anti-globalizers prefer to call 'multinationals').
- Next, I will argue that most economists today agree that trade and DFI are *economically benign* – that is, that they increase the size of the pie.
- However, many NGOs and diverse groups consider such globalization to be *socially malign* – i.e. that it produces harmful consequences for a variety of social objectives such as the reduction of gender discrimination, cultural autonomy, poverty reduction, elimination of child labour, promotion of human rights and the strengthening of democracy.

But I will argue that these malign-impact views, which are at times tied in some radical thinking to malign-intent views of globalization[1] and the multinational corporations (MNCs) and the international institutions that are viewed as the principal agents of this malign process, are often too simplistic and that, as a central tendency, it is possible to argue that globalization is even *socially benign*.

But this case for globalization, on both economic and social dimensions, is incomplete because we need to design what I call 'appropriate governance' at both domestic and international levels to manage globalization, particularly in three respects:

Handling the social downside   The benign impact of globalization on social issues can only be argued as a central tendency. It still leaves open the possibility, one that can materialize in specific circumstances, that the impact is malign. This downside must be handled and requires institutional design, at both domestic and international levels, to address it.

Accelerating the performance on social agendas   But the argument that globalization is socially benign does not mean that we ought to be content with the pace at which these social outcomes are achieved. Thus, globalization can be argued to reduce (rather than increase) the use of child labour through, for instance, the economic prosperity that it brings. But we will want to go faster. The question then is: what institutional and policy design will do that; for example the use of trade or financial sanctions (at the WTO or through trade treaties) or the use of moral suasion and harnessing of bilateral and multilateral aid and civil society groups (at the International Labour Organization (ILO), for instance) to support non-sanctions approaches to accelerate the pace of desired change?

Optimal, rather than maximal, speed of globalization   On the other hand, while we will want to accelerate the speed at which the social agendas are implemented by globalization, we must recognize that the optimal speed at which globalization is embraced through policy changes – for example, the freeing of financial flows – is not necessarily the fastest speed. Shock therapy, as evident from the East Asian financial and economic crisis and from Russian experience (and also if you think about the speed at which immigration restrictions may be removed), is not necessarily the best therapy.

Why anti-globalization? A trilogy of discontents

Before, however, I proceed narrowly with the arguments asserting the socially malign impact as outlined, which surely bear on the question as to why globalization provokes hostility (since, for instance, one cannot be happy about the phenomenon if it is socially malign), I should immediately say something more broadly about the intellectual, historical and sociological sources as to why globalization seems to provoke the outsized reactions that occasionally spill over into street theatre and into violence.

It is tempting, of course, to think that there is a primeval curse on the phenomenon. After all, if you care to count, globalization is in fact a thirteen-letter word. But, seriously, globalization has become by now a phenomenon that is doomed to unending controversy, the focal point of always-hostile passions and sometimes violent protests. It is surely a defining issue as we enter a new century. The reasons why this has happened cry out for comprehension. Without such understanding, and then informed refutation of the fears and follies that animate the anti-globalizers, we cannot adequately defend the globalization that many of us seek to sustain, even deepen.

Central to many of the protests is a linked trilogy of discontents that take the form successively of an ethos composed of anti-capitalist, anti-globalization and an acute anti-corporation mindset. These views are interlinked because globalization is seen as the extension worldwide of capitalism whereas corporations are seen as the B-52s of capitalism and its global reach. So I must begin with anti-capitalism.

Anti-capitalism

As the twentieth century ended, capitalism seemed to have vanquished its rivals. Francis Fukuyama's triumphalism in his celebrated work, *The End of History and The Last Man* (1992), was like a primeval scream of joy by a warrior with a foot astride his fallen prey. It was not just the collapse of communism in Europe and China's decisive turn away from it. As the energetic anti-globalization NGO, Fifty Years is Enough, laments, even the Swedish model had lost its appeal. The much-advertised model of 'alternative development' in the Indian state of Kerala had also run into difficulties, much as President Julius Nyerere's celebrated socialist experiment in Tanzania had run the economy into the ground. This vanishing of different possibilities has led to what I have called the 'tyranny of the missing alternative', provoking a sense of anguished anti-capitalist reactions from both the old and the young.

The old are fewer, and they matter less, than the young. They could be the generals in the war on capitalism but the young today are happy to be foot soldiers, fighting on their own. But they can make noise; and these days almost anyone who screams is likely to get, not just heard, but sometimes even listened to. The old are, of course, the anti-capitalists of the post-war years, ranging from socialists to revolutionaries. They are the ones who, especially when communists or Marxists, are captive to a nostalgia for their vanished dreams.

When the Davos meeting was held by the World Economic Forum, in February 2001, there was an anti-Davos meeting[2] held in Brazil at the same time.[3] The rhetoric in Brazil was one of revolution. I recall George Soros, who properly considers himself to be a radical thinker, a progressive financier, going into a debate from Davos on the video monitor with some of the anti-Davos participants. I recall his frustration, indeed astonishment, when he realized that he was the enemy, not a friend, much as the Democrats were chagrined that Ralph Nader thought during the [2000] US election that they were not really different from the Republicans.

Soros, who had not interacted with these groups, just did not get it. As far as these anti-capitalist revolutionaries are concerned, anyone who is in stocks and bonds should be put *into* stocks and bonds. Indeed, these groups, who were memorializing Che Guevara and listening to Ben Bella, were the exact antitheses of the Arthur Koestlers of the world who wrote of 'the god that failed'. They were working from a script titled 'The God That Failed but Will Rise Again' – they only had to keep the faith.

But the globalizers must also confront the young. And if you have watched the streets of Seattle, Washington, Prague, Quebec and Genoa where the anti-globalizers have congregated with increasing militancy, or if you see their impassioned protests on the campuses as I have watched the Anti-Sweatshop Coalition's activities at Columbia, there can be no doubt that we have here a phenomenon that is truly important in the public space and also more potent. The nostalgia of the fading generation cannot compete with the passions of the rising generation.

So, how is the discontent of the young to be explained? Of course, a rare few among them are like the old. Consider Global Exchange, an NGO that likes to describe itself as a human rights group – this is the 'in' phrase much as socialism was three decades ago and its moral resonance immediately gets you on to higher ground and gives you a free pass with the media and the unsuspecting public. It professes politics that is unmistakably in the old revolutionary corner and gets endorsements from the great linguist Noam Chomsky, among other left intellectuals. Quite stereotypically, it describes Israel as 'an exclusionary state' that 'trains other undemocratic, abusive regimes' around the world and complains that US aid to Israel 'maintains the military industrial complex here in the US'. Its pronouncements on the WTO are no less dramatic and drastic: the WTO 'only serves the interests of multinational corporations' and 'the WTO is killing people'.

But Global Exchange and its radical chic are really a fringe phenomenon. There are several other explanations of what animates the young in particular – each may explain part of the reality, while collectively they provide a more complete explanation.

Far too many among the young see capitalism as a system that cannot mean- ingfully address questions of social justice. To my generation, and that of the left-leaning intellectuals such as George Bernard Shaw that preceded it, the Soviet model was a beguiling alternative. Indeed, my early and much-trans- lated book *The Economics of Underdeveloped Countries* (1966) contains a distinct nod towards the Soviet Union: 'The imagination of many ... nations has been fired, perhaps most of all, by the remarkable way in which the Soviet Union has raised itself to the status of a great power by its own bootstraps and in a short span of time.' How appalling a misjudgement this view of the Soviet alternative seems today. How commonplace it was then.

That capitalism may be viewed instead as a system that can paradoxically destroy privilege and open up economic opportunity to the many is a thought that is still uncommon. I often wonder, for example, how many of the young sceptics of capitalism are aware that socialist planning in countries such as India, by replacing markets systemwide with quantitative allocations, worsened rather than improved unequal access because socialism meant queues that the well-connected and the well-endowed could jump whereas markets allowed a larger number to access their targets.

But the anti-capitalist sentiments are particularly virulent among the young who arrive at their social awakening on campuses in fields other than economics. English, comparative literature and sociology are fertile breeding grounds. Thus, deconstructionism, espoused by the French philosopher Jacques Derrida, has left the typical student of literature without anchor because of its advocacy of an 'endless horizon of meanings'. Terry Eagleton, the sympathetic chronicler of modern literary theory, has written:

> Derrida is clearly out to do more than develop new techniques of reading: deconstruction is for him an ultimately political practice, an attempt to dismantle the logic by which a particular system of thought, and behind that a whole system of political structures and social institutions, maintains its force. (Eagleton, 1983: 148)

True, the Derrida technique will deconstruct any political ideology, including Marxist. Typically, however, it is focused on deconstructing and devaluing capitalism rather than Marxism, often with nihilistic overtones which create the paradox that many now turn to anarchy, not from Bakunin but from Derrida. The heavy hand of Marxist texts on students of literature, on the other hand, has been beautifully captured by V. S. Naipaul in his compelling portrait (in *Beyond Belief*, 1999) of the Pakistani guerrilla Shabaz who went from studying literature in England to starting a revolution in Baluchistan that failed:

> There were close Pakistani friends at the university. Many of them were doing English literature, like Shabaz; it was one of the lighter courses, possibly the lightest, and at this time it was very political and restricted. It was encouraging Marxism and revolution rather than wide reading. So Shabaz and his Pakistani friends in their Marxist study group read the standard (and short) revolutionary texts, Frantz Fanon, Che Guevara. And while they read certain approved Russian writers, they didn't read or get to know about the Turgenev novels, *Fathers and Sons* (1862) and *Virgin Soil* (1877), which dealt with conditions not unlike those in feudal Pakistan, but questioned the simplicities of revolution. (Naipaul, 1999: 296)

As for sociology, many of its students are influenced equally by the new literary theory and the old Marxism. They stand in contempt of economic argumentation that would refute their rejectionist beliefs about capitalism by asserting that economics is about value whereas sociology is about values. But they are wrong today, on both counts.

Economists will retort that, as citizens they choose ends, but as economists they choose the (best) means. Moreover, accused of indulging the profit motive, they respond with the legendary Cambridge economist, Sir Dennis Robertson, that economics is addressed heroically to showing how man's basest instincts, not his noblest, can be harnessed through appropriate institutional design to produce public good. Adam Smith would surely have died an unsung hero if he had peddled the pedestrian argument that altruism led to public good.

And, indeed, economists' policy analysis necessarily requires the use of criteria that enable one to say that one policy is better than another. That takes them straight into moral philosophy, of course. One could thus argue that the philosopher John Rawls' input into economic theory has been as profound as that in philosophy: in fact, he drew on the economist Nobel laureate William Vickrey's concept of the 'veil of ignorance' and gave economists back the maximum principle. A fair trade, I should say.

The presumption that sociology is a better guide to ethics than economics is also misplaced. Certainly, its related discipline, social anthropology, whose many adherents now find their voice in some NGOs, foundations and in the

World Bank, traditionally leans towards *preserving* cultures whereas economics in our hands is a tool for *change*. Fascinated by social anthropology, and deeply buried in the writings of the legendary A. R. Radcliffe-Brown and many others, when I studied in England, I still wound up preferring economics for my vocation. What other choice could really have been made by a young student from a country afflicted by economic misery? Indeed, if reducing poverty by using economic analysis to accelerate growth and therewith pull people up into gainful employment and dignified sustenance is not moral, and indeed a compelling imperative, what *is*?

But I should add that many of these students are also susceptible to the bitingly critical view of economics brilliantly propounded by Rosa Luxemburg in her classic essay on 'What is Economics', the first chapter of a proposed ten-chapter work, only six of which were found in her apartment after her murder. She had argued that 'the new science of economics', which had reached the status of an academic discipline in Germany, was tantamount to an attempted legitimation of the 'anarchy of capitalist production' and was essentially 'one of the most important ideological weapons of the bourgeoisie as it struggles with the medieval state and for a modern capitalist state'. The 'invisible hand', with its rationalization of markets, had a hidden agenda, hence it lacked veracity – a *non sequitur*, of course.

But I also think that an altogether new factor on the scene that propels the young into anti-capitalist attitudes comes from a different, technological source in a rather curious fashion. This is the dissonance that now exists between empathy for others elsewhere for their misery and the inadequate intellectual grasp of what can be done to ameliorate that distress. The resulting tension spills over into unhappiness with the capitalist system (in varying forms) within which they live and hence anger at it for its apparent callousness.

Today, thanks to television, we have what I call the paradox of inversion of the philosopher David Hume's concentric circles of reducing loyalty and empathy. Each of us owes diminishing empathy as we go from our nuclear family, to the extended family, to our local community, to our state or county (say, Lancashire or Montana), to our nation, to our geographical region (say, Europe or the Americas) and then the world. What the internet and CNN have done is to take the outermost circle and turn it into the innermost, while the same technology, as Robert Putnam (1995) has told us, has accelerated our moving to 'bowling alone', glued to our TV sets and moving us steadily out of civic participation, so that the innermost circle has become the outermost one.

So, the young see and are anguished by the poverty and the civil wars and the famines in remote areas of the world but have no intellectual way of coping with these rationally in terms of appropriate action. Thus, as I watched the kids dressed as turtles at Seattle during the riotous 1999 WTO ministerial meeting, protesting against the WTO and the appellate body's decision in the shrimp-turtle case, I wondered how many knew that the environmentalists had won that decision, not lost it! When asked, of course, none knew what they were really protesting about. And when I mischievously asked some if they had read Roald Dahl's famous story about the boy who had freed the giant turtle and sailed away on it into the far ocean, they shook their turtle heads. It has become fashionable to assert that the demonstrating youth know much about the policies they protest; but that is only a sentiment of solidarity with little basis in fact. True, there are several serious NGOs with real knowledge and serious policy critiques, but they are not the ones agitating in the streets.

Overlaying the entire scene, of course, is the general presumption that defines many recent assertions by intellectuals that somehow the proponents of capitalism, and of its recent manifestations in regard to economic reforms such as the moves to privatization and to market liberalization (including trade liberalization), are engaged, as Edward Said (2001) claims, in a 'dominant discourse [whose goal] is to fashion the merciless logic of corporate profit-making and political power into a normal state of affairs'.[4] Following Pierre Bourdieu, Said endorses the view that 'Clinton–Blair neoliberalism, which built on the conservative dismantling of the great social achievements in health, education, labour and security of the welfare state during the Thatcher–Reagan period, has constructed a paradoxical *doxa*, a symbolic counter-revolution'. In Bourdieu's own words (cited in Said, 2001: 32), this is

> conservative but presents itself as progressive; it seeks the restoration of the past order in some of its most archaic aspects (especially as regards economic relations), yet it passes off regressions, reversals, surrenders, as forward-looking reforms or revolutions leading to a whole new age of abundance and liberty.

But, frankly, this view stands reality on its head. Of course, we have known since Orwell that words do matter; and the smart duellists in the controversies over public policy will often seize the high ground by appropriating to themselves, before their adversaries do, beguiling words such as 'progressive' for their own causes. Thus, believe it or not, protectionists in trade have been known to ask for 'tariff reform'; today, they ask for 'fair trade' which no one can deny except for the informed few who see that it is used in truth to justify unfair trade practices. Phrases such as 'corporate profit-making' and 'trickle down' policies do the same for the friends of Bourdieu, creating and fostering a pejorative perception of the market-using policy changes that they reject.

It is therefore not surprising that today's reformers turn to the same linguistic weapons as the anti-capitalist forces of yesterday. But let us also ask: is it 'conservative' or 'radical' to seek to correct, in light of decades of experience and in the teeth of entrenched forces, the mistakes and the excesses of past policies, no matter how well motivated? In fact, as reformers know only too well, it takes courage and élan to challenge orthodoxies, especially those that are conventionally associated with 'progressive' forces. As for the policies themselves, the fierce binary contrast drawn by Bourdieu is an abstraction that misses the central issues today. The debate is really not about conservative counter-revolution and the enlightened past order. It is rather about shifting the centre of gravity in public action, more towards the use of markets and less towards *dirigisme*. It is not about whether markets, it is about where the limits to markets must be drawn.[5]

The present-day turn towards reforms in the developing countries is also prompted by excessive and knee-jerk *dirigisme*. As I often say, the problem with many of these countries was that Adam Smith's invisible hand was nowhere to be seen! Their turn to economic reforms is to be attributed, not to the rise of conservatism, but to a pragmatic reaction of many to the failure of what many of us considered once to be 'progressive' policies that would lift us out of poverty, illiteracy and many other ills. As John Kenneth Galbraith once said about Milton Friedman, and here I take only the witticism and not sides: 'Milton's misfortune is that his policies have been tried.'

Anti-globalization

Anti-capitalism has turned into anti-globalization among the left-wing students for reasons that are easy to see but difficult to accept. After all, Lenin wrote extensively about imperialism and its essential links to capitalism. And present-day writers such as Immanuel Wallerstein have seen the growing integration of the world economy in related ways as the organic extension of national capitalism.

Lenin's views on imperialism provide an insight into a principal reason why anti-globalization is seen by those on the left so readily as following from anti-capitalism. In his famous work, *Imperialism: The Highest Stage of Capitalism* (1916), Lenin stated that the 'distinctive characteristics of imperialism' in the form of monopolies, oligarchy and the exploitation of the weak by the strong nations 'compel us to define it as parasitic or decaying capitalism'. Nikolai Bukharin, for whose work *Imperialism and the World Economy* Lenin wrote a preface, considered that imperialism with its attendant globalization of the world economy was little more than capitalism's '[attempt] to tame the working class and to subdue social contradictions by decreasing the steam pressure through the aid of a colonial valve'; that 'having eliminated [through monopolies] competition within the state, [capitalism has] let loose all the devils of a world scuffle'.

This notion therefore that globalization is merely an external attenuation of the internal struggles that doom capitalism, and that globalization is also in essence capitalist exploitation of the weak nations, provides not only an inherent link between capitalism and globalization. It also makes globalization an instrument for the exploitation of the weak nations. And this certainly has resonance again among the idealist young on the left. Capitalism seeks globalization to benefit itself but harms others abroad. The Lenin–Bukharin argument then leads, as certainly as a heat-seeking missile, to anti-capitalist sentiments.

Anti-corporations

But central to that perspective is the notion, of course, that it is the 'monopolies' – for that is indeed how the multinationals are often described even today in much of the anti-globalization literature – that are at the heart of the problem: they do not benefit the people abroad; they exploit them instead. Indeed, this notion of globalization as an exploitative force that delays the doomsday for capitalism at home and harms those abroad has captured some of the more militant among the naïve youth today.

The anti-corporation attitudes come to many others, who are not aficionados of left-wing literature, also from the obvious sense that multinationals are the B-52s of capitalism and of globalization that are the object of concern. Their proliferation has been substantial, unprecedented in history. But their strength is grossly exaggerated because few understand that they, even when huge, undercut one another in economic power because they compete against one another – economists describe this as markets being contestable – and their political power is similarly stifled by economic and national competition in many instances.

Yet others find it plausible that multinationals must necessarily be bad in a global economy because global integration without globally shared regulations must surely amount to a playing field for multinationals that seek profits by searching for the most likely locations to exploit workers and nations, thereby putting intolerable pressure on their home states to abandon their own gains in social legislation in what is feared to be a 'race to the bottom'. Indeed, this view is so credible that even a shrewd and perceptive intellectual such as Alan Wolfe, who sees through cant better than most, has recently written disapprovingly and casually of the 'policies of increasingly rapacious global corporations'.[6]

But appealing as this scenario may appear, it will not withstand scrutiny. Much recent empirical work shows that the evidence for a 'race to the bottom' is practically non-existent. The political scientist Daniel Drezner has written a whole book showing that we have here much rhetoric by both opponents and supporters of globalization, but no empirical support. Econometricians have also found little to report. This may sound contrary to common sense: surely these social scientists must be consultants to the corporations? Many are not. There are plenty of reasons why corporations do not rush in to pollute rivers and the air simply because there are no regulations. I suspect that, aside from other economic reasons for not choosing say environmentally unfriendly technology,[7] the main check is provided by reputational consequences. In today's world of CNN, civil society and democracy proliferation, the multinationals and the host governments cannot afford to do things beyond the pale.

So the obvious truth of the 'race to the bottom' in an unregulated world turns out to be not so obvious. Economists are indeed a nuisance: they complicate analysis by telling you that your gut feelings are too simplistic. This makes them particularly unpopular with the young who want to believe what seems perfectly plain but is rarely so in truth. And so, many of the young zero in, with a 'gotcha' mentality, seizing on every misdeed of a multinational they can find, seeking to validate their anti-corporation biases. This surely accounts for the return of Ralph Nader; the great scourge of misdeeds by corporations. It has also magically transformed Julia Roberts, the passable actress whose triumph was as *A Pretty Woman*, into an acclaimed actress in *Erin Brockovich*; and introduced the gifted actor Russell Crowe to celebrity on the screen in *The Insider* – both movies where a David takes on a Goliath in shape of a venal corporation.

The anti-corporation militancy that is on the rise among the young anti-globalizers is also strategic, of course. We have witnessed the brilliant way in which the anti-globalizers managed to use the meetings of the international agencies such as the World Bank, the IMF and particularly the WTO (originally the GATT), the pride of progressive architectural design regarding the management of the world economy and the permanent legacy of legendary men of vision, to protest and profess their anti-globalization sentiments. After all, these meetings were where the world's media gathered. What better place to create mayhem and get attention from the vast multitude of reporters looking for a story? So, where the old guerrillas struck where you *least* expected them, these new guerrillas strike where you *most* expect them – at these meetings.

The same strategic sense has been displayed in going after the corporations as well. Nike and Gap, two fine multinationals, now have a permanent set of critics, with newsletters and websites worldwide. With Nike and Gap being household names and having gigantic overseas operations that cannot possibly avoid lapses from whatever is defined as good behaviour (e.g. that Nike does not pay a 'living wage' as Global Exchange would define it, for instance), they represent obvious targets in a propaganda war that is stacked against them. Naomi Klein, the Canadian journalist and author of *No Logo* (2000), admitted it frankly in an article in *The Nation* (2001): faced with the amorphous but overwhelming globalization phenomenon, the only way to get at it is to latch on to something concrete and targetable. So, they go after the corporations that spread and constitute the globalization that is reprehensible. We then also see teenagers carrying placards outside Staples and demonstrating in front of Starbucks while their more militant adult friends throw stones through the coffee chain's windows at Seattle. I talk with them at every opportunity. I find enthusiasm, even idealism, but never any ability to engage concretely on the issues they take a stand on. But then the Kleins of the anti-globalization movement are not fazed; it is all strategic, it is in a good cause.

Political alliances

But the recent successes of the anti-globalization forces can also be assigned to the fortuitous alliance struck between the young agitationists and the conventional organized lobbies such as the labour unions, the new pressure groups such as the environmentalists and movements such as those for human rights. Seattle saw these groups merge and emerge as a set of coalitions. 'Teamsters and turtles' joined the unions with the students and the environmentalists. 'Green and blue' joined the environmentalists with the blue-collar unions. 'Labour standards' became 'labour rights', heralding the alliance of human rights activists and the unions. The Anti-Sweatshop movement on the campuses signified the return of several union-trained summer interns who allied themselves, and aligned their views, with the unions.

While these alliances have made the anti-globalizers more effective to date, the alliances themselves are fragile. Thus, after Black Tuesday's attack on the World Trade Centre, the alliance between the unions and the students turned brittle as the campuses turned against war and the unions for it. The turn to violence by the students at Seattle, Quebec and Genoa also prompted union misgivings: the rank and file of the unions is not sympathetic to such tactics.

The teamsters broke with the environmentalists over the Bush Administration's decision on drilling for oil in Alaska's wildlife refuge. At the WTO, the environmentalists got their agenda, in some form, onto the Doha Development Round of trade negotiations. But unions did not have their way on a social clause, so the blue-and-green alliance is likely to have a parting of the ways, much the way there is today no unified bloc of under-developed nations in international economic negotiations but only coalitions around different interests that often cut across the conventional north–south divide. The fissures are therefore many – and, in particular, the negative agenda of anti-globalization is unlikely to be sufficient glue when the disparate groups start on different trajectories of positive achievements.

Confronting anti-globalization

But that does raise the broader question: will anti-globalization then collapse? Do not count on it. It cannot happen unless we engage the anti-globalizers on many fronts. I will return to the subject as I close this chapter. But, for now, let me link up directly with, and then proceed to, the main agenda as I laid it out at the outset.

Above all, we need to use reason and knowledge, in the public policy arena, to controvert the many false and damning assumptions about capitalism, globalization and corporations that I have only sketched and which cannot be allowed to fester and turn to gangrene. It is truly astonishing how widespread is the ready assumption (that is endemic by now even in some international institutions) that if capitalism has prospered and if economic globalization has increased while some social ill has worsened as well, then the former phenomena must have caused the latter. It has almost got to a farcical level where if your girlfriend walks out on you, it must be due to globalization – after all, she may have left for Buenos Aires.

Indeed, the chief task before those who consider globalization favourably is to confront the notion, implicit in varying ways in many of the intellectual and other reasons for the growth of anti-globalization sentiments, that while globalization may be *economically benign* (in the sense of increasing the pie), it is *socially malign* (i.e. in terms of its impact on poverty, literacy, gender questions, cultural autonomy and diversity *et al.*). And we need to turn our energies seriously to managing globalization in a variety of ways, even after we have cleared up these fears and phobias.

Disaggregating globalization: focusing on trade

But, if these fears and phobias are to be addressed meaningfully, we also need to recognize what I call the 'fallacy of aggregation'. Let me remind you that globalization, even when we mean by it only its economic dimensions, embraces trade, DFI, short-term capital flows and technology transfers and flows of people across borders. Unfortunately, both proponents and (far more so) opponents of globalization lapse into talking about globalization as an undifferentiated blob. Typically, therefore, the criticisms which are valid for one kind of globalization are visited upon another kind which does not merit such a critique.

A fine example is the gung-ho financial liberalization that devastated East Asia after 1997.[8] True, there were some countries, especially Indonesia and Malaysia, which had moved to such financial liberalization pretty much on their own. But South Korea certainly had been pressured. And the pressure, coming from the IMF which was allied to the US Treasury in this instance, has been widely acknowledged by many pro-IMF economists since then. There is no doubt that the proponents of such liberalization had been imprudent in their haste and were reflecting the alliance of Wall Street interests and the US Administration with the treasury in a central role: both intertwined and amounting to what I called, in a widely cited and translated article in *Foreign Affairs* (1988) 'the Wall Street–Treasury complex', in a throwback to Eisenhower's 'military–industrial complex' and C. Wright Mills' 'power elite', both also of Columbia University. So, we have all been called the 'Columbia trio', which is the next best to being The Spice Girls.[9]

But this mismanaged financial globalization has little to do with conventional trade liberalization. It is hard to imagine trade liberalization being attended by such panic-fed massive macroeconomic disruptions of the economy. And indeed the empirical evidence shows, for no country, anything like this immense crisis following from the freeing of trade.[10] Yet, it became fashionable in the late 1990s to invoke the Asian financial and economic crisis to oppose the freeing of trade, at Seattle and elsewhere. Even an otherwise sophisticated (but misguided) sceptic on globalization such as Dani Rodrik (1998) wrote in *The New Republic* about fixing the trade system after citing the financial crisis – as good a *non sequitur* as one could find.

Of course, the *non sequitur* is far more common among non-economists. Indeed, when I was awarded by Asian NGOs the first Suh Dong Prize in Taegu, South Korea for my 1988 *Foreign Affairs* article, the many NGOs that had organized the event, including many church groups, had posters and sessions condemning the IMF in fierce terms and even asking that my good and distinguished friend Stanley Fischer, the first Deputy Managing Director of it who had been in charge during the crisis, be put into a cell alongside General Pinochet for having committed a crime against humanity. That was bad enough, but there were also demands that Seattle be rejected, equating the two forms of globalization which really have no parallel. So, taking advantage of the fact that a prize recipient, especially in Asia, can be indelicate as long as he does it with delicacy, I chose the occasion of my acceptance speech to note the asymmetry and to argue the merits of trade liberalization *despite* the financial crisis.

Is trade economically benign?

Is trade truly an engine of growth as Sir Dennis Robertson, the distinguished Cambridge contemporary of Keynes, once proclaimed? Remember, this is a question regarding central tendency, so specific exceptions will arise.

From a theoretical point of view, we cannot even guarantee that free trade is always welfare-enhancing in a static sense. For, as every serious student of the post-war theory of commercial policy knows, free trade can immiserize relative to autarky if the comparison is made subject to distortions in place. When it comes to growth, the problems are even more serious. For, growth theory turns up models (such as Robert Solow's classic 1956 model) where free trade will leave steady state growth unaffected; and where it may even reduce it (as in the Harrod–Domar model with slack labour and the distribution of income affecting the average savings ratio).

The ultimate question, then, is whether the theoretical 'exceptions' to the case for free trade are empirically compelling. Here, the post-war evidence, based on several country-length studies under large-scale research projects undertaken at the OECD and the NBER – the former directed by Ian Little, Tibor Scitovsky and Maurice Scott in the late 1960s, and the latter by myself and Anne Krueger in the 1970s – strongly underlined the fact that countries that were integrating themselves into the world economy through freer trade were doing better than import-substituting, autarky-oriented countries. Sachs and Warner (1995) have turned to cross-sectional regressions to argue the same, but laying themselves open to attack because this approach leaves too many degrees of freedom open, through choice of proxies, time periods and country samples.[11] Such cross-sectional analyses also cannot take into account the nuances and specific factors that must be understood in assessing the effects of different policies in each country. I therefore find these cross-country regressions to be treacherous and some-what mechanistic, even as I agree with the pro-trade conclusions being drawn by these distinguished economists, and no substitute for the careful analysis required to assess policies.

Nonetheless, it is interesting that it is hard to find a single example in the post-war period of an autarkic country that has managed to register sus-tained, high growth. And that, as David Dollar has noted (Dollar and Kraay, 2002), when countries are grouped whether by their shares of trade to GNP have increased significantly or not, the former group also shows significantly higher growth rates.

Besides, while the work of the historian Kevin O'Rourke (2000), published in the *Economic Journal*, argued that, in the nineteenth century, greater protection was associated with higher growth, later work by Douglas Irwin (2002) shows that this conclusion is not robust to the expansion of the sam-ple to include several omitted countries. Nor can the two (included) major countries with very high growth, Canada and Argentina, be fitted into the mould because they were outward-oriented countries instead and were, in fact, using their tariffs mainly to collect revenues rather than to protect import-competing industries.

I would therefore conclude that, while there is (as always) a small body of contrarian opinion among economists today concerning the adverse effects of protectionism, the general and indeed overwhelming consensus in the profession about the beneficial effects of free trade continues and is supported by empirical analysis. The serious questions about globalization in shape of trade continue to be those relating to its social effects.

The social effects: generally benign also?

Are these as malign as many civil society groups fear? Yes, they often appear to be plausible but, on closer examination, many turn out to be unfounded, either analytically or empirically, whereas the sceptics and critics often appear to have missed out on some of the benign effects instead. These fears relate to several areas, among them principally: accentuation of poverty in the rich and in the poor countries; erosion of unionization and other labour rights; creation of a democratic deficit; harming women; and imperilling local cultures. The culprits are twofold; globalization itself and the interna-tional agencies – chiefly the World Bank, the IMF and the WTO – that oversee and promote the globalization in turn.

I obviously cannot address these issues in depth herein (instead see Bhagwati, 2004), but let me consider briefly just three issues that are very much talked about by civil society groups.

Gender questions

Many feminist critiques of globalization can be found today. Some relate to the harmful effects on women working in export industries, often in export processing zones (EPZs) at low wages, for short periods and without skill acquisition. Others write about women migrating to First World cities to work in households and looking after other women's children while their own are looked after by yet others. It has been noted that when an economic crisis hits with force, as did the Asian financial crisis post-1997, girls are withdrawn disproportionately from schools into work, and that women tend to be fired first when there is a downturn such as that brought about by IMF-required stabilization. But the anti-globalization thrust of these arguments is mistaken. It is not that there is considerable discrimination in many, indeed all, societies and economies against women.

In fact, writing in 1973, when gender questions were simply not on the economists' radar screen, I noted, in a substantial and influential article in the Oxford magazine *World Development*, the extensive gender bias against girls in education and nutrition, citing several studies at the time in the non-economic literature. And in 1974, Padma Desai and I also examined the choice and success of (the abominably few) women in several Indian elections, breaking down the data by different political parties and finding, among other things, the puzzling paradox that the progressive left-wing parties seemed to be doing worse rather than better. The real question at hand, however, is: does globalization help or accentuate these unacceptable biases against women?

Consider that, even when young girls in EPZs are not turned into long-term employees, many come from the countryside to which they return, having acquired, not skills but an experience out of the home and even some savings that give them a certain autonomy, plus what some economists studying household behaviour today call 'bargaining power' within the household. This would have been missing if they had not left home for the globalized EPZs. Surely, this works towards feminist objectives as UNIFEM, the UN organization dealing with women's issues, recognizes.

The same goes for women in the 'global childcare chain' who go abroad for work. It is even suggested by some critics that the migrant women in such occupations lose a sense of self-respect because they work for other women's children while missing their own. But the opposite is also possible, in my experience in my own household, and seems more likely. The key is that these women come from poor and traditional, almost feudal, societies where women's rights are far less recognized, if at all. Seeing how the women they work for are treated with greater respect and dignity, and also how they themselves are generally treated by their men and women employers with a regard and courtesy that is often missing in the feudal or traditional cultures they come from, acts as an eye-opener that reinforces their search for autonomy and individuality and unsettles the straitjacket of traditional, repressive roles that they were born into and conditioned by. Also, looking at it from the viewpoint of the employing women in the rich countries, the childcare chain enables them to go to work, a feminist gain again.

Additionally, when the IMF or the World Bank induces stabilization, and is the source of the girls and the women being hurt disproportionately, the problem is the traditional, endogenous discrimination against the female gender, not the IMF or the World Bank. Besides, I should also say that, in any event, the likely counterfactual is that the crisis – and hence the distress – without recourse to the assistance that the IMF provides would have been worse, since the contraction without such assistance would have likely been worse – the crisis would have had to be coped with in any event. The one major exception seems to be the Asian financial crisis where the IMF did goof up on its policy response advice and conditionality, pushing for the adoption of a contractionary policy with high interest rates when in fact the policy should have been expansionary instead, and thereby accentuated the distress caused by panic withdrawal of funds. The IMF therefore not merely helped cause the crisis by pushing for imprudently hasty financial liberalization, it also in the first year of conditionality (until its reversal), accentuated, the distress caused by the crisis. Indeed, globalization's impact on gender issues is not that difficult to see in a favourable light once we begin to explore a variety of other themes. Take just two examples from the north.

First, in regard to wage differentials against women, two women economists, Sandra Black and Elizabeth Brainerd (1999), have used Gary Becker's theory of discrimination to hypothesize that employers in globalized industries with intensified competition will find it increasingly difficult to indulge their prejudice in favour of men and hence wage differentials will narrow faster than in non-globalized industries. Their careful econometric analysis for the United States finds, in fact, that this is so.

Second, consider the case of Japanese globalization through DFI, as Japanese multinationals poured out into the west, taking (male) executives to Paris, London, New York, etc. But the men took their wives and children with them, giving the Japanese women their first-hand exposure to how women are treated elsewhere. They would then become the subtle but firm drivers of change on returning home, as would the young female and even the male children whose mindset could no longer admit the fiercely male-dominated social and economic structuring of Japanese society. Of course, this reinforced the change that has been coming from several sources, including the vast numbers of Japanese students coming to US colleges, for instance. I have argued that these students learn, like their American counterparts, to put their feet on the table in the classroom, instead of bowing respectfully to their teachers, the *sensei*. The diffusion of values has been dramatic in recent years,[12] and the role of the spouses and the children coming with Japanese DFI globalization has added significantly to the feminist component of that change.

Poverty in rich countries

Both the International Confederation of Free Trade Unions (ICFTU) and the American Federation of Labor–Congress of Industrial Organizations (AFL–CIO) have been wedded to the notion that trade with poor countries produces poor in the rich countries. In short, trade today is resurrecting the empirically discredited nineteenth-century doctrine of the immiserization of the proletariat. As I have said, Marx is striking again, but with the aid of neoclassical weapons.[13]

There is by now an immense empirical and theoretical literature on this subject. But the overwhelming argument is in favour of the view that, at worst, trade has a minor part in the play: the pressure on real wages of the unskilled workers is very much a result of non-trade factors such as unskilled labour-saving technical change. At best, my own work exploring the Stolper–Samuelson link between trade and wages (the most plausible link, in fact) argues that trade has actually *moderated*, not even moderately accentuated, the adverse effect on wages coming from these other factors. This is also the view that emerges from the influential work of Robert Feenstra and Gordon Hanson on the effects of outsourcing of labour-intensive intermediates from the United States since the 1980s on the real wages of skilled and unskilled workers – the real wages of unskilled workers have *risen* (but, if you are interested in the different question of the wage premium for skills, the wages of the skilled have risen even faster).[14] In short, the fears of the unions regarding trade with the poor countries are very hard to sustain if we turn to empirical analysis. But few bureaucrats in the European Community (EC), few politicians in the European Union (EU), and almost no Democrats in the United States have been willing to work with their union constituencies to say so.

Nor is the other fear, about the 'race to the bottom' on standards, easy to uphold with systematic analysis. I have already indicated that. But just ask some telling questions whose answers do not require much sophistication. First, in the garment sweatshops that deface New York, and where the international competition is immense and sweatshops are supposed to be rampant abroad, is there any reason to think that these conditions have deteriorated in the last decade so that our sweatshops have become more draconian? I do not think so. In fact, the sweatshop conditions exist in the garment district of Manhattan entirely because of the influx and employment of illegal immigrants who cannot exercise any rights because a bipartisan consensus has long operated to go after them. They also exist because the US Department of Labor has long had no money to hire more than a dozen inspectors to do the job. In short, do not blame an international 'race to the bottom' for your homegrown lapses. Second, according to a General Accounting Office (US Congress) study during the year of debate prior to the passage of NAFTA, a number of small furniture firms did cross the Rio Grande because Californian legislation on lead paint was far more tough and restrictive. Did the California regulations then get emasculated? Not to my knowledge.

Third, even the decline in unionization in the United States is hard to blame on international competition with countries which suppress the right to unionize. Have those who believe otherwise never heard of the long-standing Taft–Hartley provisions on replacement workers and on sympathetic strikes that have emasculated the effectiveness of the right to strike, which is critical to successful unionization? The downward trend of unionized labour in the United States is a secular one and I have seen no analysis that ties it significantly to any kind of 'race to the bottom'. In fact, I have myself seen US campuses go head on against efforts to unionize; the issues have often had to do with outsourcing of supplies to cafeterias or the attempt to unionize teaching assistants, none of which has anything obvious to do with a 'race to the bottom' type of argument or rationale. Indeed, the campuses are rarely in globally competitive activity with campuses in poor countries where unionization is restricted. We are so far ahead as to make the assertion of a competitive race with them by the United States appear far-fetched.

So, the two main reasons why unions fear trade with the poor countries – that their lower wages abroad will drive down their own wages at home, and that the low standards abroad will lower hard-won standards at home – are not particularly compelling. The alleged social downside of global trade and DFI seems to have little support in this instance.

Poverty in poor countries

This is perhaps the least persuasive, though politically the most salient, argument of the anti-globalizers. With the Millennium Summit at the United Nations reiterating the need to remove poverty by a target date, any assertion that globalization accentuates poverty is a deadly charge. But its validity is inversely related to its salience.[15]

India and China are the two countries with immense comparative advantage in poverty and which contain the largest shares of the world's poor. China's turnaround in its performance since it forcefully started integrating into the world economy is well known. So consider India instead. During the years of virtual trade autarky, massive restrictions on incoming DFI, bloated and bleeding public enterprises that proliferated through the economy and licensing restrictions on production and investment, India's growth rate remained around 3.5 per cent per annum over a quarter century of planning.

But, starting with small reforms and large capital inflows from early 1980s and then more substantial tariff, DFI and licensing reforms starting in 1991, the average growth rate rose to over 5 per cent annually. True, India began to change, not just its inward-looking policies, but also other harmful policies in what may be described as a package of unfolding reforms. But the steady if slow opening up of the economy to the world economy was a principal component. After much debate, analysts are now broadly agreed that India's poverty has finally declined noticeably. So, the argument that outward orientation, implying a thrust to greater globalization, leads to more economic prosperity (growth) and that this, in turn, reduces poverty, is consonant with the Indian experience. As it happens this is precisely what we in India had assumed in the 1960s as we argued for the choice of a strategy to raise the incomes of the bottom third of the population to a targeted minimum level. That growth had to be the principal way of attacking poverty, when redistribution from a few rich to the many poor could not be expected to raise the incomes of the poor by more than a minuscule amount – the great Polish economist Kalecki told me in 1962, when visiting us in the Indian Planning Commission, that India's problem was that there were too few exploiters and too many exploited – was a strategy that seemed to me to make sense. Also because the few available income distribution data for different countries in different circumstances and with different policies at the time did not seem to suggest there was a magic bullet for a sustained assault on poverty other than to 'grow the pie' as the grotesque expression now goes. As it happens, that was precisely what I recommended at that time to the legendary Indian planner, Pitambar Pant, whom I was working for on the strategy to raise the standard of living of the bottom three deciles to a minimum level.

Alongside this central strategy of growth was, of course, the use of additional policy instruments such as land reforms and schemes to extend credit to the poor, which were to make the growth strategy work better at alleviating poverty by improving the access of the poor to the growth process. Moreover, the revenues generated by growth were expected to be used to provide direct benefits to the poor through primary education and health programmes. Other social agendas were also embraced: women's welfare was a principal objective and the first Indian Planning Commission's distinguished and small membership in the 1950s included a well-known and forceful social worker, a child widow, Durgabai Deshmukh. Look at the Indian plan documents, and several growth-unrelated policies are there.

As I, and many others such as T. N. Srinivasan have argued (see Srinivasan and Bhagwati, 1999) the growth strategy did not work to produce the expected outcome in reducing poverty, not because that link was misconceived, but because the growth itself did not materialize due to bad policies which included chiefly anti-globalization measures.

Today, the work of David Dollar and Aart Kraay at the World Bank has extended both (1) this early analysis of the growth-poverty linkage – what

I might immodestly call the original Bhagwati Hypothesis from the early 1960s – and (2) the work of Bela Balassa, Anne Krueger and many others involved in the projects of the OECD and NBER that I have already cited that established a link between pro-globalization policies and growth, to finding support for it worldwide in cross-country analysis (which, for different reasons, is a treacherous tool). I find particularly interesting, however, their simple but telling observation that if you were to group countries by their globalization as measured by rise in the ratio of trade to GNP, their growth rates, and their reduction of poverty, high-performance countries in one are high-performance countries in other respects as well.[16] Similar examinations of fears about the ill effects of globalization on social dimensions such as its effect on local cultures, on the democratic process *et al.*, can be undertaken – I do just that in Bhagwati (2004). As always, matters are more complex, and on balance favourable, once one does that. But let me turn now to the question of appropriate governance, the other half of this chapter.

Appropriate governance

Why must we talk about the appropriate governance of globalization?

Handling possible downsides

If globalization (on the dimensions of trade and DFI that I am focusing on) is both economically and socially benign, remember that the latter is particularly true only as what economists call a 'central tendency'. That is to say, it is not always true. Occasionally, downsides will occur. We must then be prepared to devise institutions and policy frameworks that either reduce the probability of such downsides or can be triggered so as to cope with it; preferably we should do both. Let me illustrate.

Consider the recent NGO agitations about coastal shrimp farming. I first came across it in my work for the Human Rights Watch on whose Academic Advisory Committee (Asia) I serve. That shrimp farming, which has led to substantial exports and hence contributed to enhancing India's growth and fight against poverty, was sought by local NGOs to be put on the agenda of a leading human rights agency seemed a trifle odd, to say the least. On examination, however, it was clear that this was precisely the sort of occasional downside that one had to address. What was the problem?

Coastal shrimp farming was damaging the surrounding mangroves because of discharge of chemicals and back-up of uneaten feed, damaging the livelihood of fishermen and others subsisting traditionally in the surrounding areas. It is not entirely clear whether this was an unanticipated problem or whether the shrimp firms were unaware of these consequences and caught flatfooted; the latter seems to have been the case and let me proceed on that assumption.[17] Evidently, a twofold institutional response is necessary: there must be a way for the government to compensate and assist those who have been damaged; more important, there must be the introduction of a 'polluter pays' tax on the damaging discharges and effluents.

Let me add that the optimal outcome is likely to be somewhat reduced shrimp farming, reduced damage to the mangroves and reduced numbers of fishermen and farmers subsisting therein. It is highly improbable that the solution would go to the extreme of forbidding the shrimp farming altogether. Yet that is what the NGOs wanted – globalization, i.e. shrimp exports, had been shown up to be an environmental hazard, a human rights violation, and that was *it*. Not merely did the episode provide the anti-globalizers among the NGOs with a damning, PR-relevant, gotcha-mentality-driven, example of globalization's perfidy, it also revealed among the genuinely concerned NGOs their tendency to attach an infinite weight to the groups they were taking under their wing or a zero weight to the groups who would doubtless benefit from the shrimp exports.[18]

Take yet one more example which illustrates how there should also be institutional international change to support globalization's occasional dark side. With greater openness, there often comes a sense of economic insecurity from the fear that more openness will create greater volatility of prices and hence of jobs. Even though the objective evidence for this fear is again not compelling, and recent empirical analyses suggest that labour turnover has not particularly increased in the United States and United Kingdom despite ongoing globalization,[19] the fear is palpable and prompts anti-globalization sentiments. It therefore suggests that a way to support globalization politically may well be to provide additional adjustment assistance for those laid off in a way that can be linked to such volatility from import competition. I – in *Protectionism* (1988a) and in an earlier NBER volume *Import Competition and Response* (1982) – and several others have therefore long suggested that such assistance be provided as the economy is opened up to greater trade. There are many proposals on the table, including an interesting insurance scheme by Robert Litan that would pick up a large fraction of the loss of earnings as workers are bumped into jobs with lesser remuneration due to import competition.

There is little doubt that such assistance programmes are part of purely domestic institutional support for countries increasingly integrating into the world economy. But, in my long-standing advocacy of this type of support, I am not saying that this necessarily is what happens in reality. In fact, the assertion (reflecting cross-country regression analysis) by Dani Rodrik (1998), drawing upon imaginative suggestions by the political scientist John Ruggie who was inspired in turn by Karl Polanyi, that the post-war shift to the world economy *in fact* led countries to increase spending, and social spending, relative to GNP, thus usefully 'embedding liberalism', in Ruggie's terminology, into a socially active state, has failed to persuade more sophisticated students of the rise of the welfare state in the west in its many dimensions.

I should also say that policies such as adjustment assistance to cope with openness will also require international institutional change. Poor countries cannot afford such programmes; it is necessary therefore to devise assistance triggers for this purpose. The IMF already has several programmes to handle exogenous external disturbances that lead to the need for liquidity. But we also need to bring the World Bank in so that assistance kicks in when the need for adjustment arises thanks to endogenous policy decisions to free trade. While the World Bank has occasionally done this, stepping in with assistance – as with special funds for workers to get adjustment assistance when India undertook its massive reforms during the 1991 crisis – I believe this sort of support has not been institutionalized: it needs to be.

Accelerating the pace of social change

Then again, the pace at which globalization advances social agendas need not be accepted. After all, the sustained 2 per cent growth rate annually during the Meiji era in Japan is no longer considered the miracle it once was. Today, if a developing country registers growth below 6 per cent annually, it is regarded as a failure. We have addressed much analysis and effort to securing such an accelerated growth rate. Why not the same with the speed at which we achieve social agendas?

So, we need to consider the ways in which we can reinforce the benign social effects of globalization. Thus, child labour is known to decline as economic growth occurs. But what can we do to accelerate its removal? This is where the question of appropriate choice of policy instruments, and international agencies to oversee them, becomes pertinent.

The current conflict is between those such as the ICFTU and AFL–CIO which want trade sanctions, and hence inclusion of a social clause in the WTO, to reduce child labour and to achieve other core labour standards, and those such as the Indian trade unions (whose membership exceeds 7 million, which is not a great deal below that of the AFL–CIO whose massive funds enable it to make greater noise and get larger attention) and key developing country NGOs, such as the Third World Network of Malaysia and CUTS of India, which would rather see non-sanctions-based approaches and the location of the issue at the ILO instead. My own sympathies lie with the latter position and that happens also to be the position of a great many international and developmental economists (such as Robert Baldwin, Kaushik Basu, Drusilla Brown, Alan Deardorff, Paul Krugman, Arvind Panagariya, T. N. Srinivasan and Robert Stern) and financial and economic media such as *The Economist* and *The Financial Times* who have written about this choice.[20]

Optimal, rather than maximal, speed of globalization

Again, the question of appropriate management of globalization requires attention to the speed at which globalization must be pursued. The difficulties that Russia got into under 'shock therapy' are a reminder that the best speed is not the fastest speed. Jeffrey Sachs, who favoured 'shock therapy' in Russia, used to argue by analogy: one cannot cross a chasm in two leaps. To which my wife, Padma Desai, a Russian expert whom I might beg to quote, replied: 'one cannot cross it in one leap either unless one is Indiana Jones; it is wiser to drop a bridge.' Or to use another analogy: if you kick a door open, it may rebound back and close instead.

A dramatic example of mismanagement (through excessive speed) of globalization, of course, is the imprudent and hasty freeing of capital flows that surely helped to precipitate the Asian financial and economic crisis starting 1997. Again, if one thinks of immigration, it is clear that a rapid and substantial influx of immigrants can precipitate a reaction that may make it extremely difficult to keep the door open. There is clearly prudence in proceeding with caution, even if one considers, as I do, that international migration is an economically and socially benign form of globalization.

And so, in these different ways, globalization must be managed so that its fundamentally benign effects are assured and reinforced. Without this wise management, it is imperilled and at risk.

Notes

The themes set out in this chapter have been developed more fully in Bhagwati (2004). The author thanks Matti Pohjola, Tony Shorrocks and the staff of UNU-WIDER for organizing the lecture, and Bikas Joshi and Olivia Carballo for research assistance.

1. The analytical categories-cum-phrases 'benign-impact', 'benign-neglect', 'malign-impact' and 'malign-neglect' were developed by me in 1977 when I wrote a full-length introduction to a book, *The New International Economic Order*, which I edited. They are useful in understanding and analysing the current divisions of opinion as much as they were for the analysis of the different viewpoints when the New International Economic Order (NIEO) was being forcefully argued against the Liberal International Economic Order.
2. This rival meeting, timed to parallel the Davos meeting, was held again in Porto Alegre, Brazil. It described itself as the World Social Forum, while the long-standing Davos meetings are organized by the World Economic Forum. The contrasting title is revealing: it says that 'we are for social consequences, for humanity; you are for profits, and against humanity'.
3. How many know that there is even an alternative Nobel Prize?
4. *The Nation* 17/24 September 2001.
5. See my review of Robert Kuttner's 'Everything for Sale: The Virtues and Limits of Markets', in *The Times Literary Supplement*, 21 November 1997, reprinted as Chapter 55 in Bhagwati (1998).
6. *The New Republic*, 1 October 2001.
7. These reasons have been discussed by me, jointly with T. N. Srinivasan, in Chapter 4 of Bhagwati and Hudec (1996). These reasons do not apply to small firms such as the furniture firms that moved from California to Mexico across the border; but then these small firms do not amount to a hill of beans in total magnitude of the equity investments flowing from the rich to the poor countries.

8. The emphasis here is on 'gung-ho'. The failure to put in place the domestic institutional changes required to ensure that financial liberalization would be beneficial rather than vulnerable to the kind of disaster that broke out is the issue at hand. For a critical and comprehensive account and analysis of these failings, see Desai (2003).

9. See Chapters 1–3 on this subject in my collection of public policy essays (Bhagwati, 2000).

10. This is not to deny that, in an open economy, there can be external shocks that pose severe difficulties of management. A supreme example is the fourfold oil price increase in 1973 that upset the macroeconomic situation in several countries. Countries heavily dependent on primary exports, and there still are a few left, can also experience such difficulties, as will happen when the small Caribbean countries lose their preferences from the European Union on banana exports: a problem that I turn to addressing in the section on appropriate governance.

11. Rodriguez and Rodrik (1999) have critiqued the Sachs and Warner analysis; and my sympathies are with that critique. But these authors also resort to such regressions and are equally unpersuasive in their sceptical conclusions about the effect of growth on trade, in consequence. In Srinivasan and Bhagwati (1999), a substantial riposte to Rodrik's criticisms of those who link trade to favourable growth outcomes is provided.

12. Thus, when the US–Japan summit broke down over trade issues in 1993 in Washington, I wrote in 1994 an article in *Foreign Affairs*, titled 'Samurai No More'. I was arguing that the US negotiators had miscalculated the response of the Japanese negotiators many of whom had been exposed to US behaviour and attitudes at US schools and who, like the Americans, were likely now to say 'see you in court' – i.e. at the WTO in a dispute settlement case, instead of buckling under. As I put it graphically, the Americans thought they were fighting the samurai but they were fighting GIs instead; and they came a cropper.

13. Cf. my paper with my brilliant former student, Vivek Dehejia, 'Freer Trade and Wages of the Unskilled: Is Marx Striking Again?', in Bhagwati and Kosters (1994).

14. My paper, 'Play It Again Sam: Another Look at Trade and Wages' has been reprinted in Bhagwati (2000), and the Feenstra–Hanson study is discussed in Bhagwati and Srinivasan (2002) posted on my website: http://www.columbia. edu/~jb38. A full-length review and synthesis of the vast literature on the effects of trade on (absolute) wages by myself and Arvind Panagariya will be finished shortly and will appear in a forthcoming issue of the *Journal of Economic Literature*.

15. This topic has been addressed more fully by Bhagwati and Srinivasan (1996) and in a splendid article by Dollar and Kraay (2002).

16. The comprehensive and valuable work of Alan Winters with Messrs McCulloch and Cirera for the UK's Department for International Development also supports generally the case for a positive impact of trade on poverty reduction, while also detailing ways in which that linkage can be micro-monitored.

17. If it is the former, evidently the institutional response would have to be different, holding the firms liable also for damages under torts and possibly for criminal negligence, if there is such jurisprudence on the books.

18. One sees this tendency on the part of many human rights and other NGO groups: an inability see beyond the welfare or well-being of their own constituency. Thus, Arundhati Roy, the author of *The God of Small Things* who, in opposing big dams, is aspiring to be 'The Goddess of Small Things', focuses exclusively on people

displaced by the dams, not caring a fig about the many poor who will profit from the irrigation waters.

19. See the discussion of this evidence in Chapter 1 of Bhagwati (1998).
20. The pertinent arguments need to be looked at in the original and are available in several places. My own are reprinted, for the most part, in Bhagwati (1998). See also my testimony on the US–Jordan Free Trade Agreement, where the central questions related to the inclusion of labour standards in trade treaties and institutions; available from Olivia Carballo at ocarballo@cfr.org.

References

Bhagwati, J. (1966) *The Economics of Underdeveloped Countries*, New York: McGraw-Hill.
——— (1970) *Import Competition: Adjustment and Response.*
——— (1973) 'Education, Class Structure and Income Equality', *World Development* 1(5): 21–36.
——— (ed.) (1977) *The New International Economic Order*, Cambridge, MA: MIT Press.
——— (ed.) (1982) *Import Competition and Response*, Chicago: University of Chicago Press.
——— (1988a) *Protectionism*, Cambridge, MA: MIT Press.
——— (1988b) 'The Capital Myth: The Difference between Trade in Widgets and Dollars', *Foreign Affairs* 77: 7–12.
——— (1994) 'Samurai No More', *Foreign Affairs* 73: 7–12.
——— (1998) *Stream of Windows: Unsettling Reflections on Trade, Immigration, and Democracy*, Cambridge, MA: MIT Press.
——— (2000) *The Wind of the Hundred Days: How Washington Mismanaged Globalization*, Cambridge, MA: MIT Press.
——— (2004) *In Defense of Globalization*, Oxford: Oxford University Press.
Bhagwati, J. and V. Dehejia (1994) 'Freer Trade and Wages of the Unskilled: Is Marx Striking Again?', in J. Bhagwati and M. Kosters (eds), *Trade and Wages: Levelling Wages Down?*, Washington, DC: American Enterprise Institute.
Bhagwati, J. and P. Desai (1974) 'Women in Indian Elections', in A. Field and M. Weiner (eds), *Studies in Electoral Politics in the Indian States*, Cambridge, MA: MIT Press.
Bhagwati, J. and R. Hudec (eds) (1996) *Fair Trade and Harmonization: Prerequisites for Free Trade?*, Cambridge, MA: MIT Press, 2 vols.
Bhagwati, J. and M. Kosters (eds) (1994) *Trade and Wages: Levelling Wages Down?*, Washington, DC: American Enterprise Institute.
Bhagwati, J. and A. Krueger (eds) (1974) *Foreign Trade Regimes and Economic Development: A Special Conference Series on Foreign Trade Regimes and Economic Development*, New York: Columbia University Press, for NBER.
Bhagwati, J. and T. N. Srinivasan (1996) 'Trade and the Environment: Does Environmental Diversity Detract from the Case for Free Trade?', in J. Bhagwati and R. Hudec (eds), *Fair Trade and Harmonization: Economic Analysis*, 1, Cambridge, MA: MIT Press.
——— (2002) 'Trade and Poverty', *American Economic Review, Papers and Proceedings* May, longer version available on www.columbia.edu/~jb38.
Black, S. E. and E. Brainerd (1999) 'Importing Equality? The Effects of Increased Competition on the Gender–Wage Gap', *Staff Report* 74, New York: Federal Reserve Bank of New York.
Bukharin, N. (1929) *Imperialism and the World Economy*, New York: International Publishers.

Desai, P. (2003) *Financial Crisis, Contagion, and Containment: From Asia to Argentina*, New Jersey: Princeton University Press.

Dollar, D. and A. Kraay (2002) 'Spreading the Wealth', *Foreign Affairs* 81(1), January/February: 120–33.

Drezner, D. (forthcoming) *Who Rules? State Power and the Structure of Global Regulation*, Princeton, NJ: Princeton University Press.

Eagleton, T. (1983) *Literary Theory: An Introduction*, Oxford: Basil Blackwell.

Fukuyama, F. (1992) *The End of History and The Last Man*, New York: Free Press.

Global Exchange (various) www.globalexchange.org.

Irwin, D. (2002) 'Interpreting the Tariff–Growth Correlation in the Late Nineteenth Century', *American Economic Review, Papers and Proceedings* 92(2): 165–9.

Klein, N. (2000) *No Logo: Taking Aim at the Brand Bullies*, London: HarperCollins.

———— (2001) 'Signs of the Times', *The Nation*, 22 October.

Koestler, A. (2000) *The God that Failed*, London: Hamish Hamilton.

Lenin, V. I. (1916/1997) *Imperialism: The Highest Stage of Capitalism*, New York: International Publishers.

Little, I., T. Scitovsky and M. Scott (1970) *Industry and Trade in Some Developing Countries: A Comparative Study*, Oxford: Oxford University Press, for the Development Centre of the OECD.

Luxemburg, R. (1954) *What is Economics?*, trans T. Edwards, New York: Pioneer Publishers.

McCulloch, N., X. Cirera and L. A. Winters (2001) *Trade Liberalization and Poverty. A Handbook*, London: DFID.

Naipaul, V. S. (1999) *Beyond Belief: Islamic Excursions Among the Converted Peoples*, London: Abacus.

O'Rourke, K. (2000) 'Tariffs and Growth in the Late 19th Century', *Economic Journal* 110(463): 456–83.

Putnam, R. (1995) 'Bowling Alone: America's Declining Social Capital', *Journal of Democracy* 6(1): 65–78.

Robertson, D. H. (1956) 'What Does the Economist Economize?', *Economic Commentaries*, London: Snapes.

Rodriguez, F. and D. Rodrik (1999) 'Trade Policy and Economic Growth: A Skeptic's Guide to the Cross-National Evidence', NBER Working Papers 7081, Cambridge. MA: NBER.

Rodrik, D. (1998) 'The Global Fix', *The New Republic*, 2 November.

Roy, A. (1997) *The God of Small Things*, New York: Random House.

Ruggie, J. G. (1982) 'International Regimes, Transactions and Change: Embedded Liberalism in the Post-war Economic Order', *International Organization* 36(2).

Sachs, J. D. and A. M. Warner (1995) 'Economic Reform and the Process of Global Integration', *Brookings Papers on Economic Activity* 1: 1–95.

Said, E. (2001) 'The Public Role of Writers and Intellectuals', *The Nation*, 17 September: 32.

Solow, R. (1956) 'A Contribution to the Theory of Economic Growth', *Quarterly Journal of Economics* 70(1): 65–94.

Srinivasan, T. N. and J. Bhagwati (1999) 'Outward Orientation and Development: Are Revisionists Right?', in D. Lal and R. Snape (eds), *Trade, Development, and Political Economy: Essays in Honour of Anne O. Krueger*, New York: Palgrave.

Wolfe, A. (2001) 'The Snake: Globalization, America, and the Wretched of the Earth', review of *Empire* by M. Hardt and A. Negri, *The New Republic*, 1 October: 31.

5
Horizontal Inequalities: A Neglected Dimension of Development

Frances Stewart

Introduction

Current thinking about development places individuals firmly at the centre of concern, the basic building block for analysis and policy. This is as true of the innovations led by Amartya Sen, which move us away from a focus purely on incomes to incorporate wider perspectives on well-being, as of the more traditional neoclassical welfare analysis which underpins most development policy. The present overriding concerns with reduced poverty and inequality, which stem from both types of analysis, are equally individual-focused. The Millennium Development Goals (MDGs), for example, are concerned with the *numbers* of individuals in poverty in the world as a whole, not with who they are, or where they live. Measures of inequality relate to the *ranking of individuals* (or households) within a country (or sometimes the globe). The issues of individuals' poverty and inequality are, of course, extremely important, but they neglect a vital dimension of human well-being and of social stability: that is, the group dimension.

An intrinsic part of human life is *group membership* – in fact it is this that makes up the identity (or multiple identities) of individuals – their family affiliations, cultural affinities and so on. As Gellner stated: there is a universal human need to 'belong, to identify and hence to exclude' (1964: 149). Such identities are a fundamental influence on behaviour[1] (by the individual and the group), on how they are treated by others and on their own well-being.[2] Most people have multiple affiliations and identities – some location-based, some family-based, some age- or class-based and some culturally differentiated. In this chapter I shall focus particularly on 'cultural' groups – that is, groups encompassing common cultural identities, though the argument can be extended to other forms of affiliation and group differentiation. These identities are generally based on common behaviour and values. The binding agent may be 'ethnicity' (generally associated with a common history, language, mores), or religion, or race, or region, or even class. Modern societies – in rich and poor countries – generally embody large cultural differences of this sort. In fact, they seem particularly important today, partly because ideological differences have lessened with the end of the Cold War bringing cultural differences to the fore, and partly because global migration has brought people of different cultures into physical proximity.[3] At a superficial level at least, cultural differences appear to lie behind many, perhaps most, current conflicts – huge atrocities, such as occurred in Rwanda, many civil wars, much civil disturbance and indeed today's 'war against terrorism' which comes close to Huntington's predicted 'clash of civilizations'.

Yet while it is obvious that there are – and have been historically – numerous cultural clashes within and between countries, there are also pluralistic societies that live relatively peacefully. For example, in Finland, the large Swedish minority has lived peacefully for many decades. In Tanzania, Uruguay and Costa Rica, too, multiple cultural groups have lived together without serious tensions. It is my hypothesis that an important factor that differentiates the violent from the peaceful is the existence of *severe inequalities between culturally defined groups*, which I shall define as *horizontal inequalities* (HIs), to differentiate them from the normal definition of 'inequality' which lines individuals or households up vertically and measures inequality over the range of individuals: I define the latter type of inequality as *vertical* inequality. HIs are multidimensional – with political, economic and social elements (as, indeed, are vertical inequalities, but they are rarely measured in a multidimensional way). It is my contention that HIs affect individual well-being and social stability in a serious way, and one that is different from the consequences of vertical inequality.

Unequal access to political/economic/social resources by different cultural groups can reduce individual welfare in the losing groups over and above what their individual position would merit, because their self-esteem is bound up with the progress of the group. But of greater consequence is the argument that where there are such inequalities in resource access and outcomes, *coinciding with cultural differences*, culture can become a powerful mobilizing agent that can lead to a range of political disturbances. As Abner Cohen stated:

> Men may and do certainly joke about or ridicule the strange and bizarre customs of men from other ethnic groups, because these customs are different from their own. But they do not fight over such differences alone. When men *do*, on the other hand, fight across ethnic lines it is nearly always the case that they fight over some fundamental issues concerning the distribution and exercise of power, whether economic, political, or both. (Cohen 1974: 94)

Disturbances arising from HIs may take the form of sporadic riots, as has occurred, for example, in the towns of Yorkshire in Britain or various US cities; more extreme manifestations are civil wars, such as the Biafran and

Eritrean attempts to gain independence; massacres, as occurred in Burundi and Rwanda; and local and international terrorism. Indeed, the events of 11 September 2001 can be seen as a manifestation of the force of HIs, with vast economic inequalities between the United States and the world's Moslem population coinciding with strong cultural differences between these groups.

We should not assume that it is only resentment by the deprived that causes political instability – although this certainly seems to be the case in many disputes (e.g. by the southern Sudanese; the Hutus in Rwanda; or race riots in industrialized countries). But the relatively privileged can also attack the underprivileged, fearing that they may demand more resources, and, especially, political power. Moreover, where a position of relative privilege is geographically centred, the privileged area may demand independence to protect their resource position – for example, Biafra or the Basque country.[4]

Given these extremely serious potential consequences of severe HIs, development policy ought to include policies to monitor and correct them. Yet, as noted above, this is not part of the current development agenda, which considers poverty and inequality only at the level of the individual, not as a group phenomenon.

These points will be further developed in the rest of the chapter, which will be organized as follows: the next section will further elaborate on why a group approach is important; then we will consider the processes by which cultural group identities are formed and defined, and how they act as a powerful mobilizing agent, considering whether such identities have sufficient stability to make HIs meaningful; the next section will discuss some measurement issues before providing some empirical evidence on eight cases of countries with severe HIs; finally we will draw some conclusions, including a discussion of some policy implications.

Why assessing group well-being is as important as assessing that of individuals

In the introduction, I stressed the most dramatic reason for being concerned with group well-being – that is, for social stability, which is self-evidently important in itself, and also generally as a precondition of economic development. The impact of group inequalities on social stability will be elaborated as the chapter proceeds. But there is a strong case for being concerned with groups apart from this, even from a purely individualistic perspective.[5]

First, there are *instrumental* reasons. If group inequality persists, then individuals within the depressed group may be handicapped and therefore not make the contribution to their own and society's prosperity that they might have done. For example, if one group has systematically less access to education than another, children within that group will not acquire the human resources that others of equal merit do, and not only the individuals but also society will suffer. Such inequalities may be due to the unequal distribution of public goods. In some contexts, certain public goods are exclusive to particular groups (Loury, 1988, has called these 'quasi-public goods', others name them 'club' goods). This occurs, for example, where physical infrastructure is unequally distributed across areas, and communities are clustered in these areas. Overt discrimination, where certain cultural categories are barred altogether or gain access only on prejudiced terms, is another cause of unequal group access. Networking is often group-based, so that every member of a relatively backward group has a networking disadvantage with economic and social implications that can be overcome only by group policies. Further, self-selection for cultural reasons may lead to unequal access – for example, if cultural factors mean that children attend only certain types of (inferior) school, or there is gender discrimination, or health practices that limit access to certain resources. Policies that simply address deprived *individuals* may therefore fail unless accompanied by policies directed towards group inequalities.

Another type of instrumental reason is that taking action to correct group inequalities may be the most efficient way of achieving other objectives. This occurs where differential outcomes are closely identified with group characteristics. For example, the most efficient way to achieve the objective of reducing unemployment in South Africa is through policies targeted at black youths. Or, in other contexts, poverty incidence is closely correlated with a particular region, and sometimes a particular ethnic group – for example, the Indian population in some rural areas in Peru; efficient poverty targeting may involve policies directed at a particular group. The neglect of the group as a classificatory device can therefore reduce the effectiveness of policies which in themselves are not grouped-based.

Second, there are *direct welfare* impacts of group inequalities. What happens to the group to which an individual belongs may affect that individual's welfare directly – that is, individual welfare depends not just on a person's own circumstances but the prestige and well-being of the group with which they identify. For this reason, Akerlof and Kranton have included a person's identity in the individual's utility function, arguing that 'a person assigned a category with a higher social status may enjoy an enhanced self-image' (Akerlof and Kranton, 2000: 719). One reason for this arises where people from other groups taunt members of a particular group, causing distress, even if serious violence does not occur. The Catholic schoolgirls being shouted at by Protestants in the autumn of 2001 as they travelled to school in Belfast provides a graphic example. There are negative externalities of belonging to certain groups. Membership of deprived groups can cause resentment among individuals on behalf of the group, as well as negative externalities which affect them directly. US psychologists have documented effects of racial discrimination on the mental health of the black population, finding that perceptions of discrimination are linked to psychiatric symptoms and lower levels of well-being, including depressive symptoms and reduced self-esteem; teenagers report lower levels of satisfaction with their lives (Broman, 1997; Brown, Williams *et al.*, 1999).

Limited mobility between groups enhances each of these effects. If people can readily move between groups, then groups matter much less both instrumentally and for their direct impact on welfare, since if the effects of group membership are adverse, people can shift; and groups also become ineffective targeting devices since people can readily move into any group to which benefits are targeted, thereby causing targeting errors. This chapter is primarily concerned with *limited mobility groups* because it is these groups, whose boundaries are fairly well defined, where HIs matter.

These are substantial reasons for taking the reduction of group inequalities to be an important societal objective even before we consider the implications of HIs for social stability – which forms the main theme of this chapter. It does not, however, follow that complete group equality should be the objective, for a number of reasons. One is that – like complete individual equality – it is not a meaningful objective unless one has defined the dimension: equality of inputs (e.g. access to resources) may not result in equality of outcomes (e.g. health status) because people in different groups may not make the same use of the access provided, or because their conversion from inputs to outputs differs. A second reason is that there can be trade-offs with other societal objectives – for example, near-complete group equality might be achieved only by increasing the extent of vertical inequality, or by reducing economic efficiency. A judgement has to be made on these trade-offs. Third, in the short to medium term complete equality may not be achievable given the large inherited inequalities among groups.

Making group welfare and greater group equality societal objectives does not mean that the objectives of enhancing individual capabilities or achieving vertical equality should be jettisoned. The group dimension is intended to be *added* to the individual one, not to replace it. In part, indeed, improving the well-being of deprived groups is justified because it is a way of improving individual welfare, as noted above, with the promotion of group equality tending to raise output, reduce poverty and reduce vertical inequality, because it raises the human capital of deprived groups and contributes to social stability. But there may be cases where enhancing group equality is at the expense of either output expansion or poverty reduction, when choices have to be made.

Group formation and mobilization

If group differences are to provide a useful basis for policy, group boundaries must be relatively clearly defined and have some continuity over time. People can be divided into groups in many ways – geographical, behavioural, language, physical characteristics and so on. We are concerned here with those divisions which have social significance – for example, such meaning for their members and for others in society that they influence behaviour and well-being in a significant way. Meaningful group identities are then dependent on individuals' *perceptions* of identity with a particular group – self-perceptions of those 'in' the group, and perceptions of those outside the group. The question then is why and when some differences are perceived as being socially significant, and others are not.

Anthropologists have differed sharply on this question. At one extreme are the so-called 'primordialists', who argue that 'ethnicity is a cultural given, a quasi-natural state of being determined by one's descent and with, in the extreme view, sociobiological determinants' (Douglas, 1988: 192).[6] 'Basic group identity consists of the ready-made set of endowments and identifications which every individual shares with others from the moment of birth by chance of the family into which he is born at that given time and given place' (Isaacs, 1975: 31, quoted in Banks, 1996). For primordialists, ethnic identity is etched deep in the subconscious of individuals from birth.

The primordial view, however, does not explain why ethnic groups change over time – are of pre-eminent significance at some points and then boundaries and characteristics of groups change. For example, Cohen has shown how some people moving from rural to urban Nigeria became 'detribalized', while tribal identity became more important for other urbanized Nigerians; moreover cultural characteristics among the Hausa, whose consciousness of identity increased, changed quite radically (Cohen, 1969).

It is widely agreed that many tribal distinctions in Africa were invented by the colonial powers:

> Almost all recent studies of nineteenth century pre-colonial Africa have emphasized that far from there being a single 'tribal' identity, most Africans moved in and out of multiple identities, defining themselves at one moment as subject to this chief, at another moment as a member of that cult, at another moment as part of this clan, and at yet another moment as an initiate in that professional guild. (Ranger, 1983: 248)

> Modern Central Africa tribes are not so much survivals from a pre-colonial past but rather colonial creations by colonial officers and African intellectuals. (van Binsbergen, quoted in Ranger, 1983: 248)

One example is the distinction between Hutus and Tutsis, which some historians argue was largely invented by the colonial powers for administrative convenience (de Waal, 1994; Lemarchand, 1994).

Instrumentalists see ethnicity as being used by groups and their leaders in order to achieve political or economic goals. Cohen (1969), cited above, explained the development of Hausa consciousness and customs in this way.[7] Another pre-eminent example is the work of Glazer and Moynihan who argued that ethnicity was maintained and enhanced by US migrant groups in order to promote their economic interests (Glazer and Moynihan, 1975). The colonial inventions, according to this view, served administrative purposes. In conflict, the use of ethnic symbols and the enhancement of ethnic identities, often by reworking historical memories, is frequently used as a powerful mechanism for the mobilization of support. This also represents an instrumental, or partially instrumental, perspective on ethnicity. Numerous examples have shown how ethnicity has been used by political and intellectual elites prior to, and in the course of, wars (e.g. Cohen, 1969; Turton, 1997; Alexander, McGregor and Ranger, 2000). In international wars, this takes the shape of enhancing national consciousness, with flag-waving, historical references, military parades and so on. In civil wars, it is a matter of raising ethnic or religious consciousness. For example, the radio broadcasts by the extremist Hutus before the 1994 massacre, in which the Tutsis were repeatedly depicted as subhuman, like rats to be eliminated, echoing Nazi anti-Jewish propaganda of the 1930s. Osama Bin Laden appealed to Moslem consciousness, arguing that the war was 'in essence a religious war'.[8]

Yet even instrumentalists generally recognize that there need to be some felt differences in behaviour, customs, ideology or religion to make it possible to raise ethnic or other consciousness in an instrumental way. For example, Glazer and Moynihan state that: 'For there to be the possibility for an ethnic community at all, there will normally exist some visible cultural differences or "markers" which might help to divide communities into fairly well defined groupings or ethnic categories' (Glazer and Moynihan, 1975: 379). Some shared circumstances are needed for group construction – for example, speaking the same language, sharing cultural traditions, living in the same place, or facing similar sources of hardship or exploitation. Past group formation, although possibly constructed for political or economic purposes at the time, also contributes to present differences. Whether the origins of a group are instrumental or not, the effect is to change perceptions and make the differences seem real to group members – this is why group identities are so powerful as sources of action. As Turton puts it, the power of ethnicity or 'its very effectiveness as a means of advancing group interests depends upon its being seen as "primordial" by those who make claims in its name' (Turton, 1997: 82). Hence what was a dependent variable at one point in history can act as an independent variable in contributing to current perceptions.[9]

Groups which are important for their members' self-esteem and well-being and can threaten social stability invariably have some shared characteristics which may make them easy to identify; they also have some continuity. While people have some choice over their own identities, this is not unconstrained – Kikuyu cannot decide that from tomorrow they will be part of the Luo ethnic group. Choice of identity is constrained both by characteristics of the group – its customs and symbols, norms, etc. (sometimes birth itself, sometimes language, sometimes complex customs, sometimes physical characteristics) – and by other groups' willingness to admit new members. For example, assimilation to a different culture may be a choice that outsiders wish to make, but it cannot be realized unless the insiders accept it, as the German Jews found. So there is some constancy about group boundaries. Yet there is also some fluidity in group boundaries, they do evolve over time in response to circumstances – for example, the Iwerri decided they were not after all Ibos in the middle of the Biafran war; the Telegu-speaking people who were an apparently homogeneous group seeking autonomy from the State of Madras, became quite sharply divided once they had gained this autonomy (Horowitz, 1985: 66).

The hypothesis that forms the central thesis of this chapter is that HIs matter to people in different groups. This makes sense only if the groups themselves are real to their members – which they undoubtedly are in many contexts, and it is precisely these contexts in which we would be concerned about HIs. Yet the fluidity of group boundaries can present potential problems for the approach I am advocating. If group identities can readily be chosen, the group is likely to be a much less important constraint on individual well-being and behaviour – indeed, rather than a constraint, choice of group identity could constitute an extension of capabilities. For example, a child might chose to join the Scouts, and the possibility of doing so would add to potential welfare; not being a Scout is then a chosen identity, and not a welfare constraint, for girls (although not boys). If group boundaries were all like that – open, fluid, and changing – measurement of HIs would make little sense. It is because of the discontinuities, which go along with the limited choices most people have to switch identities, that inequalities among groups becomes a source of unhappiness and resentment, and a cause of social instability. Generally speaking, it is where switching is difficult that group inequalities become relevant to social stability. In any particular case, history and social context will determine the possibilities. For example, in Europe today a change in religion is relatively easy, but this was much less so in earlier centuries when religious divisions were a major cause of conflict.[10] Although people may find it difficult to change ethnicities, they can, in Cohen's terms become 'detribalized' in some contexts, which is a form of switching. This is more likely to be the case in urban environments or in foreign countries. From our perspective, it is the conditions in which switching is difficult that are most likely to give rise to negative effects arising from HIs. Moreover, where switching is easy, group inequalities should be small, since people in the deprived group can change groups until an equilibrium is reached. Where the distinction between groups carries no political or economic baggage – i.e. does not impede opportunities – the salience of any group classification becomes much less.

In monitoring HIs, then, most concern should be with categories where switching groups is rather marginal. Nonetheless, there will always be problems of defining group boundaries with the possibility of new boundaries emerging and old ones ceasing to be significant. The choice of group boundaries is thus more problematic and arbitrary than is apparent in most conventional statistical boundaries – though the latter's 'objectivity' can be exaggerated – for example, the dividing line between 'rural' and 'urban', a very widely adopted statistical categorization, is often extremely arbitrary. While there are undoubtedly problems about defining boundaries, the issue is too important to reject the approach for this reason. What is needed is an openness to redefining boundaries as appropriate.

As we shall see in the empirical part of this chapter, when it comes to actual cases the relevant groups and boundaries are generally fairly obvious.

Measuring HIs

In the discussion that follows, I assume that the question of defining boundaries has been dealt with, and consider other important measurement issues.

To start with it is essential to re-emphasize that the HIs with which we are concerned are *multidimensional*. This multidimensionality arises with respect both to the impact of HIs on individual well-being and on social stability (the two, of course, being connected). The esteem of the group, which impacts on individual well-being, arises from the relative position of the group in a large number of areas, not just in incomes. For example, a major source of resentment among UK black youths arises from the fact that they are five times more likely to be stopped and searched by police in London than whites and four times more likely to be arrested (Cabinet Office, 2001). Equally, a range of deprivations – economic, social and political – enable political leaders to use the symbolic systems of a grouping[11] as an effective mechanism of group mobilization. In South Africa, education and jobs were among the top grievances pre-transition, while in Northern Ireland, jobs and housing were at the top of the Catholic social and economic agenda (Darby, 1999).

For simplification, we divide the various dimensions into three categories: political participation; economic (assets, incomes and employment); and social aspects, with each containing a number of elements. For example, political participation can occur at the level of the cabinet, the bureaucracy, the army and so on; economic assets comprise land, livestock, machinery, etc.

The three categories and some major elements are presented in Table 5.1, with a column for each category. Each of the categories is important in itself, but most are also instrumental for achieving others. For example, political power is both an ends and a means: control over economic assets is primarily a means to secure income but it is also an end. Clearly, as noted above, the relevance of a particular element varies according to whether it forms an important source of incomes or well-being in a particular society. The allocation of housing, for example, is generally more relevant in industrialized countries, while land is of huge importance where agriculture accounts for most output and employment, but gets less important as development

Table 5.1   Sources of differentiation among groups

Categories of differentiation	Political participation	Economic		Social access and situation
		Assets	Employment and incomes	
Elements of categories	Government ministers	Land	Incomes	Education
			Government employment	
	Parliament	Human capital	Private employment	Health services
	Civil service – various levels	Communal resources, inc. water	Elite employment	Safe water
	Army	Minerals	Rents	Housing
	Police	Privately owned capital/credit	Skilled	Unemployment
	Local government	Government infrastructure	Unskilled	Poverty
	Respect for human rights	Security of assets against theft and destruction	Informal sector opportunities	Personal and household security

proceeds. Water, as a productive resource, can be very important in parts of the world where rainwater is inadequate. Access to minerals can be a source of great wealth, and gaining such access an important source of conflict in countries with mineral resources (Reno, 1998; Fairhead, 2000).

Some important questions surface about the conditions in which HIs give rise to resentment and dissatisfaction, and to political violence, which need to be answered empirically, and have implications for appropriate measures of HIs:

- The *time dimension*: it seems plausible that HIs will be a greater source of resentment and an agent of mobilization where HIs are widening over time.
- The *consistency* issue – i.e. whether one can expect more negative consequences where HIs are consistent across categories than where they are inconsistent (for example, where one group has political dominance but is economically deprived).
- The impact of *intragroup* inequalities: can we expect greater intragroup inequalities to reduce group cohesiveness?

With these questions in mind, some issues about measurement arise:

1. Whether to develop a measure of societal welfare which is discounted to allow for group inequality. This, broadly, is the approach of Anand and Sen (1995) in connection with gender inequality, and Majumdar and

Subramanian (2001) exploring caste and rural/urban differences in India, that is:

$$W_s = K \cdot A_s \qquad (5.1)$$

where W_s = society well-being in some dimension; A_s = society average achievement in that dimensions; and K = the weighting which incorporates group differentials.

From the perspective of international (or over time) comparisons of welfare this is a useful approach, but the outcome depends on the *weighting* (i.e. the inequality aversion). From the perspective of assessing how far HIs affect social conflict, it is not helpful, since we need to have a direct measure of group differentials to identify the size and impact of HIs irrespective of average achievements.

2. For the present purpose, we need, as far as possible a *descriptive* measure rather than an *evaluative* one, since the aim is to explore the implications of the extent of HIs for outcomes of various sorts. Of course, any description involves some evaluation, so that we cannot arrive at a completely value-free description. Our aim is to measure HI as 'objectively' as possible.[12] Where different measures involve some element of valuation, then in principle (data and time allowing) we should try different descriptive measures to see whether we get robust results.

3. Since HIs are essentially multidimensional, the issue of *aggregation* arises. For many purposes, it is preferable to keep the various elements separate because among the questions to be explored are whether consistency across dimensions is important for outcomes; and whether some dimensions are more important than others. For cross-country comparisons, however, some aggregate index is needed. The nature of the aggregation exercise, of course, then affects the results. One can usefully aggregate individual categories without aggregating across them – that is, develop a separate aggregate index for each society for the three major categories of HIs – political, economic and social. This would be helpful for comparisons across countries where the precise type of information on variables within each category is likely to vary.

4. The *number and size of groups* in a society may have implications for the impact of group differences. Two different ways of measuring this have been proposed:

   • *Fragmentation indices* The index of ethnic diversity developed by Taylor and Hudson (1972) measures the probability that two randomly selected individuals will belong to different ethnolinguistic groups. Hence it is larger the more groups there are. This could, of course, be adapted to other types of group.

- *Polarization indices* (Estaban and Ray, 1994). These are greater when there are a few large groups with homogeneous characteristics within each group, and differences in a cluster of characteristics among groups. Groups of insignificant size carry little weight (the opposite of fragmentation indices).

  It seems plausible that in highly fragmented societies group differences are less salient personally and politically than in societies where there are a small number of large rivalrous groups. If leaders are using group, identities to achieve political objectives, where there are many small groups, group coalitions will be essential and cooperation rather than conflict becomes likely.[13] Similarly, numerous small groups would appear to be less likely to affect individual esteem and happiness than a few unequal groups. Hence polarization indices would seem to be more relevant than fragmentation ones. Indeed, religious polarization has been found to vary positively with civil war, while religious fragmentation does not (Reynal-Querol, 2001).

5. As noted above, we need to measure *intra*group as well as *inter*groups differentials in order to explore how intragroup differentials affect the consequences of HIs. On the one hand, it could be argued that strong intragroup differentials will reduce groups' cohesiveness and hence their ability to take coordinated action, with different social classes identifying with their counterparts in other groups rather than their own cultural group membership. On the other hand, strong intragroup differentials may provide leaders (the elite) with an opportunity and incentive to exploit group differences to avoid discontent being directed at themselves (one interpretation of the conflict in Rwanda, or Hitler's Germany).

6. It is important to bear in mind that it is *perceptions* as much as reality that is relevant to outcomes, with respect both to what differences actually are, as well as how much group members mind about the differences. While it would be valuable to draw on surveys of perceptions – and altering perceptions does constitute one aspect of policies towards HIs[14] – the basic hypothesis here is that perceptions reflect some 'reality' and it is this reality, therefore, that we should primarily aim to measure. The importance of perceptions, nonetheless, has implications for measurement. Complex measures which are not intuitively appealing are less likely to reflect perceptions of differences than more straightforward measures.

In practice, we have to work with available data. At present, because HIs have not been recognized as central to the development process, data are often quite limited, especially of a comprehensive nature and on a regular basis. But censuses and special surveys often permit some analysis, as indicated in the empirical discussion below. Most empirical work on group differences, including the material presented below, uses simple measures of differences in performance between the major groups in society, aggregating only for cross-country comparisons.

Some empirical evidence on HIs

There is a body of empirical work on the impact of group economic and social differences, mainly undertaken by sociologists. Three types of study have been carried out: statistical analysis of US black/white relationships; some cross-country regressions, primarily carried out by Gurr (1993) in the Minorities at Risk project; and case studies of particular countries. This section will present the results of a review of nine case studies I have undertaken (drawing on secondary material) as this seems a powerful way of illuminating the issues. But first I shall turn briefly to existing econometric work.

Most of the work on US black/white relationships differentiates characteristics of riot-prone and non-riot-prone cities, and explores whether riot incidence is related to the economic and social characteristics of the cities, including HIs. Generally, where statistically significant results are found, there is a positive relationship between inequalities and violence, although many studies produce insignificant results. According to McElroy and Singell (1973: 289) 'variables which measure the disparities in the distribution of income ... and divergent government expenditure levels between political subdivisions ... both discriminate effectively between riot and non-riot [cities]'. Blau and Blau (1982) find that the extent of socioeconomic inequality between races in the United States, and not poverty, helps determine the rates of violent crime.

Internationally, Gurr (1993) has produced an index of political, economic and cultural disparities for 233 groups in ninety-three countries, selected either because the group suffered systematically discriminatory treatment, or was the focus of political mobilization in defence or promotion of its interests. The sample is thus biased. Gurr finds that where there are large group grievances (i.e. major political, or economic differences and/or discrimination) *together with* strong identities, protest (violent and otherwise) is more likely. Violent protests tend to occur where expression of peaceful protest is suppressed. Strong identities are defined as shared behaviour, language and the like. This coincidence of cultural and political/economic differences is precisely what I define as HIs. Acknowledging some serious methodological problems (in sample selection, the strong element of judgement in classifying differences and reliance on simple correlation analysis), Gurr's data give strong support to the view that HIs are liable to lead to violence. Of course, as we noted in the UNU-WIDER study of complex humanitarian emergencies,[15] HIs are a predisposing factor – other elements, including political suppression or accommodation, are also clearly important.

Below I briefly review the findings from the analysis of nine cases, aimed to explore the extent of HIs, their evolution and consequences. Among the cases examined, HIs have provoked a spectrum of political reaction, including severe and long-lasting violent conflict (Northern Ireland, South Africa, Sri Lanka, Uganda), less severe rebellion (Chiapas), coups (Fiji), periodic riots and criminality (the United States), occasional racial riots (Malaysia) and a high level of criminality (Brazil).

Chiapas

The state of Chiapas in Mexico, accounting for 4 per cent of the population, contains a concentration of indigenous peoples, with the indigenous share of the total population over three times that of Mexico as a whole. This has made it possible for protests to be mobilized and united under an indigenous umbrella, with a focus on Mayan culture as well as economic and political rights. Perceptions of inequalities were stimulated by religious and activist groups.

Chiapas has long suffered serious and ongoing deprivation of a political, economic and social nature, relative to the rest of Mexico (Figure 5.1). For example, the proportion of people on incomes below the minimum wage is nearly three times greater than in Mexico as a whole, and the proportion on high incomes is less than half the all Mexican rate. The illiteracy rate in Chiapas is more than twice the Mexican rate. Within Chiapas the indigenous-speaking people are particularly deprived, with substantially lower school attendance and incomes than the rest of the state. Land presents a particular problem; the end of land reform efforts in 1972 left more land which had not been redistributed in Chiapas than elsewhere, and the indigenous population were almost entirely marginalized on poor and ecologically vulnerable land. Politically, the region, and particularly the indigenous people, has been largely excluded. It appears that these inequalities have been in evidence for a long time, with a worsening of some indicators (e.g. on

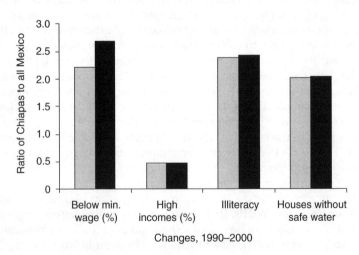

Figure 5.1   Chiapas compared with all Mexico

poverty) in recent years, a small improvement in secondary education and an improvement in the distribution of federal investment.

In 1994, the *Ejército Zapatisto de Liberación Nacional* (EZLN), with indigenous collective leadership, took control of four municipalities initiating an armed struggle against the Mexican state. The demands of the EZLN were for autonomy for the indigenous communities and the protection of their cultural heritage, as well as action towards improving economic and social conditions. Since then there have been negotiations offering greater political rights for Indians; while the armed struggle has been suspended and negotiations are ongoing, protests continue.

Fiji

In Fiji ethnic differences overlap with economic differences in a more complicated way than in Chiapas. The two major groups – indigenous Fijians and Indian-origin Fijians – were almost equal numerically in the 1970s and 1980s, with a slight majority of Indians, but as a result of political events there has been a large Indian exodus and the Fijian native population now accounts for 50 per cent of the population with the Indian-origin population at about 44 per cent.

Economically, severe imbalances exist but in different directions for different elements (see Table 5.2). The Indians are greatly favoured in education,

Table 5.2 Inequalities between Indian-origin Fijians (I) and local-origin Fijians (F)

Economic	Date	Ratio of I/F	Social	Date	Ratio of I/F
Average *per capita* income	1990	1.31	Passes in NZ school certificate	1971	2.50
			Passes in NZ university entrance	1971	2.55
Proportion of professional workers in total	1986	1.17	Households with no safe water (%)	1990	1.88
	1989	0.99	Infant mortality rate	1986	0.73
				1996	0.72
Households below food poverty line (%)	1990	0.88	Life expectancy	1986	1.00
				1996	1.00
Households below basic needs poverty line (%)	1990	1.12	*Political*		
			President/cabinet	Since independence	Fijian
			Composition of armed forces	1987	0.04

and dominate in the private sector. In the 1980s, the Fijians accounted for only about 2 per cent of the entrepreneurs (Premdas, 1993). On average Indian incomes are 30 per cent greater than Fijian and the disparity has been growing over time. But the latter own 83 per cent of the land and have a dominant position in the public sector, especially at the higher echelons. In the military, an extreme case, they account for 97 per cent of personnel. The Indian community is specially concerned with the land situation, since many of them rely on leased land for sugar production. There are severe inequalities within each community but greater in the Indian community, such that poverty levels and basic needs indicators are somewhat worse there. Yet these inequalities within each community seem to enhance the effectiveness of communal politics, not to reduce them.

At independence in 1970, Fiji inherited a constitution designed to achieve ethnic balance within parliament, with communal as well as common voting. For some years this, and informal agreements to achieve ethnic balance, preserved political peace. But again and again extremist politicians have used race successfully to undermine more moderate leaders and positions. The Fijian community is not prepared to accept an Indian-origin-dominated government, and have effected constitutional tricks and coups whenever Indian political parties gain electoral victory (1977, 1987, 2000).

The evident HIs in Fiji have made it easy for both sides to use racist politics for political purposes. 'Disparities in living standards between the races in Fiji constituted the objective basis of Fijian discontent' (Premdas 1993: 19). A major source of support for the coup against the Indian-dominated government in 1987 was the threat that the government would take away Fiji ownership and control of land (Premdas 1993: 27). Fijian-dominated governments have introduced affirmative action to assist Fijians in education, business and public employment – with some success in terms of reducing disparities. But this has increased Fijian determination not to allow an Indian-dominated government which could reverse these policies. And it has enhanced communal voting patterns among Indians, especially since their disadvantages – in land and in politics – have in no way been tackled. Despite a constitutional requirement to include major opposition parties in the cabinet, the Fijian-dominated government elected in 2000 has not done so.

Uganda

Uganda has also experienced periods where political and economic/social inequalities have been important. Economic, social and cultural divisions are broadly between the centre/south and the north, the Bantu- and non-Bantu-speaking peoples. The latter are markedly poorer than the centre/south; they are also in a minority and can attain power only with alliances and/or violence and election-rigging, facilitated in earlier years by northern domination of the army, which was a colonial heritage. Greatly oversimplifying the situation, one can say that divisions between the centre/south and the more peripheral areas, especially the north, have been at the heart of most conflicts, though, of course, specific events and personalities have been responsible for particular developments.

Uganda has suffered violent conflict on a major scale since the 1960s, including the 1970s, when Amin initiated much of the violence, and in the second Obote regime (1981–85) when Obote's forces were in conflict with Museveni's resistance movement. During these conflicts hundreds of thousands of people died. Since Museveni took over, there has been persistent fighting in the periphery of the country, especially the north, but on a much smaller scale. Museveni has aimed, far more than his predecessors, to have inclusive government; he also eschewed multiparty democracy.

There are significant, persistent horizontal inequalities in Uganda in economic and social dimensions (see Table 5.3). Average incomes are broadly twice as much in the south and centre, and social services substantially better. Yet political domination has generally been in the hands of northerners or westerners.[16] The narrowing of some differentials between 1969 and 1991 is partly the consequence of northern political domination – with some public investment favouring the north – as well as of the destruction of central facilities during the political instability and fighting (Matovu and Stewart, 2001). The dichotomy in political and economic imbalances may explain why much of the violence over the first twenty-five years was state-instigated, by the northerners who controlled the political system, directed against the

Table 5.3 Some indicators of horizontal inequality in Uganda, 1959–91[a]

	c. 1959	c. 1969	c. 1991
Economic			
Cash crops, of agricultural income (%)	—	—	0.48
Taxpayers >2500 sh. income (%)	—	0.34	—
Average household expenditure	—	—	0.59
Real GDP *per capita*	—	—	0.48
Increase in employment	—	0.77 (1962–70)	0.18 (1970–91)
Social			
Nurses per person	—	—	0.4
Distance to rural clinic	—	—	0.83
Primary enrolment	—	0.97	1.2
Secondary education[b]	—	0.71	0.67
Infant mortality	1.3	1.5	1.3
Human development index	—	—	0.67
Political			
General	Northerners	Northerners	Integrated
Military	Northerners	Northerners	Integrated

Notes: [a] Ratio of achievements of northern region to centre and south.
[b] Population having completed secondary education.

Source: Klugman, Neyapti *et al.* (1999).

economically privileged southerners. Northerners fear the economic power of the south and even more the possibility of southern political power. The National Resistance Movement – a broad-based movement with south/central support – took to arms against Obote because of election-rigging to preserve northern power.[17] Since 1986, the Museveni government has been much more inclusive; in this period, violence has mostly come from the underprivileged in the north and other peripheral areas, stimulated and supported by various outside forces, themselves reacting to Uganda's activities in the region.

Malaysia

In Malaysia, the Bumiputera, who account for the majority of Malaysia's population were at a severe economic disadvantage *vis-à-vis* the Chinese, leading to a potentially explosive situation, but systematic affirmative action has successfully diffused this tension: 62 per cent of Malaysians are indigenous (Bumiputera), 30 per cent ethnic Chinese and 8 per cent Indians. At independence, the Bumiputera were significantly less educated than the Chinese and were concentrated in agriculture. Economic and social HIs systematically favoured the Chinese; for example, Bumiputera incomes were less than half of Chinese, they accounted for only 8 per cent of registered professionals, less than 2 per cent of ownership of capital on the stock exchange and their educational enrolment rates were lower at each level of education. However, broadly democratic institutions meant that the Bumiputera, as the entrenched majority, were likely to retain political power. Serious riots in 1969 by the Bumiputera against the Chinese inspired the New Economic Policy (NEP) which was designed 'to accelerate the process of restructuring the Malaysian economy to correct economic imbalance, so as to reduce and eventually eliminate the identification of race with economic function'.[18] Another target was to eliminate poverty.

Policies that followed included quotas, targets and affirmative action with respect to education, land ownership, public service employment and ownership of quoted companies. The policies were undoubtedly successful (Figure 5.2). The proportion of Bumiputera professionals rose from 8 per cent to 54 per cent; Bumiputera students in tertiary education increased from 43 per cent to 54 per cent of the total, and there was a similar improvement at other levels of education. The Bumiputera share of corporate stock ownership rose from 1.5 per cent in 1969 to 20.6 per cent in 1995. While Bumiputeras retained their dominant position in agriculture, there was an economywide switch out of agriculture into manufacturing and services, and the Bumiputera position in these sectors improved significantly. The gap in average incomes narrowed, though was not eliminated. These achievements were paralleled by aggregate economic success. The growth of the Malaysian economy was among the highest in the world (at 6.7 per cent per annum from 1970 to 1990). Poverty fell dramatically from 49 per cent in 1970 to 7.5 per cent in 1999 and income distribution improved. The political

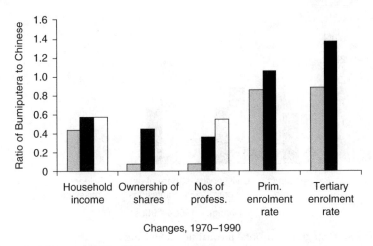

Figure 5.2 Malaysia and the NEP

success of the policies was indicated by the fact that during the economic crisis of 1997, when there were assaults on the Chinese in Indonesia, there were no such attacks in Malaysia, the only mild incidents involved Bumiputera–Indian conflict.

Sri Lanka[19]

The contrast between Sri Lanka and Malaysia is interesting. Both apparently started in a similar situation, with the political majority at an economic disadvantage, but while attempts to correct this situation in Malaysia were successful, they actually provoked war in Sri Lanka. Sri Lanka has suffered major civil war since the early 1980s, as Sri Lankan Tamils have sought political independence for the northeastern region of the country.

The situation with respect to HIs is complex. The Sri Lankan Tamil minority (accounting for 12.6 per cent of the population[20] in 1981) had been favoured by the British colonial administration, enjoying relatively privileged access to education and to government employment in the first half of the twentieth century. For example, Sri Lankan Tamils held around 40 per cent of the university places in science and engineering, medicine and agriculture and veterinary science. Tamils also gained from the use of English as the official language where they outperformed the Sinhalese majority (74 per cent of the population in 1981). Yet there was much differentiation within both communities, with intragroup differentials greatly exceeding intergroup ones (Glewwe, 1986).

When the Sinhalese gained power, they sought to correct the HIs perceived as disadvantageous to them – through educational quotas, the use

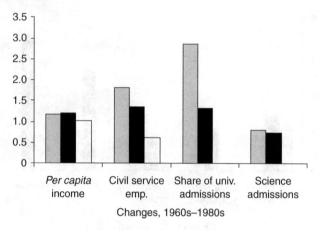

Figure 5.3   Changing horizontal inequalities in Sri Lanka

of Sinhalese as the official national language and regional investment policy. The consequence was a major change in the extent and even direction of horizontal inequalities (see Figure 5.3).[21] From 1963 to 1973, the incomes of the Sinhalese rose while those of the Tamils fell quite sharply, eliminating the previous differential between the two groups. By the end of the 1970s differentials in access to education had been eliminated, with the Sinhalese gaining more than proportionate university places, although up to 1977 Tamils continued to be favoured in science. Civil service recruitment policies, particularly the use of Sinhalese in examinations, favoured the Sinhalese – by the end of the 1970s Sinhalese recruitment in relation to population was four times more favourable than that of Tamils.

Sinhalese policies were undoubtedly effective in correcting prior HIs, but they 'overkilled', introducing new HIs in their favour. The result was to provoke the Sri Lankan Tamils, who felt excluded politically and economically threatened:

> The political impact of the district quota system [introducing quotas on university access] has been little short of disastrous. It has convinced many Tamils that it was futile to expect equality of treatment with the Sinhalese majority ... it has contributed to the acceptance of a policy campaigning for a separate state. (C. R. de Silva, quoted in Sriskandarajah, 2000: 51)

Similarly, the recruitment policies to the civil service in the 1970s, previously an important source of employment for Tamils, were strongly biased against them. Only 8 per cent of the 23,000 new teachers recruited from 1971 to 1974 were Tamils. In 1977/8 *no* Tamils succeeded in the Sri Lankan administrative service examinations (Manogoran, 1987). Moreover, political and cultural exclusion coincided with these adverse changes, making it easy for extremist leaders to use the growing resentment to gain support.

The Sri Lankan case indicates the care which is needed in pursuing policies to correct HIs. Sharp changes can create new sources of conflict, especially where they go beyond correcting prior inequalities and create new ones.

South Africa

Analysis of South Africa must obviously differentiate between the white-domination era and the situation following the transfer of power to the black majority in 1993, termed SA1 and SA2 below.

SA1 was a phase of consistent and acute HIs, which provoked rebellion. In SA2, we have a situation parallel to that of Sri Lanka and Malaysia, with the political majority facing large adverse HIs. But with the white population geographically dispersed and politically weak, their situation seems more similar to that of the Chinese in Malaysia than to the Tamils in Sri Lanka. A major problem for South Africa, however, is that strong affirmative action seems to contradict the non-interventionist market model of development they have adopted under the auspices of the international financial institutions.

SA1

The large and consistent HIs under the white-dominated government are well known (Figure 5.4). Inequalities worsened following the National Party's election in 1948. Real GDP *per capita* among blacks in 1980 was only 8 per cent of that of whites. The average monthly salary of black workers was just 20 per cent of white salaries in 1975, rising to 29 per cent by 1990. State expenditure on education per white student was fourteen times the

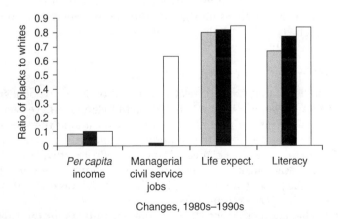

Figure 5.4 Black/white inequalities in South Africa

expenditure per black student in 1980. Infant mortality rates among blacks were six times those among whites. In 1980 adult literacy among blacks was 66 per cent compared with 97 per cent among white and life expectancy was 56 years among blacks compared with 70 among whites. Whites owned around 90 per cent of the land. The civil service was dominated by whites, who accounted for 94 per cent of the higher echelons in 1994.

Following unsuccessful peaceful protests, the sharp HIs in every dimension – political, economic and social – led to armed rebellion from 1976, until the transfer of power in 1993. Over this period there was some diminution in HIs, partly for economic reasons and in a (very) partial and unsuccessful effort to secure peace without transferring power.

SA2

An overriding objective of the post-transition government has been to reduce black/white differentials, but these efforts have been constrained by limits on government expenditure and by the economic liberalization agenda. There has been some reduction in HIs. The proportion of blacks in managerial posts in the civil service rose to 35 per cent by 1998; life expectancy and adult literacy differentials narrowed; educational differences narrowed and blacks' share of national income rose from under half in 1985 to three-quarters in 1995. Expenditures in the education and health sectors remained unbalanced, with expenditure on white students or patients exceeding those on black, but the differentials narrowed.

The differential in real adjusted GNP *per capita* had been somewhat reduced by 1996. However, efforts to 'empower' black business by increasing their role in private capital ownership have faltered with their share in stock market capitalization rising to a peak of 6 per cent in 2000 and then falling to below 5 per cent in 2001,[22] while Sherer (2000) finds evidence of persistent labour market discrimination in the post-apartheid era. Black unemployment has been rising sharply. Differentials are diminishing, but remain extremely high. While political violence has ceased, criminality remains at a very high level.

Horizontal inequalities in Northern Ireland[23]

'There is no doubt that Catholic relative deprivation is a cause of alienation and discontent' (Darby, 1999: 149). In Northern Ireland HIs have been large, persistent and consistent over all dimensions over a long time period, an example of how such inequalities can provoke violence. The case illustrates how policies to correct such inequalities can help to provide conditions supportive of peace making. It also indicates the long time horizon that is needed: while policies were initiated in the 1970s, it was only thirty years later that a fragile peace was initiated.

Considerable and consistent HIs were present throughout the twentieth century with respect to economic, social and political life (Figure 5.5).

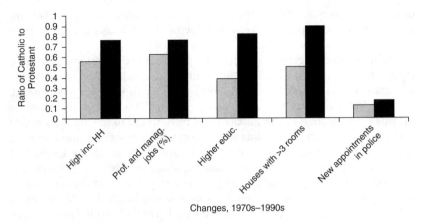

Changes, 1970s–1990s

Figure 5.5   Horizontal inequalities in Northern Ireland

Unemployment rates, for example, were consistently more than twice the rate among Catholics than Protestants; educational qualifications were worse; the employment profile strongly favoured Protestants; incomes were lower and housing access worse. As a minority in a majoritarian democracy, the Catholic community was also politically excluded when responsibility for government was devolved to the Province. They were also at acute disadvantage with respect to participation in the security forces and the police. For example, the Catholics with roughly 40 per cent of the population accounted for only 8 per cent of the membership of the Royal Ulster Constabulary (RUC). The consistency of the inequalities across political, economic and social dimensions – with most evidence suggesting little change in the first three-quarters of the twentieth century – provided fertile ground for the outbreak of the troubles in the late 1960s.

HIs in Ireland date back to the sixteenth and seventeenth centuries when Protestants took the best land for themselves, and introduced a range of legal and other sources of discrimination, preventing Catholics from owning land or acquiring wealth for example, and forcibly displacing Gaelic by English. By the end of the nineteenth century Protestants controlled the vast bulk of the economic resources of east Ulster – the best of its land, its industrial and financial capital, commercial and business networks and industrial skills (Ruane and Todd, 1996: 151). The division of the island, when the Irish Free State came into being in 1921, ensured permanent political control and continued economic dominance by the Protestants in the province of Northern Ireland, where they formed the majority. Assessments indicate no narrowing of the gap between the communities from 1901 to 1951, with Catholics disadvantaged at every level (Hepburn, 1983; Cormack and Rooney, nd, cited by Ruane and Todd, 1996). Indeed in some aspects, there appears to have been a worsening between 1911 and 1971, with a rising proportion of unskilled workers in the Catholic community and a falling proportion among Protestants; the relative unemployment ratios also appear to have worsened over this period (Ruane and Todd, 1996).

Yet the evidence suggests a reduction in HIs in many dimensions since then, especially from the mid-1980s.[24] For example, inequality in access to higher education was eliminated by the 1990s; inequality in incomes was reduced; the housing inequality was significantly reduced; the employment profile became more equal; even the imbalance in recruitment to the RUC was slowly being reversed. According to Ruane and Todd, the Catholic position remains one of relative disadvantage; Protestants are stronger at all levels, but Protestant economic power has declined significantly since the 1970s (Ruane and Todd, 1996: 177). This narrowing of HI is in part at least the outcome of British government policy, exemplified by a strengthened Fair Employment Act (1989),[25] a relatively generous housing policy and efforts to ensure equality of education among the communities.[26] Systematic efforts to correct HIs are one element explaining the readiness of the Catholic community to bring the conflict to an end. They also help explain the resistance of some Protestant groups to the more inclusive government which is being introduced.

Black/white differences in the United States

Black/white differentials in the United States have a long history, originating in slavery. They encompass all three dimensions of HIs, political, economic and social. Black households earn roughly half that of whites; asset inequality is substantially higher, with one estimate showing that the median net worth of white households was nearly twelve times that of black households; nearly three times as many blacks as whites live below the poverty line, although the population ratio is 1:6. There are numerous other examples of black/white economic differences (Figure 5.6): one minor example which must be representative of many others is that blacks have to pay up to four times higher a mark-up on car loans from Nissan.[27] Unemployment rates are twice as high among blacks; infant mortality rates two and a half times higher; high school completion rates are lower and drop out rates higher. Blacks' political participation – voting and voting registration, membership of Congress and the Senate – are all well below those of whites.

One response to these marked and consistent differences has been periodic race riots throughout the twentieth century (e.g. in Tulsa in 1921, Detroit in 1943, many cities in the 1960s, Los Angeles in 1992 and Cincinnati and Seattle in 2001); the high rates of criminality in the United States may also in part be a response to HIs (Blau and Blau, 1982).

Following the 1964 Civil Rights Act a range of affirmative actions was taken, including on employment, education and housing. In the 1980s, enforcement lapsed, but it was reasserted with the Civil Rights Restoration Act of 1991. The evidence from the aggregate changes in HIs and micro-studies is that these programmes have had a positive impact, albeit not very

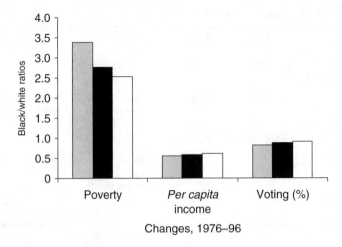

Figure 5.6 Horizontal inequalities in the United States
Source: Hamilton (2001).

large.[28] There has been a small reduction in income inequalities over the past thirty years; education completion rates have risen; the ratio of black representation in the House of Representatives to that of whites has increased from 3 per cent in 1970 to 11 per cent. Nonetheless, discrimination of many kinds persists and the HIs remain large.

Brazil

In some respects Brazil is similar to the United States, with racial inequalities originating in slavery. But it also presents a contrast – there have not been the same race riots and pressures for black liberation as in the United States. While Brazil exhibits sharp racial inequalities quite similar in level to those of the United States, despite its earlier reputation of being a non-racial society,[29] unlike the United States racial categories are fluid and there is a large amount of intermarriage. The 'mixed' or 'brown' category accounted for 43 per cent of the population in 1991, with whites at 52 per cent and blacks at just 5 per cent. The proportion in the mixed category has been rising steadily (from 27 per cent in 1950), with the proportions in white and black categories falling. Moreover, where people are classified is often somewhat arbitrary. The presence of people descended from the indigenous Indian population further complicates the racial situation.[30]

Research has shown that there *is* considerable racial inequality and discrimination – exhibited in incomes, occupations, education, mortality and political positions – for example, black family income was only 43 per cent of white family income in 1996 (see Table 5.4), years of schooling were 63 per cent and currently there are no blacks among the supreme court judges or cabinet ministers.

Table 5.4   Ratio of black/white performance in Brazil

Economic	Date	Ratio b/w	Social	Date	Ratio b/w
Per capita family income	1996	0.43	Literacy (%)	1940 1991	0.54 0.90
Wages	1991	0.59	Life expectancy	1950 1991	0.84 0.90
Female monthly wages	1987 1998	0.49 0.51			
In 'miserable' poverty (%): south northeast	1998	1.84 1.29	Human Development Index (HDI) rank	1999	0.84

Yet despite these large differences, there have not been race riots, though there has been and is a very high degree of criminality. Some argue, indeed, that the problem is not race but class – yet studies show discrimination within each class.[31] The explanation may be that because 'race' is such a fluid category and mobility from one category to another is relatively easy, it does not act as a mobilizing agent. In recent years, recognizing that there is a problem of discrimination – partly in response to the formation of an all-black political party – the government has quietly introduced a set of minor affirmative measures (including requirements for a set proportion of blacks to be included in a poverty programme, a job training scheme, and as actors in television, movies and theatre).[32]

Some conclusions from these nine cases

1. Where ethnic identities coincide with economic/social ones, social instability of one sort of another is likely – ethnicity *does* become a mobilizing agent, and as this happens the ethnic divisions are enhanced. Sri Lanka is a powerful example; Chiapas another. With more fluid boundaries, as in Brazil, mobilization is less. This is precisely the point about HIs. They are powerful because they represent the coincidence of cultural and economic/social/political inequalities, and less powerful where cultural divisions are less firm.
2. There are two distinct situations: those where political and economic/social deprivations coincide (e.g. Brazil, Chiapas, Northern Ireland, SA1, the United States) and those where the politically powerful represent the relatively deprived (Malaysia, SA2, Sri Lanka, Uganda). The first type of situation tends to lead to protests, riots or rebellion by the disempowered

and deprived whose strength depends on the relative size of the group (e.g. Chiapas at just 4 per cent of population are never going to be a strong group), and how far demands are accommodated.

In the second category, conflict may result from the politically dominant attacking the economically privileged (Fiji, Uganda, to a certain extent and, outside our sample, Rwanda). But it seems that it can be avoided by policies which strengthen the economic position of the political majority (Malaysia, SA2), if they can be introduced without provoking violent opposition, perhaps because the policies are conducted sensitively, and/or because the economically privileged group finds their situation preferable to violence.

3. Affirmative action can work and is surprisingly common. It occurred in one way or another in seven of the eight cases: most strongly in Malaysia, but also in Brazil, Fiji, Northern Ireland, SA2, Sri Lanka, Uganda and the United States. In each case, it was effective in reducing HIs, but almost never eliminated them. In Malaysia, it was probably responsible for the low level of violence; in Northern Ireland for the move towards peace; it is likely that in the United States and Fiji it reduced violence. Sri Lanka was the one exception where the policies provoked serious violence. One reason is that the policies were invasive culturally as well as economically (the language policy); another is that because of their geographic concentration in the northeast, the Tamils were in a position to demand independence in a way that others (e.g. the Indians in Fiji) could not.

   It is worth noting the political conditions in which affirmative action took place, as political factors are often cited as a decisive obstacle to it. The easiest political context is where the economically deprived are in political power, so can carry out the policies – as in Malaysia, SA2 and Sri Lanka. Northern Ireland was a case where an outside power (the UK government) imposed the policies. In other cases, affirmative action has been a response to powerful protests and liberal politics, as in the United States – but this represents the most fragile basis, which can be overturned, as is currently threatened there. Far-sighted governments may recognize that such policies ensure political stability. But democratic political competition can readily undermine such responsible leadership (as in Fiji).

   There is no evidence from these cases that affirmative action had ill effects economically. Indeed, by educating the deprived, the opposite is likely, as indicated by research on the United States. Intragroup differences were, however, generally widened by the policies even though societal equality was improved (e.g. Malaysia).

4. The problem of measurement discussed earlier as being highly problematic appears much less in actual cases. Group definitions are often obvious – where they are not obvious then HIs may matter less (as in Brazil). Simple ratios seem to be appropriate for capturing the situation, while complex formula would not seem to be helpful. Nonetheless, if we were to use

HIs for cross-country econometrics we would need to find appropriate and comparable summary measures for each country.

Conclusions

HI is an important dimension of well-being, and it has economic and political consequences which can be highly damaging to development. In this chapter I have spent a lot of time on major consequences – in particular, various forms of violent conflict. But the daily psychological consequences are also important and need more attention. For these reasons, HI ought to be an important consideration in development thinking. Yet at present it is not incorporated in development analysis, except rather randomly, or where events force it onto the agenda, as in Rwanda. In our increasingly pluralistic societies, HIs should be part of development policy for *all* societies, not just those which are currently, or have recently been, in conflict. This has implications for data and measurement as well as for policy – indeed, the latter depends on the former.

On the data side, information needs to be collected by cultural categories. This can present problems, where cultural categories are ill defined and fluid. In the United Kingdom, for example, statistics have recently begun to be collected by cultural categories, but there is much political controversy about the (many) categories presented.[33] This should not stop attempts to collect such data – as, indeed, it has not stopped other types of data collection where boundaries are fuzzy. The data on this issue need to be multidimensional: income, as argued above, is only one of many important categories. It has been argued that presenting data showing sharp HIs can itself be conflict-provoking. This seems rather unlikely as most people suffering such HIs know perfectly well what is happening; it is the outsiders, including the government, who can plead ignorance.

Where HIs are found to be large, policies are needed to correct them – from the cases above, it would appear that ratios of the deprived to the privileged of 0.7 or below (or put the other way round, 1.5 and above between the privileged and the deprived) are the sort of magnitude that creates problems. For shorthand, I have called these policies 'affirmative action'.[34] In principle, they cover political, economic and social areas. Policies of this sort are not only *not* part of the current policy debate and policy conditionality of donors, but actually conflict with some aspects of them.

On the economic side, such policies involve a range of actions including: public investment designed to reduce HIs (which may involve targeting the regional distribution of investment); public sector employment policies to do the same; group distribution requirements imposed on the private sector (e.g. shares of different groups in employment; credit allocation and so on); policies towards land reform and towards share ownership. In any particular situation, the appropriate policies will depend on the main types and sources of HIs. General anti-discrimination laws, supported by a strong judicial system with legal aid for deprived communities, can do much to help reduce HIs.

These policies are at variance with the currently recommended World Bank or IMF policy package to promote economic growth and reduce poverty. The growth policies that the international financial institutions (IFIs) advocate basically argue for reduced intervention of the state in economic matters, allowing the market to determine resource allocation. Yet policies towards HIs impose constraints on the market, as well as requirements on the public sector, which may not be strictly consistent with efficiency requirements. Nor are the policies the same as poverty-reducing policies, although they are likely to contribute to the poverty reduction objective. For one reason, some of the policies will actually help the richer sections of the deprived groups (e.g. public service employment targets). Moreover, in some contexts, more poor people are to be found in the relatively privileged group (e.g. among the Indians in Fiji), while in almost all cases, many poor people fall outside the deprived group. It is of course because poverty reduction policies do not address HIs in any systematic way that special policies are needed towards HIs. But it follows, as noted earlier, that HI policies are not substitutes for those towards poverty reduction, which will generally need to continue.

What I have termed 'social' policies encompass some – those towards human capital – with strong economic implications, which are therefore instrumentally important as well as in themselves. They include policies towards correcting HIs in education, training and health services. Again such policies may sometimes be inconsistent with economic efficiency considerations, as it is not a matter of maximizing the economic return on resource allocation but of correcting imbalances. More often, however, correcting these imbalances will raise economic returns, since systematically deprived groups are likely to contain many talented people who have been held back by discrimination. Policies towards housing are an important component of correcting imbalances especially in more developed countries, as indicated in the Northern Ireland case.

On the political side, there is a need for inclusivity. Monopolization of political power by one group or another is often responsible for many of the other inequalities, and for violent reactions, because this appears the only way to change the system. Every case of conflict we observed in the Complex Humanitarian Emergency study lacked such political inclusivity (Nafziger, Stewart and Väyrynen, 2000). Moreover, such politically inclusive policies have been adopted by well-known peace making regimes; for example, the post-Pinochet Chilean government, Museveni's government in Uganda, South Africa under Mandela and the new governance structures of Northern Ireland. This is the proposed governmental structure to ameliorate conditions in Burundi and also the type of government adopted in post-Taliban Afghanistan.

Yet achieving political inclusivity is among the most difficult changes to bring about. It is not an automatic result of democracy, defined as rule with the support of the majority, as majority rule generally leads to permanent domination by one group in situations in which one group is in a strong numerical majority. Northern Ireland and Sri Lanka are both cases of conflict that occurred in a democratic setting. Moreover, 'winner-takes-all' democracy can provoke conflicts or coups where groups fear political rule by opposing groups (as in Fiji and Uganda). There is a strong tendency for political parties in divided societies to represent and argue for particular ethnicities (Horowitz, 1985).[35] In Fiji, for example, moderate tendencies were undermined by democratic competition which led to the ethnicization of politics. In Uganda, Museveni has argued that it was this tendency that led to election-rigging and civil war and he has therefore tried to avoid multiparty democracy.

Democracy in strongly divided countries needs to be a form of *constrained democracy*, designed to ensure an inclusive system. Features of a constrained democracy include:

- strong human rights provisions to protect all groups, including outlawing discrimination
- alternative voting systems, or other forms of proportional representation
- requirements that members of each group participate in government
- job allocations to different groups
- decentralization of government so that power-sharing occurs
- inclusion of members of major groups at all levels of the civil service, the army and the police.

The appropriate political system depends on the nature of the society – for example, whether it is multipolar or bipolar, and how fragmented groups are (Bangura, 2001). However, it must be recognized that it is not at all easy to arrive at such inclusive political systems.[36] These political requirements for pluralistic societies countries *do not* currently form part of the dialogue of political conditionality adopted by many bilateral donors. The usual political conditionality includes rule with the consent of the majority, multiparty democracy and respect for human rights.[37] At times, indeed, the requirement of political inclusivity may even be inconsistent with such political conditionality, especially the requirement of multiparty democracy (Stewart and O'Sullivan, 1999). These policy conclusions, especially in the political arena, must be regarded as preliminary and tentative. The important point is that HIs should be incorporated into our thinking about development, into measurement, analysis and policy, in a way that to date they have not.

I would like to end this chapter by putting the topic into a global context. While severe HIs within countries provoke distress and instability domestically, it is increasingly the case that international HIs do the same. As communication links improve, global HIs become increasingly apparent. Today, the most apparent of these is that between Moslems and non-Moslems. It is clearly fairly easy for leaders, such as Bin Laden, to mobilize the economically deprived against the economically privileged non-Moslem world. So long as these deep economic inequalities remain, the potential for mobilization will also remain, however effective short-term measures are in apparently eliminating the 'terrorists'. Globally, as well as domestically we need to monitor and correct horizontal inequalities.

Notes

Thanks to Michael Wang and Emma Samman for research assistance.

1. Barth has argued that 'the constraints on a person's behaviour which spring from his ethnic identity ... tend to be absolute' (Barth, 1969: 17). Akerlof and Kranton (2000) have modelled how identities influence individual behaviour.
2. Groups, including families, cooperatives, governments and firms, are also of critical importance to the economy, with some groups performing efficiently and equitably, and others being inefficient and inequitable. We have attempted to analyse this elsewhere, in a UNU-WIDER project, see Heyer, Stewart and Thorp (2002).
3. For example, many would think of countries such as France and Sweden as being homogeneous – yet at least 10 per cent of the French population consider themselves first and foremost Bretons, Corsicans, Maghrebians and other nationalities (Gurr and Harff, 1994); while one-fifth of Swedes are first- or second-generation immigrants.
4. Horowitz (1985) has differentiated four situations of relative advantage/disadvantage which can lead to conflict: backward groups in backward regions, advanced groups in backward regions, backward groups in advanced regions, and advanced groups in advanced regions.
5. See Loury (1988).
6. This view has been associated with Smith (1986, 1991), for example, and also with Soviet ethnobiologists – for example, Bromley (1974).
7. Cohen argued that 'Hausa identity and Hausa ethnic exclusiveness in Ibadan are the expressions not so much of a particularly strong "tribalistic" sentiment as of vested economic interests'. The Hausa 'manipulate[d] some customs, values, myths, symbols and ceremonials for their cultural tradition in order to articulate an informal political organization' (Cohen, 1969: 214).
8. *Observer*, 4 November 2001.
9. Smith has argued that 'the [past] acts as a constraint on invention. Though the past can be read in different ways, it is not any past' (Smith, 1991: 357–8, quoted in Turton, 1997).
10. Reynal-Querol (2001: 2) argues for developing countries that 'religious divided societies are more prone to intense conflict than countries where people have conflicting claims on resources based on interest groups or in language divisions ... because religious identity is fixed and non-negotiable'.
11. 'Symbolic systems' are the values, myths, rituals and ceremonials which are used to organize and unite groups (Cohen, 1974).
12. From this perspective some measures include more evaluation than is needed or helpful – for example the Atkinson measure of inequality, or Anand and Sen's

measure of group-weighted achievements drawn from this, explicitly incorporate a valuation element (Atkinson, 1970; Anand and Sen, 1995).

13. Estaban and Ray (1999), Collier and Hoeffler (2000) and Elbadawi and Sambanis (2001) find that increased fragmentation reduces the propensity to conflict, which is greatest at an intermediate level with a few large groups. Penurbarti and Asea (1996) find polarization to be related to political violence in a sixty-three-country study.

14. Akerlof and Kranton (2000) consider policies aimed at changing perceptions as a mechanism for improving welfare.

15. Nafziger, Stewart and Väyrynen (2000). However, that study was not specifically designed to analyse HIs so the evidence is rather circumstantial.

16. Both Obote and Amin are broadly northerners and Museveni comes from the west.

17. Ginyera-Pinycwa, a Mkerere professor of political science, claimed that 'the NRM/NRA went to the bush to remove the northerners from power' (Mutibwa, 1992: 154). Omara-Otunnu, a northerner, also described the war as 'a struggle between Bantu and non-Bantu speakers and more specifically as a struggle between southerners and northerners' (Omara-Otunnu, 1987: 176). However, Museveni stated that 'we went to the bush to oppose murder, tribalism and any other form of sectarianism' (Museveni, 1992: 31).

18. *Second Malaysia Plan 1971–1975*: 1.

19. This section draws heavily on discussions with D. Sriskandarajah and his M.Phil thesis.

20. Indian Tamils in Sri Lanka account for another 5.5 per cent.

21. There are other groups within Sri Lanka – including Muslims (7.1 per cent of the population) – not included in the analysis here for the sake of simplicity.

22. *Financial Times*, 4 May 2001.

23. I am grateful to Marcia Hartwell for information about Northern Ireland.

24. The increase in the Catholic middle class has involved an expansion into occupations beyond those identified as servicing the Catholic community – teachers, doctors, lawyers and priests. Now Catholics are also substantially represented among accountants and other financial service professionals, middle managers, middle-ranking civil servants, architects and planners and university and further education lecturers.

25. This legislation was in part a response to a strong popular campaign in the United States to prevent investment in Northern Ireland unless fair employment practices were followed, as summarized in the MacBride principles (see http://irelandsown. net/macbride.html).

26. According to Ruane and Todd (1996) the British government's commitment to redressing Catholic inequality is today on a scale that is historically unprecedented (1996: 172).

27. Study reported on in *The New York Times*, 4 July 2001.

28. The preponderance of evidence suggests that activity associated with equal employment and affirmative action policies is associated with small but significant gains in a range of blue-collar and white-collar occupations', Simms (1995: 3) summarizing Badgett and Hartmann (1995).

29. F.D. Roosevelt famously stated: 'If I were to be asked to name one point on which there is a complete difference between the Brazilians and ourselves I should say it was in the attitude to the black man. In Brazil any Negro or mulatto who shows himself fit is without question given the place to which his abilities entitle him', cited in Wood and Lovell (1992: 703).

30. They would be included in the 'brown' category.
31. For example, Wood and Lovell (1992); Lovell (1999).
32. *Christian Science Monitor*, 7 August 2001.
33. Three choices are offered under the category 'white'; three under 'black or black British'; one Chinese; four various types of 'mixed'; four types of 'Asian or Asian British' and one 'other'.
34. This is a sloppy use of the term, since I have used it to cover both elimination of discrimination and providing positive bias in favour of certain groups, whereas strictly 'affirmative action' is just the latter, but it is often difficult to distinguish these two, and most commonly described affirmative actions do aim at both; see the discussion in Loury (1988).
35. 'In severely divided societies, multiethnic parties are strongly susceptible to centrifugal forces ... Parties organized nonethnically are rare or nonexistent in such societies' (Horowitz, 1985: 301).
36. Horowitz has argued that political systems can be designed which provide electoral incentives promoting ethnic peace in divided societies, yet he has been able to find very few successful cases where such incentives have worked over a long time frame.
37. See Robinson (1994); Stokke (1995).

References

Akerlof, G. A. and R. E. Kranton (2000) 'Economics and Identity', *Quarterly Journal of Economics* 115(3): 715–53.

Alexander, J., J. McGregor and T. Ranger (2000) 'Ethnicity and the Politics of Conflict: The Case of Matabeleland', in E. W. Nafziger, F. Stewart and R. Väyrynen (eds), *War, Hunger and Displacement: The Origins of Humanitarian Emergencies*, Oxford: Oxford University Press, for UNU-WIDER.

Anand, S. and A. K. Sen (1995) *Gender Inequality in Human Development: Theories and Measurement*, New York: UNDP.

Atkinson, A. B. (1970) 'On the Measurement of Inequality', *Journal of Economic Theory* 2(3).

Badgett, M. V. L. and H. L. Hartmann (1995) 'The Effectiveness of Equal Employment Opportunity Policies', in M. C. Simms, *Economic Perspectives on Affirmative Action*, Lanham, MD: University Press of America.

Bangura, Y. (2001) *Ethnic Structure and Governance: Reforming Africa in the 21st Century*, Geneva: UNRISD.

Banks, M. (1996) *Ethnicity: Anthropological Constructions*, London: Routledge.

Barth, F. (1969) *Ethnic Groups and Ethnic Boundaries*, London: George Allen & Unwin.

Blau, J. R. and P. M. Blau (1982) 'The Cost of Inequality: Metropolitan Structure and Violent Crime', *American Sociological Review* 47: 114–29.

Broman, C. (1997) 'Race-Related Factors and Life Satisfaction Among African Americans', *Journal of Black Psychology* 23(1): 36–49.

Bromley, Y. (1974) 'The Term "Ethos" and its Definition', *Soviet Ethnology and Anthropology Today*, The Hague: Mouton.

Brown, T. N., D. R. Williams *et al.* (1999) 'Being Black and Feeling Blue: Mental Health Consequences of Racial Discrimination', *Race and Society* 2(2): 117–31.

Cabinet Office (2001) *Improving Labour Market Achievements for Ethnic Minorities in British Society: Scoping Note*, London: Cabinet Office.

Cohen, A. (1969) *Custom and Politics in Urban Africa*, Berkeley: University of California Press.

Cohen, A. (1974) *Two-dimensional Man: An Essay on the Anthropology of Power and Symbolism in Complex Society*, Berkeley: University of California Press.

Collier, P. and A. Hoeffler (2000) *Greed and Grievance in Civil War*, Washington, DC: World Bank.

Cormack, R. J. and E. P. Rooney (nd) 'Religion and Employment in Northern Ireland 1911–1971', cited in J. Ruane and J. Todd, *The Dynamics of Conflict in Northern Ireland*, Cambridge: Cambridge University Press.

Darby, J. (1999) 'Northern Ireland: Beyond the Time of Troubles', in C. Young, *The Accommodation of Cultural Diversity*, London: Macmillan.

de Waal, A. (1994) 'The Genocidal State', *Times Literary Supplement* 3–4.

Douglas, W. A. (1988) 'A Critique of Recent Trends in the Analysis of Ethnonationalism', *Ethnic and Racial Studies* 11(2): 192–206.

Elbadawi, I. and N. Sambanis (2001) *How Much War Will We See? Estimating Incidence of Civil War in 161 Countries*, Washington, DC: World Bank.

Estaban, J. and D. Ray (1994) 'On the Measurement of Polarization', *Econometrica* 62(4): 819–51.

————— (1999) 'Conflict and Distribution', *Journal of Economic Theory* 87: 379–415.

Fairhead, J. (2000) 'The Conflict over Natural and Environmental Resources', in E. W. Nafziger, F. Stewart and R. Väyrynen (eds), *War, Hunger and Displacement: The Origins of Humanitarian Emergencies*, Oxford: Oxford University Press, for UNU-WIDER.

Gellner, E. (1964) *Thought and Change*, London: Weidenfeld & Nicholson.

Glazer, N. and D. Moynihan (1975) *Ethnicity, Theory and Experience*, Cambridge MA: Harvard University Press.

Glewwe, P. (1986) 'The Distribution of Income in Sri Lanka in 1969–70 and 1980–81: A Decomposition Analysis', *Journal of Development Economics* 24: 255–74.

Gurr, T. R. (1993) *Minorities at Risk: A Global View of Ethnopolitical Conflicts*, Washington, DC: Institute of Peace Press.

Gurr, T. R. and B. Harff (1994) *Ethnic Conflict in World Politics*, Oxford: Westview Press.

Hamilton, C. V. (2001) 'The United States: Not Yet "E Pluribus Unum"', Racism, America's Achilles Heel', in C. Hamilton (ed.), *Beyond Racism: Race and Inequality in Brazil, South Africa, and the United States*, Boulder, CO and London: Lynne Rienner.

Hepburn, A. C. (1983) 'Employment and Religion in Belfast, 1901–1951', in R. J. Cormack and R. D. Osborne, *Religion, Education and Employment: Aspects of Equal Opportunity in Northern Ireland*, Belfast: Appletree.

Heyer, J., F. Stewart and R. Thorp (eds) (2002) *Group Behaviour and Development – Is the Market Destroying Co-operation?*, Oxford: Oxford University Press, for UNU-WIDER.

Horowitz, D. (1985) *Ethnic Groups in Conflict*, Berkeley: University of California Press.

Klugman, J., B. Neyapti *et al.* (1999) *Conflict and Growth in Africa, 2, Kenya, Tanzania and Uganda*, Paris: OECD.

Lemarchand, R. (1994) 'Managing Transition Anarchies: Rwanda, Burundi and South Africa in Comparative Context', *Journal of Modern African Studies* 32(4): 581–604.

Loury, G. C. (1988) 'Why we Should Care About Group Equality', *Social Philosophy and Policy* 5(1): 249–71.

Lovell, P. A. (1999) 'Development and the Persistence of Racial Inequality in Brazil 1950–1991', *Journal of Developing Areas* 33: 395–418.

Majumdar, M. and S. Subramanian (2001) 'Capability Failure and Group Disparities: Some Evidence from India for the 1980s', *Journal of Development Studies* 37(5): 104–40.

Manogoran, C. (1987) *Ethnic Conflict and Reconciliation in Sri Lanka*, Honolulu: University of Hawaii Press.

Matovu, J.-M. and F. Stewart (2001) 'The Social and Economic Consequences of Conflict: A Case Study of Uganda', in F. Stewart and V. Fitzgerald, *War and Underdevelopment: Country Experience*, Oxford: Oxford University Press.

McElroy, J. L. and L. D. Singell (1973) 'Riot and Non-Riot Cities: An Examination of Structural Contours', *Urban Affairs Quarterly* 8(3): 281–302.

Museveni, Y. (1992) *What is Africa's Problem?*, Kampala: NRM Publications.

Mutibwa, P. (1992) *Uganda Since Independence*, Kampala: Fountain.

Nafziger, E. W., F. Stewart and R. Väyrynen (eds) (2000) *War, Hunger and Displacement: The Origins of Humanitarian Emergencies*, Oxford: Oxford University Press, for UNU-WIDER.

Omara-Otunnu, A. (1987) *Politics and the Military in Uganda, 1890–1985*, London: Macmillan.

Penurbarti, M. and P. Asea (1996) 'Polarization and Political Violence', paper prepared for presentation at the summer meeting of the American Political Science Methodology Meeting, Ann Arbor.

Premdas, R. R. (1993) 'Ethnicity and Development: The Case of Fiji', UNRISD Discussion Paper 46, Geneva: UNRISD.

Ranger, T. (1983) 'The Invention of Tradition in Colonial Africa', in E. Hobsbawm and T. Ranger, *The Invention of Tradition*, Cambridge: Canto.

Reno, W. (1998) *Warlord Politics and African States*, Boulder, CO: Lynne Rienner.

Reynal-Querol, M. (2001) *Ethnicity, Political Systems and Civil War*, Bellatera-Barcelona Institut d'Analisis Economic, Campus de la UAB.

Robinson, M. (1994) 'Governance, Democracy and Conditionality: NGOs and the New Political Agenda', in A. Clayton, *Governance, Democracy and Conditionality: What Role for the NGOs?*, Oxford: INTRAC.

Ruane, J. and J. Todd (1996) *The Dynamics of Conflict in Northern Ireland*, Cambridge: Cambridge University Press.

Sherer, G. (2000) 'Intergroup Economic Inequality in South Africa: The Post-Apartheid Era', *American Economic Association Papers and Proceedings* 90(2): 317–21.

Simms, M. C. (ed.) (1995) *Economic Perspectives on Affirmative Action*, Lanham, MD: University Press of America.

Smith, A. D. (1986) *The Ethnic Origin of Nations*, Oxford: Blackwell.

————— (1991) 'The Nation: Invented, Imagined, Reconstructed?', *Millennium: Journal of International Studies* 20: 353–68.

Sriskandarajah, D. (2000) *The End of Serendipity: Politico-Economic Explanations of Ethnic Conflict in Sri Lanka*, Oxford: Queen Elizabeth House.

Stewart, F. and M. O'Sullivan (1999) 'Democracy, Conflict and Development – Three Cases', in G. Ranis, S.-C. Hu and Y.-P. Chu, *The Political Economy of Comparative Development into the 21st Century: Essays in Memory of John C. H. Fei*, Cheltenham: Edward Elgar.

Stokke, O. (1995) 'Aid Conditionality: Core Issues and State of the Art', *Aid and Political Conditionality*, London: Frank Cass.

Taylor, C. and M. C. Hudson (1972) *The World Handbook of Political and Scientific Indicators*, New Haven, CT: Yale University Press.

Turton, D. (1997) 'War and Ethnicity: Global Connections and Local Violence in North East Africa and Former Yugoslavia', *Oxford Development Studies* 25: 77–94.

Wood, C. H. and P. A. Lovell (1992) 'Racial Inequality and Child Mortality in Brazil', *Social Forces* 70(3): 703–24.

6
Winners and Losers over Two Centuries of Globalization

Jeffrey G. Williamson

Introduction

The world has seen two globalization booms over the past two centuries, and one bust. The first global century ended with the First World War and the second started at the end of Second World War, while the years in between were ones of anti-global backlash. This chapter reports what we know about the winners and losers during the two global centuries, including aspects almost always ignored in modern debate – how prices of consumption goods on the expenditure side are affected, and how the economic position of the poor is influenced. It also reports two responses of the winners to the losers' complaints. Some concessions to the losers took the form of anti-global policy manifested by immigration restriction in the high-wage countries and trade restriction pretty much everywhere. Some concessions to the losers were also manifested by a 'race towards the top' whereby legislation strengthened losers' safety nets and increased their sense of political participation. The chapter concludes with four lessons of history and an agenda for international economists, including more attention to the impact of globalization on commodity price structure, the causes of protection, the impact of world migration on poverty eradication and the role of political participation in the whole process.

Globalization and world inequality

Globalization in world commodity and factor markets has evolved in fits and starts since Columbus and da Gama sailed from Europe more than 500 years ago. We begin with a survey of this history so as to place contemporary events in better perspective, and then ask whether globalization raised world inequality. This question can be split into two more: what happened to income gaps between nations? What happened to income gaps within nations? Collaborative work with Peter Lindert stresses the question about world inequality (Lindert and Williamson, 2002a, 2002b), but this chapter concentrates on the second two questions, the reason being that answers to these have more relevance for policy and for the ability of a globally integrated world to survive. Indeed, at various points in the chapter, I ask when there has been global backlash in the past – driven by complaints of the losers – and whether and how the complaints of the losers were accommodated by the winners. Finally, this chapter also stresses the contribution of world migration to poverty eradication.

Recent scholarship has documented a dramatic divergence in incomes around the globe over the past two centuries. Furthermore, all of this work shows that the divergence was driven overwhelmingly by the rise of between-nation inequality, not by the rise of inequality within nations (Berry, Bourguignon and Morrisson, 1991; Maddison, 1995; Pritchett, 1997; Bourguignon and Morrisson, 2000; Dowrick and DeLong, 2002). Figure 6.1 uses the work of Bourguignon and Morrisson to summarize these trends and confirms that changing income gaps between countries explain changing world inequality. However, the fact that the rise of inequality within nations has not driven the secular rise in global inequality hardly implies that it has been irrelevant, and for two reasons. First, policy is formed at the country level, and it is changing income distribution within borders that usually triggers political complaint and policy responses; and, second, it is the political

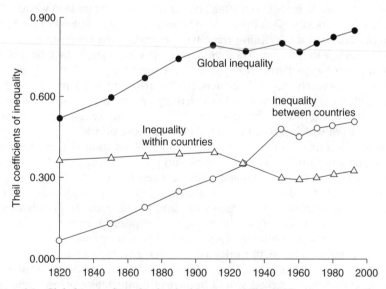

Figure 6.1 Global inequality of individual incomes, 1820–1992

Source: Adapted from Bourguignon and Morrisson (2000). The 'countries' here consist of fifteen single countries with abundant data and large populations plus eighteen other country groups. The eighteen groups were aggregates of geographical neighbours having similar levels of GDP *per capita*, as estimated by Maddison (1995).

voice of the losers that matters, and they can be at the top, the bottom, or the middle of that distribution. Furthermore, the absence of a net secular change in within-country inequality at the global level may simply reveal an equilibrium process whereby rising within-country inequality breeds policy responses that force the distribution back to some culturally acceptable steady state. That level may be far higher for the United States than for Japan, to take two modern economic giants as examples. I start by decomposing the centuries since 1492 into four distinct globalization epochs. Two of these were pro-global, and two were anti-global. I then explore whether the two pro-global epochs made the world more unequal, and whether it produced a backlash.

Making a world economy

Epoch I: anti-global mercantilist restriction, 1492–1820

The voyages of discovery induced a transfer of technology, plants, animals and diseases on an enormous scale, never seen before and maybe since. But the impact of Columbus and da Gama on trade, factor migration and globalization was a different matter entirely. For globalization to have an impact on relative factor prices, absolute living standards and GDP *per capita*, domestic relative commodity prices and/or relative endowments must be altered. True, there was a world trade boom after 1492, and the share of trade in world GDP increased markedly (O'Rourke and Williamson, 2002a). But was that trade boom explained by declining trade barriers and global integration? A pro-global decline in trade barriers should have left a trail marked by falling commodity price gaps between exporting and importing trading centres, but there is absolutely no such evidence (O'Rourke and Williamson, 2002b). Thus, 'discoveries' and transport productivity improvements must have been offset by trading monopoly mark-ups, tariffs, non-tariff restrictions, wars and pirates, all of which served in combination to choke off trade.

Since there is so much confusion in the globalization debate about its measurement, it might pay to elaborate on this point. Figure 6.2 presents a stylized view of post-Colombian trade between Europe and the rest of the world (the latter denoted by an asterisk). *MM* is the European import demand function (that is, domestic demand minus domestic supply), with import demand declining as the home market price (p) increases. *SS* is the foreign export supply function (foreign supply minus foreign demand), with export supply rising as the price abroad (p^*) increases. In the absence of transport costs, monopolies, wars, pirates and other trade barriers, international commodity markets would be perfectly integrated: prices would be the same at home and abroad, determined by the intersection of the two schedules. Transport costs, protection, war, pirates, and monopoly drive a wedge (t) between export and import prices: higher tariffs, transport costs, war embargoes and monopoly rents increase the wedge while lower barriers reduce it. Global commodity market integration is represented in Figure 6.2 by a decline in the wedge: falling transport costs, falling trading monopoly rents, falling tariffs, the suppression of pirates, or a return to peace all lead to falling import prices in both places, rising export prices in both places, an erosion of price gaps between them and an increase in trade volumes connecting them.

The fact that trade should rise as trade barriers fall is, of course, the rationale behind using trade volumes or the share of trade in GDP as a proxy for international commodity market integration. Indeed, several authors have used Maddison's (1995) data to trace out long-run trends in commodity market integration since the early nineteenth century, or even earlier (e.g. Hirst and Thompson, 1996; Findlay and O'Rourke, 2002). However, Figure 6.2 makes it clear that global commodity market integration is not the only reason why the volume of trade, or trade's share in GDP, might increase over time. Just because we see a trade boom does not necessarily mean that more liberal trade policies or transport revolutions are at work. After all, outward shifts in either import demand (to MM') or export supply (to SS') could also lead to trade expansion, and such shifts could occur as a result of population growth, the settlement of previously unexploited frontiers, capital accumulation, technological change, a shift in post-Colombian income distribution favouring those who consume imported 'exotic' luxuries and a variety of

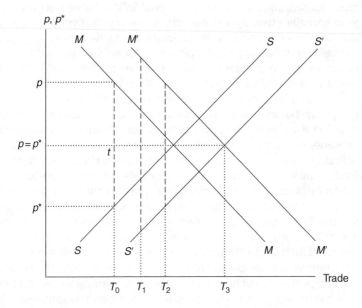

Figure 6.2 Explaining the European trade boom, 1500–1800

Source: Adapted from O'Rourke and Williamson (2002a: Figure 3).

other factors. Figure 6.2 thus argues that the *only* irrefutable evidence that global commodity market integration is taking place is a decline in the international dispersion of commodity prices, or what I call commodity price convergence. However, we cannot find it (O'Rourke and Williamson, 2002b).

If declining trade barriers do not explain the world trade boom after Columbus, what was it? Just like world experience from the 1950s to the 1980s (Baier and Bergstrand, 2001), it appears that European income growth – or growth of incomes of the landed rich – might have explained as much as two-thirds of the trade boom over the three centuries as a whole (O'Rourke and Williamson 2002a).[1] The world trade boom after Columbus would have been a lot bigger without those anti-global interventions. And labour migration and capital flows were, of course, only a trickle.

Epoch II: the first global century, 1820–1913

The 1820s were a watershed in the evolution of the world economy. International commodity price convergence did not start until then. Powerful and epochal shifts towards liberal policy (e.g. dismantling mercantilism) were manifested during that decade. In addition, the 1820s coincide with the peacetime recovery from the Napoleonic wars on the continent, launching a century of global *pax Britannica*.[2] In short, the 1820s mark the start of a world regime of globalization.

Transport costs dropped very fast in the century prior to the First World War. These globalization forces were powerful in the Atlantic economy, but they were partially offset by a rising tide of protection. Declining transport costs accounted for two-thirds of the integration of world commodity markets over the century following 1820, and for *all* of world commodity market integration in the four decades after 1870, when globalization backlash offset some of it (Lindert and Williamson, 2002a). The political backlash of the late nineteenth century and interwar period was absent in Asia and Africa – partly because these regions contained colonies of free-trading European countries, partly because of the power of gunboat diplomacy and partly because of the political influence wielded by natives who controlled the natural resources that were the base of their exports. As a result, the globalization-induced domestic relative price shocks were even bigger and more ubiquitous in Asia and Africa than those in the Atlantic economy (Williamson, 2002). Put another way, commodity price convergence between the European industrial core and the periphery was even more dramatic than it was within the Atlantic economy. In short, the liberal dismantling of mercantilism and the worldwide transport revolution worked together to produce truly global commodity markets across the nineteenth century. The persistent decline in transport costs worldwide allowed competitive winds to blow hard where they had never blown before. True, there was an anti-global policy reaction after 1870 in the European centre but it was nowhere near big enough to cause a return to the pre-1820 levels of economic isolation. On the other hand, these globalization events were met with rising levels of protection in Latin America, the United States and the European periphery, and to very high levels, as Figure 6.3 documents. However, I postpone until the end of this chapter the question as to whether it was a globalization backlash that triggered protection in the periphery or whether it was something else. If history is to offer any lessons for the present, we had better get the causes of the backlash straight.

Factor markets also became more integrated worldwide. As European investors came to believe in strong growth prospects overseas, global capital markets became steadily more integrated, reaching levels in 1913 that may not have been regained even today (Clemens and Williamson, 2001b; Obstfeld and Taylor, 2002). International migration soared in response to unrestrictive immigration policies and falling steerage costs (Hatton and Williamson, 1998; Chiswick and Hatton, 2002), but not without some backlash: New World immigrant subsidies began to evaporate towards the end of the century, political debate over immigrant restriction became very intense and, finally, quotas were imposed. In this case, it is clear that the retreat from open immigration policies to quotas was driven by complaints from the losers at the bottom of the income pyramid, the unskilled native-born (Goldin, 1994; Timmer and Williamson, 1998; Williamson, 1998; Chiswick and Hatton, 2002).

Epoch III: beating an anti-global retreat, 1913–50

The globalized world started to fall apart after 1913, and it was completely dismantled between the wars. New policy barriers were imposed restricting

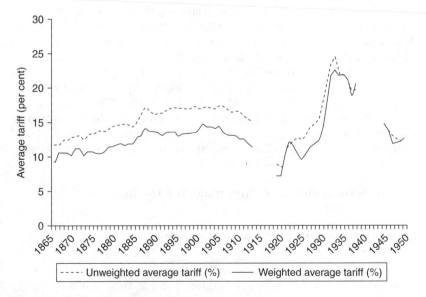

Figure 6.3 Average world tariffs, 1865–1945

Source: Adapted from Coatsworth and Williamson (2002: Figure 1).

the ability of poor populations to flee miserable conditions for something better, barriers that still exist today, a century later. Thus, the foreign-born share in the US population fell from a pre-1913 figure of 14.6 per cent to an interwar figure of 6.9 per cent. Higher tariffs and other non-tariff barriers (NTBs) choked off the gains from trade. Barrier-ridden price gaps between Atlantic economy trading partners doubled, returning those gaps to 1870 levels (Lindert and Williamson, 2002a: Table 1; Findlay and O'Rourke, 2002). The appearance of new disincentives reduced investment in the diffusion of new technologies around the world, and the share of foreign capital flows in GDP dropped from 3.3 to 1.2 per cent (Obstfeld and Taylor, 1998: 359). In short, the interwar retreat from globalization was carried entirely by anti-global economic policies.

Epoch IV: the second global century, 1950–2002

Globalization by any definition resumed after the Second World War. It has differed from pre-1914 globalization in several ways (Baldwin and Martin, 1999). Most important by far, factor migrations are less impressive: the foreign-born are a much smaller share in labour-scarce economies than they were in 1913, and capital exports are a smaller percentage of GDP in the post-war United States (0.5 per cent in 1960–73 and 1.2 per cent 1989–96: Obstfeld and Taylor, 1998: Table 11.1) than they were in pre-war Britain (4.6 per cent in 1890–1913). On the other hand, trade barriers are probably lower today than they were in 1913. These differences are tied to policy changes in one dominant nation, the United States, which has switched from a protectionist welcoming immigrants to a free trader restricting their entrance.

Ever since Eli Heckscher and Bertil Ohlin wrote almost a century ago (Flam and Flanders, 1991), their theory has taught that trade can be a substitute for factor migration. While modern theory is much more ambiguous on this point, history is not. In the first global century, before quotas and restrictions, factor mobility had a *much* bigger impact on factor prices, inequality, and poverty than did trade (Taylor and Williamson, 1997). Perhaps this explains why the second global century has been much more enthusiastic about commodity trade than about migration. In any case, I start with the more recent globalization experience, the second global century.

Did the second global century make the world more unequal?

International income gaps: a post-war epochal turning point?

The Bourguignon and Morrisson evidence in Figure 6.1 documents what looks like a mid-twentieth-century turning point in their between-country inequality index, since its rise slows down after 1950. However, the

Bourguignon and Morrisson long-period database contains only fifteen countries. Using post-war purchasing power parity (PPP) data for a much bigger sample of 115, Melchior, Telle and Wiig (2000) actually document a *decline* in their between-country inequality index in the second half of the twentieth century, and Sala-í-Martin (2002) shows the same when focusing on poverty.[3] The first three authors document stability in between-country inequality up to the late 1970s, followed by convergence. Four other studies find the same fall in between-country inequality after the early 1960s (Schultz, 1998; Firebaugh, 1999; Boltho and Toniolo, 1999; Radetzki and Jonsson, 2000).[4] Among these studies, perhaps the most useful in identifying an epochal regime switch is that of Boltho and Toniolo (1999), who show a rise in between-country inequality in the 1940s, rough stability over the next three decades, and a significant fall after 1980, significant enough to make their between-country inequality index drop well below its 1950 level. Did the post-war switch from autarky to global integration contribute to this epochal change in the evolution of international gaps in average incomes?

Trade policy and international income gaps: late twentieth-century conventional wisdom

Conventional (static) theory argues that trade liberalization should have benefited Third World countries more than it benefited leading industrial countries. After all, trade liberalization should have a bigger effect on the terms of trade of countries joining the larger integrated world economy than on countries already members.[5] And the bigger the terms of trade gain, the bigger the GDP *per capita* gain.

So much for theory: reality suggests the contrary. The post-war trade that was liberalized the most was in fact intra-OECD trade, not trade between the OECD and the rest. From the very beginning in the 1940s, the GATT explicitly excused low-income countries from the need to dismantle their import barriers and exchange controls. This GATT permission served to lower GDP in low-income countries below what it might have been, but the permission was consistent with the anti-global ideology prevailing in previously colonial Asia and Africa, in Latin America where the great depression hit so hard, and in Eastern Europe, dominated as it was by the state-directed USSR. Thus the succeeding rounds of liberalization over the first two decades or so of GATT brought freer trade and gains from trade mainly to OECD members. However, these facts do *not* suggest that late twentieth-century globalization favoured rich countries. Rather, they suggest that globalization favoured all (rich industrial) countries who liberalized and penalized those (poor pre-industrial) countries who did not. There is, of course, an abundant empirical literature showing that liberalizing Third World countries gained from freer trade after the OECD leaders set the liberal tone, after the 1960s.

First, the authors of a large National Bureau of Economic Research (NBER) project assessed trade and exchange control regimes in the 1960s and 1970s by making classic partial-equilibrium calculations of deadweight losses (Bhagwati and Krueger, 1973–76). They concluded that the barriers imposed significant costs in all but one case. However, these welfare calculations came from standard models which did not allow protection a chance to lower long-run cost curves as would be true of the traditional infant industry case, or to foster industrialization and thus growth, as would be true of those modern growth models where industry is the carrier of technological change and capital deepening. Thus, economists have looked for more late twentieth-century proof to support the 'openness-fosters-growth' hypothesis.

Second, analysts have contrasted the growth performance of relatively open with relatively closed economies. The World Bank has conducted such studies for forty-one Third World countries going back before the first oil shock (1973). The correlation between trade openness and growth is abundantly clear in these studies, as illustrated in Table 6.1. Yet, such analysis is vulnerable to the criticism that the effect of trade policies alone cannot be isolated since other policies usually change at the same time. Thus, countries that liberalized their trade also liberalized their domestic factor markets, liberalized their domestic commodity markets and set up better property rights enforcement. The appearance of these domestic policies may deserve more credit for raising income while the simultaneous appearance of more liberal trade policies may deserve less.

Third, there are country event studies where the focus is on periods when Third World trade policy regimes change dramatically enough to see their effect on growth. For example, Krueger (1983, 1984) looked at trade opening

Table 6.1   Trade policy orientation and growth rates in the Third World, 1963–92

Trade policy orientation	Average annual rates growth of GDP per capita (%)		
	1963–73	1973–85	1980–92
Strongly open to trade	6.9	5.9	6.4
Moderately open	4.9	1.6	2.3
Moderately anti-trade	4.0	1.7	−0.2
Strongly anti-trade	1.6	−0.1	−0.4

Notes: In all periods the three strongly open economies were Hong Kong, Singapore and South Korea. The identities of the strongly anti-trade countries changed over time. In 1963–73, they were Argentina, Bangladesh, Burundi, Chile, Dominican Republic, Ethiopia, Ghana, India, Pakistan, Peru, Sri Lanka, Sudan, Tanzania, Turkey, Uruguay and Zambia. For the two overlapping later periods, the strongly anti-trade countries were the previous sixteen, *plus* Bolivia, Madagascar and Nigeria, *minus* Chile, Pakistan, Sri Lanka, Turkey and Uruguay.

Sources: Adapted from Lindert and Williamson (2002a: Table 3) based on World Bank data.

moments in South Korea around 1960, Brazil and Colombia around 1965 and Tunisia around 1970. Growth improved after liberalization in all four cases. More recently, Dollar and Kraay (2000a) examined the reforms and trade liberalizations of sixteen countries in the 1980s and 1990s finding, once again, the positive correlation between freer trade and faster growth. Of course, these reform episodes may have changed more than just global participation, so that an independent trade effect may not have been isolated.

Fourth, macroeconometric analysis has been used in an attempt to resolve the doubts left by simpler historical correlations revealed by the other three kinds of studies. This macroeconometric literature shows that free-trade policies had a positive effect on growth in the late twentieth century, especially with many other relevant influences held constant. The most famous of these is by Sachs and Warner (1995), but many others have also confirmed the 'openness-fosters-growth' hypothesis for the late twentieth century (e.g. Dollar, 1992; Edwards, 1993; Dollar and Kraay, 2000a).[6] In spite of this evidence, it must be said that there are still some sceptics who doubt that support for the 'openness-fosters-growth' hypothesis is unambiguous, of which more later.

When the twentieth-century leader went open: the United States

The American surge in wage and income inequality generated an intense search for its sources. First, there were the globalization sources. These included the rise in unskilled worker immigration rates, due to rising foreign immigrant supplies and to a liberalization of US immigration policy. Increasing competition from imports that used unskilled labour intensively was added to the globalization impact, a rising competition due to foreign supply improvements (aided by US outsourcing), international transportation improvements and trade liberalizing policies. Second, there were sources apparently unrelated to globalization, such as a slowdown in the growth of per worker skill supply and biased technological change that cut the demand for unskilled workers relative to skilled workers.

The debate evolved into a 'trade versus technology' contest, although it might have learned far more by greater attention to immigration and skills (or schooling) supply, and by attention to the century *before* the 1970s. Some contestants agree with Wood (1994, 1998) that trade was to blame for much of the wage widening. Others contestants reject this conclusion, arguing that most or all of the widening was due to a shift in technology that has been strongly biased in favour of skills. Most estimates tend to resemble the guess by Feenstra and Hanson (1999) that perhaps 15–33 per cent of the rising inequality was due to trade competition. Still, everyone seems to agree that going open in the late twentieth century was hardly egalitarian for America.

William Cline offers the boldest attempt at an overall quantitative accounting of these potential sources. Cline blames globalization less than do Feenstra, Hanson and most other writers, and concludes that skill-biased technological change is bigger than any globalization effect (Cline, 1997: Table 5.1). Cline's interpretation of his own estimates is, however, very different from mine, and perhaps my longer historical perspective accounts for the difference. The proper question, it seems to me, is left unasked by Cline and other economists in the debate, namely: 'how did the period 1973–93 differ from the one that preceded it, 1953–73?' If the other sources added up to pretty much the same impact in the first post-war period, then it would be the *change* in globalization forces between the two periods that mattered. Thus, it seems to me that Cline's study illustrates how economists throw away information by confining their analysis to the recent widening of wage gaps. When the world economy became increasingly integrated in the two centuries before 1980, technology also had its factor bias, and the mismatch between technological bias and skills growth kept shifting, with inequality implications (Williamson and Lindert, 1980; Goldin and Katz, 1999, 2000; Lindert, 2000; Lindert and Williamson, 2002a). Why ignore this history?

Globalization, inequality and the OECD

The United States was not the only OECD country to undergo a rise in inequality. The trend toward wider wage gaps has also been unmistakable in Britain. Although there was less widening in *full-time labour earnings* for France or Japan, and none at all for Germany or Italy, income measures that take work hours and unemployment into account reveal some widening even in those last four cases. Burniaux *et al.*'s (1998) study surveyed the inequality of disposable household income in the OECD since from the mid-1970s. Up to the mid-1980s, the Americans and British were alone in having a clear rise in inequality. From the mid-1980s to the mid-1990s, however, twenty out of twenty-one OECD countries had a noticeable rise in inequality. Furthermore, the main source of rising income inequality after the mid-1980s was the widening of labour earnings. The fact that labour earnings became more unequal in most OECD countries, when *full-time* labour earnings did not, suggests that many countries took their inequality in the form of more unemployment and hours' reduction, rather than in wage rates.

Globalization, inequality and the Third World

The sparse literature on the wage inequality and trade liberalization connection in developing countries is mixed in its findings and narrow in its focus. Until recently, it concentrated on six Latins (Argentina, Chile, Colombia, Costa Rica, Mexico and Uruguay) and three East Asians (Korea, Singapore and Taiwan), and the assessment diverged sharply between regions and epochs. Wage gaps seemed to fall when the three 'Asian tigers' liberalized in the 1960s and early 1970s. Yet wage gaps generally widened when the six Latin American countries liberalized after the late 1970s (Wood, 1994, 1997, 1998; Robbins, 1997; Hanson and Harrison, 1999; Robbins and Gindling, 1999). Why the difference?

As Wood (1997) has rightly pointed out, historical context was important, since other things were not equal during these liberalizations. The clearest example where a Latin wage widening appears to refute the egalitarian Stolper–Samuelson prediction was the Mexican liberalization under Salinas in 1985–90. Yet this pro-global liberalization move coincided with the major entry of China and other Asian exporters into world markets. Thus Mexico faced intense new competition from less skill-intensive manufactures in all export markets. Historical context could also explain why trade liberalization coincided with wage widening in the five other Latin countries, and why it coincided with wage narrowing in East Asia in the 1960s and early 1970s. Again, timing matters. Competition from other low-wage countries was far less intense when the 'Asian tigers' pulled down their barriers in the 1960s and early 1970s compared with the late 1970s and early 1980s when the Latin Americans opened up.

But even if these findings were not mixed, they could not have had a very big impact on global inequalities. After all, the literature has focused on nine countries that together had less than 200 million people in 1980, while China by itself had 980 million, India 687 million, Indonesia 148 million and Russia 139 million. All four of these giants recorded widening income gaps after their economies went global. The widening did not start in China until after 1984, because the initial reforms were rural and agricultural and therefore had an egalitarian effect. When the reforms reached the urban industrial sector, China's income gaps began to widen (Griffin and Zhao, 1993: 61; especially Atinc, 1997). India's inequality has risen since liberalization started in the early 1990s. Indonesian incomes became increasingly concentrated in the top decile from the 1970s to the 1990s, though this probably owed more to the Suharto regime's ownership of the new oil wealth than to any conventional trade-liberalization effect. Russian inequalities soared after the collapse of the Soviet regime in 1991, and this owed much to the handing over of trading prerogatives and assets to a few oligarchs (Flemming and Micklewright, 2000).

Border effects, limited access and the Third World

Income widening in these four giants dominates global trends in within-country inequality,[7] but how much was due to liberal trade policy and globalization? Probably very little. Indeed, much of the inequality surge during their liberalization experiments seems linked to the fact that the opening to trade and foreign investment was incomplete and selective. That is, the rise in inequality appears to have been based on the exclusion of much of the population from the benefits of globalization. The question is: what accounts for the exclusion? China, where the gains since 1984 have been so heavily concentrated in the coastal cities and provinces (Griffin and Zhao, 1993; Atinc, 1997) offers a good example. Those that were able to participate in the new, globally linked economy prospered faster than ever before, while the rest in the hinterland were left behind,[8] or at least enjoyed less economic success. China's inequality had risen to American levels by 1995 (a Gini of 0.406), but the pronounced surge in inequality from 1984 to 1995 was dominated by the rise in urban–rural and coastal–hinterland gaps, not by widening gaps within any given locale. This pattern suggests that China's inequality – like that of Indonesia, Russia and other giants – has been raised by differential access to the benefits of the new economy, not by widening gaps among those who participate in it, or among those who do not. But why have the globalization-induced growth shocks favoured China's coastal provinces? How much is due to policy, and how much to border effects associated with external trade, effects that have favoured the coastal provinces for centuries?

Consider another example. In the aftermath of GATT-related liberalization in 1986 and of NAFTA-related liberalization in 1994, Mexico has undergone rising inequality, not falling inequality as most observers predicted. However, Hanson (2002) has shown that much of this result can be traced to an uneven regional stimulus and, in particular, to the boom along the US border. Is it only a matter of waiting for these 'border effects' to spread? Apparently, since Robertson (2001) has shown that the Stolper–Samuelson predictions work just fine for Mexico after 1994, if one allows for a reasonable three- to five-year lag.

Did the first global century make the world more unequal?

Global divergence without globalization

Figure 6.1 (p. 137) documents the rise of income gaps between nations since 1820. While the evidence may not be as precise, we also know that global income divergence started long before 1820. Indeed, international income gaps almost certainly widened after 1600 or even earlier. Real wages, living standards, health and (especially) output *per capita* indicators all point to an early modern 'great divergence' which took place in three dimensions – between European nations, within European nations and between Europe and Asia. Real wages in England and Holland pulled away from the rest of the world in the late seventeenth century (van Zanden, 1999; Pomeranz, 2000; Allen, 2001; Pamuk and Ozmucur, 2002; Allen *et al.*, 2002). Furthermore, between the sixteenth and the eighteenth centuries the landed and merchant classes in England, Holland, along with France, pulled far ahead of everyone – their compatriots, the rest of Europe, and probably any other region on earth. This divergence was even greater in real than in nominal terms, because luxuries became much cheaper relative to necessities (Allen *et al.*, 2002; Hoffman *et al.*, 2002), an issue with powerful contemporary analogies, as we shall see below. While we will never have firm estimates of the world income gaps between 1500 and 1820, what we do have suggest unambiguously that global inequality rose long before the first industrial revolution. Thus, industrial revolutions were never a necessary condition for widening world income gaps. It happened with industrial revolutions and it happened without them.[9]

Despite the popular rhetoric about an early modern world system, there was no true globalization move after the 1490s and the voyages of da Gama and Columbus. As I argued previously using Figure 6.2 (p. 139), intercontinental trade was monopolized, and huge price mark-ups between exporting and importing ports were maintained even in the face of improving transport technology and European 'discovery'. Furthermore, most of the traded commodities were non-competing: that is, they were not produced at home and thus did not displace some competing domestic industry. In addition, these traded consumption goods were luxuries out of reach of the vast majority of each trading country's population. In short, pre-1820 trade had only a trivial impact on the living standards of anyone but the very rich. Finally, and as I mentioned above, the migration of people and capital was only a trickle before the 1820s; true globalization began only after the 1820s.

Thus, while global income divergence has been with us for more than four centuries, globalization has been with us for fewer than two. This conflict raises serious doubts about the premise that rising world integration is responsible for rising world inequality. According to history, globalization has never been a necessary condition for widening world income gaps. It happened with globalization and it happened without it.

When the nineteenth-century leader went open: Britain

Britain's nineteenth-century free-trade leadership, especially its famous Corn Law repeal in 1846, offers a good illustration of how the effects of global liberalization depend on the leader, and how the effects of going open can be egalitarian for both the world and for the liberalizing leader. The big gainers from nineteenth-century British trade liberalization were British labour – especially unskilled labour – and the rest of Europe and its New World offshoots, while the clear losers were British landlords, the world's richest individuals (Williamson, 1990). How much the rest of the world gained (and whether British capitalists gained at all) depended on foreign trade elasticities and induced terms of trade effects. But since these terms of trade effects were probably quite significant for what was then called 'the workshop of the world', Britain must have distributed considerable gains to the rest of the world as well as to her own workers. Workers – especially unskilled workers – gained because Britain was a food importing country[10] and because labour was used much less intensively in import-competing agriculture than was land (Irwin, 1988; Williamson, 1990). Whether and how much the periphery gained also must have depended on deindustrialization there, a long-run force I explore later. History offers two enormously important cases where the world leader going open had completely different effects: pro-global liberalization in nineteenth-century Britain was unambiguously egalitarian at the national and, in the short run at least, the world level – American liberalization in the late twentieth century was not.

European followers and the New World

What about the globalization and inequality connection for the rest of Europe and its New World offshoots? Two kinds of (admittedly imperfect) evidence document distributional trends within countries participating in the global economy. One relies on trends in the ratio of unskilled wages to farm rents per acre, a relative factor price whose movements launched inequality changes in a world where the agricultural sector was big and where land was a critical component of total wealth.[11] It tells us how the typical unskilled (landless) worker near the bottom of the income pyramid did relative to the typical landlord at the top (w/r). The other piece of inequality evidence relies on trends in the ratio of the unskilled wage to GDP per worker (w/y). These trends tell us whether the typical unskilled worker near the bottom was catching up with or falling behind the income recipient in the middle.

When w/r and w/y trends are plotted for the Atlantic economy against initial labour scarcity between 1870 and the First World War (Williamson, 1997), they conform to the conventional globalization prediction (Figure 6.4). Inequality fell and equality rose in land-scarce and labour-abundant Europe due either to trade boom, or to mass emigration, or to both, as incomes of the abundant factor (unskilled labour) rose relative to the scarce factor (land). In addition, those European countries which faced the onslaught of cheap foreign grain after 1870, but chose not to impose high tariffs on grain imports (such as Britain, Ireland and Sweden), recorded the biggest loss for landlords and the biggest gain for workers. Those who protected their landlords and farmers against cheap foreign grain (such as France, Germany and Spain) generally recorded a smaller decline in land rents relative to unskilled wages. To the extent that globalization was the dominant force, inequality should have fallen in labour-abundant and land-scarce Europe. And fall it did. However, these egalitarian effects were far more modest for the European industrial leaders who, after all, had smaller agricultural sectors. Land was a smaller component of total wealth in the European industrial core where improved returns on industrial capital, whose owners were located near the top of the income distribution, at least partially offset the diminished incomes from land, whose owners tended to occupy the very top of the income distribution.

Globalization had a powerful inegalitarian effect in the land-abundant and labour-scarce New World, and for symmetric reasons. Not surprisingly,

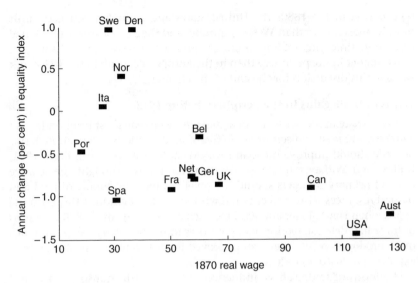

Figure 6.4   Initial real wage versus subsequent inequality trends, 1870–1913
Source: Adapted from O'Rourke and Williamson (1999: Figure 9.2).

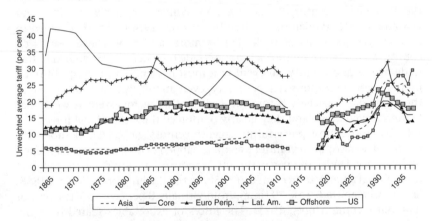

Figure 6.5   Unweighted average of regional tariffs, 1865–1939
Source: Adapted from Coatsworth and Williamson (2002: Figure 2a).

Latin America, the United States, Australia, Canada and Russia all raised tariffs to defend themselves against an invasion of European manufactures and the deindustrialization it would have caused (Blattman, Clemens and Williamson, 2002; Coatsworth and Williamson, 2002). Indeed, the levels of protection in the United States, Canada, Australia, Latin America and the European periphery were *huge* compared to continental Europe. Figure 6.5

reports that in the 1880s the United States and Latin America had tariffs *five–six* times higher than Western Europe, and the European periphery had levels *three* times higher! It is absolutely essential to know *why* tariffs were so much higher in the periphery than in the European core up to the 1930s, but we save this discussion for the end of the chapter.

Terms of trade gains in the periphery before 1913

Terms of trade movements might signal who gains the most from trade, and a literature at least two centuries old has offered opinions about whose terms of trade should improve most and why (Diakosavvas and Scandizzo, 1991; Hadass and Williamson, 2003). Classical economists thought the relative price of primary products should rise given an inelastic supply of land and natural resources. This conventional wisdom took a revisionist U-turn in the 1950s when Hans Singer and Raúl Prebisch argued that since 1870 the terms of trade had deteriorated for poor countries in the periphery – exporting primary products – while they had improved for rich countries in the centre – exporting industrial products.

The terms of trade can be influenced by changes in transport costs and changes in policy. It can also be influenced by other events, such as world productivity growth differentials across sectors, demand elasticities, and factor supply responses. But since transport costs declined so dramatically in the first global century (O'Rourke and Williamson, 1999; Findlay and O'Rourke, 2002; Williamson, 2002), this is one likely source that served to raise *everybody's* terms of trade. Furthermore, and as we have seen, rich countries such as Britain took a terms of trade hit when they switched to free trade by the mid-century, an event that must have raised the terms of trade in the poor, non-industrial periphery even more. But in some parts of the periphery, especially before the 1870s, other factors were at work that mattered even more, and they greatly reinforced these pro-global forces.

Probably the most powerful nineteenth-century globalization shock did not involve transport revolutions at all. It happened in Asia, and it happened mid-century. Under the persuasion of American gun ships, Japan switched from virtual autarky to free trade in 1858. In the fifteen years following 1858, Japan's foreign trade rose 70 times, from virtually 0 per cent to 7 per cent of national income (Huber, 1971). The prices of exportables soared in home markets, rising towards world market levels. The prices of importables slumped in home markets, falling towards world market levels. One researcher estimates that, as a consequence, Japan's terms of trade rose by a factor of 4.9 over those fifteen years (Yasuba, 1996). Thus, the combination of declining transport costs worldwide and a dramatic switch from autarky to free trade unleashed a powerful terms of trade gain for Japan.

Other Asian nations followed this liberal path, most forced to do so by colonial dominance or gunboat diplomacy. Thus, China signed a treaty in 1842 opening her ports to trade and adopting a 5 per cent *ad valorem* tariff limit. Siam adopted a 3 per cent tariff limit in 1855. Korea emerged from its autarkic 'hermit kingdom' a little later (with the Treaty of Kangwha in 1876), undergoing market integration with Japan long before colonial status became formalized in 1910. India went the way of British free trade in 1846, and Indonesia mimicked Dutch liberalism. In short, and whether they liked it or not, Asia underwent tremendous improvements in their terms of trade by this policy switch, and it was reinforced by declining transport costs worldwide.

For the years after 1870, there is better evidence documenting terms of trade movements the world around, country by country (Williamson, 2002; Hadass and Williamson, 2003). Contrary to the assertions which Prebisch and Singer made half a century ago, not only did the terms of trade improve for a good share of the non-Latin American poor periphery[12] up to the First World War, but they improved a lot more than they did in Europe. Over the four decades prior to the First World War, the terms of trade rose by only 2 per cent in the European centre, by almost 10 per cent in East Asia and by more than 21 per cent in the Southern Cone, Egypt and India combined.

Why am I able to report such different historical findings than did Prebisch and Singer, or than did W. Arthur Lewis a little later? One reason is that Prebisch and his followers were motivated by deteriorating terms of trade in Latin America, while I am casting a wider net. Another is that I have reported the terms of trade performance only during the first global century (up to 1913), not during the anti-global interlude that followed. A third reason is that the peripheral terms of trade reported here are those which prevailed in each home market (e.g. Alexandria, Bangkok or Montevideo), not the inverse of those prevailing in London or New York. In a world where transport costs plunged steeply, everybody could have found their terms of trade improving, but some primary producers in the periphery actually enjoyed the biggest pre-war improvements. If other members of the periphery did not enjoy the same big gains, it was not the fault of globalization induced by transport revolutions and liberal policy. Rather, the fault lay with the characteristics of those primary products themselves.

This pre-1913 terms of trade experience seems to imply that globalization favoured some parts of the poor periphery even more than it did the rich centre, and to that extent it must have been a force for more equal world incomes. That inference is probably false. Over the short run, positive and quasi-permanent terms of trade shocks of foreign origin will always raise a nation's purchasing power, and the issue is only how much. Over the long run a positive terms of trade shock in primary product producing countries should reinforce comparative advantage and pull resources into the export sector, thus causing deindustrialization. To the extent that industrialization is the prime carrier of capital-deepening and technological change, then economists like Singer were right to caution that positive external price shocks for primary producers might actually *lower* growth rates in the long run. Of course, small-scale, rural cottage industry is not the same as large-scale, urban factories, so industry may not have been quite the carrier of growth in the 1870 periphery that it might be in the Third World today. In any case, while nobody has yet tried to decompose the short-run and long-run components of quasi-permanent terms of trade shocks like these, there has been a recent effort to explore the possibility that positive terms of trade shocks had a negative effect around the periphery (Hadass and Williamson, 2003). Adding terms of trade variables to a now-standard empirical growth model and estimating that model for a nineteen-country sample between 1870 and 1940 confirms that an improving terms of trade augmented long-run growth in the centre. However, the same terms of trade improvement was *growth-reducing* in the periphery. It appears that the short-run gain from an improving terms of trade was overwhelmed by a long-run loss attributed to deindustrialization in the periphery; in contrast, the short-run gain was reinforced by a long-run gain attributed to industrialization in the centre.

These results imply that globalization-induced (positive) terms of trade shocks before the First World War were serving to augment the growing gap between rich and poor nations. Did the same happen after 1950 when Prebisch, Singer and other critics of conventional policy were so vocal? Maybe. Is the same true today, fifty years later? Probably not. After all, manufactures have been a rapidly rising share of developing country output and exports since the 1970s. The share of manufactures in the total commodity exports in developing countries rose spectacularly from around 30 per cent in 1970 to more than 75 per cent in 2002 (Hertel, Hoekman and Martin, 2002: Figure 2). To put it the other way around, agricultural and mineral primary product exports as a share in total exports fell from 70 to 25 per cent over the past thirty years in the Third World. Enough of the Third World is now sufficiently labour-abundant and natural resource-scarce so that their comparative advantage lies with (simple, labour-intensive) manufactures, implying that the growth of trade has helped it industrialize. The classic image of Third World specialization in primary products has almost evaporated, leaving a contracting vestige mainly just in Africa.

Rising inequality in the primary product-exporting periphery

There were powerful global forces at work before 1913 and the Third World was very much a part of it. There was commodity price convergence within and between Europe, the newly settled non-Latin countries, Latin America and Asia, and the price convergence was bigger in the periphery than it was in the core. The convergence was driven by a transport revolution that was more dramatic in the Asian periphery where, in addition, it was not offset by tariff intervention. It also appears that relative factor prices converged worldwide at the same time that average living standards and income *per capita* diverged sharply between centre and periphery.[13] The relative factor price convergence was manifested by falling wage–rental ratios in land-abundant and labour-scarce countries, and rising wage–rental ratios in land-scarce and labour-abundant countries. The convergence took place everywhere around the globe. These events set in motion powerful inequality forces in land and resource abundant areas, *especially* around the pre-industrial periphery, as in Southeast Asia and the Southern Cone. Quite the opposite forces were at work in land- and resource-scarce areas, such as East Asia.

These distributional events in the periphery were ubiquitous and powerful (Williamson, 2002). They must have had important implications for political developments which probably persisted well in to the late twentieth century, just as W. Arthur Lewis' research agenda always implied.

North–North and South–South mass migrations, with segmentation in between

North–North migrations between Europe and the New World involved the movement of something like 60 million individuals. We know a great deal about the determinants and impact of these mass migrations. South–South migration within the periphery was probably even greater, but we know very little about its impact on sending regions (such as China and India), on receiving regions (such as East Africa, Manchuria and Southeast Asia), or on the incomes of the 60 million or so who moved. As Lewis (1978) pointed out long ago, the South–North migrations were only a trickle – like today, poor

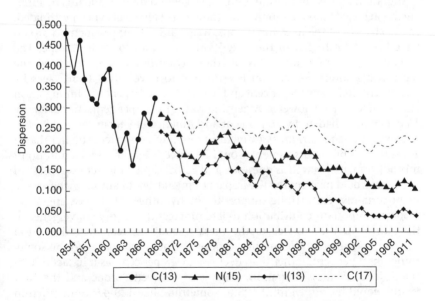

Figure 6.6 Real wage dispersion in the Atlantic economy, 1854–1913

Source: Adapted from O'Rourke and Williamson (1999: Figure 2.2).

migrants from the periphery were kept out of the high-wage centre by restrictive policy, by the high cost of the move and by their lack of education. World labour markets were segmented then, just as they are now. Real wages and living standards converged among the currently industrialized countries between 1850 and the First World War (Figure 6.6).[14] The convergence was driven primarily by the erosion of the gap between the New World and Europe. In addition, many poor European countries were catching up with the industrial leaders. How much of this convergence in the Atlantic economy was due to North–North mass migration?

The labour force impact of these migrations on each member of the Atlantic economy in 1910 varied greatly (Taylor and Williamson, 1997). Among receiving countries, Argentina's labour force was augmented most by immigration (86 per cent), Brazil's the least (4 per cent), with the United States in between (24 per cent). Among sending countries, Ireland's labour force was diminished most by emigration (45 per cent), France the least (1 per cent), with Britain in between (11 per cent). At the same time, the economic gaps between rich and poor countries diminished: real wage dispersion in the Atlantic economy declined between 1870 and 1910 by 28 per cent, GDP *per capita* dispersion declined by 18 per cent and GDP per worker dispersion declined by 29 per cent (Taylor and Williamson, 1997; Hatton and Williamson, 1998). What contribution did the mass migration make to that convergence?

Migration affects equilibrium output, wages and living standards by influencing aggregate labour supply, and these effects have also been estimated. In the absence of the mass migrations, wages and labour productivity would have been a lot higher in the New World and a lot lower in Europe. The biggest impact, of course, was on those countries that experienced the biggest migrations. Emigration is estimated to have raised Irish wages by 32 per cent, Italian by 28 per cent and Norwegian by 10 per cent. Immigration is estimated to have lowered Argentine wages by 22 per cent, Australian by 15 per cent, Canadian by 16 per cent and American by 8 per cent.

This partial-equilibrium assessment of migration's impact is higher than a general-equilibrium assessment would be since it ignores trade and output mix adjustments, as well as domestic and global capital market responses, all of which would have muted the impact of migration. In any case, the assessment certainly lends strong support to the hypothesis that mass migration made an important contribution to late nineteenth-century convergence in the North. In the absence of the mass migrations, real wage dispersion between members of the Atlantic economy would have *increased* by something like 7 per cent, rather than decrease by 28 per cent, as it in fact did. In the absence of mass migration, wage gaps between Europe and the New World would have *risen* from 108 to something like 128 per cent, when in fact they declined to 85 per cent. These results have been used to conclude that migration was responsible for *all* of the real wage convergence before the First World War and about two-thirds of the GDP per worker convergence.

There was an additional and even more powerful effect of North–North mass migrations on 'northern' income distribution. So far I have discussed only the effect of migration on convergence in per-worker averages between countries; I have not discussed the impact of migration on income distribution within the Atlantic economy as a whole. To do so, I would need to add on the large income gains accruing to the millions of poor Europeans who moved overseas. Typically, these migrants came from countries whose average real wages and average GDP per worker were perhaps only half of those in the receiving countries. These migrant gains were a very important part of the net equalizing effect on 'northern' incomes of the mass migrations.

North–North mass migrations had a strong levelling influence in the North up to 1913. They made it possible for poor migrants to improve the living standards for themselves and their children. It also lowered the scarcity of resident New World labour which competed with the immigrants, while it raised the scarcity of the poor European labour that stayed home (whose incomes were augmented still further by emigrant remittances). South–South and North–North migrations were about the same size. Until new research tells us otherwise,[15] I think it is safe to assume that South–South migrations put powerful downward pressure on real wages and labour productivity in Burma, Ceylon, East Africa, Manchuria, and other labour-scarce regions that received so many Indian and Chinese immigrants. Since the sending labour-surplus areas were so huge, it seems less likely that the emigrations significantly served to raise labour scarcity there.

The unimportance of global capital markets

Using *ceteris paribus* assumptions, I have just concluded that mass migration accounted for *all* of the real wage convergence observed in the Atlantic economy during the first global century. But *ceteris* was not *paribus*, since there were other powerful forces at work, capital accumulation responses being one of them. Capital accumulation was rapid in the New World, so much so that the rate of capital deepening was faster in the United States than in any of its European competitors, and the same was probably true of other rich New World countries. Thus, the mass migrations may have been at least partially offset by capital accumulation, and a large part of that accumulation was being financed by international capital flows which reached magnitudes unsurpassed since. One study has made exactly this kind of adjustment (Taylor and Williamson, 1997) by implementing the zero-migration counterfactual in a model where the labour supply shocks generate capital flow responses that maintain a constant rate of return on capital (e.g. perfect global capital market integration).[16] The assumed capital-chasing-labour offsets are certainly large in this experiment, but mass migration *still* explains about 70 per cent of the convergence, leaving only about 30 per cent to other forces.

Capital market responses were simply not big enough to deflate significantly the powerful income-levelling effects of mass migration within what we now call the OECD. Indeed, while it is true that global capital markets were at least as well integrated prior to the First World War as they are today (Obstfeld and Taylor, 1998, 2002), capital flows were mainly an *anti-convergence* force. This statement is, of course, inconsistent with simple two-factor theory prediction that capital should flow from rich to poor countries. It never did. As Lucas (1990) made famous, Table 6.2 shows that British capital inflows and GDP *per capita* were *positively*, not negatively, correlated just before the First World War, and that the same was true for all private capital inflows in the 1990s (Clemens and Williamson, 2001b; see also Obstfeld and Taylor, 2002). The wealth bias that Lucas and others have noticed was just as powerful a century ago, and it is explained by the fact that capital chased after abundant natural resources, youthful populations and human capital abundance. It did *not* chase after cheap labour.

International capital flows were never a pro-convergence force. They drifted towards rich, not poor, countries; they raised wages and labour productivity in the labour-scarce and resource-abundant New World, not the labour-abundant Third World. And what was true of the first global century has also been true of the second. But this does not imply that the Third World has been losing capital by export.[17] Rather, it implies that there has

Table 6.2   Wealth bias during the two global centuries

Time period	1907–13	1992–98
Dependent variable	Annual average gross British capital received (flow, in 1990 US$)	Annual average change in stock of private capital liabilities (flow, in 1990 US$)
GDP, 1990 US$	0.000208 (3.32)*** [0.534]	0.00467 (8.68)*** [0.624]
GDP *per capita*, 1990 US$	10,700 (2.43)** [0.965]	97,900 (2.20)** [0.410]
Constant	−11,100,000 (−1.06)	−44,700,000 (−0.11)
Estimator	OLS	OLS
N	34	155
R^2	0.414	0.463

Notes: *t*-statistics are in parentheses, elasticities (at average regressor values) are in square brackets. *** Significant at the 1 per cent level. ** Significant at the 5 per cent level.

Source: Adapted from Clemens and Williamson (2001b: Table 2).

always been a churning of capital among richer countries outside of Asia and Africa. Nor does it imply that global capital markets have been at fault for failing to redistribute world capital towards poor countries. Instead, it implies that, for other reasons, the poor countries have never been the best place to make investments.

Trade policy and international income gaps: why the big regime switch?

In 1972, Paul Bairoch argued that protectionist countries grew *faster* in the nineteenth century, not slower as every economist has found for the late twentieth century. Bairoch's sample was mainly from the European industrial core, it looked at pre-1914 experience only and it invoked unconditional analysis, controlling for no other factors. Like some modern studies (see Table 6.1, p. 144), Bairoch simply compared growth rates of major European countries in protectionist and free-trade episodes. More recently, O'Rourke (2000) got the Bairoch finding again, this time using macroeconometric conditional analysis on a ten-country sample drawn from the pre-1914 Atlantic economy (Australia, Canada, Denmark, France, Germany, Italy, Norway, Sweden, the United Kingdom, the United States). In short, these two scholars were not able to find *any* evidence before the First World War supporting the 'openness-fosters-growth' hypothesis.[18]

These pioneering historical studies suggest that there was a fundamental tariff–growth regime switch somewhere between the start of the First World War and the end of Second World War: before the switch, protection was associated with fast growth; after the switch, protection was associated with slow growth.[19] Clemens and Williamson (2001a) think the best explanation for the tariff–growth paradox is the fact that during the interwar years, and led by the industrial powers, tariff barriers facing the average exporting countries rose to very high levels; and since the Second World War, again led by the industrial powers, tariff barriers facing the average exporting country fell to their lowest levels in a century and a half. A well developed theoretical literature on strategic trade policy[20] predicts that nations have an incentive to inflate their own terms of trade by tariffs, but thereby to lower global welfare – a classic prisoner's dilemma. Inasmuch as favourable terms of trade translate into better growth performance and tariffs are non-prohibitive, we might expect the association between own tariffs and growth to depend at least in part on the external tariff environment faced by the country in question. After accounting for changes in world policy environment, Clemens and Williamson (2001a) show that there is no incompatibility between the positive tariff–growth correlation before 1914 and the negative tariff–growth correlation since 1970.

It has not always been true that open countries finish first, and it need not be true in the future either. There is growing evidence suggesting that the benefits of openness are neither inherent nor irreversible but rather depend upon the state of the world. When considering the move to openness, heads of state are facing a game, not an isolated decision. The low-level equilibrium of mutually high tariffs is only as far away as some big world event that persuades influential leader countries to switch to anti-global policies. Feedback ensures that the rest must follow in order to survive. Thus, today's low-tariff equilibrium was only as far away as Western coordination in the early post-war years, and the creation of transnational public institutions whose express purpose was to impede a return to interwar anti-global autarky.

But what sparks such shifts from one equilibrium to another? Why did it happen in the 1920s and 1950s? Could it happen again?

Trade policy and international income gaps: what about the pre-1940 periphery?

Were Latin America, Eastern Europe and the rest of the periphery part of this paradox, or was it only an attribute of the industrial core? While the work cited above has shown that protection fostered growth in the industrial core before the Second World War, it also shows that it did *not* do so in most of the periphery (Clemens and Williamson, 2001a; Coatsworth and Williamson, 2002). Table 6.3 reports this result, where the model estimated is of the convergence variety, but it is conditioned only by the country's own tariff rate and regional dummies. The tariff rate and GDP *per capita* level are both measured at year t, while the subsequent GDP *per capita* growth rate is measured over the half-decade following.[21] The two world wars are ignored.

The tariff–growth paradox is stunningly clear in Table 6.3. In columns (1) and (3), the estimated coefficient on log of the tariff rate is 0.14 for 1875–1908 and 0.36 for 1924–34. Thus, and in contrast with late twentieth-century evidence, tariffs were associated with *fast* growth before 1939. But was this true for all regions, or was there instead an asymmetry between industrial economies in the core and primary producers in the periphery? Presumably, the protecting country has to have a big domestic market, and has to be ready for industrialization, accumulation and human capital deepening if the long-run tariff-induced dynamic effects are to offset the short-run gains from trade given up. Table 6.3 tests for asymmetry in columns (2) and (4), and the asymmetry hypothesis wins. That is, protection was associated with faster growth in the European core and their English-speaking offshoots (the coefficient on own tariff 1875–1908 is 0.56 and highly significant), but it was *not* associated with fast growth in the European or Latin American periphery, nor was it associated with fast growth in interwar Asia (when tariffs rose even in the colonies: see Figure 6.5, p. 151). Indeed, before the First World War, protection in Latin America was associated significantly and powerfully with *slow* growth. The moral of the story is while policy makers in Latin America, Eastern Europe and the Mediterranean may, after the 1860s, have been very aware of the pro-protectionist infant-industry argument[22] offered for a newly integrated (*Zollverein*) Germany by Frederich

Table 6.3 Tariff impact of GDP *per capita* growth, by region

Dependent variable	5-year overlapping average growth rate			
	(1)	(2)	(3)	(4)
Included countries	All	All	All	All
Years per period	1	1	1	1
Time interval	1875–1908	1875–1908	1924–34	1924–34
ln GDP *per capita*	0.15	0.10	−0.73	−0.89
	1.14	*0.75*	*−1.77*	*−2.13*
ln own tariff	0.14	0.56	0.36	1.65
	1.64	*3.35*	*1.27*	*2.83*
(European periphery dummy) × (ln tariff rate)		−0.72		−2.45
		−3.32		*−3.18*
(Latin America dummy) 7× (ln tariff rate)		−0.97		0.58
		−3.15		*0.49*
(Asia dummy) × (ln tariff rate)		−0.19		−1.47
		−0.84		*−2.02*
European periphery dummy	−0.21	1.58	−0.04	6.15
	−1.24	*2.77*	*−0.08*	*3.10*
Latin America dummy	0.19	3.01	−0.73	−3.31
	0.94	*3.13*	*−1.31*	*−0.96*
Asia dummy	−0.26	0.30	−1.17	2.39
	−1.09	*0.55*	*−1.52*	*1.24*
Constant	−0.12	−0.76	5.92	3.99
	−0.11	*−0.68*	*1.55*	*1.05*
Country dummies?	No	No	No	No
Time dummies?	No	No	No	No
N	1,190	1,190	372	372
R^2	0.0357	0.0498	0.0227	0.0605
Adj. R^2	0.0317	0.0433	0.0094	0.0398

Note: *t*-statistics are in italics.

Source: Adapted from Coatsworth and Williamson (2002: Table 1).

List or for a newly independent (economically federated) United States by Alexander Hamilton, there is absolutely no evidence which would have supported those arguments in the periphery. We must look elsewhere for plausible explanations for the exceptionally high tariffs in Latin America and the European periphery during the first global century.

Lessons of history I: will there be South–North mass migration in our future?

It may be useful to repeat what we have learned about the mass European emigration: almost all of the observed income convergence in the Atlantic economy, or what we are now calling the North, was due to this North–North mass migration, and that same movement also generated more equal incomes in the labour-abundant sending regions. It is important to remember this fact when dealing today with the second global century.

Although the migrations were immense during the age of mass North–North and South–South migration prior to the First World War, there was hardly any South–North migration to speak of. Thus, while the mass migration to labour-scarce parts of the North played a big role in erasing poverty in the labour-surplus parts of the North, it did not help much to erase poverty in the South. The same is true today. Will this world labour market segmentation break down in the near future? It all depends on policy. Certainly demographic and educational forces are contributing to the breakdown of world labour market segmentation along South–North lines. As young adult shares shrink in the elderly OECD, and while they swell in the young Third World going through demographic transitions, perhaps the pressure will become too great to resist the move to a more liberal OECD immigration policy, especially in Europe and Japan. The educational revolution in the Third World (Easterlin, 1981; Schultz, 1987) has helped augment this pressure, as potential emigrants from poor countries are better equipped to gain jobs in the OECD (Clark, Hatton and Williamson, 2002; Hatton and Williamson, 2002).

The two underlying fundamentals that drove European emigration in the late nineteenth century were the size of real wage gaps between sending and receiving regions – gaps that gave migrants the incentive to move – and demographic booms in the low-wage sending regions – a force that served to augment the supply of potential movers (Hatton and Williamson, 1998). These two fundamentals are even more prominent in Africa today, and recent work suggests that Africans seem to be just as responsive to them as were Europeans a century ago (Hatton and Williamson, 2001, 2002). Although this is no longer an age of unrestricted intercontinental migration, new estimates of net migration for the SSA countries suggest that exactly the same forces are at work driving African cross-border migration today. Rapid growth in the cohort of young potential migrants, population pressure on the resource base and poor economic performance are the main forces driving African emigration. In Europe a century ago, more modest demographic increases were accompanied by strong catching-up economic growth in low-wage emigrant regions. Furthermore, the sending regions of Europe eventually underwent a slowdown in demographic growth, serving to choke off some of the mass migration. Yet, migrations were still mass. Africa today offers a contrast: economic growth has faltered, its economies have fallen further behind the leaders and there will be a demographic speed-up in the near future. The pressure on African emigration is likely to intensify, including a growing demand for entrance into the high-wage labour markets of the developed world. Indeed, if European doors were swung open, there is an excellent chance that by 2025 Africa would record far greater mass migrations than did nineteenth-century Europe.

The demographic unknown in this equation is, of course, African success in controlling the spread of the HIV/AIDS. If it is controlled early, then these emigration predictions are more likely to prevail.

This analysis for African emigration has been recently extended to US immigration by source from 1971 to 1998 (Clark, Hatton and Williamson, 2002; Hatton and Williamson, 2002). Here again, the economic and demographic fundamentals that determine immigration rates across source countries are estimated – income, education, demographic composition and inequality. The analysis also allows for persistence in these patterns as they arise from the impact of the existing immigrant foreign-born stocks, implying strong 'friends and neighbours' effects. Most of these Third World fundamentals will be serving to increase the demand for high-wage jobs in the OECD. How will the OECD respond to this challenge? If it opens its doors wider, the mass migrations will almost certainly have the same influence on levelling world incomes and eradicating poverty that it did in the first global century. It will help erode between-country North–South income gaps, and it will improve the lives of the millions of poor Asians and Africans allowed to make the move. And it will help eradicate poverty among those who will not move, making their labour more scarce at home and augmenting their incomes by remittances, forces that were powerful in pre-quota Europe a century ago.

Inequality will rise among OECD residents, of course, just as it did in the immigrant-absorbing New World a century ago.[23] Perhaps not as much, since the unskilled with whom the immigrants compete are a much smaller share of the OECD labour force today, but inequality will rise just the same. Are we ready to pay that price? Perhaps not. Indeed, we have seen how rising inequality created an anti-global backlash a century ago, a backlash that included a retreat into immigrant restriction that *still* characterizes the high-wage OECD today.

Lessons of history II: absolute or relative income? Nominal or real income?

The debate over the impact of globalization on world inequality almost always measures performance in relative terms. The questions posed are: Have international income gaps between poor and rich countries widened with globalization? Has inequality within countries widened with globalization? Something is very wrong with these questions and the measures they imply. Here are better questions: If gaps between rich and poor countries have widened, and if globalization is the cause, is it because poor countries have not gained from going global, or is it because they have actually lost? If the gaps between rich and poor within countries have widened, and if globalization is the cause, is it because poor citizens have not gained by their country going global, or is it because they have actually lost? To the extent that policy is driven by the *absolute* losses to vocal citizens and/or vocal nations, rather than relative losses, it is all the more amazing that so many contemporary economists insist on using relative inequality measures. Economic historians know better. I offer two examples.

Example 1

During the great British political debates over a move to free trade in the decades before the 1846 Repeal of the Corn Laws, predicted impact was *always* assessed by reference to *both* nominal incomes on the employment side *and* to consumption goods prices on the expenditure side. Indeed, free-traders called the high duties on agricultural imports 'bread taxes' (Williamson, 1990), and thought that the relative price of this wage good (grain) was central to working-class living standards. And they were absolutely right. Since grain – and its derivative, bread – made up such an enormous share of working-class budgets, the falling relative price of this importable made a fundamental contribution to the rise in real wages and the living standards of the poor.

Example 2

During the great rise in European inequality between 1500 and 1800, when Malthusian forces dominated the closed European economy (O'Rourke and Williamson, 2002a, 2002c), staple food and fuels became more expensive, while luxury goods, like imported exotics and domestic servants, became cheaper (Hoffman *et al.*, 2002). These relative price changes served to augment rising nominal inequality – and, indeed, to reduce living standards of the working poor. What happened in the nineteenth century when Europe went open? The price of imported food fell, contributing to the absolute real wage gains associated with the industrial revolution, and to an absolute decline in land rents. What had been a pre-globalization inegalitarian price effect was converted into a post-globalization egalitarian price effect. And since the poor devote such a large share of their budget to food, the poorest gained the most.

Economic historians cannot take all the credit for asking the right questions, since one can also find a few rare examples in the huge literature on the current globalization–inequality connection. Dollar and Kraay (2000b) report from late twentieth-century country cases and cross-country analysis that globalization leads to poverty reduction in poor countries, and that trade openness benefits the poor as much as it benefits all others.[24] Of course, it may not be the poor who vote, and thus the impact of going open on their economic performance may be unimportant to policy formation in poor countries and thus to the survival of global liberalism there.

The two historical examples from the first global century suggest an agenda for the second. If 'going global' has had a real impact on participating economies over the past three decades, then we should see its impact on relative commodity prices in home markets: the price of importables should have fallen relative to the price of exportables and perhaps even relative to the price of non-tradables. What do the rich and poor consume in these countries? What happened to the cost of their consumption market baskets when their country went open? Did the price movements on the expenditure side serve to reinforce or offset income movements on the employment side? The answers to these questions are very hard to find in the literature on the second global century. True, some time ago William Cline (1980) asked whether world commodity price shocks had much to do with within-country nominal income inequality, concluding 'not much' while, as I pointed out above, Robertson (2001) asked the same question of Mexico since NAFTA, concluding a 'great deal'.[25] But do global-induced relative commodity changes induce uneven *real income changes on the expenditure side* to the extent that the poor consume a very different market basket than the rich? They certainly did for Vietnam in the 1990s. According to Edmonds and Pavcnik (2002), during the liberal period between 1993 and 1998 the price of rice rose by 29 per cent relative to the Vietnamese consumer price index (CPI), and this relative price change must have had important inegalitarian effects on the expenditure side since the budget of the poor in that country is so dominated by rice.

It seems to me that economists should be searching for contemporary cases where the expenditure budgets of the rich and poor are very different, and where the rich consume in large proportions skill- and capital-intensive importables plus the services of the poor, and where the poor consume in large proportions land-intensive food and housing. They should also search for countries that have a recent history of switching from anti-global to pro-global policies. The best places to find both conditions satisfied are, of course, poor countries in Asia and Africa.

Lessons of history III: accommodating the losers with safety nets and suffrage

Any force that creates more within–country inequality is automatically blunted today – at least in the OECD, a point that is sometimes overlooked in the inequality debate. That is, any rise in the inequality of households' net disposable post-fisc income will always be less than the rise in gross pre-fisc income inequality. Any damage to the earnings of low-skilled workers is partially offset by their lower tax payments and higher transfer receipts, such as unemployment compensation or family assistance. Broadening the income concept therefore serves to shrink any apparent impact of globalization on the inequality of living standards. And by muting their losses, such safety nets also, presumably, mute any political backlash.

So far, so good. But does globalization destroy these automatic stabilizers by undermining taxes and social transfer programmes? In a world where businesses and skilled personnel can flee taxes they don't like, there is the well-known danger that governments may compete for internationally mobile factors by cutting tax rates and thus social spending. As Rodrik (1997, 1998) and Agell (1999, 2000) have stressed, however, the relationship between a country's vulnerability to international markets and the size of its tax-based social programmes is *positive*, not negative as a 'race to the bottom' would imply. Thus, countries with greater global market vulnerability have higher taxes, more social spending and broader safety nets. Furthermore, 'vulnerability' to global market changes is in part an endogenous policy choice: there is a trade-off between going open and investing in safety nets. In any case, while there may be other reasons for the positive correlation between openness and social programmes, there is no apparent tendency for globalization to undermine the safety nets.

While these stabilizers certainly prevail in the OECD today, one might suppose they were not common during the first global century when such safety nets were not yet in place. One might also suppose that there was no trade-off between going open and investing in safety nets at that time in what we now call the OECD. If one were inclined to make those suppositions, one would be very wrong. Europe was globalized by 1913, and the increased market vulnerability created greater wage and employment instability. Huberman (2002) and Huberman and Lewchuk (2001) show that authorities responded to workers' complaints by establishing labour market regulations and social insurance programmes, and by giving them the vote. Empirical analysis of seventeen European countries shows that the legislation gave workers reason to support free trade. Thus, globalization was compatible with government intervention before 1913, just as it has been since 1950. And, to repeat, the first global century was also one during which the vote was extended increasingly to the previously disenfranchised (Acemoglu and Robinson, 2000; Huberman and Lewchuk, 2001). It also appears that the two were related. The interesting question is: how long it will take poor nations today to put the same modern safety nets in place and to empower all citizens in the debate over global policy choices?

Lessons of history IV: why do countries protect?

What better place to end this chapter than to ask: why do countries protect? I am aware that the 1990s generated a flourishing theoretical literature on endogenous tariffs. That literature is primarily motivated by recent OECD, and mainly US, experience, thus ignoring the enormous variance over time and across regions with very different endowments, institutions and histories.

Look again at Figure 6.5, where the enormous variance in levels of protection is documented for both the first global century and for the interwar years, and where three big facts are revealed. First, tariffs in the independent periphery (Latin America, the non-Latin European offshoots and the European periphery) were vastly higher than they were in the European core. Second, in an apparent – but maybe not real – globalization backlash, tariffs rose *much* more steeply in the periphery than in the European core during the first globalization century up to the First World War. Third, what made the interwar years so autarkic was not a move towards protection in the periphery – since tariffs in Latin America, the European periphery and the non-Latin offshoots were just about as high in the 1930s as they were before the First World War.[26] What made the interwar years so autarkic was the rise of protection in the European core and the United States.

Economists need to confront these facts and to offer explanations for them. When one does so for Latin America from 1820 to 1950, one finds that the motivations for protection were very complex and changed over time (Coatsworth and Williamson, 2002). Those exceptionally high Latin American tariffs were driven up by government revenue needs, strategic tariff reactions to trading partner policy (e.g. very high tariffs in the United States), Stolper–Samuelson lobbying forces and protection of the local manufacturing industry. Before we can be confident about what causes the globalization backlash today, we need to know what caused it in the past. Over the century 1820–1913,[27] only a (perhaps small) part of the anti-global policy in Latin America was driven by development goals, by deindustrialization fears, or by the complaints of the losers. Furthermore, these determinants changed over time: revenue goals diminished in importance as Latin America became better integrated with global capital markets, as *pax americana latina* diminished the need for and thus the financial burden of standing armies and as these young countries developed less distorting internal tax revenue sources. Economists need to make the same kind of assessment for the second global century if we are to understand the sources of the globalization backlash better.

Notes

Thanks are due to Michael Clemens, John Coatsworth, Tim Hatton, Peter Lindert and Kevin O'Rourke for collaboration, Barbara Fagerman and Tony Shorrocks of UNU-WIDER for organization and the support of the US National Science Foundation (SES-0001362).

1. The causality is worth stressing here. While the modern globalization–inequality debate chases the causation from globalization to within-country inequality, the period 1500–1800 was characterized by population pressure on the land which raised land rents and thus the incomes of Europe's rich. Rising inequality increased the demand for imported luxuries, causing a trade boom. It also caused a boom in all well-placed European ports around the Atlantic economy. It seems to me that a paper by Acemoglu, Johnson and Robinson (2002) has the causality wrong.
2. For an excellent survey, see Findlay and O'Rourke (2002).
3. This benign interpretation certainly has its critics, most recently from the World Bank itself (Milanovic, 2002).
4. They all use PPP data for which the fall is far clearer. Indeed, it disappears in studies that use income data in US dollars (Melchior, Telle and Wiig, 2000: 16).
5. For example, when Mexico joined NAFTA in 1994, its economy was only about 6 per cent the size of the United States. Furthermore, only about 9 per cent of US

trade was with Mexico, while about 75 per cent of Mexican imports and 84 per cent of Mexican exports involved the United States (Robertson, 2001: 1). These shares suggest that Mexico satisfied the 'small-country assumption' and took North American market prices as given, thus getting the full measure of terms of trade gains by going open.

6. For an excellent critical survey, see Dowrick and DeLong (2002).
7. The giants also dominate trends in between-country inequality. Much of the fall in the between-country inequality index offered by Melchior, Telle and Wiig (2000: 15) is due to the fact that the populations in Japan and the United States are getting relatively fewer and less rich, while those in China and India are getting richer and more populous.
8. Migration from the hinterland to the cities was pretty much prohibited before the mid-1990s.
9. Granted, nineteenth-century industrial revolutions greatly contributed to an acceleration in the growing gap between industrial core and pre-industrial periphery (e.g. Pritchett, 1997).
10. Labour would not have gained much from free trade on the continent since, among other things, agriculture was a far bigger employer, so big that the employment effects (the nominal wage) dominated the consumption effects (the cost of living). See O'Rourke (1997).
11. Agricultural output and land input shares are certainly smaller today even in the Third World, but to ignore them in the inequality debate is a big mistake. It is also a mistake to ignore self-employment income in the large service sector. Yet, economists studying the modern Third World seem to have an obsession with earnings distributions of hired labour.
12. In two of the studies cited (Williamson, 2002; Hadass and Williamson, 2003), the periphery sample is limited to nine – Argentina, Burma, Egypt, India, Japan, Korea, Taiwan, Thailand and Uruguay – which, of course, excludes non-Southern Cone Latin America where the terms of trade appear to have fallen most dramatically. This small sample from the periphery is augmented by twelve more countries in a third study: Brazil, Ceylon, Chile, China, Colombia, Cuba, Greece, Indonesia, Mexico, the Philippines, Peru and Turkey (Blattman, Clemens and Williamson, 2002).
13. These facts deserve stress. While there was income *per capita* and living standards divergence between centre and periphery in the first global century, there was powerful convergence in *relative* factor prices. One wonders whether the same has been true in the second global century – and, if so, why economists have not noticed it.
14. Figure 6.6 plots convergence in the Atlantic economy for sample sizes of 13, 15 and 17. The largest sample includes: Argentina, Australia, Brazil, Canada, the United States; Belgium, Denmark, France, Germany, Great Britain, Ireland, Italy, the Netherlands, Norway, Portugal, Spain, Sweden (Williamson, 1996; O'Rourke and Williamson, 1999).
15. Timothy J. Hatton and I are embarking on that South–South migration project, covering the years from about 1850 to the present.
16. Davis and Weinstein (2002) do the same for the United States today, agreeing that all factor inflows, capital and labour, should be looked at together.
17. Apparently, Africa has suffered significant capital flight in recent times. Indeed, as of 1990, Africans placed a huge 39 per cent of their wealth portfolios outside the region, a year when the figure was 3 per cent for South Asia, 6 per cent for East Asia and 10 per cent for Latin America (Collier and Gunning, 1999: 92). This is hardly surprising given that the region has suffered negative terms of trade shocks, civil war and confiscation.

18. There are two additional studies worth mentioning here. Capie (1983) found support for the Bairoch hypothesis using event analysis with a pre-1914 European sample of four (Germany, Italy, Russia and the United Kingdom). Vamvakidis (2002) could not find any interwar evidence supporting the 'openness-fosters-growth' hypothesis either, although it was (once again) based on a small, mostly OECD sample.

19. In an influential article, Rodriguez and Rodrik (2001) have argued that the late twentieth-century evidence allows us to say only that free trade was not harmful for growth.

20. Exemplified by Dixit (1987) and surveyed in Bagwell and Staiger (2000).

21. Thus, the last pre-Second World War observation is 1934, which relates to growth between 1934 and 1939, and the last pre-First World War observation is 1908, which relates to growth between 1908 and 1913.

22. Late nineteenth-century Latin American policy makers certainly were so aware (Bulmer-Thomas, 1994: 140). However, it is important to stress 'late' since the use of protection specifically and consciously to foster industry does not occur until the 1870s or 1890s: for example Argentina with the 1876 tariff; Mexico by the early 1890s; Chile with its new tariff in 1897; Brazil in the 1890s; and Colombia in early 1900s (influenced by the Mexican experience). So, the qualitative evidence suggests that domestic industry protection becomes a motivation for Latin American tariffs only in the late nineteenth century.

23. I stress 'residents' here, since the addition of low-wage immigrants (especially those without the vote) at the bottom of a country's income distribution has far less politically explosive implications than their presence may have on the wages of low-skilled 'residents' (who *do* have the vote). A look at the structure of wages will control for this important distinction in immigrant countries, but a look only at the country's income distribution may not.

24. A more recent study by Sala-i-Martin (2002) is more descriptive, asking only what happened from 1970 to 1998, assigning no blame or applause to causes. He shows that while poverty rates have fallen since 1970, within-country inequality has increased. See also Chen and Ravallion (2001).

25. To quote Robertson (2001: 3): 'When Mexico joined the GATT, it opened its borders to trade with an arguably labour-abundant world, which may explain why it protected less-skill-intensive industries. Joining NAFTA, however, deepened integration with [the] skill-abundant … US and Canada. The relative price of skill-intensive goods reversed its rise. As suggested by the Stolper–Samuelson theorem, relative wages also reversed their trend.'

26. Figure 6.5 measures 'protection' by average tariff levels only, thus ignoring NTBs. NTBs were on the rise in the interwar years, so the indicator in Figure 6.5 understates the anti-global regime switch.

27. Blattman, Clemens and Williamson (2002) expand the historical analysis from Latin America to the rest of the world between 1870 and 1937.

References

Acemoglu, D. and J. Robinson (2000) 'Why Did the West Extend the Franchise? Democracy, Inequality, and Growth in Historical Perspective', *Quarterly Journal of Economics* 461: 1167–99.

Acemoglu, D., S. Johnson and J. Robinson (2002) 'The Rise of Europe: Atlantic Trade, Institutional Change and Economic Growth', paper presented to the Economic History Workshop, Harvard University, 5 April.

Agell, J. (1999) 'On the Benefits from Rigid Labour Markets: Norms, Market Failures and Social Insurance', *Economic Journal* 108: F143–F164.

———— (2000) 'On the Determinants of Labour Market Institutions: Rent Sharing vs. Social Insurance', CESifo Working Paper 384, Munich: University of Munich.

Allen, R. C. (2001) 'The Great Divergence: Wages and Prices from the Middle Ages to the First World War', *Explorations in Economic History*, 38: 411–47.

Allen, R. C. *et al.* (2002) 'Preliminary Global Price Comparisons, 1500–1870', paper presented at the XIII Congress of the International Economic History Association, Buenos Aires, 22–26 July.

Atinc, T. M. (1997) *Sharing Rising Incomes: Disparities in China*, Washington, DC: World Bank.

Bagwell, K. and R. W. Staiger (2000) 'GATT-Think', NBER Working Paper 8005, Cambridge, MA: NBER.

Baier, S. J. and J. H. Bergstrand (2001) 'The Growth of World Trade: Tariffs, Transport Costs, and Income Similarity', *Journal of International Economics* 53: 1–27.

Bairoch, P. (1972) 'Free Trade and European Economic Development in the Nineteenth Century', *European Economic Review* 3: 211–45.

Baldwin, R. and P. Martin (1999) 'Two Waves of Globalization: Superficial Similarities, Fundamental Differences', NBER Working Paper 6904, Cambridge, MA: NBER.

Berry, A., F. Bourguignon and C. Morrisson (1991) 'Global Economic Inequality and Its Trends since 1950', in L. Osberg (ed.), *Economic Inequality and Poverty: International Perspectives*, Armonk, NY: M. E. Sharpe.

Bhagwati, J. and A. O. Krueger (eds) (1973–76) *Foreign Trade Regimes and Economic Development*, multiple volumes with varying authorship, New York: Columbia University Press, for the NBER.

Blattman, C., M. A. Clemens and J. G. Williamson (2002) 'Who Protected and Why? Tariffs the World Around 1870–1937', paper presented at the conference on The Political Economy of Globalization, Dublin, 29–31 August.

Boltho, A. and G. Toniolo (1999) 'The Assessment: The Twentieth Century – Achievements, Failures, Lessons', *Oxford Review of Economic Policy* 15(4): 1–17.

Bourguignon, F. and C. Morrisson (2000) 'The Size Distribution of Income among World Citizens: 1820–1990', Washington, DC: World Bank, mimeo.

Bulmer-Thomas, V. (1994) *The Economic History of Latin America Since Independence*, Cambridge: Cambridge University Press.

Burniaux, J.-M. *et al.* (1998) 'Income Distribution and Poverty in Selected OECD Countries', OECD Economics Department Working Paper 189, Paris OECD.

Capie, F. (1983) 'Tariff Protection and Economic Performance in the Nineteenth Century', in J. Black and L. A. Winters (eds), *Policy and Performance in International Trade*, London: Macmillan.

Chen, S. and M. Ravallion (2001) 'How Did the World's Poorest Fare in the 1990s?', *Review of Income and Wealth* 47: 283–300.

Chiswick, B. R. and T. J. Hatton (2002) 'International Migration and the Integration of Labor Markets', in M. D. Bordo, A. M. Taylor and J. G. Williamson (eds), *Globalization in Historical Perspective*, Chicago: University of Chicago Press.

Clark, X., T. J. Hatton and J. G. Williamson (2002) 'Where Do US Immigrants Come From, and Why?', NBER Working Paper 8998, Cambridge, MA: NBER.

Clemens, M. A. and J. G. Williamson (2001a) 'A Tariff-Growth Paradox? Protection's Impact the World Around 1875–1997', NBER Working Paper 8459, Cambridge, MA: NBER.

———— (2001b) 'Wealth Bias in the First Global Capital Market Boom, 1870–1913', unpublished manuscript.

Cline, W. R. (1980) 'Commodity Prices and the World Distribution of Income', *Journal of Policy Modeling* 2(1): 1–17.

——— (1997) *Trade and Income Distribution*, Washington, DC: Institute for International Economics.

Coatsworth, J. H. and J. G. Williamson (2002) 'The Roots of Latin American Protectionism: Looking Before the Great Depression', NBER Working Paper 8999, Cambridge, MA: NBER.

Collier, P. and J. W. Gunning (1999) 'Explaining African Economic Performance', *Journal of Economic Literature* 37: 64–111.

Davis, D. and D. Weinstein (2002) 'Technological Superiority and the Losses from Migration', Columbia University Department of Economics Discussion Paper 0102–60, New York: Columbia University.

Diakosavvas, D. and P. L. Scandizzo (1991) 'Trends in the Terms of Trade of Primary Commodities, 1900–1982: The Controversy and Its Origin', *Economic Development and Cultural Change* 39: 231–64.

Dixit, A. (1987) 'Strategic Aspects of Trade Policy', in T. F. Bewley (ed.), *Advances in Economic Theory: Fifth World Congress*, New York: Cambridge University Press.

Dollar, D. (1992) 'Outward-Oriented Developing Economies Really Do Grow More Rapidly: Evidence from 95 LDCs, 1976–1985', *Economic Development and Cultural Change* 40: 523–44.

Dollar, D. and A. Kraay (2000a) 'Trade, Growth, and Poverty', Washington, DC: World Bank, mimeo.

——— (2000b) 'Growth *is* Good for the Poor', Washington, DC: World Bank, mimeo; published in A. Shorrocks and R. van der Hoeven (eds), *Growth, Inequality and Poverty: Prospects for Pro-Poor Economic Development*, Oxford: Oxford University Press, for UNU-WIDER, 2004.

Dowrick, S. and J. B. DeLong (2002) 'Globalization and Covergence', in M. D. Bordo, A. M. Taylor and J. G. Williamson (eds), *Globalization in Historical Perspective*, Chicago: University of Chicago Press.

Easterlin, R. A. (1981) 'Why isn't the Whole World Developed?', *Journal of Economic History* 41: 1–19.

Edmonds, E. and N. Pavcnik (2002) 'Does Globalization Increase Child Labor? Evidence from Vietnam'; NBER Working Paper 8760, Cambridge, MA: NBER.

Edwards, S. (1993) 'Openness, Trade Liberalization, and Growth in Developing Countries', *Journal of Economic Literature* 31: 1358–94.

Feenstra, R. C. and G. H. Hanson (1999) 'The Impact of Outsourcing and High-Technology Capital on Wages: Estimates for the United States, 1979–1990', *Quarterly Journal of Economics* 114: 907–40.

Findlay, R. and K. H. O'Rourke (2002) 'Commodity Market Integration, 1500–2000', in M. D. Bordo, A. M. Taylor and J. G. Williamson (eds), *Globalization in Historical Perspective*, Chicago: University of Chicago Press.

Firebaugh, G. (1999) 'Empirics of World Income Inequality', *American Journal of Sociology* 104(6): 1597–630.

Flam, H. and M. J. Flanders (1991) *Heckscher–Ohlin Trade Theory*, Cambridge, MA: MIT Press.

Flemming, J. S. and J. Micklewright (2000) 'Income Distribution, Economic Systems, and Transition', in A. B. Atkinson and F. Bourguignon (eds), *Handbook of Income Distribution*, 1, Amsterdam: Elsevier Science.

Goldin, C. (1994) 'The Political Economy of Immigration Restriction in the United States, 1890 to 1921', in C. Goldin and G. D. Libecap (eds), *The Regulated Economy: A Historical Approach to Political Economy*, Chicago: University of Chicago Press.

Goldin, C. and L. F. Katz (1999) 'The Returns to Skill in the United States across the 20th Century', NBER Working Paper 7126, Cambridge, MA: NBER.

———— (2000) 'Decreasing (and Then Increasing) Inequality in America: A Tale of Two Half Centuries', in F. Welch (ed.), *Increasing Income Inequality in America*, Chicago: University of Chicago Press.

Griffin, K. and R. Zhao (eds) (1993) *The Distribution of Income in China*, New York: St Martin's Press.

Hadass, Y. S. and J. G. Williamson (2003) 'Terms of Trade Shocks and Economic Performance 1870–1940: Prebisch and Singer Revisited', *Economic Development and Cultural Change* 51: 629–56.

Hanson, G. (2002) 'Globalization and Wages in Mexico', paper presented at the IDB Conference on Prospects for Integration in the Americas, Cambridge, MA: Harvard University, 31 May–1 June.

Hanson, G. and A. Harrison (1999) 'Trade Liberalization and Wage Inequality in Mexico', *Industrial and Labor Relations Review* 52: 271–88.

Hatton, T. J. and J. G. Williamson (1998) *The Age of Mass Migration*, Oxford: Oxford University Press.

———— (2001) 'Demographic and Economic Pressure on African Emigration', NBER Working Paper 8124, Cambridge, MA: NBER.

———— (2002) 'What Fundamentals Drive World Migration?', paper presented at the WIDER Conference on Poverty, International Migration and Asylum, Helsinki, 27–28 September; published in G. J. Borjas and J. Crisp (eds), *Poverty, International Migration and Asylum*, Basingstoke: Palgrave Macmillan, for UNU-WIDER, 2005.

Hertel, T., B. M. Hoekman and W. Martin (2002) 'Developing Countries and a New Round of WTO Negotiations', *World Bank Research Observer* 17: 113–40.

Hirst, P. Q. and G. Thompson (1996) *Globalization in Question: The International Economy and the Possibilities of Governance*, Cambridge: Polity Press.

Hoffman, P. T., D. S. Jacks, P. A. Levin and P. H. Lindert (2002) 'Real Inequality in Europe since 1500', *Journal of Economic History* 62: 322–55.

Huber, J. R. (1971) 'Effects on Prices of Japan's Entry into World Commerce after 1858', *Journal of Political Economy* 79: 614–28.

Huberman, M. (2002) 'International Labor Standards and Market Integration Before 1913: A Race to the Top?', paper presented to the conference on the Political Economy of Globalization, Dublin, 29–31 August.

Huberman, M. and Wayne Lewchuk (2001) 'The Labor Compact, Openness and Small and Large States Before 1914', University of Montreal, mimeo.

Irwin, D. A. (1988) 'Welfare Effects of British Free Trade: Debate and Evidence from the 1840s', *Journal of Political Economy* 96: 1142–64.

Krueger, A. O. (1983) 'The Effects of Trade Strategies on Growth', *Finance and Development* 20: 6–8.

———— (1984) 'Trade Policies in Developing Countries', in R. Jones and P. Kenan (eds), *Handbook of International Economics*, 1, Amsterdam: North-Holland.

Lewis, W. A. (1978) *The Evolution of the International Economic Order*, Princeton, NJ: Princeton University Press.

Lindert, P. H. (2000) 'Three Centuries of Inequality in Britain and America', in A. B. Atkinson and F. Bourguignon (eds), *Handbook of Income Distribution*, 1, Amsterdam: Elsevier Science.

Lindert, P. H. and J. G. Williamson (2002a) 'Does Globalization Make the World More Unequal?', in M. D. Bordo, A. M. Taylor and J. G. Williamson (eds), *Globalization in Historical Perspective*, Chicago: University of Chicago Press.

———— (2002b) 'Mondialisation et inégalité: une longue histoire', *Revue d' économie du developpement*, 10(1–2): 7–51.

Lucas, R. (1990) 'Why Doesn't Capital Flow from Rich to Poor Countries?', *American Economic Review* 80: 92–6.

Maddison, A. (1995) *Monitoring the World Economy, 1820–1992*, Paris: OECD.

Melchior, A., K. Telle and H. Wiig (2000) 'Globalization and Inequality: World Income Distribution and Living Standards, 1960–1998', *Studies on Foreign Policy Issues* Report 6B, Oslo: Royal Norwegian Ministry of Foreign Affairs.

Milanovic, B. (2002) 'The Ricardian Vice: Why Sala-í-Martin's Calculations of World Income Inequality Cannot Be Right', Washington, DC: World Bank, mimeo.

Obstfeld, M. and A. M. Taylor (1998) 'The Great Depression as a Watershed: International Capital Mobility over the Long Run', in M. D. Bordo, C. Goldin and E. N. White (eds), *The Defining Moment: The Great Depression and the American Economy in the Twentieth Century*, Chicago: University of Chicago Press.

———— (2002) 'Globalization and Capital Markets', in M. D. Bordo, A. M. Taylor and J. G. Williamson (eds), *Globalization in Historical Perspective*, Chicago: University of Chicago Press.

O'Rourke, K. H. (1997) 'The European Grain Invasion, 1870–1913', *Journal of Economic History* 57: 775–801.

———— (2000) 'Tariffs and Growth in the Late 19th Century', *Economic Journal* 110: 456–83.

O'Rourke, K. H. and J. G. Williamson (1999) *Globalization and History*, Cambridge, MA: MIT Press.

———— (2002a) 'After Columbus: Explaining Europe's Overseas Trade Boom, 1500–1800', *Journal of Economic History* 62: 417–56.

———— (2002b) 'When Did Globalization Begin?', *European Review of Economic History* 6(1): 23–50.

———— (2002c) 'From Malthus to Ohlin: Trade, Growth and Distribution Since 1500', NBER Working Paper 8955, Cambridge, MA: NBER.

Pamuk, S. and S. Ozmucur (2002) 'Real Wages and Standards of Living in the Ottoman Empire, 1489–1914', *Journal of Economic History* 62: 293–321.

Pomeranz, K. (2000) *The Great Divergence: China, Europe, and the Making of the Modern World Economy*, Princeton, NJ: Princeton University Press.

Pritchett, L. (1997) 'Divergence, Big Time', *Journal of Economic Perspectives* 11: 3–18.

Radetzki, M. and B. Jonsson (2000) 'The 20th Century – the Century of Increasing Income Gaps. But How Reliable Are the Numbers?', *Ekonomisk Debatt* 1: 43–58.

Robbins, D. J. (1997) 'Trade and Wages in Colombia', *Estudios de Economia* 24: 47–83.

Robbins, D. J. and T. H. Gindling (1999) 'Trade Liberalization and the Relative Wages for More-Skilled Workers in Costa Rica', *Review of Development Economics* 3: 140–54.

Robertson, R. (2001) 'Relative Prices and Wage Inequality: Evidence from Mexico', St Paul, MN: Macalester College, mimeo.

Rodriguez, F. and D. Rodrik (2001) 'Trade Policy and Economic Growth: A Skeptic's Guide to the Cross-National Evidence', in B. S. Bernake and K. Rogoff (eds), *NBER Macroeconomics Annual 2000*, 15, Cambridge, MA: MIT Press.

Rodrik, D. (1997) *Has Globalization Gone Too Far?*, Washington, DC: Institute for International Economics.

———— (1998) 'Why Do More Open Economies Have Bigger Governments?', *Journal of Political Economy* 106: 997–1033.

Sachs, J. D. and A. Warner (1995) 'Economic Reform and the Process of Global Integration', *Brookings Papers on Economic Activity* 1: 1–53.

Sala-í-Martin, X. (2002) 'The Disturbing "Rise" of Global Income Inequality', NBER Working Paper 8904, Cambridge, MA: NBER.

Schultz, T. P. (1987) 'School Expenditures and Enrollments, 1960–1980: The Effects of Income, Prices, and Population Growth', in D. G. Johnson and R. D. Lee (eds), *Population Growth and Economic Development: Issues and Evidence*, Madison: University of Wisconsin Press.

———— (1998) 'Inequality in the Distribution of Personal Income in the World: How Is It Changing and Why?', *Journal of Population Economics* 11: 307–44.

Taylor, A. M. and J. G. Williamson (1997) 'Convergence in the Age of Mass Migration', *European Review of Economic History* 1: 27–63.

Timmer, A. and J. G. Williamson (1998) 'Immigration Policy Prior to the 1930s: Labor Markets, Policy Interactions, and Globalization Backlash', *Population and Development Review* 24: 739–71.

Vamvakidis, A. (2002) 'How Robust Is the Growth–Openness Connection? Historical Evidence', *Journal of Economic Growth* 7: 57–80.

van Zanden, J. L. (1999) 'Wages and the Standard of Living in Europe, 1500–1800', *European Review of Economic History* 3: 175–98.

Williamson, J. G. (1990) 'The Impact of the Corn Laws Just Prior to Repeal', *Explorations in Economic History* 27: 123–56.

———— (1996) 'Globalization, Convergence, and History', *Journal of Economic History* 56: 277–306.

———— (1997) 'Globalization and Inequality: Past and Present', *World Bank Research Observer* 12: 117–35.

———— (1998) 'Globalization, Labor Markets and Policy Backlash in the Past', *Journal of Economic Perspectives* 12: 51–72.

———— (2002) 'Land, Labor, and Globalization in the Third World 1870–1940', *Journal of Economic History* 62: 55–85.

Williamson, J. G. and P. H. Lindert (1980) *American Inequality: A Macroeconomic History*, New York: Academic Press.

Wood, A. (1994) *North-South Trade, Employment and Inequality*, Oxford: Clarendon Press.

———— (1997) 'Openness and Wage Inequality in Developing Countries: The Latin American Challenge to East Asian Conventional Wisdom', *World Bank Economic Review* 11: 33–57.

———— (1998) 'Globalization and the Rise in Labour Market Inequalities', *Economic Journal* 108: 1463–82.

Yasuba, Y. (1996) 'Did Japan Ever Suffer from a Shortage of Natural Resources Before World War II?', *Journal of Economic History* 56: 543–60.

7
Global Labour Standards and Local Freedoms
Kaushik Basu

Introduction

For some time I have been working on the problem of international labour standards, labour rights and child labour, and in particular the tensions between global intentions and local aspirations and freedoms. This gives rise to a host of practical problems concerning what the ILO should do, what the WTO could potentially do and what the global policy options are for the US government or the Finnish government. But I plan to dwell relatively little on these practical matters and spend more time on the abstruse theoretical questions that underlie this practical debate. I believe the theoretical debate is important to ensure that our interventions do not go wrong, do not hurt the very constituencies they are meant to help. The impatience that international bureaucrats and policy makers show with abstract debates in their muscular desire to get on with the business of legislating and crafting policy can do much harm. And UNU-WIDER, perched uncomfortably between academe and the world of policy, is a good place to debate some of the abstract principles of economics that underlie global and national-level interventions to uphold minimal labour standards and worker rights.

In the city of Calcutta, a large area called Salt Lake, which was originally a salt marsh, was developed by the local government, with the idea of enabling relatively worse off people to own land and houses. So plots were sold off at a subsidized rate. But it then struck the government that these people to whom the plots were sold could, in the future, lose their land to rich buyers offering to pay a lot more. So a law was enacted to disallow the sale of these Salt Lake plots to private buyers. The law was meant to help the disadvantaged people to whom the land was first sold. When I tell economists about this policy, they laugh. Surely, a person who wishes to sell their land will be better off by being able to sell it. So stopping a person from doing so can hardly be justified on the grounds of *helping* them.[1]

This is part of a larger principle in economics that virtually all economists are brought up on. A contract between two consenting adults, that has no negative fallout on an uninvolved third person, is their business. Government has no reason to intervene and stop such a contract – if anything, government should provide the machinery needed for enforcing such contracts. This 'principle of free contract' is, in turn, derived from a more fundamental axiom of normative economics, the Pareto principle, which asserts that any change which leaves one or more persons better off and no one worse off is a desirable change and ought not to be thwarted.

While most economists subscribe to the principle of free contract many, often unwittingly, support legislative interventions which seem to violate this principle. The same people who laugh at the folly of the government that enacted the Salt Lake legislation frequently support global conventions that disallow workers in poor countries from working at jobs that expose them to significant health hazards or from getting into bonded labour contracts with employers. A 'bonded labour' contract is one in which a worker receives an upfront payment (usually from a big landlord) and promises to pay it back by working for as long as necessary, often lasting several years and maybe even a lifetime, during which time he receives negligible wages (Genicot, 2002).

Banning these contracts is often justified by hand-waving references to the ubiquitous 'externality' that economists so often use as an alibi for intervention. I want to argue in this chapter that we need to be more circumspect in justifying bans on such market activity than we have been thus far. The world has gone through a phase of overvigilant government and over-regulated markets *within nations*. This has given rise to the chorus of demand for economic reform and liberalization. What we are risking now is the same mistake at a *global level*.

Thanks to globalization, it is now easier to intervene in one another's nations and there is a genuine risk of overdoing this. I am not arguing against intervention *per se*. Governments and international organizations have important roles to play in controlling the market. But interventions have to be evaluated against some well-defined normative principles before they are put into effect.[2] This is necessary to ensure that the agenda of global intervention is not hijacked by lobbies of northern protectionism, or elite interest groups in the south, and we do not end up with wanton interventionism.

The difficulty of the problem is best illustrated by John Stuart Mill's attempt to grapple with the issue of voluntary slavery. In his *Principles of Political Economy* (1848), after making a spirited case for the principle of free contract, Mill realized that it could take him into troubled waters. In particular, he was uneasy about the fact that some people, driven by their immediate poverty, might be willing to become slaves for life. This dilemma subsequently came to be known as the problem of 'voluntary slavery' or 'waranteeism' (Engerman, 1973). While slavery is usually rooted in an initial act of coercion (such as taking people prisoners by force), this is not necessary. There have been times when people, driven by poverty, would opt to become slaves. In the US state of Louisiana, for instance, legislation was passed in 1859 which allowed people the freedom to select masters and become slaves for life.[3] Mill wanted to articulate a principle that would disallow waranteeism and so he argued that very long-term contracts, even if they were voluntary, should not be allowed.[4] This does not seem like a compelling argument to me. It is too ad hoc. Besides, it could make it impossible to a get a thirty year mortgage for buying a house.

It is easy for all of us to agree that no worker should have to expose themself to excessive health hazards, and that no one should have to contract away their future labour so as to survive the day. But this does not mean that hazardous work should be banned and bonded labour contracts disallowed. Of course, no one should be poor enough to have to enter into these kinds of contracts. But if people *are* that poor, it is not evident that banning is the right response. There may, nevertheless, be a case for some of these bans but such a case has to be constructed much more carefully and checked against well-articulated principles, before they are put into effect. And we may also have, on occasion, to shelve the idea of a ban in favour of more nuanced policy interventions or even no policy intervention at all.

My aim here is to develop criteria against which potential interventions in the market will need to be checked, and to isolate conditions that must be fulfilled before we sanction the use of a legislative intervention in the market. But I want to begin by showing why wanton global intervention is especially risky in today's world.

Globalization and the retreat of democracy

One matter that has received little attention in the economics or the political science literature, and yet is important for understanding the tensions that can arise between global policy and local freedoms, is the intricate relation between globalization and democracy.[5] This is an important precursor to the analysis of labour standards and so worth recounting, however briefly.

While much has been written in the economics literature on the benefits of globalization (see Bhagwati, 1995, 2004; and discussion in Basu, 2004), it is important to recognize that one concomitant of globalization is that, *ceteris paribus*, it tends to erode global democracy. This has either not been noticed or has been hushed up by those who did notice it in order not to sully the reputation of globalization. But globalization has many benefits to offer and we would be helping sustain it if we looked its negative fallout in the eye and worked to counter it, instead of glossing over it.

Democracy entails many things – the existence of a variety of political and legislative institutions, avenues for citizens to participate in the formation of economic policies that affect their lives and, in the ultimate analysis, a certain mindset. Yet at its core, democracy requires that people should have the right to choose those who rule them and who have influence over their lives and well-being, and the principle that the vote of one person should count as much as that of another persons.

Next, note that globalization, almost by definition, means that nations and people can exert a greater influence on other nations and the lives of citizens in other nations. Moreover, it is a fact that the power of one nation to influence another is by no means symmetric. The United States, for instance, can cut off the trade lines of Cuba. It can do so not only by curtailing its own trade with Cuba but by threatening punitive action against those who trade with or invest in Cuba. This is not just a hypothetical possibility, the US Helms–Burton Act is testimony to how it can actually happen. Cuba, on the other hand, can do little to hurt the American economy or polity. Likewise, China can do things to Taiwan, which Taiwan can in no way reciprocate and India to Nepal that Nepal would find hard to counter.

If we now bring the 'axioms' of the two previous paragraphs together, the 'proposition' is obvious: as the world shrinks and powerful governments develop a variety of instruments and ways to influence the lives of citizens in other nations, it is no longer enough for people to be able to choose the leaders of their own nations. Since democracy requires the ability to choose the leaders who have influence over your life, in a globalizing world such as today's citizens, especially those of poorer, weaker nations, need to be able to vote in the elections of the rich and powerful nations. Since such transnational voting does not happen (and even its hypothetical suggestion sounds absurd to us), globalization is bound to cause a diminution of global democracy. This is the 'dismal proposition' that I had tried to establish and warn against in Basu (2002a).

Fortunately or unfortunately, in today's world, to have influence in the affairs of another nation it is no longer necessary to occupy the other nation's land or even to go to war with it. There are, today, a variety of instruments that nations can use to influence outcomes elsewhere. Foremost among these is money. Thanks to the ease of instantaneous electronic links and the improving system of global guarantees, capital has flown across national boundaries as never before. And a rapid withdrawal of such capital can have devastating effects on the debtor nations, as we saw in 1997 when the Asian super-performing economies succumbed to financial crisis (Rakshit, 2002).

Like capital, international trade (after a slowdown in the years between the two world wars) has risen steadily. These global linkages have fuelled unprecedented growth rates of national incomes (during the 1990s, China grew at around 8 per cent per annum and India at 6.5 per cent) but they have also created new vulnerabilities. Governments and international organizations can now use the threat of disrupting these flows (or the lure of releasing greater flows of money or goods) to enforce conformity to certain kinds of behaviour. And such threats have been used. International organizations have given money while insisting that the developing countries fulfil certain conditions, many of which have had nothing to do with ensuring repayment. These conditionalities have, at times, even been contradictory, such as requiring the debtor nation to practise democracy and for it to privatize certain key sectors, unmindful of the fact that this was often against the collective wishes of the people.

Some of these conditions have been blatantly in the interest of the donor nation. In 1998, during the Asian crisis, the rescue package put together with money from several industrialized nations, most prominently Japan and the United States, had clauses that required Korea to lift bans on imports of certain Japanese products (which Japan had for long been trying to sell to Korea) and to open up its banking sector to foreign banks (an item that had long been on America's bilateral agenda with Korea).[6]

Given that the benefits of democracy are ample, as modern research has shown, this erosion of global democracy must have negative fallouts. Indeed, it is arguable that the rise in global unrest and political instabilities are a manifestation of this retreat of democracy. And the inchoate demands of the protestors in the streets of Seattle and Washington may be founded in an intuitive but ill-articulated perception of this erosion of democracy. This is a large and important problem, but not one that I am concerned with in this chapter.

Given that cross-country voting is unrealistic and not likely to happen, our best option is to strengthen global governance and make international organizations and global agreements sensitive to the needs of the poor in developing nations. Global conventions signed by ILO member countries, international agreements on non-proliferation of arms, global treaties on the environment, the semblance of global law that is beginning to emerge as the WTO passes judgements on nations' trading practices and the International Criminal Court (ICC) established following the Rome Treaty of 1998, can all have a major role to play in influencing behaviour in distant lands and villages.[7] The status of women in an African village and working conditions in a Vietnamese factory can be influenced by a global treaty on the rights of women and a global convention on labour. Hence, these global arrangements can have a major influence on global democracy and local freedoms. In crafting global conventions and agreements we have to keep in mind this larger role that they can and do play. It is with this awareness in the background that I want to enter the arena of global labour standards and local freedoms and well-being.

Three examples of labour standards in developing countries

Let us consider three rather controversial matters of international labour standards, where people are often tempted to intervene globally in local practices in developing countries. These are three of several possible contentious matters confronting international policy makers today.

Labour rights in export processing zones

Many countries have done very well in the export market by creating special EPZs, where firms that produce, exclusively or primarily, for international markets are given special land and benefits by governments. Mexico's *maquiladoras*, China's special economic zones (SEZs), and Malaysia's numerous EPZs and 'licensed manufacturing warehouses', are examples of this. One of the things that multinationals working in these zones do not want is labour trouble and the disruption of work. To ensure this, some countries require workers in these zones to give up their collective bargaining rights and desist from trade union activity, and suspend the application of minimum wage laws (which are frequently the source of worker–management dispute), which may be effective elsewhere in the nation. That is, workers wanting to work in these zones have to relinquish some of the rights that other workers in other parts of the country can take for granted.

This has led to protests that EPZs that indulge in such practices are anti-labour and should be closed down. I do not think, however, that such a conclusion can be reached quite so easily. This is because no one is compelled to work in an EPZ. If a worker chooses to work in one and is accepted by a firm, then presumably both the worker and the employer like it that way and the principle of free contract seems to kick in. As Judge Robert Sweet, presiding over the case in which McDonald's was sued for causing obesity said, in dismissing the case, 'nobody is forced to eat at McDonald's'.[8]

Moreover, investigations by the US Department of Labor (1990) confirm what most of us suspected – that, overall, workers in EPZs are better off than their counterparts elsewhere. It is true that in some countries workers in EPZs may have fewer rights, but typically they get higher pay and have superior working conditions.[9] It is not surprising that many people would choose to work in an EPZ. Banning the practice of curtailing worker rights in EPZs is thus certainly not axiomatic, especially for the policy maker who values the Pareto criterion. There may be arguments for a ban but, to be compelling, such arguments need a great deal more sophistication than we have seen thus far. Moreover, we may need to distinguish between different kinds of cases.

The US Department of Labor (1990) study on EPZs reports a case in the Guangdong province of China, where some foreign-owned export firms were allegedly offered forced prison labour for work in the SEZs. The prisoners, mainly female prostitutes, would not be paid a salary but earn points towards their release, while the salary on their behalf would be collected by the Provincial Security Bureau. The firms reportedly rejected the offer so the scheme was not put into effect. But even if the firms had accepted it, such a contract quite obviously could not be defended under the principle of free contract. The fact that the workers in this case were being forced into this kind of work meant that the Pareto criterion would not apply here,[10] and so we can rule this kind of practice in an EPZ as wrong without having to look for further justification. But a situation where workers have the option of not working in an EPZ, but nevertheless choose to work in one, is the context where one needs to have more sophisticated arguments for banning the EPZ, and also be prepared for the fact that there may not be such arguments. So we may have no good reason for interfering in the market in these developing nations. In a later section, I shall show how a case for intervention in some free-market transactions can be developed and how we may use it as a litmus test to decide which free-market agreements in labour markets can be construed as not permissible.

Lest it be thought that having special provisions for the export sector is a prerogative of less developed nations, let me emphasize that that is certainly not the case. The idea of export zones with special rights and privileges originated, in all likelihood, in Ireland and quickly took the form of an actual EPZ around Shannon airport in 1960. Moreover, the general phenomenon of having special laws for exporting firms has a long history in industrialized nations. In the United States, typically, there are very stiff anti-trust laws for firms indulging in collusive activity. However, there is another law, the Webb–Pomerene Act of 1918, which exempts firms from the jurisdiction of anti-collusion law if they can show that the bulk of their production is for the export market. In Japan, firms have similar exemptions, and in fact an exporting firm that breaks a cartel can actually be punished by government.

Child labour

A lot has been written about the reprehensible practice of child labour. But should it be banned? Should we stop the import of products that are made with child labour? I think the answers are not as obvious as may at first sight appear.

Before going into a discussion of these questions, let me briefly recount some of the facts. According to ILO (2002) estimates, there are currently 186 million child labourers in the world.[11] Child labour is notoriously difficult to measure and any estimate can be subjected to criticism. The ILO estimate tends to overcount in some ways and undercount in some. It counts a child below the age of 12 as a labourer if the child reports having done paid work (or work towards producing a good that is sold on the market) for more than one hour in the previous reference period.[12] What constitutes a 'reference period' can, however, vary – it can be a day or even a week. When it is a week, this amounts to a child doing 10 minutes or more work per day as being counted as a child labourer. This would seem to me to be too undemanding a condition: virtually every child in poor regions, if he or she reports truthfully, would be counted as a labourer. On the other hand, domestic work, some of which can be onerous and hazardous does not count as labour. This leads to serious undercounting of child labour and, especially, 'girl labour'.

Not having any other statistics to hand and given that the above estimate is subject to both an overcount and an undercount, it seems reasonable at this stage to go along with the ILO estimates. It is evident that the incidence of child labour is very high and, in the twenty-first century with technology surging and human wealth reaching for the skies, this cannot but be a source of some embarrassment.

From this it is easy to jump to the conclusion that child labour should be banned. If, however, these children who work do so because they prefer to work and escape acute poverty then it is not obvious that there is a moral case for legislatively banning child labour. I shall show later that there may in some cases be a justification for a legislative ban (Basu and Van, 1998) but the argument is a complex one, resting on the possibility of multiple equilibria in the labour market, and whether or not this multiple equilibria argument applies in a particular situation is ultimately an empirical matter. I shall return to this later.

As one might suspect, what policy stand we take on child labour depends crucially on what causes it, and the causes of child labour are many. In a region where schools are unavailable or of poor quality, the level of child labour is usually found to be high.[13] In regions where schools provide incentives such as midday meals or other subsidies, there tends to be a lower level of child labour (Drèze and Kingdon, 1999; Ravallion and Wodon, 2000; Bourguignon, Ferreira, and Leite, 2003). Rural households that have more land often have their children working harder than households with no land (Bhalotra and Heady, 2003). However, the most compelling reason for child labour is undoubtedly poverty. If a household is sufficiently prosperous, it will not send its children to work, whether or not there is a school in the neighbourhood and whether or not it owns land. Barring rare exceptions, poverty seems a necessary condition for child labour, and there is now an enormous amount of micro and macro evidence on this.[14]

A single, elegant exercise that sums the situation up well is a figure that occurs is Humphries (2003), based on an earlier scatter diagram due to Krueger (1997: 281–302). The figure has GDP *per capita* on the horizontal axis and the percentage of children aged 10–14 years who work on the vertical axis. On this is plotted a point for each country in 1992. The scatter is a nicely declining one and a line fitted to this is a monotonically downward-sloping one, going from a child labour participation rate of nearly 50 per cent for very poor countries to nearly zero for countries with *per capita*-income above US$20,000. In the same figure, Humphries inserts points representing the United Kingdom over time, in 1800, 1840 and 1870. During this period the United Kingdom was becoming richer, of course, and we find child labour falling.[15] One can fit a virtual straight line through these points. Once again, we get a monotonically downward-sloping line, suggesting that as people become richer, child labour decreases. But the United Kingdom over time line is significantly above the cross-country line for 1992. What does this tell us? That both lines are downward-sloping suggests that a greater income causes child labour to fall (in other words, poverty is a major cause of child labour) but the fact that in the nineteenth century child labour was greater than in 1992 for comparable *per capita* incomes reveals that income alone is not sufficient to explain child labour. It is possible that social norms matter (Basu, 1999; Lopez-Calva, 2003) and nineteenth-century Britain had norms that tolerated more child labour. Or that technology matters, and today's world has technology that discourages child labour (Humphries, 2003; Tuttle, 1999). One can think of many other factors.

However, if the primary reason for child labour is poverty, as seems to be the case, then the use of a legislative ban is harder to justify. One can say that no one should be poor enough to have to make their children work. But the fact is that many people *are* that poor. And then what? If we cannot obliterate poverty, should we tolerate child labour? The answer that I have given is that we should, in that case, try to improve adult wages and employment. This will on its own cause a lot of child labour to go away. But what happens if it turns out to be impossible to raise adult wage and employment? This is very possible in contexts where poverty itself is stubborn. Should we then legislatively ban child labour? My answer would be, typically, not even then. But the qualification, 'typically', is important because there are significant exceptions.

One possible exception, and therefore a case for a ban, would occur if we had evidence that children were being forced to work by their parents, guardians or whoever, because the use of force immediately puts such work outside the ambit of the principle of free contract. What constitutes forced labour in the context of *children* can be a philosophically tricky question (see Satz, 2003), since children are treated by us as not always able to judge their own interest.[16] Children often have to be compelled to go to school by their parents – and the parents could be acting entirely in the interest of the children. Should schooling in such cases be described as 'forced schooling'? And even if the answer to that is 'yes', should we treat that as bad just because it is forced? It will be too much of a digression to go into these issues here, and it must suffice to have raised this problem and move on.

The other possible exception where legislative bans may be justified is the case where we may have reason to believe that there are multiple equilibria in the child labour market. I shall examine the importance of this argument later.

Forced labour

A topic where the difficulties of crafting global legislation is amply evident concerns forced labour. Stopping forced labour is part of the four core international labour standards that various global organizations have been campaigning for.[17] But our understanding of 'forced labour' is predicated on our understanding of coercion and voluntariness. This is a topic on which economists have had very little to say, but there is a need to articulate the principles involved more clearly. In economics we make repeated reference to the free choice of agents, on how if people *voluntarily* choose something they must be better off with that thing, and so on. The principle of free contract mentioned at the start of this chapter makes critical use of the idea of *voluntary* choice and coercion. But economists have spent very little time on trying to understand what exactly these terms mean. Even in the world of policy making, these terms frequently crop up. We think poorly of *forced* labour. The ILO has begun work on counting the number of people who can be thought of as 'forced labourers' and enacting conventions to stop this practice – see ILO (2001) for a discussion. A commendable US law, the so-called Sanders' Amendment (1997), has ruled that the United States will not import products that are made using *forced* child labour.

But to have such policies work effectively and in the interest of the common person, we need to be clear about what the terms mean. Without that, there is a risk that these policies will be hijacked by those who have the best lawyers on their team, and the reference to force and voluntariness will become alibis for powerful lobbies to justify whatever it is that they wish to do.[18] If we are to stop genuine forced labour and not just be an unwitting instrument of protectionism or partisan interest, we need to understand better what forced labour is.

Much of the early Chicago school writings erred on the side of voluntariness. As long as a person's decision is voluntary, most of us agree that the state should keep away. If we can claim that virtually all adult decisions are voluntary, then we can argue against government intervention virtually everywhere. And this fitted well with the Chicago school's market-fundamentalist predilection. Voluntary choice was often thought of by those belonging to this school of thought as equivalent to having choice, and being able to reject alternatives. But clearly, if one thinks it through a little, one realizes that this cannot be so. When one gives away one's watch to a mugger in response to the mugger having pulled out a gun and asked for the watch, one exercises choice. One did have the option of holding on to the watch and getting shot. But no one would think of a person parting with his watch at gun point as doing so voluntarily, unless one is under the sway of a completely tautological definition (Basu, 2000).

Likewise, many have erred on the side of 'force' – finding compulsion and force everywhere. If a worker accepts a low wage, it is because they are forced to do so. If a woman does not go to work, it must be because she is forced to stay at home. And if she does go to work, this is evidence that she is forced to go to work. To use these all-encompassing categories is to rob this important phenomenon of meaning and significance. If we are to stop coercion and force, we must move away from the traps of tautology on either side. I bring the example of forced labour here not to offer any answers but to impress on the reader that these problems of great legislative urgency can be matters of some analytical intricacy. Policy makers, impatient to get on with the task on hand, may not like to pause over such abstruse matters. But it is incumbent on us to think this, and other topics of labour legislation, through very carefully before we pass laws or plan interventions.

When can we intervene?

The topic of international labour standards belongs to the larger subject of the role of intervention in the functioning of markets. In particular, we are concerned here with global interventions in, typically, Third World markets. Should there be interventions and, if so, how should they be enforced? Should trade sanctions be used to punish a country that violates minimal labour standards? Naturally, this has been a very contentious subject[19] and this is not the occasion for me to enter the fray. What I want to do here is simply outline three general principles against which a potential market intervention needs to be tested before it is put into effect.

Irrationality and behavioural economics

Human beings are often irrational. We are frequently impatient and willing to make disproportionate sacrifices to make good things happen soon. We lack self-control. We often count wrong, especially where returns *over time* are concerned. In particular, we are atrocious at understanding the implications of interest rates, where compounding is involved. In Indian villages I have noticed that the higher interest rates are usually quoted in per-month terms or per-week terms, whereas the lower interest rates are quoted in per-annum terms. Though I have never put this to the test, my hunch is that stating it in terms of a month or a week allows the lender to camouflage the enormity of the interest rate.[20] Modern behavioural economics has drawn the attention of economists to these systematic 'irrationalities' and opened a welcome chapter in economics. It is a bit dismaying, though, that economists *needed* behavioural economics to realize that people are not always rational.

The assumption of total rationality has played a major distorting role in our view of the role of government. One of the major achievements of modern society is that we do not have continuously to fear physical assault and the loss of our belongings and property. Most of the time when we go out for dinner we do so without having to fear that we will have to evict the people who may have moved into our homes during our absence. When we walk with a briefcase, we typically do not fear that it will be taken away by force. One reason for this great improvement on primitive life is that society recognizes the use of force and physical appropriation of another's belongings as wrong.

What, however, continues to happen nowadays is that people get duped out of their wealth. I am not using the word 'duped' here to mean obvious cheating, such as selling adulterated goods or defective products or misinforming the consumer. Against these, in principle, there is recourse. I am referring here to deals in which there is no cheating involved as such, and all information is put on the table. The duping here occurs in more subtle ways, by using the inability of agents fully to comprehend the information that is made available to them or the complications of the contract about to be signed, and also because of some common irrationalities. For instance, complex financial deals and sophisticated contracts, which are difficult for the common person to understand, make lots of people routinely lose out. The main reason society does not provide enough safeguards against this, in the same way that it prevents the physical appropriation of property, is the success of economists in persuading the policy maker that no one ever *does* get duped because human being are always rational.

When a villager regularly takes loans at the interest rate of 10 per cent or more per month, as I saw happen regularly during my field work in Jharkhand (see n. 20), economists explain this in terms of the alleged fact of a high default rate or monopoly pricing or fragmented credit markets. What we do not do is to allow for the fact that the borrower may not understand what '10 per cent per month' means in terms of the enormity of the repayment burden. Until recently, a paper that made such an assumption would be unlikely to get past the journal refereeing process. Fortunately, this is beginning to change now.

In reality, a failure to understand the meaning of interest rates is one of the major factors behind the prevalence of high rates in rural areas. I also believe that some of the poorest people are poor because of the lopsided deals they have made over the years. And it is possible that the people who become moneylenders in rural areas are, maybe through a process of natural selection, individuals who are better at understanding the details of intertemporal deals.

The US Federal Trade Commission has brought to our attention the phenomenon of 'predatory lending'. This refers to the practice of (predatory) lenders locating an attractive property, typically with a single, elderly person living in it who, in their opinion, will be unable to pay back a large loan, and then offering them a large loan for home improvement at seemingly attractive terms. The aim here is to work into the contract exorbitant charges in the event of a default and even attempt to foreclose on the property when the person fails to pay back the loan.[21] If borrowers assessed their ability to repay loans realistically, then there would be no scope for this phenomenon. Hence, the existence of predatory lending suggests a less than full rationality on the borrowers' part. Once this is recognized, there arises scope for legislative action that could not have been justified otherwise. Consider, for instance, hazardous work. If there is reason to believe that workers do not fully comprehend the long-run harm done to their health through certain kinds of hazardous work, then there could be a case for legally banning certain kinds of such work or fixing, legislatively, the amount of compensation that a worker who is involved in this kind of work must be paid. Presumably this will be an amount greater than what would occur naturally through the market, since the latter relies on the worker's perception of the hazard.

If we could show that parents do not understand the loss of human capital or damage to health that occurs in a child who works, then again this could be a reason to ban child labour. We must be careful, however, to recognize that it is not enough to show that a child's health is hurt through labour or that there is loss of human capital (even if this is huge). This argument is predicated on our being able to show that parents underestimate these costs of child labour, and that adults in hazardous work underestimate the long-run costs of such work.

The recognition of less than full rationality and the inability to calculate among ordinary people also opens the door for better redress for those who are tricked into accepting deals that hurt them. This is, however, a very difficult and risky area for government to get involved in, for it can easily lead to excessive intrusion in free-market decisions. Hence, this is a future policy option for us to keep in mind and discuss but not one on the basis of which I would at this stage encourage interventions in labour markets.

Multiple equilibria

A general case where a legislative intervention in free-market contracts may be justified without having to disregard the Pareto principle is one where we have multiple equilibria. This idea has been used in several areas of development economics, from the theory of child labour to the analysis of policies for releasing a nation caught in the vicious circle of poverty.[22] The idea is simplest to outline in a game-theoretic setting. Consider the problem of hazardous labour (though this could equally apply to child labour, or statutory limits on hours of work, or a worker's right to be part of a union). Let us consider a case where there are no government restrictions on hazardous work. Each worker looks around the labour market, at the wages that prevail for 'safe' work (S) and 'hazardous' work (H), and decides which to opt for. The worker, in other words, has a right to a safe environment but this is not an inalienable right. If he wishes to divest himself of this right in order to earn some more money (since, presumably, hazardous work will command a higher wage than safe work), he has the freedom to do so.

Now, without going into the details of the economy, it seems reasonable to posit that what a person wishes to do could depend on what others do, since what others do could affect the wages that hazardous work and safe work command. Improvising a bit on standard game-theory notation, let me denote by $B(H, H)$ the payoff that a worker gets if she does hazardous work and all other workers do hazardous work. The first H in $B(H, H)$ denotes what the worker does and the second H denotes what everybody else does. Likewise, I shall use $B(H, S)$ to denote the payoff that a worker expects to earn if she does hazardous work while everybody else does safe work. $B(S, H)$ and $B(S, S)$ are interpreted similarly. These are all net payoffs, and so take account of the pleasure of the income that such work brings and also the cost of leisure and hazard associated with this work. Let us now consider a case where the following assumptions are true:

$$B(H, H) > B(S, H) \tag{7.1}$$

and

$$B(S, S) > B(H, S) \tag{7.2}$$

It is true that I have not specified the full game because it has not been stated what the payoff to an individual would be if half the remaining population does safe work and half does hazardous work, and so on. But even without going into this, it is evident that the assumptions of the payoffs just specified give rise to at least two Nash equilibria – one in which everybody chooses hazardous work and another in which no one does. For simplicity, let us assume that these are the only Nash equilibria of this game. Assumptions (7.1) and (7.2) in themselves do not tell us anything about the relative values of $B(H, H)$ and $B(S, S)$. Let us now assume that:

$$B(S, S) > B(H, H) \tag{7.3}$$

Now, let us consider an equilibrium in which everybody chooses to do hazardous work. Note that each individual, if asked separately what she prefers, hazardous work or safe work, will say 'hazardous' (this follows from (7.1)). Nevertheless, there is a case here for banning hazardous work. Such a ban would give rise to the outcome in which everybody does safe work. And since this is a Nash equilibrium, if people were *now* given the freedom to choose between safe and hazardous work, they would choose safe work. Moreover, by (7.3), they are all better off in this new equilibrium than the old one. Disallowing free contract, far from leading to a Pareto suboptimal outcome, has taken the economy to a Pareto superior outcome. Hence, if some economy has the characteristics just described, a legislative ban on hazardous work will be justified and, in fact, be required under the Pareto principle.

Another interesting possibility occurs if some people satisfy (7.3) but others satisfy the opposite inequality. Assume, for example, that there are two kinds of people in society: type R and type P. We may think of R as 'rich' and P as 'poor'. Suppose now that everybody satisfies (7.1) and (7.2) but types R and P evaluate outcomes (S, S) and (H, H) differently. Assume, in particular, that:

$$B_P(S, S) > B_P(H, H) \tag{7.4}$$

and

$$B_R(S, S) < B_R(H, H) \tag{7.5}$$

In this economy, once again, there are two Nash equilibria – one where everybody chooses *S* and another everybody chooses *H*. But neither of these two states Pareto dominates the other. Hence, if beginning from a state where everybody chooses *H*, the state bans *H* (and so deflects society to the equilibrium where all choose *S*), this will not be a policy in violation of the Pareto principle. In the context of child labour (see Basu and Van, 1998; Basu, 1999) it can be shown, by constructing a full-fledged economic model, that multiple equilibria (namely, payoffs that have the above characteristics)[23] could well occur under realistic conditions. It will be interesting to attempt the same for hazardous work.[24] Only after one has done so can one make a case for placing legislative restrictions on workplace hazard.

At times, we find some economists expressing scepticism about these kinds of multiple equilibria results, and the policies that arise from them, on the ground that we do not as yet have empirical evidence of there being multiple equilibria. This, however, is a fallacy because, just as we may not have evidence of multiple equilibria, we do not have hard evidence of the non-existence of multiple equilibria either. Even if we observe an economy in one equilibrium, we cannot assume from this that the economy has a unique equilibrium. Hence, at least for the time being, the actual crafting of policy has to depend on the demonstration of theoretical possibilities and the marshalling of circumstantial empirical evidence, since empirically we have no reason for favouring one assumption over the other.[25]

I want to end this section with two observations about law. Legal intervention in a multiple-equilibrium model is very different from what we see in standard models of law and economics. In the standard model, when a law is needed to change behaviour, one needs the persistent presence of the law. For instance, if you declare parking on a busy road illegal and subject to a fine, you will have to involve the law perennially there if you wish to prevent cars from being parked on that road. However, in the above model, once hazardous work has been banned for a while, even if the law is revoked, the economy does not return to the original situation, since the new outcome is an equilibrium in its own right. In Basu and Van (1998), we had called this a *benign* legal intervention. The advantage of economies with appropriate multiple equilibria is that we may not need perennial legal or government intervention. A benign intervention may be enough to 'cure' the problem once and for all.

The second point that it is important to keep in mind, especially in the context of this chapter, is that the efficacy of a nation's law depends critically on the extent of globalization. I have glossed over this in the model specified here, but in a more fully specified model, with globally mobile capital, the wage that workers in a nation can command will depend on the extent of capital attracted into the country.

The basic point is intuitively obvious. Consider a closed economy that bans hazardous work. This will have a certain effect on the wage rate that prevails for safe work, because presumably capital that supported firms involved in hazardous work will move over to non-hazardous work and likewise labour will move from one sector to another. Presumably, something like this occurs behind the sparse-game model described above. Now suppose the same ban occurs in an open and globally integrated economy. It is entirely possible that capital will now shift not just to another sector but out of the country to another nation where there is no such law. And given that labour is not so mobile between nations, this will cause the 'safe' wage in this country (post-ban on hazardous work) to be lower than what it would be in a closed economy. Hence, a government concerned about labour welfare will find it harder to enact certain laws, effectively, in a more globalized environment. This is a theme that will be picked up later.

The large numbers problem

Let me finally turn to a theoretically more intricate route for justifying interventions to stop *certain kinds* of free-market contracts in the labour market. In economics, we often go from reasoning about a single contract or a limited number of contracts to taking a position on such contracts in general. As we have seen earlier, economists often argue that if a rational person wants to sell his house voluntarily and another rational person wants to buy it, then these two persons must be better off by the exchange, and since no one else has any obvious negative externality from this, it constitutes a Pareto improvement and so the state should not intervene. From this, they jump to the conclusion that the state should not stop individuals from selling their homes. An intervention that disallows such sales, they argue, is wrong.

This deductive jump is, however, not as innocuous as it may seem at first sight. Can we always go from arguing about the moral status of each single transaction to the moral status of a *class* of such transactions? This is a philosophically difficult question that economists tend to gloss over by answering or implicitly assuming the answer to be 'yes'. A serious investigation into this was undertaken by a philosopher. Derek Parfit, in his celebrated book on moral reasoning (Parfit, 1984), answers this question in the negative. That is, he argues that there are certain actions such that each one may be morally acceptable, but the totality of these actions may not be.[26]

At one level, Parfit's answer seems in easy accord with general-equilibrium theory, in particular, the concept of pecuniary externalities. Each single person signing an agreement to do hazardous work or to give up the right to join a trade union or the right to be protected against sexual harassment in the workplace may have no externalities since, by assumption, wages and prices are not affected by a single person's behaviour. So, a single person signing such a contract voluntarily must lead to a Pareto improvement (that person and his/her employer are better off and there is no effect on anybody else). But if lots of people sign such contracts, wages get affected and this could hurt the welfare of uninvolved individuals, thereby rendering the new outcome Pareto non-comparable to the old outcome.

Let me call this standard general-equilibrium (GE) proposition the 'GE reversal claim', or GERC. The paradoxical conclusion that GERC enables us to reach is this: if we are committed Paretians (and I maintain that we ought to be), then we should not object to individual workers agreeing to sign away their right not to be sexually harassed in the workplace, or their right not to expose themselves to large health hazards at work, or their right to collective bargaining in order to get some benefit in exchange – for instance, being able to work in an EPZ where work conditions may be particularly nice or simply to earn a higher wage. But we may nevertheless, without having to face the charge of inconsistency, enact a law that prohibits sexual harassment in the workplace or excessive health hazard at work or forbids everyone from giving up his/her right to bargain collectively, whether or not an individual worker and an employer find such a contract worthwhile. This is because the enactment of a law amounts to banning a whole *class* of actions or contracts, and we can, by GERC, take a different normative stand on a class of actions and on each action in the class.

It is interesting to note that the justification for this kind of a legislative ban is very different from the ones commonly proposed. Here, the case for the ban is founded on the harm it does to 'others' – those who suffer the pecuniary externalities of many people doing some kind of trade and exchange.[27] Hence, if a firm offers job contracts which involve high wages but require workers to forgo the right not to be sexually harassed at work (and this is made clear to the worker at the time of her taking up employment), the reason why this should be stopped is not to protect individual workers from being harassed by this entrepreneur, but because of what firms offering such contracts do to wages and the well-being of workers – and, in particular, to the well-being of those who are especially strongly averse to harassment. This principle sounds inimical to our common sense, simply because we have reasoned so poorly for so long in these difficult areas of labour rights. But this is a very sensible way to understand why we may wish to legislate against EPZs where workers have to give up their rights or against contractual sexual harassment in the workplace, or against hazardous work.

The discerning reader will have noted that allowing workers the freedom to forgo a certain right does not lead to a Pareto improvement – does not mean that workers should *not* be allowed to forgo the right. All that we have shown is that, when the GERC principle holds we do not, on purely Paretian grounds, have a case for either upholding the right as inalienable or permitting workers to trade the right away. And, equivalently, upholding the right and not upholding it are both compatible with Paretianism. To go from this to a definite prescription, we need further moral axioms.

One route to such a further axiom is to note that we, quite naturally, think of certain human preferences as (morally) fine – or what will be here called 'morally maintainable' – and others as not. A person's racist preference for giving jobs only to whites would be considered by most people as 'wrong' or not morally maintainable. On the other hand, we would consider a person's propensity not to work four days a week as fine – that is, morally maintainable. We would agree that this is likely to be harmful for the person themself, but not a preference that most of us would consider morally wrong.

Now among preferences that we consider morally maintainable, it seems possible to make some further distinctions. I have argued (Basu, 2003) that there are certain morally maintainable preferences, which are special in the sense that most of us would agree that not only do people have the right to have these preferences but, in addition, no one should have to pay a penalty for having such a preference. These may be called 'inviolable preferences'. Thus, while we agree that it is fine for Rip to want to sleep all day, four days a week, we at the same time see nothing wrong in the fact that Rip will have to pay the price of poverty for having this preference. On the other hand, most of us would agree that no one should have to pay a price for being averse to being sexually harassed or bullied. Hence, the preference not to be sexually harassed is an *inviolable preference*.

What exactly is considered an inviolable preference is of course not given *a priori*. Being a normative matter, there may also be disagreement between different societies about what should fall under the description of 'inviolable preference'. Is a father's aversion to letting his child do hard labour an inviolable preference or merely a morally maintainable preference? What about the preference not to be exposed to health hazards at work?

These could, of course, be contentious matters.[28] But most of us would agree that there exist preferences that are inviolable. And this enables us to reach clear conclusions in choosing between certain Pareto non-comparable alternatives. Suppose states x and y are Pareto non-comparable but in x some people who are especially averse to being sexually harassed have to pay a special price for having this preference. We should in that case consider y superior.

The use of the GERC, along with the normative criterion of marking certain preferences as morally inviolable, could allow us to reach policy prescriptions about labour rights – in particular, to treat certain rights as inalienable.

It is worth noting that the moral criterion developed here belongs to neither welfarism nor deontological ethics. It involves a blending of welfarism and non-welfarist considerations.[29] I shall call it here a 'miscible moral'. What I am arguing is that we should be welfarists in applying the Pareto criterion (that is, use individual welfare data to check if, between states x and y, everybody is at least as well off in x as in y and there exists one person who is better off in x than in y and, if so, to declare x to be socially superior to y) but among alternatives that are Pareto non-comparable we should be prepared go beyond people's welfare information. We should look at the basis of, or what *underlies*, a person's preference or welfare. If in state x, person i is unable to go to the cinema and so i prefers state y to x, and in state y, person j is exposed to large workplace health hazard or faces sexual harassment at work and so j prefers x to y, then in deciding between x and y, society has to look beyond is and js welfare intensities. Society should choose x because y results in a violation of what we consider (to the extent that we do) to be someone's inviolable preference. The reason why this argument is partly welfarist is because it fully heeds the Pareto principle. But it is not entirely welfarist because non-welfare considerations kick in when the Pareto principle gives us no verdict. Observe that under this miscible moral system if an adult says that she hates to be harassed but is willing to put up with it (because of the higher wage promised by the sleazy employer),[30] society has no authority to stop this transaction by saying that the harassment hurts her.

In the existing literature there is some discussion on unacceptable preferences, and this has led to the suggestion of using preference-based welfare criteria but only after the 'purification' of individual preferences (see Sen, 1997, for a discussion on this). It seems to me that such 'purification' should be allowed only in the event of Paretian non-comparability. Suppose a person gets pleasure (as an end in itself) from hurting others and suppose that this person plans to hurt another person. Should this be permitted? Or, more specifically, should this be allowed if the pleasure the 'hurter' gets is very large compared to the pain the 'hurtee' feels?[31] My response will be: 'no, this should not be allowed, no matter how big the pleasure and how small the hurt'.[32] But now consider another case where the hurter offers to pay money to a free person in order to inflict pain on him and suppose the latter, after properly thinking it through, considers the offer acceptable. Should this transaction be allowed? Under the miscible moral system that I have proposed, the answer is 'yes'.

There is also an important theoretical agenda that this inquiry opens up, which I want to mention here only in passing. The possibility of there being transactions which by themselves are Pareto improving but in their collectivity may lead to a Pareto non-comparable or Pareto inferior state arises by the GERC. The claim is of course standard and is to be found in our textbooks. But that is no reason for accepting it. Is it really a reasonable principle? If each of a class of actions lead to a welfare increase, can all the actions together cause welfare to decline in any meaningful sense? The fact that this is assumed to happen in GE theory is no real consolation. Can such a theory be founded in a consistent logic? We know from the works of Aumann (1964) and Hildenbrand and Kirman (1988) that this is possible in a society with uncountably many individuals. I tried to show in Basu (1994) that in certain game-theoretic situations we can get such results with a countably infinite number of individuals. But evidently this is a topic that deserves further investigation.[33]

Notes on international labour standards

It is time to return to the mundane. Given the above problems and arguments, what is to be done? How can we have global labour standards that do not trample on local freedoms? This needs to be approached with an open mind. We should be prepared to do whatever is necessary, including doing nothing. The human mind has a natural propensity to prompt us, wherever we see a problem, to do something. In reality, there are lots of problems about which nothing can be done, or at least nothing can be done without making matters worse. The recognition that we live in a necessarily second-best world is important for realistic and successful policy making.

Some of the problems of labour standards are a concomitant of poverty. The only way to fight these is to fight poverty and we will be successful to the extent that we can be successful in mitigating global poverty.

Also worth keeping in mind is what mainstream economics keeps telling us – that much of what workers have achieved over the twentieth century has been achieved by virtue of the greater demand for labour and the consequent, automatic empowering of labourers. The power of what can be achieved by creating new legal rights may be small compared to what can be achieved by ensuring that labour demand keeps rising, which would enable workers on their own to ask for more and get it. This implies that trade channels ought to be left open. The use of trade sanctions to achieve certain ends should be discouraged. A direct implication of this is that labour standards should be in the charge of the ILO and not the WTO.

Further, the culture of contracts – whereby consenting adults can in general make agreements among themselves and have reasonable expectations that the agreements will be fulfilled because the state will help uphold such contracts or, more minimally, not negate them – can play an important role in improving living standards. The significance of this is routinely underestimated by policy makers.

Nevertheless and despite all the above caveats, as we have already seen there can be contexts where we may legitimately intervene in free-market contracts and exchange and do so without abandoning the Pareto axiom. The Pareto reversal proposition explains why we may want to legislate against certain classes of actions that may, on their own, seem to be Pareto improving. We have also seen that the existence of multiple equilibria provides a powerful case for banning certain voluntary, free-market exchanges. But all this applies to any legitimate governing authority. There is nothing special here about global interventions. But, interestingly, the multiple equilibria argument developed above can be taken further to provide a new justification for and give new meaning to the idea of *international* labour standards. As has already been pointed out in the discussion on hazardous work, in a world with globally mobile capital a ban on certain labour market practices may not succeed in deflecting the economy to the 'good equilibrium' the way it would have done in an economy where firms were country-specific. This is because every new, unilateral act of labour legislation would typically be expected to cause some flight of capital.

The only way to get around this is to have all countries – or, at least, all similarly placed countries – legislate simultaneously. This would limit the flight of capital associated with new legislation or government intervention. This is the principle reason why we need *international* labour standards as opposed to purely idiosyncratic and country-specific laws. But this also means that, when talking of international labour standards in poor countries, the initiative and the specific details of what goes into a package of international standards must come from developing countries and not from the governments or lobbies of industrialized nations, no matter how well-meaning they are.

I also hesitate about the use of consumer sanctions in industrialized countries to improve labour standards in poor nations. Moral monitoring through consumer activism runs the risk of playing into the hands of big businesses that have the power to direct opinion. Also, there is the genuine risk of witch-hunting – the criticism of some companies for violating labour codes that takes the form of hysteria and has very little actual basis. Given that labour standards in poor nations will be lower than in rich nations (not to allow for this is to hurt the poor nations), it is easy for people in industrialized nations to be misled into thinking that a firm that pays much lower wages in Vietnam compared to the United States is violating a moral standard.

Once the initiative gets passed onto poor countries and gives voice to workers and the dispossessed in those nations, we may end up getting a very different package of labour standards than the ones that are currently favoured. We may reach the conclusion that in very poor countries, such as Ethiopia and Nepal, where more than 40 per cent of children in the age group 10–14 years are labourers, child labour should not be banned, because this could cause deaths from starvation or drive children to other more dangerous livelihoods. We may reach the conclusion that employers must provide bathrooms for women close to the workplace because people close to the grassroots know that this is a major reason why women cannot take on certain kinds of jobs. It may be agreed upon that there should be no minimum wage laws in the poorest nations.

Giving voice to the Third World means risking that the agenda of international labour standards that we come up with will be significantly different from what would have emerged under the old order. But that is what global democracy is all about.

Notes

The author thanks Tony Shorrocks for comments, and Alaka Basu, Gayatri Koolwal and Lorraine Telfer-Taivainen for editorial suggestions.

1. I have written about this Salt Lake phenomenon in Basu (2003).
2. This becomes especially important if we view development as essentially an expansion in the freedoms of the people concerned (Sen, 1999). Then, the curbing of free transactions in markets in the name of encouraging development has to be carefully crafted and justified so as not to be a self-contradictory policy.
3. It is interesting to note, however, that the Louisiana legislators were rather partial and granted this freedom only to persons of colour.
4. In later work Mill (1859) took a somewhat more sophisticated position on this, but never really managed to outline a compelling general principle for the exceptions.
5. I have discussed this at length in Basu (2002a).
6. The pressures on poor nations are not always in the deliberate self-interest of the donors and the industrialized nations. Many of the issues championed in various international fora are (as I discuss below) meant to be for the good of the poor nations. So my concern is not with the specific demands but with the mechanism through which these are brought to bear on the world. Once we create an effective mechanism, this can become a conduit for exploiting poor nations and bending them against their political will. The global mechanisms that are made available thus need to have built-in safeguards to prevent anti-democratic uses.
7. Shadows were cast on this process when the US administration sought to withdraw from some major international treaties. On 6 May 2002, for instance, the US administration announced its intention to withdraw from the Rome Treaty and has actually worked to undermine the ICC by striking bilateral deals with nations to bypass the court, such as that signed with India on 26 December 2003.
8. See *USAToday*, 22 January 2003: www.usatoday.com/money/industries/food/2003-01-22-mcdonalds-lawsuit_x.htm.
9. See Kabeer (2000) for an excellent analysis in the context of Bangladeshi workers.
10. That is, the signing of this contract between the prison authority and a firm in the EPZ would not automatically lead to a Pareto improvement, since there is no reason to believe that the workers would be better off by this.
11. A 'child' for this purpose is someone below the age of 15 years.
12. For someone between the ages of 12 and 15 years, 14 hours or more work in the reference period has him/her classified as a child labourer.
13. For analyses of the relation between schooling and child labour, see Levison, Moe and Knaul (2001) and Rosati and Rossi (2003).
14. See, for instance, Krueger (1997), Ray (2000), Humphries (2003), Edmonds (2005). For surveys of some of this evidence, see Basu and Tzannatos (2003) and Brown, Deardorff and Stern (2003).
15. The claim is not without controversy, since child labour data, prior to 1951, was very uneven in Britain. Humphries' (2003) numbers are based on her own computations.
16. Note that we typically speak about the rights of 'consenting *adults*' and not '*people*'.
17. The other three being the stoppage of child labour, prevention of discrimination in the workplace and upholding of workers' rights to form unions and bargain collectively.

18. There is some evidence that this happening, as, for instance, when Sanders' Amendment was cited in the charge that was brought in the United States against Brazil's juice exporter, Sucocitrico Cutrale Ltd.

19. See, for example, Bhagwati (1995, 2004), Maskus (1997), Chau and Kanbur (2002), Kanbur (2003), Singh (2003), Winters (2003), Bhagwati (1995, 2004) and Satz (2004).

20. In the village of Nawadih, in the state of (now) Jharkhand, in eastern India, where I did four field trips in the early 1990s, I found that whenever interest rates crossed 100 per cent per annum, it would typically be stated in per month terms. Lots of poor farmers told me, for instance, that they had got loans from local landlords or money lenders at 10 per cent per month. I have my doubts if they realized that this amounted to an interest rate of over 200 per cent per annum.

21. 'Predatory lending' has been the subject of very good analysis by the US Federal Trade Commission. See, for instance, www.ftc.gov/os/2000/05/predatorytestimony.htm.

22. See, for instance, Rosenstein-Rodan (1948); Nurkse (1953); Murphy, Shleifer and Vishny (1989); Matsuyama (1992); Basu and Van (1998); Hoff and Stiglitz (2001); Emerson and Souza (2002); Lopez-Calva (2003); Edmonds and Pavcnik (2005).

23. That model corresponds to the case described by (7.1), (7.2), (7.4) and (7.5).

24. If we build a competitive model with hazardous work and multiple equilibria, one important distinction will be that no equilibrium will Pareto dominate another equilibrium. This is because by the first fundamental theorem of welfare economics we know that each equilibrium must be Pareto optimal. However, our main claim would remain valid despite this. If, starting from an equilibrium where some workers do hazardous work, a ban is imposed on hazardous work and the economy moves to another equilibrium, we can be sure that this ban does not lead to a Pareto inferior outcome, since the new equilibrium must also be Pareto optimal.

25. In the context of child labour, we now know that both of these are available. In fact, the theoretical possibility of multiple equilibria occurs not only in models with exogenous law but even in models where child labour regulation is an endogenous choice of the citizenry (Doepke and Zilibotti, 2004).

26. See also Neeman (1999), Genicot (2002), Basu (2002b).

27. Needless to say, this is only for freely entered upon, contractual exchange. In coercive situations, one can appeal directly to the welfare loss of the aggrieved party.

28. This should not surprise us. We are trying to develop a normative policy principle. From Hume's law we know that we can never reach such a principle from propositions of pure facts and logic. When, on occasion, we feel we have done so, it must be that we have unwittingly slipped a normative axiom into the discourse. All I am doing here is confronting the unavoidable normative axiom directly.

29. Welfarism has been critiqued effectively in the literature and in many different ways (see Sen, 1997, 2003). The critique being presented here is, however, different because it is based on rejecting welfarism only in the event of Paretian reticence.

30. The argument that she may be opting for this because of poverty is clearly no reason to stop the transaction. I would consider it a case for doing some thing to eradicate poverty so that no one has to make awful choices like this. But if someone is so poor as to wish to make this choice, clearly she would be even worse off if she were not allowed to do it.

31. I am grateful to Abhijit Banerjee for drawing my attention to this moral quandary.

32. Note that in making this statement we have gone beyond welfarism, because if the same welfare profile were generated through another underlying story – for instance, the first person wanting to listen to music which the second person does not like – we might have reached a different prescription.
33. Following Parfit's (1984) lead I have, in Basu (2002b), explored some possibilities of such reversal results in finite societies, but this has to be viewed as no more than a beginning.

References

Aumann, R. (1964) 'Markets with a Continuum of Traders', *Econometrica* 32: 39–50.
Basu, K. (1994) 'Group Rationality, Utilitarianism and Escher's Waterfall', *Games and Economic Behavior* 7: 1–9.
——— (1999) 'Child Labor: Cause, Consequence and Cure with Remarks on International Labor Standards', *Journal of Economic Literature* 37: 1083–1119.
——— (2000) *Prelude to Political Economy: A Study of the Social and Political Foundations of Economics*, Oxford: Oxford University Press.
——— (2002a) 'The Retreat of Global Democracy', *Indicators* 1: 1–10.
——— (2002b) 'Sexual Harassment in the Workplace: An Economic Analysis with Implications for Worker Rights and Labor Standards Policy', Department of Economics Working Papers 02–11, Cambridge, MA: MIT.
——— (2003) 'The Economics and Law of Sexual Harassment in the Workplace', *Journal of Economic Perspectives* 17: 141–57.
——— (2004) 'Globalization and Development: A Re-examination of Development Policy', in A. Kohsaka (ed.), *New Development Strategies: Beyond the Washington Consensus*, Basingstoke: Palgrave Macmillan.
Basu, K. and Z. Tzannatos (2003) 'The Global Child Labor Problem: What do we Know and What Can We Do?', *World Bank Economic Review* 17(2): 147–73.
Basu, K. and P. H. Van (1998) 'The Economics of Child Labor', *American Economic Review* 88(3): 412–27.
Bhagwati, J. (1995) 'Trade Liberalization and "Fair Trade" Demands: Addressing the Environmental and Labor Standards Issues', *World Economy* 18: 745–59.
——— (2004). *In Defense of Globalization*, New York: Oxford University Press.
Bhalotra, S. and C. Heady (2003) 'Child Farm Labor: The Wealth Paradox', *World Bank Economic Review* 17(2): 197–228.
Bourguignon, F., F. H. G. Ferreira and P. G. Leite (2003) 'Conditional Cash Transfers, Schooling, and Child Labor: Microsimulating Brazil's Bolsa Escola Program', *World Bank Economic Review* 17(2): 229–54.
Brown, D., A. Deardorff and R. M. Stern (2003) 'Child Labour: Theory, Evidence and Policy', in K. Basu, H. Horn, L. Roman and J. Shapiro (eds), *International Labour Standards*, Malden, MA: Blackwell.
Chau, N. and R. Kanbur (2002) 'The Adoption of International Labor Standards: Who, When, and Why', *Brookings Trade Forum 2001*, Washington, DC: Brookings Institution.
Doepke, M. and F. Zilibotti (2004) 'The Macroeconomics of Child Labor Regulation', Los Angeles: UCLA, mimeo.
Drèze, J. and G. Kingdon (1999) 'School Participation in Rural India', Development Economics Discussion Paper 18, London: LSE.
Edmonds, E. (2005) 'Does Child Labor Decline with Improving Economic Status?', *Journal of Human Resources* 40(1): 77–99.

Edmonds, E. and N. Pavcnik (2005) 'Child Labor in the Global Economy', *Journal of Economic Perspectives* 19(1): 199–220.

Emerson, P. M. and A. P. Souza (2002) 'Is There a Child Labor Trap? Intergenerational Persistence of Child Labor in Brazil', *Economic Development and Cultural Change* 51(2): 375–98.

Engerman, S. (1973) 'Some Considerations Relating to Property Rights in Man', *Journal of Economic History* 33: 43–65.

Genicot, G. (2002) 'Bonded Labor and Serfdom: A Paradox of Voluntary Choice', *Journal of Development Economics* 67(1): 101–27.

Hildenbrand, W. and A. Kirman (1988) *Equilibrium Analysis*, Amsterdam: North-Holland.

Hoff, K. and J. Stiglitz (2001) 'Modern Economic Theory and Development', in G. Meier and J. Stiglitz (eds), *Frontiers of Development Economics*, Oxford: Oxford University Press.

Humphries, J. (2003) 'The Parallels between the Past and the Present', in K. Basu, H. Horn, L. Roman and J. Shapiro (eds), *International Labour Standards*, Malden, MA: Blackwell.

ILO (2001) *Stopping Forced Labour*, Geneva: ILO.

───── (2002) *Every Child Counts: New Global Estimates on Child Labour*, Geneva: ILO.

Kabeer, N. (2000) *The Power to Choose: Bangladeshi Women and Labor Market Decisions in London and Dhaka*, London: Verso.

Kanbur, R. (2003) 'On Obnoxious Markets', in P. K. Pattanaik and S. Cullenberg (eds), *Globalization, Culture, and the Limits of the Market: Essays in Economics and Philosophy*, New Delhi: Oxford University Press.

Krueger, A. (1997) 'International Labor Standards and Trade', *Annual World Bank Conference on Development Economics 1996*, Washington, DC: World Bank.

Levison, D., K. Moe and F. Knaul (2001) 'Youth Education and Work in Mexico', *World Development* 29: 167–88.

Lopez-Calva, L.-F. (2003) 'Social Norms, Coordination and Policy Issues in the Fight against Child Labour', in K. Basu, H. Horn, L. Roman and J. Shapiro (eds), *International Labour Standards*, Malden, MA: Blackwell.

Maskus, K. (1997) 'Should Core Labor Standards be Imposed through International Trade Policy', Washington, DC: International Trade Division, World Bank, mimeo.

Matsuyama, K. (1992) 'The Market Size, Entrepreneurship and the Big Push', *Journal of Japanese and International Economics* 6: 347–64.

Mill, J. S. (1848) *Principles of Political Economy*, 1970 edn, Harmondsworth: Penguin.

───── (1859) *On Liberty*, London: Parker.

Murphy, K. M., A. Shleifer and R. Vishny (1989) 'Industrialization and the Big Push', *Journal of Political Economy* 97(5): 1003–26.

Neeman, Z. (1999) 'The Freedom to Contract and the Free-Rider Problem', *Journal of Law, Economics and Organization* 15(3): 685–703.

Nurkse, R. (1953) *Problems of Capital Formation in Underdeveloped Countries*, New York: Oxford University Press.

Parfit, D. (1984) *Persons and Reasons*, Oxford: Clarendon Press.

Rakshit, M. (2002) *The East Asian Currency Crisis*, New Delhi: Oxford University Press.

Ravallion, M. and Q. Wodon (2000) 'Does Child Labor Displace Schooling? Evidence on Behavioral Responses to an Enrollment Study', *Economic Journal* 110: 158–76.

Ray, R. (2000) 'Analysis of Child Labor in Peru and Pakistan: A Comparative Study', *Journal of Population Economics* 13(1): 3–19.

Rosati, F. C. and M. Rossi (2003) 'Children's Working Hours and School Enrollment: Evidence from Pakistan and Nicaragua', *World Bank Economic Review* 17: 283–96.

Rosenstein-Rodan, P. N. (1948) 'Problems of Industrialization in Eastern and South Eastern Europe', *Economic Journal* 53: 202–11.

Satz, D. (2003) 'Child Labor: A Normative Perspective', *World Bank Economic Review* 17: 297–310.

———— (2004) 'Noxious Markets: Why Should Some Things Not Be for Sale?', in P. K. Pattanaik and S. Cullenberg (eds), *Globalization, Culture, and the Limits of the Market: Essays in Economics and Philosophy*, New Delhi: Oxford University Press.

Sen, A. (1997) 'Individual Preference as the Basis of Social Choice', in K. J. Arrow, A. Sen and K. Suzumura (eds), *Social Choice Re-examined*, London: Macmillan.

———— (1999) *Development as Freedom*, New York: Alfred Knopf.

———— (2003) 'Processes, Liberty and Rights', in A. Sen (ed.), *Rationality and Freedom*, Cambridge, MA: Harvard University Press.

Singh, N. (2003) 'The Theory of International Labour Standards', in K. Basu, H. Horn, L. Roman and J. Shapiro (eds), *International Labour Standards*, Malden, MA: Blackwell.

Tuttle, C. (1999) *Hard at Work in Factories and Mines: The Economics of Child Labor during the British Industrial Revolution*, Boulder, CO: Westview Press.

US Department of Labor (1990) 'Worker Rights in Export Processing Zones', *Foreign Labor Trends* 90-32, Washington, DC: US Department of Labor.

Winters, L. A. (2003) 'Trade and Labour Standards: To Link or Not to Link?', in K. Basu, H. Horn, L. Roman and J. Shapiro (eds), *International Labour Standards*, Malden, MA: Blackwell.

8
Rethinking Growth Strategies
Dani Rodrik

A brief roadmap

This chapter focuses on growth because we can all agree that achieving sustained poverty reduction around the world will be practically impossible unless economic growth is achieved in poor countries. In addressing *rethinking* economic growth strategies I will explain in greater detail that the kind of certainty and consensus that existed in the mid-1990s about the appropriate policy framework for economic growth has almost disappeared. And it is not clear what is going to replace it. I therefore make the case for a particular way of thinking about designing growth strategies. These ideas are still in their early stages of development and have been undertaken jointly in work with a number of my colleagues at Harvard, including, most significantly, Ricardo Hausmann, Lant Pritchett and Andres Velasco. I would like to acknowledge their contribution upfront.

Let me offer an overview of the chapter: the groundwork covers a number of propositions which I believe almost everybody agrees on by now, and I will try to cover this in a non-controversial way because I think that starting from such a common ground is important. I shall argue that there are basically two ways that one can go from here. The more conventional way, which has now been developing for some time, is what I call the *Augmented Washington Consensus*, which is the old Washington Consensus augmented, enlarged and expanded with a number of deeper institutional/governance reforms. I shall argue that this is not a very helpful way of thinking about growth strategies, for a number of reasons. Then I shall present an alternative, which I think is more practical, and is likely to be more productive. Before I get into that alternative approach, I shall take a quick detour and say something about an empirical effort to identify some of the correlates of what we call *growth accelerations*; periods of increased economic growth sustained over the medium term. This is important empirical background to the alternative framework that I am going to outline at the end of the chapter.

This alternative framework is really a diagnostic strategy; so, unlike the Washington Consensus or the Augmented Washington Consensus, it is not a list of dos and don'ts. It is a framework for *figuring out* what to do (and maybe what not to do) in different kinds of cases and different kinds of countries. It is a strategy for identifying areas where the greatest returns to economic reform are. I shall illustrate the power of that strategy with a couple of country cases at the end of the chapter.

The common ground

Let me start with where I think that we stand at present. First, I think that everybody would accept that a lot of reform has actually taken place since the 1980s. This is particularly true in Latin America. Figure 8.1 shows an index of structural reform that was computed at the Inter-American Development Bank. Latin America is the region where the accepted wisdom about what to do to achieve economic growth was adopted with the greatest amount of enthusiasm. I think it is also fair to say that if we had a similar index of how much reform has taken place in SSA, we would find that there was a lot of 'structural' reform in SSA as well. Markets are freer, economies are more open and inflation is lower in most SSA countries today than was the case in the 1980s. I think that most people would agree that when we evaluate the nature of policies today in Latin America and in most of SSA, then – by the conventional standards of how much liberalization, how much privatization, how much macroeconomic stabilization, how much

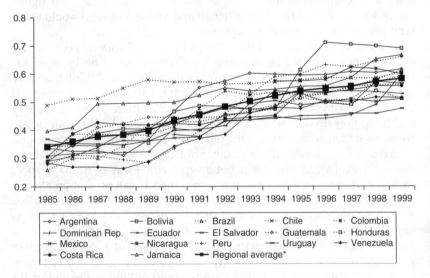

Figure 8.1 Structural reform index for Latin American countries, 1985–99
Source: Lora (2001).

openness to trade has actually taken place – the quality of policies in these two important regions is much better than it was in the 1970s and 1980s. A lot of reform *has* taken place.

But, over time, there has been a growing recognition that the response to these reforms has been less than spectacular. There have been many efforts in the literature to try to estimate the contribution to economic growth of the conventional economic reforms inspired by the Washington Consensus. Without going into the details of that literature, I think it is now commonly accepted that the countries that adopted this agenda have underperformed. The simplest way to see this is to focus on the experience of Latin America.

Latin America at the beginning of the 1990s faced a bigger convergence gap with the advanced industrial countries than it did in the previous three or four decades. So just on account of the convergence factor alone we would have expected Latin America to grow faster in the 1990s, without making allowance for the 'improved' nature of Latin America's policies. As we can see from Figure 8.2, during the 1990s Latin America grew more slowly not only compared to other parts of the world, in particular Asia, but also compared to its own performance in the 1960s and 1970s. That is a *striking* empirical fact, the importance of which is hard to downplay. After all, the Latin America of the 1960s and 1970s was a region of import substitution, macroeconomic populism and protectionism, while the Latin America of the 1990s was a region of openness, privatization and liberalization. The cold fact is that *per capita* economic growth performance was abysmal during the 1990s by any standards. That is also true of productivity performance, so one

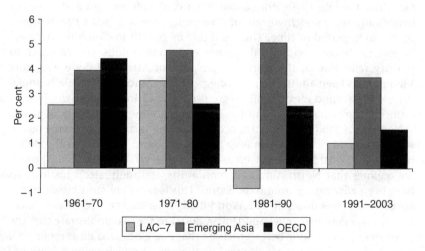

Figure 8.2   Response to reforms has been weak at best

Notes: Regional GDP *per capita*. Asia includes Indonesia, Korea, Malaysia, the Philippines and Thailand. The LAC–7 (Latin America and Caribbean 7) comprise Argentina, Brazil, Chile, Colombia, Mexico, Peru, Venezuela.

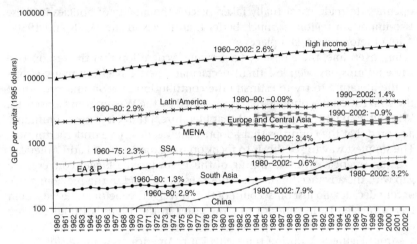

Figure 8.3   Economic performances, 1960–2002

cannot simply ascribe this to the adverse short-run effects of economic reform. When one looks at economywide TFP growth in Latin America, one finds that it was considerably lower than in the 1950s or 1960s or 1970s – periods of import substitution.

The good news of course is that, while Latin America and Africa have done very poorly, some of the poorest parts of the world have in fact done extremely well (Figure 8.3). In particular, China increased its *per capita* growth rate since the late 1970s from about 3 per cent to 8 per cent and more – a historically unprecedented rate of economic growth, when sustained over such a long period of time. The rapid rate of growth in China is extremely important because growth there makes a tremendous contribution to poverty reduction in the world. Other parts of Asia have done well, too: Vietnam has been another very strong performer since the late 1980s; India, the world's second most populous country after China, has also doubled its economic growth since around 1980 which is another source of good news.

Now this is good news in terms of outcomes but it contributes to the puzzle with respect to *policies*. There is at best an awkward fit between the policy regimes that exist in the most successful countries of the world and the policy regimes that North American economists and multilateral institutions have been advocating around the world. This is probably most visible in the area of trade liberalization. The World Bank did a study called *Globalization, Growth, and Poverty* (Collier and Dollar, 2001) to try to demonstrate that the countries that had done best were those that had globalized most rapidly. Of course, if one defines 'globalization' as the rate at which countries expand their trade volumes, the rate at which they are attracting foreign investment – that is, if one defines globalization by *outcomes* rather than prevailing policy

Table 8.1 World Bank's 'star globalizers'

Country	Growth rate (1990s)	Trade policies
China	7.1	Average tariff rate 31.2 per cent, NTBs; not a WTO member
Vietnam	5.6	Tariffs range between 30 per cent and 50 per cent, NTBs and state trading, not a WTO member
India	3.3	Tariffs average 50.5 per cent (the highest but one in the world)
Uganda	3.0	Moderate reform

Source: Collier and Dollar (2001: 6).

frameworks – then this conclusion is absolutely right. So one finds that the World Bank's star globalizers – China, India, Uganda and Vietnam – have all increased very rapidly their volumes of foreign trade and in most cases their volumes of inward foreign investment as well. But, of course, if one thought that this was achieved through policies of rapid and across-the-board import liberalization, one would end up very much off the mark (Table 8.1).

In fact, countries such as China, Vietnam and India maintained high rates of import barriers including quantitative restrictions (QRs) until relatively late. Vietnam to this day is not a member of the WTO. And there is something ironic, to say the least, in the empirical reality that the countries that seem to be turning out the best performance in trade are the ones that are playing by different rules: let us call them the 'GATT rules' rather than the WTO rules of world trade. This is just another instance of the paradox that policy regimes in the most successful countries have been highly unorthodox.

Another illustration comes from India (Figure 8.4). India is commonly presented as a case where the standard story fits rather well. The conventional account is that India was a 'sleeping giant' that woke up and started to grow rapidly once there was internal and external liberalization, with the decisive break in policy stance taking place in 1991. The trouble with this story is that it gets the dates and sequence quite wrong. We do not have to carry out any fancy econometrics to realize that rapid economic growth in India started a *full decade* before the liberalization of 1991. Whatever it is that doubled India's economic growth rate, starting some time around 1980, it certainly could not have been the 1991 liberalization. There is a puzzle here, for sure.

One could also expand the discussion to the earlier period of growth miracles and talk about the 'East Asian tigers' of Taiwan and Singapore, where the policy frameworks were also quite anomalous, essentially combining many of the orthodox ideas about outward orientation and the importance of the private sector with considerable microeconomic interventions, industrial policies, trade protection and so forth (Table 8.2). But those stories are quite well known and I do not need to repeat them here.

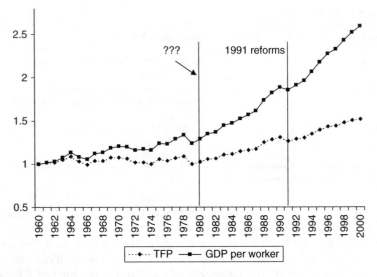

Figure 8.4 The Indian economic take-off, 1960–2000
Source: Bosworth and Collins (2003).

Table 8.2 East Asian anomalies

Institutional domain	Standard ideal	'East Asian' pattern
Property rights	Private, enforced by the rule of law	Private, but government authority occasionally overrides the law (especially in Korea)
Corporate governance	Shareholder ('outsider') control, protection of shareholder rights	Insider control
Business–government relations	Arms' length, rule-based	Close interactions
Industrial organization	Decentralized, competitive markets, with tough anti-trust enforcement	Horizontal and vertical integration in production (*chaebol*); government-mandated 'cartels'
Financial system	Deregulated, securities-based, with free entry Prudential supervision through regulatory oversight	Bank-based, restricted entry, heavily controlled by government, directed lending, weak formal regulation
Labour markets	Decentralized, de-institutionalized, 'flexible' labour markets	Lifetime employment in core enterprises (Japan)

Continued

Table 8.2 Continued

Institutional domain	Standard ideal	'East Asian' pattern
International capital flows	'Prudently' free	Restricted (until 1990s)
Public ownership	None in productive sectors	Plenty in upstream industries

I said that the successful countries followed unorthodox policy agendas. But as these summaries indicate, one can characterize what they did, at a sufficiently high level of generality, as deploying unorthodox policies in the service of orthodox ends – such as openness, macroeconomic stability, private entrepreneurship and so on. Hence I think that it is possible to come up with certain general principles that have applied in all of these cases: all successful countries have, in one form or another, provided for effective property rights protection and contract enforcement; all successful countries have maintained macroeconomic stability; they have all sought to integrate into the world economy; they all have had a supportive environment for private enterprise and private investment; they have all provided for effective prudential regulation of their financial sectors; etc. One can indeed generate a list of commonalities in these countries; however, we cannot take these relatively abstract ends – such as property rights protection, effective prudential regulation, sound money and sustainable public finance, support of private investment – and come up with well-defined policy prescriptions that are valid for all countries at all times. Another way of stating this is that we can have a relatively easy time specifying the desirable functions that good institutions and appropriate reform agendas must produce, but we have a very difficult time specifying the form or the design that such arrangements have to take. The blueprints that we are looking for seem to be highly context-specific.

Let me illustrate that point more concretely by quoting at length an interesting passage from a lecture that Larry Summers gave in 2003. His theme was economic growth and he was trying to make the argument that we actually do know a fair bit about what produces it. The operative part of his lecture went as follows:

> I will suggest that the rate at which countries grow is substantially determined by three things: their *ability* to integrate with the global economy through trade and investment; their *capacity* to maintain sustainable government finances and sound money; and their *ability* to put in place an institutional environment in which contracts can be enforced and property rights can be established. I would challenge anyone to identify a country that has done all three of these things and has not grown at a substantial rate. (Summers, 2003, emphasis added)

I have italicized some key words here because what Summers is really telling us is that we can only specify some abstract general abilities and capacities to achieve certain outcomes, and not specific policies. Does the ability to integrate with the world economy come necessarily with openness to imports and capital flows? Does sustainable government finance and sound money imply independent central banks, floating exchange rates and inflation targeting? Does a good institutional environment mean an Anglo-American-type corporate governance regime, or even a legal regime based on private property? Not if the experience of the growth champions of the last half-century is any guide. So we can agree with Larry Summers that property rights and contract enforcement, openness, sound money and sustainable fiscal balances are important. But that still leaves a whole lot unanswered as to how we can achieve these things. If the example of China, India and Vietnam, and before them other successful Asian countries, is any guide, these outcomes can be achieved – and, indeed, typically are achieved – through highly divergent or heterodox institutional arrangements.

I would like to illustrate this further with the experience of China, because China makes such a good example (Table 8.3). Consider the following thought experiment; suppose you were asked to go and advise the Chinese government in 1978 about the reforms they should undertake. The first thing that you would find is that China is mostly a rural country and the vast majority of the poor live in the countryside. You would immediately note that the reason for poverty is low agricultural productivity. What might the solution be? It would not take long to realize that the problem is largely one of central planning: farmers are told how much to produce and at what price. So the first recommendation is to *liberalize the price system* and to allow farmers to produce and sell at market-determined prices. But that would not be enough because, after all, these are farmers who do not own their own means of production, land. Market pricing alone does not give farmers the right incentives to improve productivity and make the right production and saving decisions. So price liberalization would have to be supplemented with the *privatization of*

Table 8.3 The indeterminacy of institutional forms: a Chinese counterfactual

Problem	Solution
Low agricultural productivity	Price liberalization
Private incentives	Land privatization
Fiscal revenues	Tax reform
Urban wages	Corporatization
Monopoly	Trade liberalization
Enterprise restructuring	Financial sector reform
Unemployment	Safety nets
And so on ...	

land. You cannot stop there either, because the moment you eliminate central planning, institute market pricing and privatize land, you immediately run into a public finance problem. The problem is that the government relies on the implicit tax that it derives from purchasing crops from the communes at low prices and selling them at somewhat higher prices in urban areas. If you simply get the government out of this, then you have the problem that the underlying fiscal revenue of the government will collapse and you will face a macroeconomic problem. So the next recommendation on your list has got to be *tax reform*: to find alternative tax instruments in order to make up for the lost revenue that privatization and price liberalization entail.

But the problems are not over yet. The moment that you liberalize prices and abolish the state order system, workers in urban areas no longer have access to food rations at below market prices in government-run stores. Now they will want higher wages in order to deal with higher food prices, and that means that you will have to provide urban enterprises with the ability to pay higher wages. Because these are state enterprises, you will have to give them some autonomy with which they can decide on their wage and price decisions and respond to demands for higher wages. This calls for *corporatization of state enterprises*, at the very least. This creates another problem. The state enterprises are huge behemoths that can exercise monopoly power if given the freedom to raise prices. How are you going to deal with that? The easiest way is to import price discipline from abroad through *trade liberalization*. But once you liberalize trade you have to worry about the problem of inefficient enterprises. How are they going to be restructured? That obviously requires in turn *financial sector reforms* so you can lubricate the process of restructuring. And if you are restructuring you are also going to get unemployment and so you had better have some *safety nets* in place to deal with that. And so on and so forth.

By the time you have run through these things and you look at everything that you have to do you have basically arrived at the standard Washington Consensus agenda. My first conclusion from this thought experiment is to underscore the point that the Washington Consensus agenda is not silly. When you think systematically about how different areas of reform are related to each other, you end up with a list of reforms that are quite similar, as we have just seen in the context of China's reforms. The policy advisor who went through this process would be entirely justified in feeling really good about a job well done, having actually foreseen *ex ante* how each one of these things is complementary and how some of them would not work without the others. On the other hand, you can also imagine how the Chinese government might have reacted to this long list of reforms; they would likely have thought: this reform business is really tricky; maybe we should not do it for another ten years.

The Chinese experience is interesting because we know what actually happened. We know that the Chinese government did reform, but they did not do any of what we have just discussed. What the Chinese government did was entirely different (Box 8.1). Rather than liberalizing the markets wholesale and

210   Rethinking Growth Strategies

Box 8.1 Chinese shortcuts

- *Household responsibility system* and *TVEs* obviate the need for ownership reforms
- *Two-track pricing* insulates public finance from the provision of supply incentives
- *Federalism, 'Chinese-style'* generates incentives for policy competition and institutional innovation.

---

eliminating central planning, what they did was institute a two-track pricing system and then grafted a market pricing system on top of the state order system. The nice thing was that two-track pricing insulates public finance from the provision of private incentives. This was a practical solution that they arrived at experimentally, by having confidence in their ability to generate home-grown reforms. The reason that two-track pricing insulates public finance from the provision of supply incentives is that incentives matter only at the margin: so as long as farmers can trade at the margin at market-determined prices it does not matter if inframarginal units have to be sold to the state at below-market prices. So you get efficiency but you also maintain the existing form of public finance for the state.

Similarly in the area of property rights, rather than institute private ownership in land and in industry, the Chinese government instead implemented various institutional innovations, such as the 'household responsibility system' and township and village enterprises (TVEs). TVEs are particularly interesting. They were able to elicit inordinate amounts of private investment and acted as the engine of growth for the economy throughout the mid-1990s. They were thus clearly effective in providing some form of property rights and in stimulating private entrepreneurship, and one wonders how exactly that was achieved in the absence of *private* property rights. One possible explanation is that in the absence of a well-functioning judiciary, private entrepreneurs are better protected through alliances with local government – their most likely expropriator – than through the legal system. A private property rights system, which is the default mode of legal reform, relies on efficient third-party enforcement of contracts. In advanced industrial countries, this is achieved through the courts. In a transitional economy, courts can hardly be expected to work well. Consider Russia, for example, which tried to do property rights reform the conventional way and generated very little real, effective property rights because of the inefficiency and corruption of its judiciary. The comparison between the two transitional economies shows that it might be a lot easier to achieve effective property rights when entrepreneurs ally themselves with local governments than when they throw themselves on the mercy of the courts.

The point is not that China did everything right and that all countries have to imitate them. What I am trying to illustrate is a much more general issue about the multiplicity, or the non-uniqueness, of institutional arrangements that achieve desirable ends. So if our objective is to achieve productive efficiency (whether of the static or dynamic kind), there are some universal principles such as property rights, market-oriented incentives and the rule of law. These are 'universal' in the sense that you can just get off the plane in any country that you have never been to, knowing nothing about that country, and still come out and prescribe property rights, incentives and the rule of law. There is no chance you could possibly be wrong, since it is difficult to think of circumstances under which the pursuit of these ends (in the appropriate manner of course) could be bad for the economy. The real issue is not these general principles but how we are going to accomplish them. The operational question is: how do we map these principles into practical guidelines? By 'non-uniqueness', what I have in mind is that these principles do not map uniquely into specific designs. We need reform strategies that are sensitive to domestic opportunities and constraints. That is the essential lesson of the Chinese strategy.

I turn now to the last point on which I think that by now there is fair amount of agreement. Since we know less than we thought we did, and since a lot of the actual success on the ground depends on how we craft these highly specific policies, then it is going to be desirable to allow national governments to have some degree of *space* and room for manoeuvre for policy experimentation. We see this new-found emphasis on experimentation in a number of different ways. We see it in academic work, which is increasingly emphasizing the amorphous nature of institutions and the need for policy experimentation. We also see it at the level of international lending agencies, where there is much more talk about 'country ownership'. Poverty reduction and growth strategies (PRSPs) are now supposed to be the result of some domestic deliberative process.

There is a groping toward an alternative, but what that alternative is remains unclear. There is, in fact, the danger that one can take the kind of arguments I have been outlining here and end up with a nihilistic attitude which suggests there is very little that economists, as development professionals, can actually do to help governments. I am going to argue that this is not the right way to go, either. 'Anything goes' is not the right policy message.

The false alternative

One alternative that has been shaping up for some time is what I call the *Augmented Washington Consensus* (Table 8.4). The idea here is that we basically keep adding things on to the policy agenda as prevailing policies continue to disappoint. Sometimes this agenda is called 'second-generation reforms'. I remember a Latin American finance minister explaining, in all seriousness, how his country had done all the second-generation reforms, and even the third-generation ones, and now was on to the fourth generation. The economy of this country was stagnant.

Table 8.4 The Washington Consensus and 'Augmented' Washington Consensus: what to avoid

Original Washington Consensus	'Augmented' Washington Consensus ... the previous ten items, plus
1 Fiscal discipline	11 Corporate governance
2 Reorientation of public expenditures	12 Anti-corruption
3 Tax reform	13 Flexible labour markets
4 Interest rate liberalization	14 Adherence to WTO disciplines
5 Unified and competitive exchange rates	15 Adherence to international financial codes and standards
6 Trade liberalization	16 'Prudent' capital account opening
7 Openness to DFI	17 Non-intermediate exchange rate regimes
8 Privatization	18 Independent central banks/ inflation targeting
9 Deregulation	19 Social safety nets
10 Secure property rights	20 Targeted poverty reduction

This is actually quite a widespread phenomenon: as the growth response to the standard reforms ends up being very weak, we have the tendency to say that obviously this was not enough and we need to do more. So if trade liberalization did not work well, this must be because labour markets were not flexible enough, with the implication that the next set of reforms have to be in the area of labour markets. If opening up the financial markets did not work, it was because prudential regulation was weak, so now we are in need of international financial codes and standards and improved financial governance. If privatization did not work well, maybe that was because we lacked good enough social safety nets. People who lost their jobs became upset, which undercut the legitimacy of privatization. So social safety nets need more attention; and so on.

With the list of reforms augmented in this fashion, the immediate issue is how one *prioritizes* them. The current approach can be summarized, with little exaggeration, as one of: *do whatever you can as much as you can as quickly as you can.* As a matter of basic economics this represents a faulty strategy. When we are in second-best situations, it is simply not true that any reform is good; or that the more areas are reformed or the deeper the reform in a single area, the better off you are. This is just a simple matter of second-best economics.

What I am going to suggest here is an alternative, focused on trying to identify the most binding constraints on economic growth. What we should be after are the *distortions* that hurt the most at any point in time.

The empirics of growth accelerations

Before I get into a discussion of growth diagnostics, let me take a quick detour through some empirical work. I want to ask what happens when countries all of a sudden start to grow. While there is a huge literature on cross-country growth empirics, surprisingly none of this literature has actually looked at what happens just around the time when countries start to grow. The basic theory of economic growth is that if you have a really meaningful economic reform at time t, then that is going to be rewarded by a significant increase in the economic growth rate at that time t (Figure 8.5). If you are in the world of neoclassical growth models with diminishing returns to reproducible factors of production, then the growth bonus will be temporary. If you are in the world of endogenous growth models where there are no diminishing returns, then this growth effect could be permanent. But, in either case, if you want to see what kind of things actually cause increases in growth, you should look at what happens just when these growth accelerations take place. The standard growth regressions do not do this. They simply stack different time periods on top of each other, with five or ten-year averages. They do not look for the *turning points in growth*.

So the exercise that I want to report on is one that looks at what happens during these periods of growth acceleration. First, I need to define what 'growth acceleration' is. In joint work with Ricardo Hausmann and Lant Pritchett (2004), we defined a growth acceleration as an increase in a country's growth rate by at least 2 percentage points per annum. We also required that growth be at least 3.5 per cent per annum subsequent to the acceleration. Finally, since we do not want to pick up cases of rebound after prolonged crises, we also required that the level of income exceed the pre-acceleration peak level. Our time horizon is eight years, so we look for

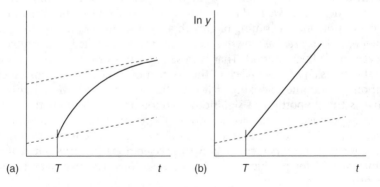

Figure 8.5 Growth accelerations: what does the theory say? Effect of improvement in growth fundamentals at time t. (a) Neo-classical growth model; (b) Endogenous growth model

increases in growth rates of 2 percentage points per annum that are maintained for at least eight years.

The first question is how many countries have actually experienced these significant growth accelerations. The surprise, to me at least, was that these things happen very frequently (Table 8.5). When we exclude the eight years at the beginning and eight years at the end of our time sample, we are left with the period between 1957 and 1992 over which we can search for growth accelerations. The pleasant surprise was that we identified no fewer than eighty-three cases of growth acceleration over this period. These were drawn from all parts of the world, including SSA. Even though they are concentrated in the 1960s and 1970s in SSA rather than in more recent decades, it is striking that even here there is a large number of countries that managed to experience these growth accelerations. The minimum increase in growth we required is 2 percentage points, but in practice many of these growth accelerations involved jumps in the growth rate of a much larger magnitude – up to 8 or 9 percentage points. These are huge increases in economic growth. Of course, most of these accelerations were not sustained. If we add the more demanding requirement that these growth accelerations be sustained not for most of the decade, but for two decades, then basically around half of them disappear. Nevertheless, getting such an increase in growth for the better part of a decade is not a bad thing. The question is: what causes these growth accelerations?

The disappointing part of the empirical exercise was to find that these growth accelerations tend to be highly unpredictable (Table 8.6). We grouped the potential determinants of growth accelerations under three headings. One is *economic* reform – that is, economic liberalization in the conventional sense of opening up and stabilizing the economy. The second is changes in the nature of *political* regime. The third is changes in *external circumstances*, which we captured by changes to the terms of trade. Focusing on economic liberalization, what we find is that the match between significant economic liberalization and the timing of growth accelerations is *extremely* imperfect. *Fewer than 15 per cent of* growth accelerations were preceded or accompanied by economic liberalization. That is to say that the vast majority of growth accelerations *do not* take place in the context of standard economic liberalization programmes. Looking at it the other way around, we can also ask: what is the proportion of significant economic liberalizations that subsequently produced growth accelerations? There, the ratio is less than one in five. So only about 18 per cent of significant economic liberalizations are subsequently accompanied by growth accelerations. It turns out that our principal tool for producing growth accelerations has very weak leverage over the desired outcome.

One plausible reading of this evidence is that we need to think about growth-stimulating policies in a different way. What the numbers suggest is that growth accelerations are actually not that difficult to produce: if we take

Table 8.5 Episodes of rapid growth, by region, decade and magnitude of acceleration, 1957–92

Region	Decade	Country	Year	Growth before	Growth after	Difference in growth
SSA	1950s,	Nigeria	1967	−1.7	7.3	9.0
	1960s	Botswana	1969	2.9	11.7	8.8
		Ghana	1965	−0.1	8.3	8.4
		Guinea Bissau	1969	−0.3	8.1	8.4
		Zimbabwe	1964	0.6	7.2	6.5
		Congo	1969	0.9	5.4	4.5
		Nigeria	1957	1.2	4.3	3.0
	1970s	Mauritius	1971	−1.8	6.7	8.5
		Chad	1973	−0.7	7.3	8.0
		Cameroon	1972	−0.6	5.3	5.9
		Congo PR	1978	3.1	8.2	5.1
		Uganda	1977	−0.6	4.0	4.6
		Lesotho	1971	0.7	5.3	4.6
		Rwanda	1975	0.7	4.0	3.3
		Mali	1972	0.8	3.8	3.0
		Malawi	1970	1.5	3.9	2.5
	1980s,	Guinea Bissau	1988	−0.7	5.2	5.9
	1990s	Mauritius	1983	1.0	5.5	4.4
		Uganda	1989	−0.8	3.6	4.4
		Malawi	1992	−0.8	4.8	5.6
South Asia	1950s 1960s	Pakistan	1962	−2.4	4.8	7.1
	1970s	Pakistan	1979	1.4	4.6	3.2
		Sri Lanka	1979	1.9	4.1	2.2
	1980s	India	1982	1.5	3.9	2.4
East Asia	1950s,	Thailand	1957	−2.5	5.3	7.8
	1960s	Korea	1962	0.6	6.9	6.3
		India	1967	−0.8	5.5	6.2
		Singapore	1969	4.2	8.2	4.0
		Taiwan	1961	3.3	7.1	3.8
	1970s	China	1978	1.7	6.7	5.1
		Malaysia	1970	3.0	5.1	2.1
	1980s,	Malaysia	1988	1.1	5.7	4.6
	1990s	Thailand	1986	3.5	8.1	4.6
		Papua New Guinea	1987	0.3	4.0	3.7
		Korea Rep.	1984	4.4	8.0	3.7
		India	1987	3.4	5.5	2.1
		China	1990	4.2	8.0	3.8
Latin America and Caribbean	1950s, 1960s	Dominican Rep.	1969	−1.1	5.5	6.6
		Brazil	1967	2.7	7.8	5.1
		Peru	1959	0.8	5.2	4.4
		Panama	1959	1.5	5.4	3.9

Continued

Table 8.5 Continued

Region	Decade	Country	Year	Growth before	Growth after	Difference in growth
		Nicaragua	1960	0.9	4.8	3.8
		Argentina	1963	0.9	3.6	2.7
		Colombia	1967	1.6	4.0	2.4
	1970s	Ecuador	1970	1.5	8.4	6.8
		Paraguay	1974	2.6	6.2	3.7
		Trinidad & Tobago	1975	1.9	5.4	3.5
		Panama	1975	2.6	5.3	2.7
		Uruguay	1974	1.5	4.0	2.6
	1980s,	Chile	1986	−1.2	5.5	6.7
	1990s	Uruguay	1989	1.6	3.8	2.1
		Haiti	1990	−2.3	12.7	15.0
		Argentina	1990	−3.1	6.1	9.2
		Dominican Rep.	1992	0.4	6.3	5.8
Middle East	1950s,	Morocco	1958	−1.1	7.7	8.8
and North	1960s	Syria	1969	0.3	5.8	5.5
Africa		Tunisia	1968	2.1	6.6	4.5
		Israel	1967	2.8	7.2	4.4
		Israel	1957	2.2	5.3	3.1
	1970s	Jordan	1973	−3.6	9.1	12.7
		Egypt	1976	−1.6	4.7	6.3
		Syria	1974	2.6	4.8	2.2
		Algeria	1975	2.1	4.2	2.1
	1980s, 1990s	Syria	1989	−2.9	4.4	7.3
OECD	1950s,	Spain	1959	4.4	8.0	3.5
	1960s	Denmark	1957	1.8	5.3	3.5
		Japan	1958	5.8	9.0	3.2
		USA	1961	0.9	3.9	3.0
		Canada	1962	0.6	3.6	2.9
		Ireland	1958	1.0	3.7	2.7
		Belgium	1959	2.1	4.5	2.4
		New Zealand	1957	1.5	3.8	2.4
		Australia	1961	1.5	3.8	2.3
		Finland	1958	2.7	5.0	2.2
		Finland	1967	3.4	5.6	2.2
	1980s,	Portugal	1985	1.1	5.4	4.3
	1990s	Spain	1984	0.1	3.8	3.7
		Ireland	1985	1.6	5.0	3.4
		UK	1982	1.1	3.5	2.5
		Finland	1992	1.0	3.7	2.8
		Norway	1991	1.4	3.7	2.2

Source: Hausmann, Pritchett and Rodrik (2004).

Table 8.6   Predictability of growth accelerations

(a) All growth episodes

Proportion of growth accelerations that are preceded or accompanied by:

Economic liberalization	14.5
Political regime change	50.6
External shock	27.5

Proportion of occurrences of column variable that is accompanied or followed by growth accelerations:

Economic liberalization	18.2
Political regime change	13.6
External shock	5.1

(b) Sustained growth episodes only

Proportion of growth accelerations that are preceded or accompanied by:

Economic liberalization	16.2
Political regime change	56.8
External shock	23.5

Proportion of occurrences of column variable that is accompanied or followed by growth accelerations:

Economic liberalization	9.1
Political regime change	7.1
External shock	1.4

Notes: Figures are percentages. As in the probits, we allow for a five-year lag between a change in the underlying determinant and a growth acceleration. The timing of the growth acceleration is the three-year window centred on the initiation dates shown in Table 8.5.

Source: Hausmann, Rodrik and Velasco (2004).

our numbers at face value what they imply is that a country has a one-in-five chance of achieving a growth acceleration in any decade. So these things are not that difficult to achieve, but what sets them off is apparently not ambitious economic reform programmes but highly idiosyncratic changes. In all of these cases something happened that unleashed growth, at least for a certain period of time, and what that was seems highly dependent on the conditions of the different countries.

A diagnostic strategy for reforms

So this is where the diagnostic approach to growth strategies comes from. The idea is to identify, for each country, the area where the 'biggest bang' for the reform buck lies. *A priori* there is no reason to think that these areas are going to be identical in different countries. If we actually were able to undertake such a diagnostic exercise, we would then have a pointer to the distortions that we need to tackle first to get the largest response in terms of economic growth.

Let me briefly outline how such a growth diagnostic could be done:

$$\underbrace{g}_{\text{growth}} = \sigma \left\{ \underbrace{\left(\left(\underbrace{\frac{1 - \tau}{\text{appropriability}}\right) \times \underbrace{\rho}_{\text{social return}} \right)}_{\text{private return to accumulation}} - \underbrace{r}_{\text{cost of financing accumulation}} \right\}$$

The equation comes from any standard model of economic growth, and says that along a balanced-growth path, the rate at which an economy is growing depends on three things:

- The *social return to accumulation* in its broad sense; that is, the return from accumulating physical capital, human capital, entrepreneurship, technology and so forth
- The extent to which the social return is *appropriable by private entrepreneurs*, which we call appropriability
- The cost of *financing accumulation*.

Obviously the higher the social return, the higher the accumulation and the growth rate of the economy. But you could be in an economy where the underlying productivity was very high, but investors could not appropriate the private returns because taxes were high, property rights were not well protected, macroeconomic risk was too high and so on, such that private appropriability was low. Then the economy would grow slowly despite the high social returns. On the other side of the ledger, growth could also be depressed because the cost of capital was too high. Obviously the higher the cost of capital, the more scarce are investible resources in the economy, and the lower will be the amount of investment that can be financed. The equation provides us with a taxonomy that differentiates, at the most aggregate level, among three different reasons why the rate of growth of an economy is low. It could be that the cost of capital is too high, or the social return to investment is too low, or appropriability is low.

The first step in the analysis is to try to figure out which among these three seem to be the *most binding constraint*. Is growth low because of inadequate social returns to investment, inadequate private appropriability of the returns, or inadequate access to finance? You can think of this exercise as going through a decision tree (Figure 8.6). Depending on which branches of this decision tree we choose, different areas of reforms are implicated and different policies called for. So if the problem is one of low private returns and we decide that the issue is one of poor appropriability, we want to ask next whether the problem originates with micro-risks or macro-risks. If it is micro-risks, is it a question of property rights, corruption, or taxes? If it is a question of macro-risk, is it something to do with financial markets and

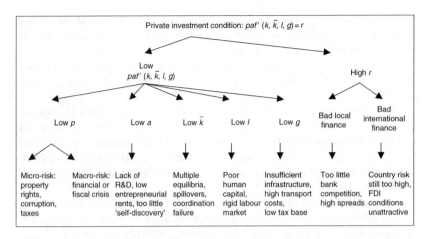

Figure 8.6   Problem: low levels of private investment and entrepreneurship

Notes: p private appropriability; a total factor productivity; k individual capital stock; l labour input; $\bar{k}$ aggregate capital stock; g government-provided infrastructure; r domestic lending rate.

Source: Hausmann, Rodrik and Velasco (2004).

probability of fiscal crises? If this is a case of low social returns, is it due to poor infrastructure, low level or poor quality of complementary factors of production (such as skills), or poor geography? If it is low appropriability, maybe it has to do with externalities of some kind rather than poor institutions or macro-risk *per se*, so we may want to examine things such as information spillovers or coordination failures. On the other hand, if it is a question of high cost of capital, or a scarcity of investible resources, then we need to ask whether the problem originates from low savings domestically, poor domestic intermediation, or poor integration with the international financial markets (for example, collateral constraints and other items that reduce a country's access to foreign borrowing).

Fundamentally if we are able to carry out this exercise, then we would have a much better ability to focus our effort. We could focus political capital and administrative resources on areas where the returns were the largest. So a country where private returns are very high but investment is constrained by lack of investible resources and very high cost of capital, for example, will respond very differently to the provision of foreign aid than an economy where the problem is not access to investible resources or low savings or high cost of capital, but either low social returns to capital or low appropriability by private investors of the existing returns. In that second type of economy, foreign aid is not going to achieve much. Or foreign aid would be much better targeted at increasing appropriability for private investors instead of supplementing domestic saving. If private returns are low due to disadvantageous geography, poor infrastructure, or low levels of complementary factors of production such as human capital, we would want to focus instead on education, or on improving public infrastructure and transport links with the rest of the world. Poor property rights or high taxes will call for yet another focus. These are very obvious things, but it is remarkable how little these kinds of ideas have actually been put into practice when designing country programmes.

Let me give a couple of concrete illustrations of how this kind of approach can be useful. Hausmann, Rodrik and Velasco (2004) lay out the theoretical foundations for the diagnostic approach, and discuss a number of empirical illustrations. In that paper, we report mini-case studies of Brazil, the Dominican Republic and El Salvador. Here I focus on the first two which will be adequate to make the point.

El Salvador and Brazil look, in some respects, very similar because they both have low investment-to-GDP ratios (relative to their own historical averages) and they have both been growing recently at low rates, again relative to their historical trends. But when looking closely, following the diagnostic approach and running through the decision tree, it turns out that they are suffering from very different problems. The nature of the 'binding constraints' is very different.

El Salvador is an economy where the problem cannot be a high cost of capital or low access to investible resources. This is an economy with low real interest rates, where the banking system is flush with liquidity and where banks cannot find enough borrowers domestically and are actively looking for customers outside the country. It is an economy which receives more than 10 per cent of GDP as transfer of resources from abroad in the form of remittances; yet whenever remittances increase it is not investment that goes up, but domestic savings that goes down. So El Salvador has all the symptoms of an economy where the problems lie not with the high cost of capital, or lack of investible funds, but with poor returns. So, are the poor returns due to poor social returns, or to low appropriability? And if it is low appropriability, does that arise from poor institutional structures and poor property rights or does it arise from some inherent market externalities that reduce the private return of investment even though social returns are high.

It is relatively easy to rule out the hypothesis of poor institutions, since El Salvador is ranked relatively highly in terms of institutional capability by both the World Bank and by private surveys. It cannot be high taxes, either; the country has one of the lowest tax ratios in the continent. It cannot be macroeconomic instability, because the economy is dollarized and has low inflation. So our diagnostic strategy leads us to eliminate most of the likely suspects for low private returns.

Our conclusion in this case, arrived largely through a process of ruling out other explanations, was that El Salvador suffers from lack of incentives for private entrepreneurs to invest in non-traditional areas – too few incentives for 'self-discovery'. This is the result of limitations inherent to a system that is fairly laissez faire in its orientation. One problem is information externalities: investors that undertake forays into new areas generate useful cost information to imitators, and their rents, when successful, are dissipated through imitative entry. Another is coordination failures: the initial investor in, say, pineapples cannot make money unless there are enough other simultaneous investments. One can easily convince oneself that in an economy like El Salvador the most binding constraint is the low return to private investment, which in turn arises from market imperfections that block economic diversification. And this conclusion leads us to think of a proactive role for the government focused on fostering entrepreneurship in non-traditional areas. It leads us, in short, to a rather heterodox agenda of policy reform.

The situation in Brazil is very different. Brazil has all the symptoms of an economy where private returns are very high. In El Salvador, when entrepreneurs were asked what they would do if we gave them US$50 million dollars to invest, we elicited in response mostly silence (and occasionally a suggestion that they would put the money in Miami). In Brazil, there is no problem with figuring out areas where there are profitable investment opportunities: the private sector is teeming with such ideas. If investment is not higher, the reason is that real interest rates are extremely high. It is in fact amazing that there is so much investment in Brazil in view of how high real interest rates are. Investment demand is high, but it is constrained by low domestic saving and a binding external borrowing constraint. So in Brazil it seems to be the financing constraint that binds. That conclusion in turn leads to a policy agenda that is very different from that in El Salvador. The problem is not how to increase returns to investment, but how to reduce the cost of capital. We need to enhance domestic savings, improve domestic intermediation in the banking system and ultimately also increase the value of the collateral that Brazil presents to the international financial market so that the external financing constraint can become less binding.

I hope these two vignettes illustrate how the diagnostic approach can lead to a policy agenda that is much more much focused on the apparent constraints and which therefore economizes on scarce political and administrative resources of the government.

Finally, a word on the Dominican Republic: an example of an economy which grew fairly rapidly until 2002, at which time it collapsed as a result of a financial crisis. Growth in the Dominican Republic was stimulated by removing obstacles that a few key sectors faced, essentially tourism and *maquilas*. When a crunch developed in the financial markets, there was not enough regulatory capacity to prevent a Ponzi scheme from spreading in the financial system. The result was a financial crisis and the end of growth. This is a case that shows how the binding constraint to growth changes over time. In the Dominican Republic, the quality of institutions and of the regulatory system (particularly with respect to financial markets) eventually became the binding constraint. So implementing a growth strategy cannot be a one-time thing. If, say, poor labour skills are not a constraint at the moment, they will surely become one eventually with sufficient growth (if investment in human capital does not keep up).

The diagnostic approach is a useful way of thinking about designing growth strategies, both because it is practical and because it essentially encompasses most existing policy orientations. So if you think that the key to development is greater economic aid, this framework tells you under exactly what circumstances that is true. Maybe there are indeed some countries where economic aid is key, but El Salvador is one case where we can be fairly certain that aid is not going to do much. For those who think that the key lies with the quality of institutions and of governance, the approach helps us figure out the circumstances under which that is indeed true. In neither Brazil, nor El Salvador does this policy agenda seem to be particularly growth-promoting at the moment. The Dominican Republic, by contrast, shows the costs of delaying regulatory reforms once growth has picked up.

Concluding remarks

I hope that I have convinced you that the diagnostic approach is a useful way of looking at growth issues. This approach helps us become more selective and focus our energies on where the returns seem to be the greatest. In this regard, it presents a great advantage relative to the Washington Consensus (in its many variants) with its 'laundry-list' approach to reforms. It also makes better use of what economists have to offer: it asks economists for their guesses of shadow prices of various constraints, and not their subjective evaluation of the political feasibility of different kinds of reforms (which is how the Washington Consensus often gets implemented in practice).

Having said all this, let me end by reminding everyone that I and my colleagues have so far only scratched the surface of this alternative approach. Much more work needs to be done; we are continuing our work on this, and my hope is that we will be joined by others on this productive agenda.

Note

The author thanks Tony Shorrocks for the invitation to present this paper.

References

Bosworth, B. and S. M. Collins (2003) 'The Empirics of Growth: An Update', Washington, DC: Brookings Institution, unpublished paper, 7 March.
Collier, P. and D. Dollar (2001) *Globalization, Growth, and Poverty: Building an Inclusive World Economy*, New York: Oxford University Press for the World Bank.
Hausmann, R., L. Pritchett and D. Rodrik (2004) 'Growth Accelerations', Cambridge, MA: Harvard University, mimeo.

Hausmann, R., D. Rodrik and A. Velasco (2004) 'Growth Diagnostics', Cambridge, MA: Harvard University, mimeo.

Lora, E. (2001) *Structural Reforms in Latin America: What has been Reformed and How to Measure It*, Washington, DC: Inter-American Development Bank, December.

Summers, L. (2003) 'Godkin Lectures', Cambridge, MA: John F. Kennedy School of Government, Harvard University.

Index

Aaberge, R., *et al.* (1997)   51, 70
  Björklund, A.   70
  Jäntti, M.   70
  Pedersen, P. J.   70
  Smith, N.   70
  Wennemo, T.   70
accounting   45(n24)
Acemoglu, D.   167(n1)
actions, class of   191, 193, 194
adaptive efficiency   8, 10–15
  ideology, choices and   11–13
  path dependence   13–14
  transition economies   14–15
Adelman, I.   69(n1)
adjustment assistance (to workers)
  95, 96
adults   187, 193, 194, 196(n16)
affiliations, multiple   101
affirmative action   116, 118, 121,
  124, 126, 127, 128, 132(n28),
  133(n34)
Afghanistan   129
Africa   22, 106, 140, 143, 154, 159, 165,
  168(n17), 179, 204
  migration   162, 163
Agell, J.   70(n7, n10), 166
aggregation   111
'aggregation fallacy' (Bhagwati)   86
agriculture   118, 168(n10–11)
  'basic breakthrough' in economic
    history   7–8
  courses   119
  import-competing   149–50
  reforms   147
aid   23, 76, 220, 222
aid agencies   39
aid donors   xviii, 128, 130, 179,
  196(n6)
air pollution   40–1, 83
airlines   34
Akerlof, G. A.   22, 61, 62, 104, 131(n1),
  132(n14)
Alaska   85
Alesina, A.   43(n7)

Alexander, J.   107
Alexandria   153
Algeria   216t
alienation   122
'alternative development'
  (Kerala model)   77
American Federation of Labour –
  Congress of Industrial Organizations
  (AFL-CIO)   91, 96
Amin, I.   117, 132(n16)
Anand, S.   110, 131–2(n12)
Anand and Sen's measure of
  group-weighted achievements
  131–2(n12)
anthropologists
  'primordialists' versus
    'instrumentalists'   106–7
anthropology   61
anti-capitalism   76–82, 97(n2–5)
anti-corporations   83–5, 97(n6–7)
anti-dumping   34, 45(n26)
anti-globalization   74, 82–3, 93, 95,
  140, 166, 167
  backlash 1913–50 (Williamson)   xix,
    136m 153, 163
  confronted   85–6
Anti-Sweatshop Coalition
  77, 85
anti-trust laws   34, 35, 181
appropriability   218, 219f, 220
'appropriate governance' (Bhagwati)
  of globalization   94–7,
    98–9(n17–20)
  handling possible downsides   94–6,
    98–9(n17–19)
  social change (pace accelerated)   96,
    99(n20)
Argentina   18, 19f, 26t, 88, 144n, 146,
  156, 168(n12, n14), 169(n22), 202f,
  203f, 216t
armed forces   109, 110t, 115t, 116,
  117f, 130
arson   3, 6
Asea, P.   132(n13)

Asia   xx, 5, 87, 140, 143, 148, 151f,
    152, 153, 154, 159, 160, 161t,
    165, 203, 204
    economic performance (1960–2002)
    204f
    emerging   203f
Asian crisis (1997–8)   *see* East Asian crisis
Asian tigers   146, 147, 205
Asians (in UK)   133(n33)
asset inequality   124
asset prices   24
assets   44(n19)
assets and liabilities, corporate   29
assignment models   70(n6)
assumptions   57, 61, 85, 157, 189
    more realistic   58
    total rationality   185
Atkinson, Sir Anthony   xiii, xvii–xviii,
    49, 52n, 53, 54n, 59n, 66, 74
Atkinson measure of inequality
    131–2(n12)
Atlantic economy   140, 142, 150, 156,
    157, 161, 168(n14)
    real wage dispersion (1854–1913)
    155f
atrocities   102
Attack on Inflation (Labour Government,
    UK, 1975)   63
auctions   33, 39
auditing   27
'Augmented Washington Consensus'
    (Rodrik)   201, 202, 211, 212t
Aumann, R.   193
Australia   34, 43(n6), 151f, 151, 159,
    168(n14), 216t
autarky   87–8, 92, 143, 152, 160, 167
automation   53
autonomy   115, 209

'baby-boom' generation (USA)   23
Badgett, M. V. L.   132(n28)
Bagwell, K.   169(n20)
Bairoch, P.   159, 169(n18)
Bakunin, M.   79
Balassa, B.   94
Baldwin, R.   96
Baluchistan   79
Banerjee, A.   197(n31)
Bangkok   153
Bangladesh   144n, 198(n9)

bank lending   28
banking/banking system   24, 179, 219f,
    220, 221
    liberalization   28
    re-capitalization   27
banking crises   25, 26t, 26f, 29
bankruptcy   3, 31
    'firm failures'   24
banks   18, 27–9, 206t
Banks, M.   106
bargaining   60–1
bargaining power   3–4, 89
Barro, R.   21, 43(n8)
Barth, F.   131(n1)
basic needs/necessities   115t,
    116, 149
Basque country   103
Basu, A.   196n
Basu, K.   xiii, xix-xx, 96, 177, 178,
    189, 192, 193, 196(n1, n5, n14),
    197(n22), 197(n26), 198(n32)
Bayet, A.   54n
Becker, G.   90
Becker, I.   52n, 70(n11)
behaviour   101, 105–6, 107, 113,
    131(n1)
    standards   12
behavioural economics   185–7,
    197(n20–1)
Belfast   104
Belgium   151f, 168(n14), 216t
beliefs   12, 15
Ben Bella, M. A.   77
Bernstein, J.   56n
Berry, A.   69(n1)
Bhagwati, J. N.   xiii, xviii, 57, 86–7,
    89, 93–5, 97n, 97(n1, n5, n7),
    98(n9, n11, n13–15), 99(n19–20),
    177, 197(n19)
Biafra   102–3, 108
bias   113, 133(n34)
bilateralism   196(n7)
Bin Laden, O.   107, 131
Björklund, A.   70
Black, S.   90
blacks   125, 132(n29)
    South Africa   121
    UK   133(n33)
Blair, A. C. L.   81
Blanchard, O.   44(n13)

Blattman, C. 168(n12), 169(n26)
Blau, J. R. 113
Blau, P. M. 113
Bolivia 144n, 19f, 202f
Boltho, A. 143
bonded labour 176, 177
border effects 147–8, 168(n7–8)
borrowing 24, 36, 45(n28), 219, 221
  maturity structure 44(n12),
    44–5(n20)
Bosworth, B. 206n
Botswana 215t
Bourdieu, P. 81, 82
Bourguignon, F. 66, 69(n1), 137, 137n,
    142–3
'bowling alone' (Putnam) 80
Brainerd, E. 90
Brazil 6, 18, 19f, 42(n2), 43(n6),
    45(n22), 77, 145, 168(n12, n14),
    169(n22), 197(n18), 202f, 203f,
    215t, 220–2
  black/white inequalities 125, 126f
  horizontal inequalities 114, 125–6,
    127, 132–3(n29–32)
'bread taxes' 164
Bretons 131(n3)
Brightlingsea: Aldous Shipyard 58
Britain *see* United Kingdom
Bromley, Y. 131(n6)
Brown, D. 96, 196(n14)
Bruno, M. 21, 39
budget deficits xvii, 18, 20, 23–4, 31,
    42(n2), 43–4(n8–10, n12)
  'fiscal deficits' 31, 45(n24)
  optimum level (no simple formula)
    23, 43–4(n10)
  see also government budgets
budget surpluses 19
Buenos Aires 86
Bukharin, N. 82–3
Bulgaria 26t
Bumiputera (indigenous peoples of
    Malaysia) 118–19
Burma 157, 168(n12)
Burniaux, J.-M. 146
Burtless, G. 53
Burundi 103, 129, 144n
Bush administration (2001–) 85
business 116
  'big business' 195

business cycles 24
business–government relations 206t

cabinet 109, 110t, 115t, 116, 125
Calcutta: Salt Lake 175, 176, 196(n1)
California 92, 97(n7)
Cameroon 215t
Canada 43(n6), 51–2, 54f, 64–6, 88,
    151f, 151, 156, 159, 168(n14),
    169(n25), 216t
Capie, F. 169(n18)
capital 8, 9, 26, 55, 70(n4), 110t, 118,
    123, 159, 168(n16), 178, 189–90
  access to 27
  cost of 218, 219, 220, 221
  globally-mobile 195
  industrial 150
  international 23
  private 122
  providers of 45(n31)
  social returns 220
capital account transactions 28
capital accumulation 37, 139, 157, 218
capital allocation/misallocation
    28, 32, 42
capital deepening 144, 153, 157
capital exports 142
capital flight/migration 67–8, 149,
    168(n17), 195
capital flows 44(n12), 97, 140, 142,
    158, 158t, 208
  international 157, 207t
  short-term 86
capital incomes 50
capital markets 27, 32, 62, 70(n4), 156
  global 141, 157–9, 167, 168(n16–17)
capital restraints 44(n12)
capital stock 12, 219f
capital transactions 45(n24)
capitalism 5, 44(n16), 76, 78–9, 81–3,
    85–6
  contradictions 10
capitalists 149
Caprio, G. 26n
Carballo, O. 97n, 99(n20)
carbon dioxide emissions 40–1
Caribbean countries 98(n10), 203f,
    215–16t
cartels 181, 206t
cash crops 117f

cash flow   24, 44(n14)
cash transfers   64
caste   111
Catholics   104, 109, 122, 123, 124,
    132(n24, n26)
  schoolgirls   104
censuses   112
Central Africa   106
central banks   43(n7), 208, 212t
central planning/command economy
    15, 208, 209, 210
'central tendency'   94
Centre for Economic Policy
    Research (CEPR) bulletin
    (1999)   54
centre-periphery   150–4, 168(n13)
centrifugal forces   133(n35)
Chad   215t
chaebol   17, 206t
change   80
Chau, N.   197(n19)
cheap labour
  not chased by capital   158
cheating   2, 3, 186
chemicals   94
Chen, S.   169(n24)
Chiapas (Mexico)   113, 114–15,
    126, 127
Chicago School   184
child labour   xix, xx, 75, 96, 175,
    181–3, 189, 196(n11–16),
    196(n17), 197(n25)
  causes   182–3, 196(n13)
  forced   184
  legislative ban   182, 183, 187
  multiple equilibria   183
children   89, 90, 91, 103–4, 108, 157,
    181, 192
Chile   19f, 26t, 129, 144n, 146,
    168(n12), 169(n22), 202f,
    203f, 216t
China   32, 54, 76, 92, 147, 152,
    155, 168(n7), 168(n12), 178,
    180, 204, 215t
  coastal provinces   148
  economic performance (1960–2002)
    204f
  'essential lesson'   211
  indeterminacy of institutional forms
    (counterfactual)   208–11

'puzzle' (for traditional economics)
    32–3
  shortcuts   210b
  World Bank 'star globalizer'
    205t, 205
Chinese
  in Indonesia   119
  in Malaysia   118, 121
  in UK   133(n33)
  migrants   157
Chinese government   210
Chipman, J. S.   57
choice   4, 6, 184
  enforced   105, 197(n30)
  political   3
Chomsky, N.   78
church groups/churches   6, 87
Cincinnati   124
Cirera, X.   98(n16)
cities   102, 113, 148
Civil Rights Act (USA, 1964)   124
Civil Rights Restoration Act (USA, 1991),
    124
civil servants/bureaucrats   xx, 39, 91,
    132(n24), 175
civil service/bureaucracy   10, 37, 109,
    110t, 130
civil service employment   119–22
civil society   76, 83, 88
civil war   80, 102–3, 107, 112, 117, 119,
    130, 168(n17)
Clark, T.   52n
Clemens, M. A.   158, 158n, 159, 167n,
    168(n12), 169(n26)
climate change   40
Cline, W. R.   146, 165
Clinton, W. J.   81
Clinton Administration (1993–2001)
    43(n7)
closed economy   189–90
'club' goods   104
CNN [Cable News Network]   80, 83
coastal shrimp farming   94–5, 98(n17)
Coatsworth, J. H.   141n, 151n,
    161n, 167n
Cobb–Douglas production function   37
codes of conduct (self-imposed)   4–5,
    13–14
coercion   4, 176, 183, 184, 197(n27)
Cohen, A.   106, 107, 108, 131(n7)

collective bargaining   63, 180, 191,
    196(n17)
Collier, P.   132(n13), 204, 205n
Collins, S. M.   206n
Colombia   19f, 42(n2), 145, 146,
    168(n12), 169(n22), 202f, 203f, 216t
colonialism   116, 119, 152, 153
    invention of 'tribes'   106–7
colonies   140, 160
Columbus, C.   136, 138, 140, 149
commodities   154
    non-competing   149
commodity markets
    domestic   144
    global/world   136, 140
    international   138
commodity price convergence
    (Williamson)   xix, 140, 154
commodity prices
    divergence   xix
    domestic relative   138
    relative   164–5
    world   165
commodity trade   142
common knowledge   46(n33)
common sense   83, 191
communalism   116
communes   209
communications   131
communism
    collapse   76, 102, 147
    demise (Eastern Europe, 1989)   14
communists   77
communities   104, 129
Community Reinvestment Act (USA,
    1977)   27
companies/firms   1, 6, 9, 18, 24, 29, 41,
    44(n14, n20), 60–1, 70(n9),
    99(n17–18), 131(n2), 180, 191, 195,
    198(n10)
    domestic   30, 45(n26)
    exporting   181
    foreign-owned export   180
    overlending to   17
    private   32
    public   32
    small   97(n7)
comparative advantage   30, 92,
    153, 154
compensation   94–5

competition   2, 19, 27, 28, 29–35,
    43(n3), 45(n22–6), 49, 53, 56, 68,
    82–3, 90–2, 145, 147
    'central to success of market economy'
        (Stiglitz)   29
    domestic and international   34
    free trade promotion   30–1,
        45(n22–3)
    further research required   31
    imperfect   58
    privatization facilitated   31–3,
        45(n24–5)
    regulation   34
competition policy   16, 21, 34–5, 42,
    45(n26)
competitors   3, 6
Complex Humanitarian Emergency
    study   xviii, 113, 129, 132(n15)
computer industry   34
conditionality   90, 128, 130, 132(n25),
    178–9
confidence   27, 29, 44(n18)
conflict   112, 130, 132(n13)
    sources   110
    violent   117, 128
conflict situations (Horowitz)   131(n4)
Congo   215t
Congo PR   215t
consensus   39, 201
Conservative Government (UK)   63
constrained democracy   130
'constrained Pareto efficient'   44(n15)
constraints   2, 5, 32, 43(n7), 131(n1),
    218, 222
    informal   1, 6, 7, 10, 12–14
    institutional   6, 7, 45(n25)
consumer protection   27
consumer sanctions   195
consumers   30, 31
consumption   30, 33, 165, 168(n10)
consumption goods   136, 149, 164
contract/s   3, 31, 63, 175–6, 186, 190,
    191, 196(n4), 197(n27), 198(n9)
    bonded labour   176, 177
    classes of   xix, 191
    free-market   187, 188, 194
    incomplete   27
contract-enforcement   2–3, 4–5, 11, 61,
    176, 207, 208, 210
contracting-out   39

conventions xvii, 4, 13–14, 50, 60,
    68, 69
Cooper, R. A. 58
cooperation 112
cooperatives 1, 131(n2)
coordination 7
  devices used in 'purely instrumental
    manner' 61
coordination failures/problems 4, 219,
    219f, 221
Copenhagen x
core–periphery 140, 152–6, 159–61,
    166–7, 168(n9)
  Uganda 116–18, 132(n16–17)
Corn Law repeal (UK, 1846) 149, 164
Cornia, G. A. xx, 69n, 69(n1)
corporate governance 17–18, 31, 206t,
    208, 212t
corporate restructuring 209
corporate stock ownership 118, 119f
corporatization 32, 209
corruption 33, 39, 210, 212t, 219, 219f
Corsicans 131(n3)
Costa Rica 102, 146, 202f
Côte d'Ivoire 26t
cottage industry 154
counter-revolution 81, 82
countries
  foreign 108
  high-wage 136
  poor 88, 96, 97(n7), 101, 152, 156,
    158, 159, 163, 164, 166, 176,
    195, 201
  rich 88, 90, 97(n7), 101, 152, 156,
    158, 163
  rich and poor (growing gap) 154
  richer 159
country event studies 144
country samples 88
coups 113, 116, 130
credit 17–18, 24, 27, 93, 110t, 128, 186
crime 6, 113
crimes against humanity 87
criminal negligence 98(n17)
criminality 114, 122, 124, 126
cross-country analysis 70(n3), 94–5,
    111–13, 164
cross-sectional regressions 88
Crowe, R. 84
Cuba 168(n12), 178

cultural differences 102, 103, 107
culture 5, 12, 39, 75, 80, 86, 88, 94,
    101, 104, 108, 113, 115, 127, 128,
    131(n7)
  Mayan 114
currency 23–4, 29
  depreciation 67
  devaluation 29
  mismatches 45(n20)
current account balances 42
current account deficit 23–4,
    44(n10–12)
  optimal level 44(n10–11)
customs (traditions) 68, 107, 108
CUTS (Indian NGO) xi, 96
Czech Republic 14, 32

Dahl, R. 81
dams 98(n18)
data deficiencies 43(n6), 64, 70(n3, n5),
    93, 111, 112, 150, 182, 196(n15)
data-mining 43(n5)
'David and Goliath' 84
Davis, D. R. 56–7, 168(n16)
Davos: World Economic Forum (2001)
    77, 97(n2)
Deardorff, A. 96, 196(n14)
death 195
debt
  short-term 29
  short-term dollar-denominated
    23–4
  'subordinated bank debt' 39
debt-deflation models 44(n14)
debtor nations 178
decentralization 3, 130
deconstructionism 78
default 186
Dehejia, V. 98(n13)
deindustrialization 150, 151, 153, 154,
    169(n26)
DeLong, J. B. 168(n6)
demand elasticities 152
democracy 14, 75, 84, 179
  erosion xix
  global 195
  globalization and retreat of 177–9,
    196(n5–7)
  majority rule (permanent domination)
    130

democracy – *continued*
  multi-party 117, 130
  political competition versus
    responsible leadership (Fiji) 127
  'winner-takes-all' (can provoke
    conflict) 130
democratic deficit 88
democratic development 16
Democratic Party (USA) 77, 91
democratic process 94
democratization 40
demographic transition 162
demography 162, 163
Denmark 51, 151f, 159, 168(n14), 216t
Denmark: Royal Ministry of Foreign
  Affairs x
deontological ethics 192
deposit insurance 24, 39
deposits, short-term 29
deprivation 114–15
  relative 122
deregulation 19, 34, 212t
  overnight 28
Derrida, J. 78
Desai, P. 74, 89, 97, 98(n8)
Deshmukh, D. 93
'detribalization' 106, 108
Detroit 124
devaluation 19
  inflation effects 45(n21)
developed countries 54, 129
  'advanced (industrial) countries' 62,
    203, 210
  'First World' 89
  'industrial countries' xvii, 34, 36,
    37, 41, 51, 55, 103, 143, 156,
    181, 195
  see also OECD countries
developing countries xvii, xix, xx, 22,
    24, 28, 30, 34, 36, 37, 41, 42, 49, 54,
    69(n1), 82, 96, 131(n10), 146, 154,
    178–9
  inflation rates (1985, 1995) 22f
  labour standards (three examples)
    179–85, 196–7(n8–18)
  'less-developed nations' 181
  see also Third World
development 17, 196(n2)
  equitable, democratic 40
  long-term 29

non-interventionist market
  model 121
objectives broadened 16
development analysis 128
development economics 187
development goals 167
development goals (broadened) 40–2
  education (improvement) 40
  environmental policy/protection
    40–2
  multiple goals 40–1
  participation (increased) 41–2
  technology (investment) 41
  trade-offs 41–2
development policy xviii, 103
Dewatripont, M. 53
DFI *see* foreign direct investment (FDI)
Dickens, W. 22
diminishing returns 213
direct foreign investment (DFI) *see*
  foreign direct investment
dirigisme 82
discrimination 90, 104, 113, 123, 125,
    126, 130, 133(n34), 196(n17)
  labour market (SA2) 122
disease 138
distortions 212
distribution 45(n25)
distribution system 34
distribution theory 50
diversity 86
divided countries/societies xviii, 130,
    133(n35–6)
Dixit, A. K. 57, 169(n20)
Doha Development Round 85
Dollar, D. 88, 93–4, 98(n15), 145, 164,
    204, 205n
Dominican Republic 144n, 202f, 215t,
    216t, 220, 221, 222
Dowrick, S. 168(n6)
Drezner, D. 83
duping 185–6

e-mail 99(n20)
Eagleton, T. 78
earnings/pay 124, 180
  cross-country data 70(n3)
  individual gross 52
  mean 70(n6)
  see also pay norms; salaries; wages

earnings continuum (Atkinson) 50, 58–60
earnings distribution 59, 168(n11)
earnings/skill nexus, 'tilt' in 50
East Africa 155, 157
East Asia xvii, 19, 23, 27, 30, 36, 40, 147, 155, 168(n17), 215t
  anomalies 206–7t
  inflation (1980–95) 20f
  public sector deficits 19f
  volatility of GDP growth (1970–95) 25f
East Asia and Pacific (EA&P) 204f
East Asian crisis (1997–8) 28, 76, 86, 87, 89, 90, 97, 178, 179
  'heart of problem' 17–18
  lessons (Stiglitz) 17–18, 42(n1)
East Asian Miracle (World Bank, 1993) 17, 42
Easterly, W. 21, 23, 43(n9)
Eastern Europe 14, 22, 143, 160
econometrics 83, 90, 128, 205
economic cycle 23
economic development 2, 40, 103
economic diversification 221
economic downturn 23, 32, 44(n10), 89
  'recessions' 21
  social and economic costs 24, 44(n13)
economic growth xviii, 6, 7, 8, 11–12, 16, 19, 22, 30, 36, 40, 42, 43(n7), 49, 80, 87, 94, 129, 154
  accelerations xx
  alternative framework (Rodrik) xx, 217–22
  balanced 218
  binding constraints 222
  China 32, 33
  constraints on 212
  effects on trade 98(n11)
  faster 145
  import-substitution policies 45(n22)
  India 92–3
  'little evidence that inflation under 40% is costly' 21
  long-term xvii, 24–5, 28
  Meiji Japan 96
  most binding constraint 218
  per capita 204

performance 144, 203
  rate 153, 178, 218
  tariffs 159–60
  turning points 213
  see also rethinking growth strategies
economic growth accelerations 201, 213–17
  episodes (1957–92) 215–16t
  predictability 217t
  sustained 217t
economic growth-poverty linkage 93–4, 98(n16)
economic historians 164
Economic Journal 88
economic liberalization 217t
  agenda 122
  'no clear link' with economic growth accelerations xx
  standard programmes 214
economic opportunity 78
economic performance xvi, 1–2, 3, 5, 7, 12, 16, 22, 23, 162, 204f
economic planning (India) 92
economic policy
  'not just a matter for technical experts' (Stiglitz) 21
economic prosperity 75
economic reform 176, 202, 213, 214
  adverse short-run effects 204
  diagnostic strategy 217–22
economic revolution
  second 7–10, 12, 13
economic slump 29
economic stabilization 214
economics 78, 79, 80, 175, 177, 184, 189, 190, 194, 212
  new institutional 1–15
Economics of Underdeveloped Countries (Bhagwati, 1966) 78
economies, labour-scarce 142
economies of scale 10
economies of scope 13, 14
Economist 96
economists 50, 61, 84, 89, 96, 144, 146, 164, 167, 168(n11, n13), 175, 176, 184–6, 189, 204, 222
  agenda 136
  approach to pay determination 60
  classical 152
  ends and means 79

economy, the 131(n2), 211
  hybrid areas 34
Ecuador 202f, 216t
Edlin, A. 32
Edmonds, E. 165, 196(n14), 197(n22)
education 7, 17, 19, 35, 81, 89, 103,
    104, 109, 110t, 114–19, 121–5, 129,
    156, 162, 163
  improvement (achievement of
    multiple goals) 40
  primary 23, 36, 93
  secondary 115
  tertiary 37, 118, 119f
  tertiary (science and engineering) 38f
  tertiary technical 41
educational attainment 115t, 123f,
    123, 124
Edwards, S. 145
efficiency xviii, 18, 21, 31, 33–6,
    105, 129
egalitarianism xix, 16, 17, 149, 150
Egypt 153, 168(n12), 216t
Eisenhower, D. D. 86
Ejército Zapatisto de Liberación Nacional
    (EZLN) 115
El Salvador 202f, 220, 221, 222
Elbadawi, I. 132(n13)
elderly persons/the old 77, 162, 186
  retired people 50
election campaigns 68
election-rigging 116, 118, 130
Eleventh of September (2001) 85, 103
elites 107, 112, 176
'embedding liberalism' (Ruggie) 95
Emerson, P. M. 197(n22)
empiricism 4, 21, 24, 29, 43(n7), 53,
    58–9, 69, 83, 87, 88, 91, 95, 143,
    154, 166, 182, 189, 203, 205
  growth accelerations 201, 213–17
  horizontal inequalities 103, 109,
    110, 112, 113–28, 132–3(n15–32)
employers 62, 67, 70(n8), 90, 176, 190,
    193, 195
employment/jobs 24, 49, 60, 80,
    91–2, 95, 109, 110t, 117f, 123f,
    123, 124, 130, 132(n25, n28),
    164, 165, 166, 183
  public sector 116, 128, 129
  relative demand shift (skilled versus
    unskilled workers) 53, 66, 68,
    145–6

End of History and the Last Man
    (Fukuyama, 1992) 76
endogenous growth models
    213, 213f
ends and means 29–30, 38, 79
energy 23
enforcement 13–14
  rules and constraints 1
engineering 38f, 119
England 79, 80, 148
English literature 79
entrepreneurs 6, 7, 25, 33, 37, 116,
    218, 221
entrepreneurship 11, 207, 210, 218,
    219f, 221
environment (institutional) xx,
    207, 208
environment (natural) 10, 35, 40, 81,
    85, 179
  policy implementation (achievement
    of multiple goals) 40–1
  shrimp farming 94–5
  trade-offs 41–2
Epland, J. 52n
equality
  group 105
  individual 105
Erin Brockovich 84
Eritrea 103
Estaban, J. 112, 132(n13)
Ethiopia 23, 144n, 195
ethnic groups 102, 104
  change over time 106
ethnicity 101, 106, 107
  Fiji 115–16
  'switching' 108
ethnobiologists 131(n6)
Euro Zone (EZ) 55, 57, 63
  Common Agricultural Policy
    (CAP) 58
  European Monetary Union (EMU) 67
Europe 44(n13), 50, 55, 57, 58, 66, 76,
    80, 108, 136, 148, 149, 150–2, 153,
    155, 156, 157, 159, 160, 161t, 162,
    164, 166
  industrial core 150
  openness-fosters-growth hypothesis
    (lack of supporting evidence)
    169(n18)
  trade boom (1500–1800) 138–40,
    167(n1)

Europe and Central Asia   24
  economic performance (1960–2002)
    204f
  volatility of GDP growth (1970–95)
    25f
European centre   153
European periphery   141, 151f,
  151, 152
European Union   91, 98(n10)
exchange   4
  channels of,   5
  impersonal   2, 10, 15
  personal   15
exchange controls   143, 144
exchange problems   12
exchange process   9
exchange rates   44(n20), 45(n21),
  67, 212t
  floating   208
'exit' (Hirschman)   68
exogenous, inevitable events   68
expenditure   136, 165
experience   89
exploitation   9, 82, 83, 93, 107, 196(n6)
export industries   63, 89
export markets   147
export prices   139
export sector   153
export supply   139
export-processing zones (EPZs)   89, 191
  labour rights   180–1, 196(n8–10)
exports   18, 30, 63, 95, 98(n10), 138,
  140, 154, 159, 168(n5)
externalities   36, 37, 190, 219

factor endowments   57
factor markets   2, 9, 11, 144
factor migration   138, 142
factor mobility   xix, 7, 67, 142
factor prices   142
  equalization   57–8
  integrated worldwide   141
  relative   138, 154, 168(n13)
factor supply   152
factor-intensity reversals   57
factors of production   9, 55, 67,
  168(n16), 213, 213f, 219
Fagerman, B.   167n
failures, elimination of   3, 11
Fair Employment Act (UK, 1989)   124,
  132(n25)

fair trade   34–5, 79, 81
Fairly Conventional Woman (Shields)   68
fairness/equity (fairness)   3, 31, 39,
  61, 63
family   4, 10–11, 12, 24, 36, 101,
  106, 131(n2)
family assistance   165
Family Expenditure Survey (FES)   52n
Family Resources Survey   52n
Fanon, F.   79
farmers   95, 197(n20)
Fathers and Sons (Turgenev, 1862)   79
Federal National Mortgage Association
  (USA)   27
federalism, Chinese-style   210b
Feenstra, R. C.   91, 98(n14), 145, 146
feminism   89, 91
feudalism   6, 79, 89
Fifty Years is Enough (NGO)   77
Fiji
  constitution   116
  horizontal inequalities   113, 115–16,
    127, 129, 130
finance
  international   219f
  local   219f
financial accumulation   218
financial crisis   219f, 222
financial governance   212
financial liberalization   28, 76
  'gung-ho'   75, 86, 98(n8)
  mismanaged   86, 90
financial markets   xvii, 19, 23, 24, 26,
  212t, 219, 222
  international   219, 221
  sound   29
financial monitoring   26
financial panics   24–5
financial reform process   25–9,
  44–5(n15–21)
  general points   28
financial regulation   16, 18
financial sector   19, 21, 27, 29, 207
  reform   208t, 209
  regulation   42
  vibrant   28
financial standards   212t, 212
financial system   25, 27, 28, 29, 42,
  44(n13), 206t
Financial Times   96
Findlay, R.   139, 167(n2)

Finland   ix, 51, 64, 65f, 66, 67, 74, 102, 175, 216t
   Swedish minority   102
Finland: Ministry of Foreign Affairs x
firms   *see* companies
first global century (world inequality, 1820–1913) (Williamson)   xix, 136, 140–1, 148–67, 167(n2), 168–9(n9–27)
   big tariff-growth regime switch 159–60, 169(n26)
   European followers and New World 150–2
   global divergence without globalization   148–9
   lessons of history   161–7
   North–North and South–South migrations   155–7
   pre-1940 periphery   160–1
   rising inequality in primary product-exporting periphery 154–5
   terms of trade gains in periphery before 1913   152–4
   trade policy and international income gaps   159–61
   unimportance of global capital markets   157–9
   United Kingdom (when nineteenth-century leader went open) 149–50
fiscal crises   219, 219f
fiscal discipline   xx, 212t
fiscal policy   24, 66–7
fiscal prudence   17
fiscal redistribution   68
fiscal revenues   208t, 209
Fischer, S.   21, 43(n5, n9), 87
fishermen   94–5
food   149, 164, 165, 209
forced labour   183–5, 197–8(n17–18)
Foreign Affairs   86, 87, 98(n12)
foreign direct investment (FDI/DFI) xviii, 23, 37, 74, 75, 86, 90–4, 212t, 219f
   'economically benign'   75
foreign exchange   42(n1), 44(n11)
foreign investment   147, 204, 205
Fortin, N. M.   61
Fortune 500 companies   45(n26)

France   43(n6), 51, 52f, 52, 54f, 55, 56f, 59, 66, 146, 148, 150, 151f, 156, 159, 168(n14)
   immigration   131(n3)
fraud   27
free market   xix
free trade   30–1, 42, 45(n22–3), 57, 75, 88, 140, 142, 143, 152, 153, 164, 166, 168(n10), 169(n19)
   further research required   31
free trade episodes   159
free-market decisions   187
free-trade leadership   149–50, 168(n10)
Friedman, M.   82
Friez, A.   56n
fuels   164
Fukuyama, F.   76
furniture firms   92, 97(n7)

gains from trade   142, 143
Galbraith, J. K.   82
Gama, V. da   136, 138, 149
game theory   187, 188, 193
Gap   84
garment sweatshops   91–2
GATT   34, 84, 148, 169(n25)
'GATT rules'   205
GDP   18, 19f, 20f, 22f, 23, 25, 26t, 26f, 33, 42(n2), 139, 142, 220
   government spending as share of   35
   world   30, 138
GDP growth (volatility, 1970–95)   25f
GDP *per capita*   17, 137n, 138, 144f, 156, 158, 158t, 160, 169(n21), 182, 203f
   gain   143
   real   121
GDP per capita growth   160–1, 169(n21)
   tariff impact   161t
GDP per worker   156–7, 206f
Gellner, E.   101
gender   75, 86, 89–91, 98(n12), 104, 110
general equilibrium (GE)   190–1, 193
general-equilibrium reversal claim (GERC)   191, 193
Genicot, G.   197(n26)
Genoa   77, 85
geography   105, 121, 219, 220
   'place'   106, 107

Germany   43(n6), 52f, 52, 54f, 65f,
  70(n11), 80, 112, 146, 150, 151f,
  159, 160–1, 168(n14), 169(n18)
  Jews   107, 108
  Nazi era   14, 107
  Western *Länder*   51
getting prices right   16
Ghana   144n, 215t
Gini coefficient   51, 52f, 53, 64, 65f, 65,
  66, 70(n3)
Ginyera-Pinycwa, A. G. G.   132(n17)
Glazer, N.   106–7
'global childcare chain'   89
global commodity market integration
  139–40
global development
  wider perspectives   xvi–xx
Global Exchange   77–8, 84
global integration   74, 143
global labour standards and local
  freedoms (Basu)   175–200
  further investigation required   193
  globalization and retreat of democracy
    177–9, 196(n5–7)
  international labour standards   194–5
  intervention (appropriate occasions)
    185–93, 197–8(n19–33)
  labour standards in developing
    countries (three examples)
    179–85, 196–7(n8–18)
  theoretical questions   175
globalization   xix, 74, 85, 95, 153, 163,
  164, 166, 204
  change   146
  economic   70(n4)
  economic ('needs to be disaggregated')
    75
  economically-benign   75, 86
  finance   xvii
  national law   189
  'needs to be disaggregated'   xviii
  'never a necessary condition for
    widening world income gaps'
    (Williamson)   149
  optimal speed   76
  'proper question'   146
  retreat of democracy   177–9,
    196(n5–7)
  socially-benign   75, 88–94, 96
  socially-malign   75, 86

trade   xvii, xviii, 49
wise management   97
globalization: disaggregation (focus on
  trade)   86–7
globalization: winners and losers over
  two centuries (Williamson)   136–74
  backlash   137, 140
  first global century (world inequality)
    148–67, 168–9(n9–27)
  globalization and world inequality
    136–8
  making a world economy   138–42,
    167(n1–2)
  second global century (world
    inequality)   142–8, 162, 167,
    167–8(n3–8)
globalization and appropriate
  governance (Bhagwati)   74–100
  anti-capitalism   76–82, 97(n2–5)
  anti-corporations   83–5, 97(n6–7)
  anti-globalization   82–3
  anti-globalization (confronted)   85–6
  appropriate governance   94–7,
    98–9(n17–20)
  disaggregating globalization (focusing
    on trade)   86–94, 98(n8–16)
  gender questions   89–91, 98(n12)
  globalization speed (optimal rather
    than maximal)   96–7
  political alliances   85
  poverty in poor countries   92–4,
    98(n15–16)
  poverty in rich countries   91–2,
    98(n13–14)
  social effects (generally benign)
    88–94, 96, 98(n12–16)
  trade (economic benignity)   87–8,
    98(n11)
  'ultimate question'   87
globalization epochs (Williamson)
  138–42
  anti-global mercantilist restriction
    (1492–1820)   138–40, 164,
    167(n1)
  beating an anti-global retreat
    (1913–50)   140, 141–2, 153, 163
  first global century (1820–1913)
    140–1, 167(n2)
  second global century (1950–2002)
    142

Globalization, Growth, and Poverty
(Collier and Dollar, 2001) 204
globalization–inequality connection
164, 167(n1)
GNP 8, 18, 88, 94, 95, 122
God of Small Things (Roy) 98(n18)
Goodman, A. 52n
goods 57, 58, 60, 178
non-traded 58
tradable 55
goods and services 2, 9, 39, 67
non-traded 55, 58
governance 222
'appropriate' (Bhagwati) 94–7,
98–9(n17–20)
global 179
international xviii
national xviii
reforms 201
government 10, 209
'got out of way' 16
inclusive 117, 124
optimal size 23
government budgets 51, 64, 66
redistributive 68–9
see also budget deficits
government intervention 44(n15),
45(n27), 166, 176, 189, 195
central question 35–6
government procurement 39
government role 21, 42, 221
governments xvii, 10, 19, 28, 30, 33,
44(n20), 45(n24), 67, 69, 84, 94–5,
126, 128, 131(n2), 165–6, 176,
178, 180, 185, 187, 190, 195, 209,
211, 221
acting as complement to markets
35–8, 45–6(n27–33)
'do too little rather than too much'
17
effectiveness 38–40
freedom of policy choice 67–8
human capital 36, 45(n29)
technology transfer 36–8,
45–6(n30–3)
grain 150, 164
Great Britain 59n
Great Depression 44(n14), 143
great powers 78
Greece 168(n12)

greenhouse gases 40–1
Greenwald, B. 44(n14, n16)
group behaviour xviii
group boundaries 108–9
group coalitions 112
group definition 127–8
group identity 107–8
group inequalities 103–4, 105, 110
group membership 101
group mobilization 109, 110
group prestige 102, 104
group size 127
group well-being (importance) 103–5,
131(n5)
direct welfare impacts 104–5
instrumental reasons 103–4
groups xviii, 1, 13, 103, 113, 131(n2,
n11), 133(n34)
formation and mobilization 105–9,
131(n6–10)
fragmentation indices 111, 132(n13)
Gurr's index of disparities 113
limited mobility 105
marginalized 43(n4)
number and size 111–12
polarization indices 112, 132(n13)
political dominance versus economic
deprivation 110
relatively-privileged 129
growth accounting 37
Guangdong: Provincial Security
Bureau 180
Guatemala 202f
Guevara de la Serna, E. ('Che Guevara')
77, 79
Guinea Bissau 215t
gunboat diplomacy 140, 152
Gurr, T. R. 113

Hadass, Y. S. 168(n12)
Haiti 216t
Hamilton, A. 161
Hanson, G. H. 91, 98(n14), 145,
146, 148
Happenstance (Shields, 1991) 68
Harrod-Domar model 87
Hartmann, H. L. 132(n28)
Hartwell, M. 132(n23)
Hatton, T. J. 167n, 168(n15)
Hausa 106, 131(n7)

Hauser, R.   52n, 70(n11)
Hausmann, R.   201, 213, 216n,
    219n, 220
Hayek, F. A. von   3, 12
health   35, 40, 81, 93, 104, 105, 110t,
    122, 129, 148, 187
health hazards   41–2, 176, 177, 191,
    192, 193
Heckscher–Ohlin model   30–1, 54–5,
    57–8, 69, 142
Helms–Burton Act (USA, 1996)   178
Helsinki   i, ix, x
Helsinki School of Economics   xx
Heyer, J.   131(n2)
hierarchy   10, 32
high inflation/low growth trap   21
high technology   55, 58
high technology goods   63
high technology sector   60, 70(n6)
high-earners   50
high-income countries   13, 24
    volatility of GDP growth (1970–95)
    25f
Hildenbrand, W.   193
Hirschman, A. O.   68
Hirst, P. Q.   139
history   xviii–xix, 5, 6, 7–8, 11–12,
    39, 101, 106–7, 108, 131(n9), 141,
    145, 146, 147, 149, 150, 161t,
    169(n18), 220
    'two basic breakthroughs'   7–8
    two centuries of globalization
    (winners and losers)   136
Hitler, A.   112
HIV/AIDS   163
Hoeffler, A.   132(n13)
Hoff, K.   197(n22)
Honduras   202f
Hong Kong   38f, 144n
horizontal inequalities (HIs) (Stewart)
    101–35
    aggregation   111
    categories   109, 110t
    conclusions   128–31, 133(n33–7)
    consistency issue   110
    context   108, 130–1
    cultural   116, 121, 126
    definition   102, 113
    descriptive, rather than evaluative,
    measure   111, 131–2(n12)

economic   115t, 116–17, 120, 122–4,
    126–9, 131
empirical evidence   113–28,
    132–3(n15–32)
extent, evolution, consequences   113
global   130–1
group formation and mobilization
    105–9, 131(n6–10)
group well-being (importance)
    103–5, 131(n5)
intra-group   110, 112, 119, 127
measurement   109–12, 127–8,
    131–2(n11–14)
multi-dimensionality   109
political   115t, 116–17, 120–4,
    126–8
politically dominant versus
    economically privileged   127
'precisely the point'   126
sharp changes (new sources of
    conflict)   121
social   115t, 116–17, 122–4, 126–9
societal objectives   105
weighting   111
horizontal inequalities: case studies
    (Stewart)   113, 114–28,
    132–3(n16–32)
Brazil   114, 125–6, 127,
    132–3(n29–32)
Chiapas (Mexico)   113, 114–15,
    126, 127
conclusions   126–8
Fiji   113, 115–16, 127, 129, 130
Malaysia   114, 118–19, 121, 126, 127,
    132(n18)
Northern Ireland   113, 122–4, 126,
    127, 129, 130, 132(n23–6)
South Africa   104, 109, 113,
    132(n22); apartheid era (1948–93)
    121–2, 126; post-apartheid era
    (1993–)   122, 126, 127, 129
Sri Lanka   113, 119–21, 126, 127,
    132(n19–21)
Uganda   113, 116–18, 126, 127, 129,
    130, 132(n16–17)
United States (black/white difference)
    113, 114, 124–5, 126, 127,
    132(n27–8)
Horowitz, D.   131(n4), 133(n36)
hours of work   187

household disposable income 51, 52, 146
household expenditure 117f
household responsibility system (China) 210b, 210
household size 69(n2)
households 89, 102, 115t
  ranking 101
  rural 182
  working-age 66
housing 109, 110t, 123f, 123, 124, 129, 165, 175, 177
Huberman, M. 166
Hudec, R. 97(n7)
Hudson, M. C. 112
human capital xvii, 6, 37, 42, 44(n13), 103–4, 105, 110t, 158, 160, 187, 218, 219f, 222
human development index (HDI) 117f, 126t
human interaction 6, 12
human preferences 191–3
  'inviolable' 192, 193
  'purification' 193
human rights 75, 77, 85, 98(n18), 110t, 130
Human Rights Watch: Academic Advisory Committee (Asia) 94
humanitarian emergencies xviii, 113, 129, 132(n15)
humanity 97(n2)
Hume, D. 80
Hume's law 197(n28)
Humphries, J. 182, 196(n14–15)
Hungary 26t
Huntington, S. 102
Hutus 103, 106, 107
hysteresis effect 44(n13)

Ibadan 131(n7)
Ibos 108
idealism 84–5
ideas 13
  importance 6, 12
  'like a candle' (Jefferson) 37
identities 113
  coincidences 126
  economic/ social 126
  ethnic 126, 131(n1)
  group 112

multiple 101, 106
  perceptions 106
  tribal 106
ideology 3, 5, 11–13, 79, 80, 102, 107
  anti-global 143
illiteracy, 82, 114, 114f
immigration xix, 76, 97, 136, 142, 156, 162
  illegal 91–2
  liberalization (USA) 145
  unrestrictive 141
  unskilled workers 145
'immiserization' of proletariat (Marx) 91
Imperialism: Highest Stage of Capitalism (Lenin, 1916) 82
Imperialism and World Economy (Bukharin) 82
import barriers 143, 205
Import Competition and Response (Bhagwati, 1982) 95
import demand 139
import liberalization 205
import prices 139
import-substitution 45(n22), 87, 203, 204
  'ineffective strategy for development' 30
imports 18, 29, 30, 70(n4), 138, 145, 149, 165, 168(n5), 181, 184, 208
  agricultural 164
incentive incompatibilities 10, 11
incentives 9, 10, 18, 28, 29, 32, 33, 37, 43(n3), 46(n33), 208, 208t, 221
  individual 61
  private 210
income 18, 87, 101, 110t, 114, 114f, 123f, 123, 125, 128, 153, 167(n4)
  absolute or relative 163–5, 169(n24–5)
  disposable 51, 52, 53, 64–7, 69, 69(n2), 146, 165
  global divergence 137
  gross 69(n2)
  nominal or real 163–5, 169(n24–5)
  per capita 37, 115t, 116–17, 120–2, 125f, 126t, 154, 168(n13), 183
  real 33
income deciles 52, 55, 56f, 59–60, 70(n3), 147

income distribution   169(n23)
    determinants   69(n1)
income gaps   118, 119f, 125, 147
    global   148–9, 168(n9)
    North-South   163
    post-war epochal turning point?
        142–3, 167(n3–4)
income gaps (international)   159–61,
        169(n18–22)
    conventional wisdom   143–5,
        167–8(n5–6)
    trade policy and   143–5, 167–8(n5–6)
income inequality, rising (Atkinson)
        xvii–xviii
    alternative approach   58–64,
        70(n5–10)
    changes (1977–99)   52f
    critique of 'Transatlantic Consensus'
        49–73
    differences in definition   69(n2)
    'episodes'   53
    France and USA (1977–99)   56f
    'inevitability' disputed   49, 69
    model 'needs to be richer'   58, 69
    national government freedom   67–8
    redistributive experience   64–7,
        70(n11)
    redistributive impact of budgets
        (1977–97)   65f
    reputational approach   61–4,
        70(n7–10)
    tilt (UK, 1977–98)   59f
    unresolved questions   56–8
    wage differentials (determinants)
        60–1
incomes policy (governmental)   63
independence   103
India   77, 78, 92, 94, 144n, 147, 153,
        155, 168(n7, n12), 178, 185,
        196(n7), 197(n20), 204, 208, 215t
    economic performance (1960–2002)
        204f
    economic take-off (1960–2000)
        205, 206f
    elections   89
    reform (1980s–)   93
    reforms (1991)   96, 206t
    rural/urban differences   111
    World Bank 'star globalizer'
        205t, 205

Indian Planning Commission   93
Indians
    in Fiji   115–16, 127, 129
    in Malaysia   118, 119
    migrants   157
    see also Tamils
indigenous peoples   114, 115, 125
    see also 'horizontal inequalities
        (case studies)'
individuals   xviii, xix, 1, 11, 12, 13, 61,
        102, 103, 104, 193
    numbers in poverty   101
    ranking   101
Indonesia   19f, 44(n18), 86, 119, 147,
        148, 153, 168(n12), 203f
industrial policy   17, 205
industrial revolutions   149, 164,
        168(n9)
industrialization   36, 49, 144, 154, 160
industries
    import-competing   88
    less-skill-intensive   169(n25)
industry   169(n22), 210
inequality   xviii, 40, 41, 101, 142, 146,
        155, 163, 168(n11), 188
    between-country   168(n7)
    China   148
    cultural   113
    economic   103, 109, 110t, 111, 113
    global   148–9, 168(n9)
    hinterland-coastal (China)   148
    intra-group   116
    liberalization connection (Europe and
        New World)   150–2, 168(n11)
    'normal definition' (Stewart)   102
    political   111, 113
    primary product-exporting periphery
        154–5, 168(n13)
    racial   125
    relative measures   164
    social   109, 110t, 111
    socioeconomic   113
    urban–rural   148
    vertical   105
    wage and income (USA)   145
    within-country   147, 165, 167(n1),
        169(n24)
    world   163
inequality aversion   111
inequality changes   150

Inequality of Pay (Phelps Brown, 1977)
60
inequality surge   147
infant industry   144, 160
infant mortality   115t, 117f, 122, 124
inflation   xvii, 16, 17, 19, 20, 25, 29,
39, 42, 43(n4), 202, 221
accelerationist hypothesis   22
control   21–2, 43(n5–7)
increases 'costly to reverse'   21
Latin America versus East Asia
(1980–95)   20f
'precipice' theory (rejected)   45(n21)
inflation rates (developing countries,
1985, 1995)   22f
inflation targeting   208, 212t
influence   177–8
information   12, 18, 27, 128, 146, 186
imperfect   36
incomplete   27, 44(n15)
localized   39
information asymmetry   xvii, 37
information costs   13
information externalities   221
information feedback   11, 13
information spillovers   219
information technology (IT)   xvii, 53
infrastructure   219, 219f, 220
government-provided   219f
governmental   110t
institutional   31
physical   23, 104
innovation/s   3, 30, 37, 41,
45(n31), 101
institutional   210b, 210
input   46(n33), 105
input-output   9, 37
Insider, The   84
institutional change   5–7
agents   5, 6–7
direction   5, 7
path dependence   5, 7
sources   5, 6
institutional development   27
institutional framework   13, 14
institutional structures   32, 220
institutions   xvii, 11, 12, 14, 39,
99(n20), 211, 222
adaptively efficient   3
change   5–7

composition   3–5
differ from 'organizations'   1
economic   2, 12–13
efficient   6
efficient markets   1–7
financial   25
flexibility   10
functions   5
international   50, 86
legislative   177
multilateral   204
political   2, 177
poor   219
quality   38
stability characteristics   5–6
theory of   xvi
insurance, private   70(n7)
intellectual property (IP)   45(n31),
46(n33)
intellectuals   81, 106
Inter-American Development Bank   202
interest groups   13–14, 131(n10)
interest payments   18, 44(n14)
interest rate liberalization   212t
interest rates   20, 23, 28, 29, 39,
44(n18–20), 90, 185, 219f
annual/monthly   197(n20)
real   221
intermarriage   125
International Criminal Court (ICC)
179, 196(n7)
international agencies   96
International Confederation of Free
Trade Unions (ICFTU)   91, 96
international financial institutions
121, 129
International Labour Organization (ILO)
76, 96, 175, 179, 181, 182, 184, 194
International Monetary Fund (IMF)   18,
29, 42, 43(n7), 50, 84, 86, 87, 88,
89, 90, 96, 129
International Statistics Database   19n
internet   80
investment   7, 9, 24, 92, 97(n7),
132(n25), 142, 159, 218–22
federal (Mexico)   115
low-productivity   26
national   23
private   207, 210, 219f, 220, 221
public   42, 117f, 128

investment – *continued*
  regional distribution   128
  returns   23
investors   16, 27, 218, 220, 221
invisible hand   80, 82
Ireland   123, 150, 156, 168(n14),
  181, 216t
irrationality and behavioural economics
  185–7, 197(n20–1)
irrigation   99(n18)
Irwin, D.   88
Isaacs, H. R.   106
Isham, J.   39
Israel   26t, 78, 216t
Italy   x, 43(n6), 146, 151f, 156, 159,
  168(n14), 169(n18)
Iwerri [ethnic group, Ibos]   108

Jamaica   202f
Jäntti, M.   70
Japan   5, 38f, 43(n6), 55, 138, 146, 152,
  153, 162, 168(n7, n12), 179, 181,
  206t, 216t
  Meiji Era   96
Jefferson, T.   37
Jharkhand (India)   186, 197(n20)
job-search literature   61
Johnson, S.   167(n1)
Jones, I.   97
Jordan   216t
Joshi, B.   97n
Journal of Economic Literature   98(n14)
journals   186
judges   4, 125
judiciary   2, 39, 210
Julhès, M.   54n, 56n
jurisprudence   98(n17)

Kabeer, N.   198(n9)
Kahn, L. M.   63
Kalecki, M.   93
Kalt, M.   4
Kanbur, R.   69(n1), 197(n19)
Kangwha Treaty (1876)   153
Karoly, L. A.   54n
Kerala model   77
Keynes, Lord   12, 87
Kikuyu   107
kinship ties   2
Kirman, A.   193

Klein, N.   84
Klingebiel, D.   26n
Klugman, J.   117n
Knaul, F.   196(n13)
knowledge   3, 7, 23, 37, 40
  misdirected energies   46(n33)
  'scientific'   12
knowledge dissemination   42
knowledge 'price'   46(n33)
knowledge spillovers   24
knowledge stock   8
Koestler, A.   77
Koolwal, G.   196n
Korea, Republic of (South Korea)   17,
  19f, 37, 38f, 43(n7), 86, 144n, 145,
  146, 168(n12), 179, 203f, 206t, 215t
Kosters, M.   98(n13)
Kraay, A.   93–4, 98(n15), 145, 164
Kranton, R. E.   104, 131(n1), 132(n14)
Krueger, A. O.   87, 94, 144, 182,
  196(n14)
Krugman, P.   55, 56, 60, 96
Kuttner, R.   97(n5)
Kuznets, S.   49

labour   9, 81, 87, 154, 156, 157, 158,
  168(n10–11, n16), 219f
  British   149
  hazardous versus safe   186–7, 187–90,
    195, 197(n24)
  landless   150
  low-skilled   165, 169(n23)
  'simple' skilled/unskilled distinction
    abandoned   58, 69
  skilled   55, 57–8
  unskilled   54, 55, 57–8, 149, 150, 163
labour earnings (full-time)   146
labour economics   60
labour force   8, 43(n4)
Labour Government (UK, 1970s)   63
labour markets   63, 68, 181, 187, 195,
  206t, 212t, 219f
  flexible,   212t
  multiple equilibria in   182
  world   156, 162
labour migration   xix, 67–8, 140
Labour Party (UK)   63
labour rights   85, 88, 175, 191, 192
  export-processing zones   180–1,
    196(n8–10)

labour scarcity 150
labour skills 222
labour standards xix-xx, 85, 92, 96, 99(n20), 175–200
  international 194–5
  see also global labour standards
labour standards: appropriate occasions for intervention (three general principles) 185–93, 197–8(n19–33)
  irrationality and behavioural economics 185–7, 197(n20–1)
  large numbers problem 190–3, 197–8(n26–33)
  multiple equilibria 187–90, 194, 197(n22–5)
labour standards in developing countries (three examples) 179–85, 196–7(n8–18)
  child labour 181–3, 196(n11–16)
  forced labour 183–5, 197–8(n17–18)
  labour rights in export-processing zones 180–1, 196(n8–10)
labour welfare 190
labour-abundance/scarcity 155, 157, 158, 162, 169(n25)
LAC-7 (Latin America and Caribbean 7) 203f
Lancashire 80
land 55, 109, 116, 122, 123, 140, 150, 154–5, 165, 167(n1), 168(n11), 175, 180, 182, 210
  inelastic supply 152
  privatization 208t, 208–9
land reform 93, 114, 128
land rents 150, 164, 167(n1)
land–labour ratio 6, 154–5
landlords 148, 149, 150, 176, 197(n20)
land ownership 118
language 78, 101, 106–8, 113, 114, 116, 119, 120, 123, 127, 131(n10), 132(n17), 160
large numbers problem 190–3, 197–8(n26–33)
Latin America xx, 11, 19, 30, 38, 141, 143, 146–7, 151–4, 160–1, 166, 167, 168(n12, n17), 169(n22, n26), 202–4, 211, 215–16t
  economic crises (1980s) xvii
  economic performance (1960–2002) 204f

experience (1980s) 18
  inflation (1980–95) 20f
  public sector deficits 19f
  structural reform index (1985–99) 202f
  volatility of GDP growth (1970–95) 25f
law 4, 5, 6, 129, 179, 189–90, 191, 197(n25)
law courts 5, 210
law and order 35
lawyers 184
learning by doing 7
legal aid 129
legal framework/structures 28, 31, 32, 34
legal system 14, 27, 210
legislation 43(n7), 83, 136, 144n, 177, 183, 186, 188, 191, 195
legislatures 1, 32
Lemieux, T. 61
Lenin, V. I. 82–3
Lesotho 215t
Lester, R. A. 60
level playing field 27
Levison, D. 196(n13)
Lewchuk, W. 166
Lewis, Sir Arthur 153, 155
liberal arts 37
Liberal International Economic Order 97(n1)
liberal policy 153
liberalism, Dutch 153
liberalization 21, 150, 176, 202, 203
  global 149
  India 205
liberalization–inequality connection
  Europe and New World 150–2, 168(n11)
liberty, personal xix
'licensed manufacturing warehouses' (Malaysia) 180
licensing 9, 93
life expectancy 17, 121f, 122, 126t
lifetime employment 206t
limited access [to globalization benefits] 147–8, 168(n7–8)
Lindert, P. H. 136, 144n, 167n
liquidity 26, 220
List, F. 160–1

244   *Index*

Litan, R.   95
literacy   86, 121f, 122, 126t
literary theory   79
literature   78
Little, I.   87
livestock   109
living costs   168(n10)
living standards   xvii, xviii, 37, 40,
    45(n30), 93, 116, 138, 148, 149,
    154, 156, 157, 165, 168(n13), 194
  working class   164
LO (trade union federation, Norway)
    63
loans   18, 186, 197(n20)
  government-directed   17
local government   110t, 175, 210
logic   193, 197(n28)
Lommerud, K. E.   70(n7)
London   90, 109, 153
Lopez-Calva, L.-F.   197(n22)
Lora, E.   202n
Louisiana   177, 196(n3)
Loury, G. C.   104, 131(n5), 133(n34)
Lovell, P. A.   132(n29), 133(n31)
low technology   60
low-income countries   xvi, xx, 22n, 33,
    36, 39, 143
  volatility of GDP growth (1970–95)
    25f
low-wage economies   49, 147
lower middle-income countries
  volatility of GDP growth (1970–95)
    25f
loyalty   2
Lucas, R.   158
Lundborg, P.   70(n10)
Luo ethnic group   107
Luxemburg, R.   80
luxury goods   139, 149, 164, 167(n1)

MacBride principles   132(n25)
machinery   109
macroeconometric analysis   145, 159
macroeconomic disruption   86–7
macroeconomic issues   xvi
macroeconomic policy   19, 20, 24, 29,
    43(n9), 44(n12)
macroeconomic populism   203
macroeconomic problems   209
macroeconomic situation   98(n10)

macroeconomic stability   xvii, 16, 21–5,
    24, 25, 29, 31, 42, 202, 207, 221
  budget deficit   23–4, 43–4(n8–10, n12)
  current account deficit   23–4,
    44(n10–12)
  inflation control   21–2
  long-run growth   24–5
  output stabilization   24–5
  second generation of reforms   18
Madagascar   144n
Maddison, A.   137n, 139
Madras (state)   108
Maghrebians   131(n3)
Major, J. (now Sir John)   53
Majumdar, S.   110–11
Malawi   215t
Malaysia   19f, 26t, 86, 157, 180,
    203f, 215t
  Asian crisis (1997–8)   119
  economic growth   118
  horizontal inequalities   114, 118–19,
    121, 126, 127, 132(n18)
Mali   215t
Malthus, T. R.   7
Malthusian forces   164
managers   28, 32
Manchuria   155, 157
Mandela, N. R.   129
mangrove   94–5
Manning, A.   70(n9)
manorialism   6
manufactures/manufacturing   118, 147,
    151, 154, 167
maquiladoras   180
maquilas,   222
market, the   36, 129, 181
  'under-provides technology'   37
market discipline   32
market economy   xvii, 10, 13, 14, 15,
    19, 29–30, 34
market externalities   220
market forces   55, 60, 68
market failures/imperfections   xvii,
    36, 221
market income   65f, 65, 66
  difference from disposable
    income   64
  inequality   64
market inequality   69
market information   39

market liberalization 81
market prices 168(n5), 209
market segmentation 162
market size 2
market-like mechanisms 39
markets 16, 36, 78, 80, 82, 152, 185, 196(n2), 202
  competitive xvii, 11, 31, 42, 206t
  contestable 83
  domestic 160
  efficient 1–7, 10
  functioning 22
  global/world 147, 166
  home 153
  incomplete 27, 44(n15)
  international 166
  made to work better 18–21, 42–3(n2–4)
  over-regulated within nations 176
  potential interventions in 177
Marshallianism 57
Martinez, M. 66
Marx, K. H. 8, 12, 91
Marxism/Marxists 10, 77, 79
Maskus, K. 197(n19)
massacres 103, 107
Matsuyama, K. 197(n22)
Mauritius 215t
McCulloch, N. 98(n16)
McDonald's 180
McElroy, J. L. 113
McGregor, J. 107
media xviii, 78, 84, 96
medicine 119
Mediterranean 160
Melchior, A. 143, 168(n7)
mercantilism, dismantling of 140
mercantilist restriction
  anti-global (1492–1820) 138–40
Mexico 26t, 43(n6), 97(n7), 146, 147, 165, 167–8(n5), 168(n12), 169(n22, n25), 180, 202f, 203f
  Chiapas 113, 114–15
  US border 148
Miami 221
Micklewright, J. 54n, 59n
microeconomics 29, 39, 205
Middle East and North Africa 24, 25f, 204f, 216t
middle-income countries 22b

migration xviii, xix, 89, 137, 142, 149, 150, 156, 157
  hinterland-coastal (China) 168(n8)
  income-levelling effects 158
  international 97, 141
  North–North 156, 157, 161, 162
  North–North and South–South (with segmentation in between) 155–7, 168(n14–15)
  receiving regions 155
  rural–urban 106
  sending regions 155
  South–North 161–3, 169(n23)
  South–South 157, 162, 168(n15)
  see also immigration
Milanovic, B. 167(n3)
military expenditure 32–3, 167
military-industrial complex (Eisenhower) 78, 86
Mill, J. S. 176, 196(n4)
Millennium Development Goals (MDGs) 101
Mills, C. Wright 86
minerals 110t, 110
minimum wage 55, 57, 58, 114, 114f, 180, 195
Minorities at Risk project 113
minority groups xviii, 27
minority shareholders 27, 28
'miscible moral' system (Basu) 192, 193
Mishel, L. 56n
Moe, K. 196(n13)
monetary policy 43(n4)
  counter-cyclical 24
money 18, 178
money creation 23
money supply growth 20
moneylenders 186, 197(n20)
monitoring 28, 29, 42
monopolies 30, 31, 34, 82, 83, 138, 139, 208t, 209
Montana 80
Montevideo 153
moral axioms/standards 191–2, 195, 197(n28)
moral hazard 44(n17)
moral monitoring 195
moral reasoning/suasion 75, 190
Morocco 216t
Morrisson, C. 69(n1), 137, 137n, 142–3

mortality   125
mortgages (housing)   177
Moslems   103, 107, 131
motion pictures   126
motivation   70(n8)
Moynihan, D.   106–7
multinational companies (MNCs)   75,
    83, 84, 85, 90, 180
multiple equilibria   187–90, 194,
    197(n22–5), 219f
multiple goals (PWC)   40–1
  achieved through environmental
      policy (joint implementation)
      40–1
  achieved by improving
      education   40
murder   132(n17)
Murphy, K. M.   197(n22)
Museveni, Y. K.   117, 118, 129, 130,
    132(n16–17)
music   198(n32)
Muslims (in Sri Lanka)   132(n21)
myths   131(n11)

Nader, R.   77, 84
Nafziger, E. W.   132(n15)
Naipaul, V. S.   79
Napoleonic wars   140
Narayan, D.   39
Nash equilibria   188, 189
Nation   84
National Bureau of Economic Research
    (NBER)   87, 94, 95, 144
National Resistance Movement
    (NRM/NRA, Uganda)   118,
    132(n17)
National Science Foundation (USA)
    167n
nations   178
  income gaps between   136–7,
      137f, 142–3
  income gaps within   136–8
  industrialized   196(n6)
  poor   196(n6)
  rich   195
natural resources   40, 140, 152,
    154, 158
Nawadih (Indian village)   197(n20)
Neeman, Z.   197(n26)
Nelson, D.   4

neoclassical economics   2–3, 11, 14, 91
  growth model   213
  welfare analysis   101
neoliberalism   81
Nepal   178, 195
Netherlands   51–3, 54f, 148, 151f,
    168(n14)
Netherlands: Central Bureau of
    Statistics,   52n
network externalities   13, 14
networking/networks   104, 123
New Earnings Survey (UK, 1998)   59n
New Economic Policy (Malaysia,
    1970–90)   118
new institutional economics
    (D. C. North)   1–15
  adaptive efficiency and modern
      technology   10–15
  fundamental policy issue   14
  ideology, choices and adaptive
      efficiency   11–13
  institutional change   5–7
  institutions and efficient markets
      1–7
  path dependence   13–14
  second economic revolution   7–10,
      12, 13
  understanding transition economies
      14–15
New International Economic Order
    (Bhagwati, 1977)   97(n1)
New Republic   87
New World   6, 149, 150–2, 155–8, 163
  immigration subsidies   141
New York   90, 153
New York: Manhattan   91
New York Times   132(n27)
New Zealand   34, 51, 52f, 52, 54f, 216t
newly-industrializing countries (NICs)
    53, 55, 57, 58, 68, 70(n4)
Neyapti, B.   117n
NHO (employers' organization,
    Norway)   63
Nicaragua   202f, 216t
Nigeria   106, 215t
nihilism   79, 211
Nike   84
Nissan   124, 132(n27)
nitrogen dioxide   40
No Logo (Klein, 2000)   84

Nobel Prize xiv, 74
alternative Nobel Prize 97(n3)
Nokia 74
non-governmental organizations
(NGOs) 39, 75, 77, 79, 81, 87, 94,
95, 96
non-tariff barriers (NTBs) 138, 142,
169(n26), 205t
Nordic countries 51
Norman, V. 57
normative principles 176, 196(n2)
norms 4, 39, 107, 183
behaviour 13–14
informal 14
shifting 69
social xvii, xviii, 5, 69
'North' 155–7, 161, 162, 163,
168(n14–15), 176
North, D. C. xiii-xiv, xvi-xvii
North America: economic performance
(1960–2002) 204f, 204
North American Free Trade Agreement
(NAFTA) 51, 92, 148, 165,
167–8(n5), 169(n25)
North–South divide 85
Northern Ireland/Ulster 109
horizontal inequalities 113, 122–4,
126, 127, 129, 130, 132(n23–6)
Norway 26t, 51, 52f, 52, 54f, 63, 151f,
156, 159, 168(n14), 216t
Norway: Royal Ministry of Foreign
Affairs x
Nurkse, R. 197(n22)
Nyerere, J. K. 77

Obote, A. M. 117, 118, 132(n16)
Obstfeld, M. 158
OECD 50, 87, 94, 158, 160, 162, 163,
165, 166, 169(n18)
author/data source 53, 54n
globalization, inequality, and 146
trade 143
OECD countries 26f, 49–51, 64, 66, 68,
69, 70(n11), 203f, 216t
'two distinct groupings' 55
see also developed countries
OECD residents 163, 169(n23)
oil 85, 98(n10), 144, 147
oligarchs/oligarchy 82, 147
Omara-Otunnu, A. 132(n17)

open economy 70(n10), 98(n10),
144n, 202
openness 95, 159–60
openness-fosters-growth hypothesis
144, 145
lack of supporting evidence 159,
169(n18)
opportunism 2, 9
opportunity costs 41
Oracle x
organization 10
organizational dilemmas 9–10
bureaucracy 10
external effects 10
increased resources 9
strategic behaviour 9
worker alienation and shirking 9
organizations 6
differ from 'institutions' 1
economic 1
hierarchical 10
international xviii, 178
political 1
O'Rourke, K. H. 88, 139, 139n, 151n,
155n, 159, 167n, 167(n2), 168(n10)
Orwell, G. 81
Oslo x
outcomes 7, 12, 13, 36, 105, 111, 112,
204, 208
output 21, 22, 32, 60, 105, 154, 156
per capita 148
per man-hour 37
output stabilization 24–5
outsourcing 91, 92, 145
Oxford 89

Pakistan 79, 144n, 215t
Panagariya, A. 96, 98(n14)
Panama 215t, 216t
Pant, P. 93
Papua New Guinea 215t
Paraguay 216t
parents 183, 187
fathers 192
Pareto principle 27, 31, 44(n15), 176,
180, 187–90, 192–4, 197(n24, n29),
198(n10)
Parfit, D. 190, 198(n32)
Paris 90
parliaments 110t, 116

participation (trade-offs)   41–2
path dependence   5, 7, 13–14, 15
Pavcnik, N.   165, 197(n22)
Pax Americana Latina   167
Pax Britannica   140
pay norms   50, 61, 62, 66–7, 69, 70(n8)
   egalitarian   63, 67
   redistributive   63–4, 68
   shifting   63
pay policy   62
payoffs   187, 189
payroll taxes   67
peace   122, 127, 129, 133(n36),
   139, 140
pecuniary externalities (concept)
   190, 191
Pedersen, P. J.   70
pensions   50
Penurbarti, M.   132(n13)
perception   1, 3, 6, 12, 13, 112,
   132(n14)
   racial discrimination   105
performance contracting   39
performance-related pay   64
periphery   150, 168(n12)
   poor   153
   pre-industrial   155, 168(n9)
   pre-1940   160–1, 169(n21–2)
   primary product-exporting (rising
      inequality in)   154–5, 168(n13)
   terms of trade gains (before 1913)
      152–4, 168(n12)
Perry, G.   22
Peru   144n, 168(n12), 202f, 203f, 215t
   Indian population   104
Phelps Brown, E. H.   60
Philippines   19f, 168(n12), 203f
Phillips curve   22, 43(n6)
physical capital   6, 218
physical characteristics   108
physical proximity   102
Piketty, T.   66
Pinochet Ugarte, A.   87, 129
pirates   138, 139
Pohjola, M.   xx, 69n, 74, 97n
Polanyi, K.   95
police   109, 123f, 123, 130
policy competition   210b
policy ownership   42
policy paradox   205

policy principles   192, 197(n28)
policy 'puzzles'   204, 205
policy-makers   14, 19, 175, 185, 186, 194
   'decision-making'   3, 11, 40
political alliances   85
political capital   219
political economy   14, 15, 33, 67
political inclusivity   129–30, 133(n36)
political instability   8, 13, 42(n1),
   103, 179
political judgements   43(n7)
political participation   109, 110t,
   124–5, 130, 136
political parties   1, 6, 89, 126, 130,
   133(n35)
political regime change   217t
political rights   115
political stability   40, 127
political structures/systems   78,
   133(n36)
political suppression/accommodation
   113
political will   196(n6)
politicians   91, 116
politics   14, 68, 114, 115, 131(n7),
   137–8
   ethnicization   130
   liberal   127
   racist   116
polity   5, 12, 14
'polluter pays' tax   95
pollution   9, 40–1, 83
Ponzi scheme   221
poor, the   93, 99(n18), 136, 142, 164,
   165, 188, 208
poor communities   27
population   137n, 139, 147, 158, 162,
   167(n1), 168(n7)
   growth or decline   6
population versus resources
   (Malthus)   7
Porto Alegre (Brazil): World Social Forum
   77, 97(n2)
ports   149, 152
Portugal   151f, 168(n14), 216t
Post-Washington Consensus: more
   instruments and broader goals
   (Stiglitz)   16–48
   budget deficit   23–4, 43–4(n8–10,
      n12)

Post-Washington Consensus – *continued*
  competition 29–35, 45(n22–6)
  'confusion between means and ends'
    (Stiglitz) 29–30, 38
  current account deficit 23–4,
    44(n10–12)
  East Asian crisis (lessons) 17–18,
    42(n1)
  development goals (broadened) 40–2
  economic growth (long-run) 24–5,
    44(n13–14)
  financial reform process 25–9,
    44–5(n15–21)
  further research/humility required
    31, 42
  government acting as a complement
    to markets 35–8, 39,
    45–6(n27–33)
  government effectiveness 38–40
  inflation 21–2, 43(n5–7)
  macroeconomic stability 21–5
  markets made to work better 18–21,
    42–3(n2–4)
  output stabilization 24–5,
    44(n13–14)
  principles 42
poverty 17, 24, 82, 86, 88, 103, 104,
    110t, 115, 116, 125f, 142, 143,
    176–7, 183, 192, 194, 197(n30), 208
  acute 182
  in poor countries 92–4, 98(n15–16)
  in rich countries 91–2, 98(n13–14)
  vicious circles 187, 197(n22)
poverty line 124
  basic needs 115t
  food 115t
poverty rates 169(n24)
poverty-elimination/eradication xx,
    92, 118, 136, 197(n30), 163
poverty-reduction 18, 43(n4), 75, 80,
    93, 94, 101, 105, 129, 137, 164, 201,
    204, 211, 212t
  'anti-poverty programmes' 41
power 116
  economic 83, 102
  political xviii, 68, 81, 83, 102, 103,
    118, 129
'power elite' (Wright Mills) 86
power-sharing, 130
PPP 167(n4)

Prague 77
Prebisch, R. 152, 153, 154
predatory lending 186, 197(n21)
pressure groups/lobbies 4, 85, 184, 195
Pretty Woman 84
price liberalization 208, 208t
price mark-ups 149
price stability 43(n7)
prices 9, 30, 31, 44(n14), 95, 136, 142,
    190, 208, 209
  convergence 154
  export and import 138
  factors 58
  goods 58
  relative 57, 60, 63, 152, 164
  relative changes 5, 6, 12
pricing 186
  two-track 210b, 210
primary products 98(n10), 152, 153
principal–agent problems 9, 10
'principle of free contract' 176, 180,
    183, 184
Principles of Political Economy
    (Mill, 1848) 176
priorities 212
prison authorities 198(n9)
prisoner's dilemma 159
Pritchett, L. 24, 39, 168(n9), 201,
    213, 216n
private ownership 210
private property 208
private returns 218, 220, 221
private sector 17, 28, 33, 36, 39, 42,
    45(n28), 116, 128, 205, 221
privatization xvii, 11, 14, 17, 19, 21,
    31–3, 42, 43(n3), 45(n24–5), 81,
    179, 202, 203, 212t, 212
  sequencing and scope 33
  voucher system 32
privilege xviii, 78, 103
product differentiation 58
product markets 2, 9, 11
production 45(n25), 92
production chain 9
production costs xvi, 1
production functions 57
production possibilities curve 45(n25)
production possibility frontier (PPF)
    30–1
productive capacities 57

productive potential 8
productivity 7, 38, 58, 60, 61–2, 63,
    70(n9), 152, 156, 157, 158, 203,
    208, 218
productivity gap 37
products, industrial 152
professionalism 39
professionals 118, 119f
profit-maximization 31
profitability 67
profits 62, 79, 81, 83, 97(n2)
'progressive' forces 82
project implementation
  community participation
    39–40
propaganda 84
property rights 2, 3, 5, 11, 13,
    14, 31, 206t, 207, 210, 212t,
    218–20
  enforcement 144
proportional representation 130
prosperity 103
protection 138, 140–1, 144, 160,
    169(n22, n25), 205
protectionism 30, 45(n22–3), 81, 142,
    159, 176, 184
  reasons 166–7, 169(n26–7)
Protectionism (Bhagwati, 1988) 95
protest 76, 113, 179
Protestant ethic 5
Protestants 104, 123, 124
protests 114, 115, 126, 127
proxies 88
PRSPs (poverty reduction strategy
    papers) 211
psychologists 104–5
public choice 68
public debt–GDP ratio 23
public economics 60
public enterprises 92
public expenditure 18, 212t
  'government expenditure/spending'
    23, 113, 122
  share of GDP 35
public finance 210b, 210
  sustainable 207, 208
public goods 36, 37, 79, 104
public officials 39
public opinion 78
public ownership 207t

public sector 28, 116, 128, 129
  deficits (Latin America versus East
    Asia) 19f
  financial reorganization 45(n24)
  pay policy 64
public service employment 118
Putnam, R. 80

quality (institutions) 38
quality of output 9
quality standards 18
quantitative restrictions (QR1) 205
quasi-public goods (Loury) 104
quasi-rents 61
Quebec 77, 85
queues 78
quotas 141, 142

race 101, 113, 116, 125, 132(n30)
race riots 103, 124, 125, 126
'race to bottom' 83–4, 92, 166
'race towards top' (Williamson) 136
racism 192
  effects on mental health 104–5
Radcliffe-Brown, A. R. 80
radio 107
Ranger, T. 106, 107
rational choice, 11–13, 14
ratios
  investment to GDP 220
  trade to GNP 88, 94
  unskilled wages to farm rents 150
  unskilled wages to GDP 150
  wage–rental 154–5
Ravallion, M. 169(n24)
Rawls, J. 79
Ray, D. 112, 132(n13)
Ray, R. 196(n14)
Reagan, R. W. 81
real estate 17, 24, 28
real income
  changes on expenditure side 165
rebellion 113, 121, 122, 126
Reder, M. W. 62
redistribution 62, 69, 93
redistributive experience 64–7,
    70(n11)
redistributive policy 51
redundancies 95
reforms 203

regions   101, 104, 119, 120, 127, 128,
     132(n16–17)
   Uganda   116–18
   uneven stimulus   148
regulation   33, 35, 197(n25)
   effective   21
   establishment   34
   'four purposes in financial
     markets'   27
   prudential   27, 28, 206t, 207, 212t
regulations   9, 10, 83
   labour markets   166
regulatory bodies   6
regulatory capacity   xvii
regulatory framework   28
regulatory reforms   222
regulatory structure   34
regulatory system   222
religion   107, 112, 114
   cause of conflict   108, 131(n10)
remittances   157, 163, 220
remuneration in kind   70(n5)
rent (economic)   30, 33, 138, 139, 221
rent-seeking   28, 42, 45(n23)
Republican Party (USA)   77
reputation   61–4, 70(n7–10), 83
research and development (R&D)   24,
     37, 219f
   returns (individual and social)   36
research expenditure   46(n33)
resentment   104, 108, 110
resource access   102, 105
resource-allocation   16, 25, 39, 129
resources, claims on   131(n10)
retaliation   4
rethinking growth strategies (Rodrik)
     201–23
   common ground   201, 202–11
   diagnostic strategy for reforms
     217–22
   empirics of growth accelerations   201,
     213–17
   false alternative   211–12
   further research required   222
   roadmap   201–2
revolution   77, 79
Reynal-Querol, M.   131(n10)
Ricardian equivalence   43(n8)
rice   165
rich, the   149, 165, 167(n1), 188

Rio Grande   92
riots   102, 113, 126
   racial   114, 118
risk   26, 27, 28, 41, 44(n12), 61, 177
   macroeconomic   218–19, 219f
   microeconomic   219, 219f
risk premiums   39
risk-aversion   42
risk-taking   3
rituals   131(n11)
rivers   83
roads   23, 35
Roberts, J.   84
Robertson, Sir Dennis   79, 87
Robertson, R.   148, 165, 169(n25)
Robinson, J.   167(n1)
Robinson, M.   133(n37)
Robinson, S.   69(n1)
Rodriguez, C.   23
Rodriguez, F.   98(n11), 169(n19)
Rodrik, D.   xiv, xx, 87, 95, 98(n11),
     166, 169(n19), 213, 216n,
     219n, 220
Rome Treaty (1998)   179, 196(n7)
Roosevelt, F. D.   132(n29)
Rosati, F. C.   196(n13)
Rosen, S.   63
Rosenstein-Rodan, P. N.   197(n22)
Rossi, M.   196(n13)
Roy, A.   98–9(n18)
Roy model   70(n6)
Royal Economic Society   53
Royal Ulster Constabulary (RUC)
     123, 124
Ruane, J.   123–4, 132(n26)
Ruggie, J.   95
rule of law   14, 206t
rules   9, 10, 39
   efficient   14
   formal   11
   political   6
rules, formal   1, 5, 7, 10, 12, 13, 14
   contracts   3
   economic   3
   function   4
   political   3
rules of game   1, 3, 6
'rural' versus 'urban'
   dividing line 'arbitrary'   109
rural areas   89, 117f, 147, 186, 208

Russia/Russian Federation   14, 32,
    33, 76, 96–7, 147, 148, 151,
    169(n18), 210
  'puzzle' (for traditional economics)
    32–3
  see also Soviet Union
Rwanda   102, 103, 106, 112, 127,
    128, 215t

sabotage   6
Sachs, J. D.   88, 97, 98(n11), 145
safety nets   136, 165–6, 208t, 209,
    212t, 212
Said, E.   81
Sala-í-Martin, X.   143, 169(n24)
salaries   121
Salinas de Gortari, C.   147
Sambanis, N.   132(n13)
Samman, E.   131n
sample selection (methodological
    problems)   113
sanctions/embargoes   96, 138, 185, 194
  societal   4, 5
  trade or financial   75
Sanders' Amendment (USA, 1997)   184,
    197(n18)
Sapir, A.   53
Sappington, D.   31
Sattinger, M.   70(n6)
Satz, D.   183, 197(n19)
savings   25, 42, 87, 89, 219–21
  domestic   221
  national   23
Schelling, T. C.   62
Schmidt-Hebbel, K.   23
schooling   3, 183
schools   182, 196(n13)
  midday meals   182
science   7, 8, 37, 38f, 40, 119,
    120f, 120
Scitovsky, T.   87
Scott, M.   87
Scouts   108
Seattle   77, 80–1, 84, 87, 124, 179
'second generation reforms'   211
second global century (1950–2002):
    world inequality   142–8, 167,
    167–8(n3–8)
  border effects, limited access, and
    Third World   147–8, 168(n7–8)

globalization, inequality and OECD
    146
globalization, inequality and Third
    World   146–7
international income gaps (post-war
    epochal turning point?)   142–3,
    167(n3–4)
trade policy and international income
    gaps: late twentieth century
    conventional wisdom   143–5,
    167–8(n5–6)
when twentieth-century leader went
    open: the USA   145–6
second-best situations   212
sectarianism   132(n17)
securities markets   28
security, personal and household   110t
security forces   123
seigniorage   18
Sekkat, K.   53
self-employment   168(n11)
self-esteem/self-image   102, 104,
    107, 112
self-selection   104
Sen, A. K.   101, 110, 131–2(n12), 193,
    197(n29)
Senegal   26t
sensei   91
separation of powers   39
service sector   118, 168(n11)
sexual harassment   190–1, 193
Shabaz (Pakistani guerrilla)   79
shadow prices   222
Shannon Airport   181
shareholders   32, 74, 128, 206t
Shaw, G. B.   78
Sherer, G.   122
Shields, C.   68
shirking   2, 3, 6, 9, 10
Shleifer, A.   32, 197(n22)
shock therapy   76, 96–7
shocks   62, 98(n10), 140, 144, 148,
    152–4, 157, 165, 168(n17), 217t
Shorrocks, A.   i, xx, 97n, 167n,
    196n, 222n
shrimp-turtle case   80–1
Silberberg, E.   4
Silva, C. R. de   120
Simms, M. C.   132(n28)
Singapore   37, 38f, 144n, 146, 205, 215t

Singapore: Ministry of Education 38n
Singell, L. D. 113
Singer, H., 152, 153, 154
Singh, N. 197(n19)
Sinhalese people 119–21
skill-pay relation 69
skills 7, 45(n32), 62, 63, 89, 219
  industrial 123
slavery 6, 124, 125
  'voluntary' ('waranteeism') 176–7,
    196(n3)
'small-country assumption' 168(n5)
Smeeding, T. 51
Smith, A. 79, 82
Smith, A. D. 131(n6, n9)
Smith, N. 70
social agendas 75–6
social anthropology 79
social change (pace accelerated) 96,
  99(n20)
social class 101, 112, 126, 132(n24)
  landed 148
  merchant 148
  working 82, 164
social codes 50, 61, 62, 70(n8)
social cohesion xviii
social conflict 111
social contradictions 82
social institutions 78
social policy 27
social programmes 166
social protection 35, 68
social returns 218, 219, 220
social scientists 83
social security taxes 51
social services 117, 117f
social spending 166
  relative to GNP 95
social stability 101, 103, 105, 107, 108
social status 104
social transfer programmes 165–6
social transfers xviii, 64, 66, 67, 69
social welfare 35, 43(n5), 110
social welfare function 44(n10)
socialism 77, 78
society 7, 12, 14, 37, 39, 60, 111, 112,
  185, 188–9, 192, 193, 198(n32)
  egalitarian 40
  fragmented 112
  pluralistic 128

restructuring 8, 10, 14–15
  urban 10
sociology/sociologists 60, 61,
  78, 79
solidarity 81
Solow, R. 37, 87
Soros, G. 77
sound money 207, 208
'South' 155–7, 162, 163, 168(n14–15),
  176
South Africa
  black business empowerment (South
    Africa) 122
  black/white inequalities (1980s–1990s)
    121f
  horizontal inequalities 104, 109,
    113, 121–2, 132(n22)
  post-transition government 122
  SA1 (apartheid era, 1948–93)
    121–2, 126
  SA2 (post-apartheid era, 1993–) 121,
    122, 126, 127, 129
South Asia 168(n17), 215t
  economic performance (1960–2002)
    204f
  volatility of GDP growth (1970–95)
    25f
Southeast Asia 155
Southern Cone 153, 155
Souza, A. P. 197(n22)
Soviet Union/USSR 32–3, 78,
  131(n6), 143
  collapse (1991) 147
  end of Cold War 102
  'former Soviet Union' (FSU) 14,
    22, 33
  see also Russia
space 211
Spain 26t, 150, 151f, 168(n14), 216t
sparse-game model 190
Special Economic Zones (SEZs, China)
  180
specialization/division of labour 2, 8,
  9, 10, 11
speculation (economic) 44–5(n20)
Spice Girls 86
Sri Lanka/Ceylon 26t, 144n, 157,
  168(n12), 215t
  horizontal inequalities 113, 119–21,
    126, 127, 132(n19–21)

Srinivasan, T. N.   93, 96, 97(n7),
    98(n11, n14–15)
Sriskandarajah, D.   120, 132(n19)
stability   5–6
stabilization   22, 89, 90
stagnation   11–12, 30
Staiger, R. W.   169(n20)
Staples   84
Starbucks   84
starvation/famine   80, 195
state, the   129, 184, 190, 194, 210
    non-interventionist   35
state institutions   xvii
state intervention   17
    central question   35
state sector   18
state transfers   50–1
state-owned enterprises xvii, 32,
    45(n24), 209
    state monopolies   31
statistical analysis   113
Statistics Canada   52n, 65n
Statistics Finland   65n
steel   17, 33
Stern, R. M.   96, 196(n14)
Stewart, F.   xiv, xviii, 69(n1), 131(n2),
    132(n15)
Stiglitz, J. E.   xiv, xvii, 21, 24, 31, 32, 34,
    42(n1), 43(n6–7), 44(n14, n16),
    45(n21, n27), 74, 197(n22)
Stockholm School of Economics   x
stock market capitalization   122
stock options   63, 70(n5)
stocks and bonds   77
Stokke, O.   133(n37)
Stolper–Samuelson theorem   147, 148,
    167, 169(n25)
    trade and wages   91
strategic behaviour   9
strikes   92
Strøm, B.   63
students   80, 82, 85, 90, 118, 122
Sub-Saharan Africa (SSA)   24, 36, 162,
    202, 214, 215t
    volatility of GDP growth (1970–95)
        25f
subjectivity   11–12, 13
Subramanian, S.   111
subsidies   18, 182
Sucocitrico Cutrale Ltd   197(n18)

Sudan   144n
    southern Sudanese   103
suffrage   165–6, 169(n23)
    voters/voting   4, 67, 116, 124,
        125f, 130
    trans-national   178, 179
sugar   116
Suh Dong Prize   87
Suharto regime   147
sulphur dioxide   40
Summers, L.   43(n7), 44(n13), 62,
    207–8
superstar theory (Rosen)   63
supply   63, 145
supply and demand   xvii, 50, 60,
    69, 138
supply incentives   210b
sustainable development   xx,
    16, 40
Sweden   26t, 28, 51, 150, 151f, 159,
    168(n14)
    immigration   131(n3)
Sweden: International Development
    Cooperation Agency (Sida)   x
Swedes (in Finland)   102
Swedish model   77
Sweet, Judge R.   180
'symbolic systems'   109, 131(n11)
Syria   216t

Taegu (South Korea)   87
Taft–Hartley Act (USA, 1947)   92
Taiwan   37, 38f, 38n, 45(n22), 146,
    168(n12), 178, 205, 215t
Tamils (in Sri Lanka)   119–21, 127,
    132(n20)
Tanzania   77, 102, 144n
tariff rates   205t
tariff reductions   xix
tariff reform   81, 93
tariff–growth correlation/paradox
    159, 160
tariffs   xix, 34, 88, 138, 139, 141f, 142,
    150–4, 159, 160, 161t, 161, 164,
    166, 167, 169(n22), 205t
tax base   18, 67, 219
tax competition
    real   67
    virtual   67–8
tax reform   208t, 209, 212t

taxation 23, 51, 64, 69, 165–7, 209, 218–21
  corporate 68
  direct 65
  on income xviii, 60, 64, 66
  indirect 65
  lower 68
  personal 68
  progressive 66, 67
taxpayers 117f
Taylor, A. M. 158
Taylor, C. 111
Taylor, J. 52n
technical change 37
  bias towards skilled labour 53, 68, 145–6
  unskilled-labour-saving 91
technological change 49, 139, 144, 153
technological development 55
technological frontier 37
technology xviii, 7, 8, 19, 37, 69, 80, 83, 182, 183, 218
  adaptive efficiency 10–15
  changes in 45(n30)
  military 6
  new xvii, 30, 34, 142
  trade-offs 41
technology gap 17
technology-transfer 16, 36–8, 41, 42, 45–6(n30–3), 86, 138
telecommunications 34
Telegu language 108
television 80, 126
Telfer-Taivainen, L. 196n
Telle, K. 143, 168(n7)
terms of trade 143, 149, 153, 154, 159, 168(n12, n17), 214
  gains 152–4, 168(n5, n12)
  Japan 152
terrorism/terrorists 103, 131
Thailand/Siam 17, 19f, 23–5, 28, 44(n18), 153, 157, 168(n12), 203f, 215t
Thatcher, M. H. (Baroness Thatcher) 81
theatre 126
Third World 13, 14, 143, 144, 154, 158, 162, 163, 168(n11), 185, 195
  border effects, limited access 147–8, 168(n7–8)
  globalization, inequality, and 146–7

trade-policy orientation and growth rates (1963–92) 144f
Third World Network (Malaysian NGO) 96
Thompson, G. 139
Thorp, R. 131(n2)
Thurow, L. 45(n26)
time 1–2, 3, 9, 11–12, 14–15, 51, 59, 62, 66, 67, 69(n2), 78, 88, 105, 106, 108, 111, 116, 122, 133(n36), 139, 167, 185, 203, 204, 212, 213, 213f, 217, 222
  horizontal inequalities 110
time and motion 9
time and space 2, 5
timing 147
Tinbergen, J. 55
'tipping' (Akerlof/Schelling) 62
Todd, J. 123–4, 132(n26)
Toniolo, G. 143
tort 98(n17)
total factor productivity (TFP) 24, 27, 37, 45(n30), 204, 206f, 219f
tourism 222
township and village enterprises (TVEs) 210b, 210
trade xviii, xix, 50, 54, 69, 70(n6), 91, 95, 138, 147–50, 152–3, 154, 156, 178, 205, 207
  disaggregation of globalization 86–7, 98(n8–10)
  economic benignity 87–8, 98(n11)
  'economically benign' 75
  elasticities 149
  freer 74, 145
  gains from 31
  general equilibrium theory (Krugman) 56–7
  impact on poverty-reduction 98(n16)
  intercontinental 149
  international 60
  share in GDP 139
  short-term gains 160
  standard model 67
  two-country model 56
trade barriers/restrictions 136, 139, 140, 142
trade competition 145
trade deficits 20
trade economists 74

trade and factor flows   xviii–xix
trade issues   98(n12)
trade liberalization   16, 19, 21, 30, 31,
    53, 68, 81, 86–7, 143, 148, 204,
    208t, 209, 212t
  moments   144–5
  wage inequality   146–7
trade openness   144, 164, 166, 194,
    203, 207, 208
  see also openness
trade policy   34
  'big tariff-growth regime switch'
    159–60, 169(n18–20), 169(n26)
  international income gaps   143–5,
    159–61, 167–8(n5–6),
    169(n18–22)
  late twentieth century conventional
    wisdom   143–5, 167–8(n5–6)
  liberal   147
'trade versus technology' contest   145
trade theory   63, 69
  enhanced   58
  see also Heckscher–Ohlin model
trade treaties   75, 99(n20)
trade unions   1, 6, 85, 88, 91, 92, 96,
    180, 187, 190, 196(n17)
  egalitarian wage policies   70(n7)
  membership   61
  power   61
trade volume   139, 204
trade-offs   16, 20, 27, 40, 43(n7),
    105, 166
  environmental protection versus
    increased participation   41–2
  investment in technology   41
transaction costs   xvi, 1, 11, 13
  cost of measuring attributes   2
  enforcement   2
  ideological attitudes   3
  measurement and enforcement
    problems   9
  size of market   2
transactions
  class of   190
  free   196(n2)
'Transatlantic Consensus' (Atkinson)
    49–73
  background   53–6, 70(n4)
  rising inequality   51–3, 69–70(n1–3)
  unresolved questions   56–8

transfer payments   66
transition economies   xvi–xvii, 30, 210
  problem   1–15
  understanding   14–15
transparency   16, 27
transport   145, 149, 153, 220
transport costs   xix, 58, 138, 139, 140,
    152, 153, 219f
treaties   196(n7)
tribalism   132(n17)
trickle-down   41, 81
Trinidad and Tobago   216t
Tulsa   124
Tunisia   145, 216t
Turgenev, I. S.   79
Turkey   144n, 168(n12)
Turton, D.   107, 131(n9)
Tutsis   106
'tyranny of missing alternative'
    (Bhagwati)   77
Tzannatos, Z.   196(n14)

Uganda   215t
  horizontal inequalities   113, 116–18,
    126, 127, 129, 130, 132(n16–17)
  World Bank 'star globalizer'
    205t, 205
uncertainty   2, 3, 9, 24
underdevelopment   8, 85
unemployment   21, 24, 37, 43(n4),
    44(n13), 55, 57, 58, 61, 68, 69,
    70(n8), 104, 110t, 122, 123, 124,
    146, 208t, 209
unemployment benefit/insurance
    50–1, 66, 165
United Kingdom   x, xvii, 49, 51–3, 54f,
    64–7, 69(n2), 95, 102, 124, 128, 142,
    146, 151f, 152, 156, 158, 158t, 159,
    164, 168(n14), 169(n18), 182–3,
    196(n15), 216t
  cultural categories   128, 133(n33)
  free-trade leadership   149–50,
    168(n10)
  governmental incomes policies
    (1970s)   63
  tilt in earnings distribution (1977–98)
    59f
  wage–rank relationship   59f, 59–60
United Kingdom: Department of
    Employment   54n, 59n

United Kingdom: Department for
International Development
98(n16)
United Kingdom: Office for National
Statistics 65n
United Kingdom government 127,
132(n26)
United Nations
Millennium Summit (2000) 92
UNESCO 38n
UNICEF xiv
UNIFEM xii, 89
United Nations University: World
Institute for Development
Economics Research, Helsinki,
Finland (UNU-WIDER, 1984–) i, ix,
x, 97, 131(n2), 175
Annual Lecture (1997–) ix, x,
xvi–xx, 49, 74, 97n, 167n
core issues xvi, xvii, xx
publications i–ii
study of humanitarian emergencies
xviii, 113, 129, 132(n15)
United States of America xvii, 5, 8, 18,
26t, 28, 33, 34, 36, 38f, 43(n6),
45(n30), 49–59, 63, 69(n2), 90–1,
95, 102–4, 132(n25), 138, 141, 148,
151–2, 156, 157, 159, 161, 163, 166,
167, 167–8(n5), 168(n7, n14, n16),
169(n25), 178, 179, 181, 184, 195,
196(n7), 197(n18), 216t
aid to Israel 78
black/white differences (horizontal
inequalities) 113, 114, 124–5,
126, 127, 132(n27–8)
foreign-born share of population 142
national mortgage system, 45(n28)
'proper question' 146
savings and loans débâcle 25,
44(n19)
wage and income inequality (sources)
145
'when twentieth-century leader went
open' 145–6
universities 37, 79, 115t, 132(n24)
admissions 119, 120f, 120
'campuses' 78, 85, 92
Cambridge xiii, 87
Columbia xiv, 77, 86
Copenhagen x

Cornell xiii
Florence xx
Harvard xiv–xv, 201
Oslo x
Oxford xiii, xiv
St Louis xiii
United States 90–1
upper middle-income countries 25f
urban areas 106, 108, 147, 209
Uruguay 26t, 102, 144n, 146,
168(n12), 202f, 216t
US Congress 4, 6, 124
General Accounting Office 92
House of Representatives 125
Senate 124
US Constitution 11
US Council of Economic Advisers (US
CEA) 43(n4)
US Department of Commerce 52n, 53
US Department of Labor 92, 180
US dollar 23–4, 67, 167(n4)
dollarization 221
US election (2000) 77
US Federal Reserve Bank ('US Fed')
43(n5), 44(n19)
charter 43(n7)
US Federal Trade Commission 186,
197(n21)
US government 45(n28), 175
'US migrant groups' 107
US Treasury 86
US–Japan summit (1993) 98(n12)
US–Jordan Free Trade Agreement
99(n20)
USAToday 196(n8)
USSR *see* Soviet Union
Uusitalo, H. 66

values/ethics 4, 12, 43(n7), 79, 91, 101,
131(n11)
Vamvakidis, A. 169(n18)
Van, P. H. 189, 197(n22)
van Binsbergen, W. M. J. 106
Väyrynen, R. 132(n15)
veil of ignorance (Vickrey/Rawls) 79
Velasco, A. 201, 219n, 220
Venezuela 19f, 202f, 203f
vertical inequality (Stewart) 102
veterinary science 119
Vickers, J. 43(n3)

Vickrey, W.   79
Vietnam   179, 195, 204, 208
   Consumer Price Index (CPI)   165
   economic performance (1960–2002)
      204f
   World Bank 'star globalizer'
      205t, 205
villages/villagers   185, 186, 197
violence   76, 85, 104, 113, 116,
   127, 129
   political   110, 122, 132(n13)
Virgin Soil (Turgenev, 1877)   79
Vishny, R.   32, 197(n22)
'voice' (Hirschman)   68
voice   195
Volcker, P.   44(n19)
voluntariness   183, 184, 194

wage compression   70(n7)
wage convergence   156–7, 157–8
wage costs   67
wage differentials   xvii–xviii, 90
   determinants   60–1
   'range theory'   60
   see also income inequality
wage distribution, tilt   59, 59f,
   67, 69
wage gaps   146–7, 156, 162
wage inequality–trade liberalization
   connection   146–7
wage rates   55, 146, 189–90
wage risk, insurance against   70(n7)
wage-earnings dispersion   49, 55, 56,
   59, 61, 63, 69, 156
wage/skill nexus   66
wages   30, 39, 58, 70(n9), 84, 98(n14),
   126t, 166, 169(n23), 183, 187, 189,
   190, 191, 193, 209
   efficiency   63
   fair   70(n10)
   high   57, 156, 162, 163
   low   89, 162, 169(n23), 184
   lower   92
   nominal   168(n10)
   real   60, 91, 148, 151f, 156, 157, 164
   real gains   164
   relative   169(n25)
   trade union premium   61
   unskilled   150
   urban   208t

'Wall Street-Treasury complex'
   (Bhagwati)   86
Wallerstein, I.   82
Wang, M.   131n
war   85, 138
'war against terrorism'   103
'waranteeism'   176–7
Warner, A. M.   88, 98(n11), 145
warranties   9
wars   107
Washington Consensus   xvii, 201, 202,
   203, 209, 212t, 222
   'does not offer answers' (Stiglitz)   20
   'incomplete, misguided, misleading'
      (Stiglitz)   21, 42
   issues 'not addressed' (Stiglitz)   33
   Ricardian equivalence issue 'not
      explicitly addressed' (Stiglitz)
      43(n8)
   'simplicity' (Stiglitz)   20
   'smaller state, better state'   35
   see also 'Augmented Washington
      Consensus'; Post-Washington
      Consensus
Washington D.C.   77, 179
waste   9, 31
watchdogs   39
water   39, 110t, 110, 114f, 115t
wealth   110, 168(n7)
wealth bias   158, 158t
wealth-creation   33, 42
wealth-maximization   5, 6, 11
Webb, S.   52n
Webb–Pomerene Act (1918),   181
Weber, M.   5
websites   84, 98(n14), 196(n8),
   197(n21)
Weinstein, D.   168(n16)
welfare economics   30, 197(n24)
welfare state   55, 67, 81, 95
   benefit coverage/levels   55, 64
welfarism   192, 193, 197(n29, n32)
well-being/welfare   xviii, 102, 104–8,
   111, 128, 178, 191
   improvement   132(n14)
   individual   109
   society   111
Wennemo, T.   70
West Indies   6
Western Europe   152

Western world 5, 6, 8, 10, 13, 95
'What is Economics' (Luxemburg) 80
whites
  in South Africa 121
  in UK 133(n33)
Wiig, H. 143, 168(n7)
Williamson, J. 16
Williamson, J. G. xiv–xv, xviii–xix,
  139n, 141n, 144n, 151n, 155n, 158,
  158n, 159, 161n, 168(n12, n15),
  169(n26)
Winters, L. A. 98(n16), 197(n19)
witch-hunting 195
Wolfe, A. 83
women 88, 89, 90, 93, 184, 195, 196(n7)
Wood, A. 145, 147
Wood, C. H. 132(n29), 133(n31)
words/linguistic weapons 81–2
work hours 146
work conditions 191
worker alienation 9
worker rights xix
workers 8, 39, 60–1, 62, 70(n3, n8), 83,
  96, 150, 166, 176, 194, 195,
  197(n24), 198(n9), 209
  blue-collar 132(n28)
  compensation 186–7
  low-paid 57, 63, 68
  male earnings 54n, 70(n3)
  marginal 63
  median 50, 55, 56f, 59, 60
  professional 115t
  self-selection 70(n6)
  skilled 50, 55, 91, 145
  unskilled 50, 55, 59, 66, 91, 124,
    141, 145
  well-being 191
  white-collar 8, 132(n28)
working conditions xx, 180
workplace harassment xx
World Bank 18, 27, 29, 41, 42,
  43(n6), 80, 84, 88, 90, 93, 96,
  129, 167(n3), 220
  author/data source 17, 20n, 22n,
    25n, 144, 144n, 204
  'star globalizers' 205t, 205

World Development 89
World Development Report 1997 (World
  Bank) 38
world economy 82, 84, 87, 92, 93, 95,
  143, 146
  'global economy' xx
  integration into 207, 208
world factor market 136
world inequality xix
  globalization and 136–8
  individual incomes (1820–1992) 137f
world integration 149
world trade 30, 56
  share in world GDP 138
world trade boom (1500–1800)
  138–40
  causality 167(n1)
World Trade Organization (WTO) 34,
  75, 78, 80–1, 84, 88, 96, 175, 179,
  194, 205t, 205
  disciplines 212t
  dispute settlement 98(n12)
  rules 205
world wars
  inter-war years 142, 159, 160, 167,
    169(n18, n21, n26), 178
  post-war era (1945–) 77, 88, 95, 142,
    143, 146, 159, 160
  pre-World War I era 136, 142, 153,
    154, 156, 159, 160, 162, 166–7
  World War I 136, 159
  World War II 136, 159

Yarrow, G. 43(n3)
Yorkshire 102
Young, A. 45(n30)
youth/the young 77, 78, 80, 81, 83,
  84, 85, 158, 162
  black (South Africa) 104
  black (UK) 109
  teenagers 105

Zambia 144n
Zimbabwe 215t
Zollverein 160
Zupan, M. 4